CW01291963

BEN JONSON IN CONTEXT

Bringing together a group of established and emergent Jonson scholars, this volume reacts to major new advances in thinking about the writer and his canon of works. The study is divided into two distinct parts: the first considers the Jonsonian career and output from biographical, critical and performance-based angles; the second looks at cultural and historical contexts, building on rich interdisciplinary work. Social historians work alongside literary critics to provide a diverse and varied account of Jonson. These are less standard surveys of the field than vibrant interventions into current critical debates. The short-essay format of the collection seeks less to harmonize and homogenize than to raise awareness of new avenues of research on Jonson, including studies informed by book history, cultural geography, the law and legal discourse, the history of science and interests in material culture.

JULIE SANDERS is Professor of English Literature and Drama at the University of Nottingham. She is the author of *Ben Jonson's Theatrical Republics* (1998) and has recently edited *The New Inn* for The Cambridge Edition of the Works of Ben Jonson.

Portrait of Benjamin Jonson, by Abraham van Blyenberch

BEN JONSON IN CONTEXT

EDITED BY
JULIE SANDERS

CAMBRIDGE
UNIVERSITY PRESS

CAMBRIDGE UNIVERSITY PRESS
Cambridge, New York, Melbourne, Madrid, Cape Town, Singapore,
São Paulo, Delhi, Dubai, Tokyo

Cambridge University Press
The Edinburgh Building, Cambridge CB2 8RU, UK

Published in the United States of America by Cambridge University Press, New York

www.cambridge.org
Information on this title: www.cambridge.org/9780521895712

© Cambridge University Press 2010

This publication is in copyright. Subject to statutory exception
and to the provisions of relevant collective licensing agreements,
no reproduction of any part may take place without the written
permission of Cambridge University Press.

First published 2010

Printed in the United Kingdom at the University Press, Cambridge

A catalogue record for this publication is available from the British Library

ISBN 978-0-521-89571-2 Hardback

Cambridge University Press has no responsibility for the persistence or
accuracy of URLs for external or third-party internet websites referred to in
this publication, and does not guarantee that any content on such websites is,
or will remain, accurate or appropriate.

*To the venture tripartite – David Bevington, Martin Butler
and Ian Donaldson – with respect and thanks*

Contents

List of illustrations	*page* x
Notes on contributors	xiii
Acknowledgements	xix
Note on editions used	xx
Chronology by Sarah Grandage	xxi

Introduction — 1

PART I LIFE, WORKS AND AFTERLIFE — 3

1. Tales of a life — 5
   Richard Dutton

2. Jonson in the Elizabethan period — 15
   Matthew Steggle

3. Jonson in the Jacobean period — 23
   Andrew McRae

4. Jonson in the Caroline period — 31
   Martin Butler

5. Genre — 39
   Katharine Eisaman Maus

6. Friends, collaborators and rivals — 48
   Michelle O'Callaghan

7. Jonson and Shakespeare — 57
   Mark Robson

8. Editions and editors — 65
   Eugene Giddens

9	Critical reception *James Loxley*	73
10	Performance afterlives *Lois Potter*	84

PART II CULTURAL AND HISTORICAL CONTEXTS 95

11	London and urban space *Adam Zucker*	97
12	The Globe Theatre and the open-air amphitheatres *Tiffany Stern*	107
13	The Whitefriars Theatre and the children's companies *Lucy Munro*	116
14	The Blackfriars Theatre and the indoor theatres *Janette Dillon*	124
15	Provinces, parishes and neighbourhoods *Steve Hindle*	134
16	The court *Malcolm Smuts*	144
17	Masques, courtly and provincial *Karen Britland*	153
18	Music *David Lindley*	162
19	Dance *Barbara Ravelhofer*	171
20	Manuscript culture and reading practices *James Knowles*	181
21	Print culture and reading practices *Alan B. Farmer*	192
22	Visual culture *John Peacock*	201
23	The body *Ben Morgan*	212

24	Law, crime and punishment *Lorna Hutson*	221
25	Religion *Julie Maxwell*	229
26	Politics *Andrew Hadfield*	237
27	Rank *Clare McManus*	245
28	Households *Kate Chedgzoy*	254
29	Foreign travel and exploration *Rebecca Ann Bach*	263
30	Domestic travel and social mobility *Julie Sanders*	271
31	Money and consumerism *Christopher Burlinson*	281
32	Land *Garrett A. Sullivan, Jr*	289
33	Patronage *Helen Ostovich*	296
34	Architecture *Mimi Yiu*	304
35	Food *Robert Appelbaum*	314
36	Alchemy, magic and the sciences *Margaret Healy*	322
37	Clothing and fashion *Eleanor Lowe*	330
38	Gender and sexuality *Mario DiGangi*	339

Further reading   348
Index   360

Illustrations

For kind permission to reproduce the images and for supplying photographs, the Editor would like to thank the following libraries and museums: The Bridgeman Art Library; The British Library; Chatsworth House; the Courtauld Gallery; English Heritage; and the National Portrait Gallery, London; as well as the Royal Bank of Scotland Group, Sophie Baker Photography and John Higham for additional images, plus Cambridge University Press for the permission to reproduce the map which appears as Figure 12.1. Every effort has been made to secure necessary permissions to reproduce copyright material in this work. If any omissions are brought to our notice, we will be happy to include appropriate acknowledgements in any subsequent edition.

	Portrait of Benjamin Jonson by Abraham van Blyenberch © National Portrait Gallery, London.	ii
5.1	Frontispiece to Ben Jonson's 1616 folio *Workes* © The British Library Board, All rights reserved. Shelfmark C39.k.9.	40
6.1	Bust of Apollo, from the Apollo Room, Fleet Street. Reproduced by kind permission of The Royal Bank of Scotland Group © 2009.	54
6.2	Verses over the door in the Apollo Room, Fleet Street. Reproduced by kind permission of The Royal Bank of Scotland Group © 2009.	55
10.1	David Garrick with William Burton and John Palmer in *The Alchemist* by Ben Jonson, 1770, by Johann Zoffany (1733–1810) © Private Collection/The Bridgeman Art Library. Nationality/copyright status: English/out of copyright.	92
10.2	1977 Royal Shakespeare Company production of *The Alchemist* © Sophie Baker Photography, London.	93

List of illustrations

12.1	Map showing principal public and private theatres in London, *c.* 1560–1640. Reproduced by kind permission of Cambridge University Press. This map first appeared in *The Cambridge Companion to English Renaissance Drama,* ed. A. R. Braunmuller and Michael Hattaway (Cambridge University Press, 1990).	108
14.1	Study of a seated actor by Rembrandt Harmenszoon van Rijn © The Samuel Courtauld Trust, Courtauld Gallery, London.	125
19.1	Inigo Jones, final design for Prince Henry as Oberon © Devonshire Collection, Chatsworth. Reproduced by permission of Chatsworth Settlement Trustees. Photo: Photographic Survey Courtauld Institute of Art.	176
19.2	Fabritio Caroso's circular choreography from *Nobiltà di dame* (1600) © The British Library Board. All rights reserved. Shelfmark case 7.d.12.	178
21.1	Title page to the third edition of *The comicall Satyre of Euery Man Out of His Humor* © The British Library Board. All rights reserved. Shelfmark C.57.c.22.	195
22.1	Inigo Jones, a sheet of sketches for characters in the anti-masques of *Britannia Triumphans* (1637) © Devonshire Collection, Chatsworth. Reproduced by permission of Chatsworth Settlement Trustees. Photo: Photographic Survey Courtauld Institute of Art.	203
27.1	Quack addressing a crowd, by Rembrandt Harmenszoon van Rijn © The Samuel Courtauld Trust, Courtauld Gallery, London.	249
30.1	Woodcut frontispiece to Henry Peacham's *Coach and Sedan, Pleasantly Disputing for Place and Precedence,* 1636 © The British Library Board. All rights reserved. Shelfmark 012314.e.88.	273
33.1	Lucy (Percy) Hay, Countess of Carlisle by Pierre Lombart, after Sir Anthony Van Dyck © National Portrait Gallery, London.	303
34.1	View out from the Little Castle, Bolsover, Derbyshire. Photo: John Higham. Produced by kind permission of English Heritage.	309
34.2	Painted panels in the Little Castle, Bolsover, Derbyshire. Photo: John Higham. Produced by kind permission of English Heritage.	310

34.3 Panel in the Pillar Chamber in the Little Castle, Bolsover, Derbyshire. Photo: John Higham. Produced by kind permission of English Heritage. 310

38.1 Old man with a long coat and a large hat by Rembrandt Harmenszoon van Rijn © The Samuel Courtauld Trust, Courtauld Gallery, London. 338

Contributors

ROBERT APPELBAUM is Senior Lecturer in Renaissance Studies at Lancaster University. He is the author of *Aguecheek's Beef, Belch's Hiccup, and Other Gastronomic Interjections: Literature, Culture, and Food Among the Early Moderns,* winner of the 2007 Roland H. Bainton Prize.

REBECCA ANN BACH is Professor of English at the University of Alabama at Birmingham. She is the author of *Shakespeare and Renaissance Literature before Heterosexuality* (2007) and *Colonial Transformations: The Cultural Production of the New Atlantic World, 1580–1640* (2000).

KAREN BRITLAND is Associate Professor at the University of Wisconsin-Madison. She is the author of *Drama at the Courts of Queen Henrietta Maria* (Cambridge University Press, 2006) and is an associate editor on The Cambridge Works of Ben Jonson.

CHRISTOPHER BURLINSON is Fellow in English at Jesus College, Cambridge. His recent publications include *Allegory, Space, and the Material World in the Writings of Edmund Spenser* (2006) and, with Andrew Zurcher, *Edmund Spenser: Selected Letters and Other Papers* (2009).

MARTIN BUTLER is Professor of English Renaissance Drama at the University of Leeds. With David Bevington and Ian Donaldson, he is General Editor of The Cambridge Edition of the Works of Ben Jonson (forthcoming, 2010). His most recent book is *The Stuart Court Masque and Political Culture* (Cambridge University Press, 2008).

KATE CHEDGZOY is Professor of Renaissance Literature at Newcastle University. She is co-editor, with Susanne Greenhalgh, of *Shakespeare and the Cultures of Childhood,* a special issue of the journal *Shakespeare* (2006), and, with Susanne Greenhalgh and Robert Shaughnessy, of

Shakespeare and Childhood (Cambridge University Press, 2007). She is currently working on children and cultural production in the early modern period.

MARIO DIGANGI is Professor of English at Lehman College and the Graduate Center (CUNY) and is the author of *The Homoerotics of Early Modern Drama* (Cambridge University Press, 1997). He has edited *Romeo and Juliet* and *A Midsummer Night's Dream* for the Barnes & Noble Shakespeare, and *The Winter's Tale* for Bedford's Texts and Contexts series. He is currently completing a study of sexual types in early modern drama.

JANETTE DILLON is Professor of Drama at the University of Nottingham. Her recent publications include *The Cambridge Introduction to Early English Theatre* (Cambridge University Press, 2006) and *The Cambridge Introduction to Shakespeare's Tragedies* (Cambridge University Press, 2007). She is currently working on a Leverhulme-funded research project on space and place in medieval and early modern court performance.

RICHARD DUTTON is Humanities Distinguished Professor and Chair of the Department of English at Ohio State University. He has written three books on Jonson, including *Ben Jonson, 'Volpone', and the Gunpowder Plot* (Cambridge University Press, 2008). His most recent publication is *A Handbook on Early Modern Theatre* (2009).

ALAN B. FARMER is Assistant Professor of English at the Ohio State University. He has published widely on Renaissance drama and the English book trade and is co-editor, with Adam Zucker, of *Localizing Caroline Drama: Politics and Economics of the Early Modern English Stage, 1625–42* (2006). He is currently completing a monograph on playbooks, newsbooks and the politics of the Thirty Years' War in England.

EUGENE GIDDENS is Skinner-Young Professor in Shakespeare and Renaissance Literature at Anglia Ruskin University. He is one of the general editors on the Arts and Humanities Research Council-funded Complete Works of James Shirley project. He is also an associate editor on The Cambridge Edition of the Works of Ben Jonson. He is currently preparing a Revels Plays edition of James Shirley's *Hyde Park*.

SARAH GRANDAGE is a postgraduate teaching fellow in the School of English Studies at the University of Nottingham. Her research interests centre on the intersection of language and drama.

Notes on contributors

ANDREW HADFIELD is Professor of English at the University of Sussex. He is the author of a number of works on early modern literature and culture including *Shakespeare and Republicanism* (Cambridge University Press, 2005) and *Shakespeare and Renaissance Politics* (2003). He is currently working on a biography of Edmund Spenser.

MARGARET HEALY is Reader in English and Director of the Centre for Early Modern Studies at the University of Sussex. She is currently completing *Shakespeare, Alchemy and the Creative Imagination: 'Sonnets' and 'A Lovers Complaint'*.

STEVE HINDLE is Professor of History at the University of Warwick. He is the author of *The State and Social Change in Early Modern England, 1550–1640* (2000) and *On the Parish? The Micro-politics of Poor Relief in Rural England, c. 1550–1750* (2004). He is currently editor of the *Economic History Review*.

LORNA HUTSON is Berry Professor and Head of the School of English at the University of St Andrews. Her books include *The Usurer's Daughter: Male Friendship and Fictions of Women in Sixteenth Century England* (1994) and *The Invention of Suspicion: Law and Mimesis in Shakespeare and Renaissance Drama* (2007).

JAMES KNOWLES is Professor of Medieval and Renaissance Literature and Head of the School of English at University College Cork. He has edited *Four City Comedies* (2001) and *The Key Keeper* (2002) (Jonson's *Entertainment at Britain's Burse*, the extant manuscript of which he identified). He has also contributed several of the editions of masques and entertainments for The Cambridge Edition of the Works of Ben Jonson.

DAVID LINDLEY is Professor of Renaissance Literature, University of Leeds. Recent publications include an edition of Shakespeare's *The Tempest* for New Cambridge Shakespeare and *Shakespeare and Music* (2006). Editions of eleven Jonson masques will be included in the forthcoming The Cambridge Edition of the Works of Ben Jonson.

ELEANOR LOWE is Lecturer in Drama at Oxford Brookes University. She has edited two plays for the Arts and Humanities Research Council-funded project, The Complete Works of Richard Brome Online, as well as working as the post-doctoral research fellow on that project for three years. She is currently preparing a critical edition of George Chapman's *A Humorous Day's Mirth*.

JAMES LOXLEY is Senior Lecturer in the School of Literatures, Languages and Cultures at the University of Edinburgh. He is the author of *Performativity* (2007) and *The Complete Critical Guide to Ben Jonson* (2002). He is currently working on a manuscript relating to Jonson's walk to Scotland (in collaboration with Julie Sanders) and has a forthcoming book on *Shakespeare, Jonson and the Claims of the Performative* with Mark Robson.

KATHARINE EISAMAN MAUS is the James Branch Cabell Professor of Renaissance Literature at the University of Virginia. Among many other works, she was the author of *Ben Jonson and the Roman Frame of Mind* (1985) and a co-editor of *The Norton Shakespeare* (1997; 2nd edn, 2008). She is currently working on *The Oxford English Literary History, 1603–60*.

JULIE MAXWELL worked on Jonson during a Junior Research Fellowship at New College, Oxford. Her novel, *You Can Live Forever* (2007), was inspired partly by Jonson's play *Bartholomew Fair*.

CLARE MCMANUS is Reader in English Literature at Roehampton University, London. She publishes on early modern women's performance and the theatrical woman. She is author of *Women on the Renaissance Stage* (2002) and editor of *Women and Culture at the Courts of the Stuart Queens* (2003) and is currently editing John Fletcher's *Island Princess*.

ANDREW MCRAE is Professor of Renaissance Studies at the University of Exeter. His publications include *Literature, Satire and the Early Stuart State* (Cambridge University Press, 2005) and *Literature and Domestic Travel in Early Modern England* (Cambridge University Press, 2009).

BEN MORGAN is Williams Fellow and Tutor in English at Exeter College, Oxford.

LUCY MUNRO is Senior Lecturer in English at Keele University. Her publications include *Children of the Queen's Revels: A Jacobean Theatre Repertory* (Cambridge University Press, 2005) and an edition of *Pericles* for *William Shakespeare: Complete Works,* edited by Jonathan Bate and Eric Rasmussen (2007).

MICHELLE O'CALLAGHAN is Reader in the Department of English and American Literature, University of Reading. She is the author of *The English Wits: Literature and Sociability in Early Modern England*

(Cambridge University Press, 2007) and *Thomas Middleton, Renaissance Dramatist* (2009).

HELEN OSTOVICH is Professor of English at McMaster University. She is founding editor of the journal *Early Theatre* and a general editor of The Revels Plays, as well as the electronic series, Queen's Men Editions. She edited *The Magnetic Lady* for The Cambridge Edition of the Works of Ben Jonson, *The Late Lancashire Witches* and *A Jovial Crew* for The Complete Works of Richard Brome Online and co-edited a volume of essays, *Locating the Queen's Men, 1583–1603: Material Practices and Conditions of Playing* (2009).

JOHN PEACOCK was Reader in English at Southampton University, where he is now a visiting fellow. His monograph *The Look of Van Dyck: The 'Self-Portrait with a Sunflower' and the Vision of the Painter* was published in 2006. At present he is writing a book on Van Dyck's aristocratic portraits and ideas of nobility in the early modern period.

LOIS POTTER is Ned B. Allen Professor Emeritus of the University of Delaware. Her most recent book is the Shakespeare in Performance volume on *Othello* (2002), and she has written many theatre reviews for *The Times Literary Supplement* and *Shakespeare Quarterly*.

BARBARA RAVELHOFER is Reader in English Literature at Durham and a research associate of the Centre for History and Economics, Cambridge. Her most recent book, *The Early Stuart Masque: Dance, Costume, and Music* (2006), studies illusionistic theatre of the Renaissance with documentary evidence from Germany, France, Italy and the Ottoman Empire.

MARK ROBSON is Associate Professor at the University of Nottingham. His recent publications include *The Sense of Early Modern Writing* (2006) and *Stephen Greenblatt* (2008). Forthcoming publications include (with James Loxley) *Shakespeare, Jonson and the Claims of the Performative* (2010).

JULIE SANDERS is Professor of English Literature and Drama at the University of Nottingham. She is the author of *Ben Jonson's Theatrical Republics* (1998) and has recently edited *The New Inn* for The Cambridge Edition of the Works of Ben Jonson.

MALCOLM SMUTS is Professor of History at the University of Massachusetts Boston and North American head for the Society for Court Studies. His publications include *Court Culture and the Origins of a Royalist Tradition in Early Stuart England* (1987) and *Culture and Power in England, 1585–1685* (1999).

MATTHEW STEGGLE is Reader in English at Sheffield Hallam University. His publications include *Wars of the Theatres: The Poetics of Personation in the Age of Jonson* (1998) and *Laughing and Weeping in Early Modern Theatres* (2007). He has co-edited, with Eric Rasmussen, *Cynthia's Revels* for the forthcoming The Cambridge Edition of the Works of Ben Jonson.

TIFFANY STERN is Professor of Early Modern Drama at Oxford University and the Beaverbrook and Bouverie Fellow and Tutor in English Literature at University College, Oxford. She is the author of *Rehearsal from Shakespeare to Sheridan* (2000), *Making Shakespeare* (2004), *Shakespeare in Parts* (2007, co-written with Simon Palfrey, and winner of the 2009 David Bevington Award for Best New Book in Early Drama Studies) and *Documents of Performance in Early Modern England* (Cambridge University Press, 2009).

GARRETT A. SULLIVAN, JR is Professor of English at Pennsylvania State University. He is the author of *The Drama of Landscape: Land, Property, and Social Relations on the Early Modern Stage* (1998) and *Memory and Forgetting in English Renaissance Drama: Shakespeare, Marlowe, Webster* (Cambridge University Press, 2005). He has co-edited, with Mary Floyd-Wilson, *Environment and Embodiment in Early Modern England* (2007).

MIMI YIU is Assistant Professor of English at Georgetown University. She is currently working on a book manuscript entitled *Building Platforms: Staging the Architecture of Early Modern Subjectivity*.

ADAM ZUCKER is Assistant Professor of English at the University of Massachusetts, Amherst. He is the co-editor, with Alan B. Farmer, of *Localizing Caroline Drama: Politics and Economics of the Early Modern Stage, 1625–42* (2006). His current book project is entitled *The Places of Wit in Early Modern Comedy* (forthcoming).

Acknowledgements

The editor would like first and foremost to thank the contributors to this volume. It has been a huge undertaking made lighter and more enjoyable by the wit and good grace of the contributors. I could not have seen the project through its final few months without the sterling assistance of my research assistant, Sarah Grandage, who worked above and beyond the call of duty and to whom endless thanks are due. Any remaining errors are wholly my responsibility. I am grateful to the University of Nottingham's School of English Studies, in particular the then Head of School, Dominic Head, who made that research assistance possible, and to all my colleagues who have been tirelessly supportive and encouraging at key moments in the process.

The volume was commissioned by Sarah Stanton at Cambridge University Press, and she has remained wholly engaged in the process from start to finish. I am deeply grateful for her insight and support at all times. It is something of an honour that these chapters will appear in print in close proximity to the monumental new Cambridge University Press edition of Jonson's works. It is a project on which I consider myself as having served a remarkable apprenticeship, and I am glad to have the opportunity to thank the three general editors, David Bevington, Martin Butler and Ian Donaldson, here by means of the dedication not only for their work on that project but also for their support and encouragement at numerous stages of my career in the considerable shadow of Ben Jonson.

Finally, there is the man behind the scenes. To John Higham, thanks and love as always.

Note on editions used

The edition of Jonson referred to throughout, unless otherwise indicated, is *The Cambridge Edition of the Works of Ben Jonson,* general editors David Bevington, Martin Butler and Ian Donaldson. The edition is due to be published by Cambridge University Press in 2011, and I am grateful to the editors and the Press for advance access to the edition at proof stage.

Chronology

Date	Jonson's life and works	Events
1572	Ben Jonson born.	
1587		Rose Theatre built.
1588		Defeat of Spanish Armada.
1589		James VI travels to Denmark to marry Princess Anna of Denmark.
1595		Swan Theatre built.
1596		Second Blackfriars Theatre built.
1597	*The Case is Altered* performed. *The Isle of Dogs* [lost play] performed.	*Isle of Dogs* controversy.
1598	*Every Man In His Humour* performed. Jonson imprisoned over death of actor Gabriel Spencer in a duel. Narrowly escapes hanging. Branded with T for Tyburn.	Material from The Theatre transported for reconstruction as Globe Theatre.
1599	*Every Man Out of His Humour* performed.	
1600	*Cynthia's Revels (The Fountain of Self-Love)* performed?	Fortune Theatre built. Second Blackfriars Theatre first used.
1601	*Poetaster, or The Arraignment* performed. *Every Man In His Humour* Quarto published.	Essex rebellion (fails).

1602	Additions to *The Spanish Tragedy* written?	
1603	*A Particular Entertainment at Althorp.*	Death of Elizabeth I.
	Sejanus His Fall performed?	Accession of James VI of Scotland as James I of England.
1604		James VI adopts title 'King of Great Britain, France and Ireland'.
1605	*The Masque of Blackness* performed.	Gunpowder Plot.
	Eastward Ho! performed.	
1606	*Hymenaei* performed.	?Whitefriars Theatre built (not in use until 1609).
	Volpone performed.	
1607	*An Entertainment at Theobalds* performed.	John Smith settles Jamestown, Virginia.
1608	*The Masque of Beauty* performed.	
	The Haddington Masque performed.	
1609	*The Masque of Queens* performed.	
	The Entertainment at Britain's Burse performed.	
	Epicene, or The Silent Woman performed.	
1610	*The Alchemist* performed.	
1611	*Oberon, The Fairy Prince* performed.	
	Love Freed From Ignorance and Folly performed.	
	Catiline His Conspiracy performed.	
1612	'To Penshurst' written.	Death of Henry, Prince of Wales.
1614	*Bartholomew Fair* performed.	
1615	*Mercury Vindicated from the Alchemists at Court* performed.	Inigo Jones appointed Surveyor of the King's Works.
1616	*The Golden Age Restored* performed.	Death of Shakespeare.
	Every Man In His Humour folio published.	

Chronology

	Epigrams published.	
	The Forest published.	
	The Devil is an Ass performed.	
	Christmas His Masque performed.	
1617	*The Vision of Delight* performed.	James VI and I visits Scotland.
	Lovers Made Men performed.	
1618	*Pleasure Reconciled to Virtue* performed.	
	For the Honour of Wales performed.	
	Jonson's walk to Scotland.	
1619	*Informations to William Drummond* (published 1711).	Death of Queen Anna.
1620	*News From the New World Discovered in the Moon* performed.	
	The Cavendish Christening Entertainment performed.	
1621	*Pan's Anniversary, or The Shepherd's Holiday* performed.	
	The Gypsies Metamorphosed performed.	
1622	*The Masque of Augurs* performed.	
1623	*Time Vindicated to Himself and to His Honours* performed.	
1624	*Neptune's Triumph for the Return of Albion* planned but unperformed.	
1625	*The Fortunate Isles and Their Union* performed.	Death of James VI and I; accession of Charles I. Charles I marries Henrietta Maria.
1626	*The Staple of News* performed.	
1629	*The New Inn* performed.	Charles dissolves parliament: beginning of eleven-year period of 'personal rule' without parliament.
1631	*Love's Triumph through Callipolis* performed.	
	Chloridia performed.	

1632	*The Magnetic Lady* performed.	
1633	*A Tale of a Tub* performed.	Charles I visits Scotland for his coronation.
	The King's Entertainment at Welbeck performed.	
1634	*Love's Welcome at Bolsover* performed.	
1637	*The Sad Shepherd* written (unfinished at time of death).	
	Ben Jonson dies.	
	(*The Underwood* and *Timber, or Discoveries* published in 1640–41.)	

Introduction

Ben Jonson has always been many things to many people. For the playwright Edward Bond, who in his 1973 play *Bingo* depicted him in the midst of a heavy drinking session with his rival William Shakespeare, he was a cantankerous old man, hateful of his rivals and the very art form in which he was required to work, as well as himself.[1] For the poet U. A. Fanthorpe, speaking on behalf of William Drummond of Hawthornden, with whom Jonson stayed during his 1618 trip to Scotland (he walked there and back, a considerable feat of performance in itself), he is a swaggerer and a bully who is nevertheless the creator of sweet and tender verse.[2] Fanthorpe herself would regularly select Jonson poems when asked to contribute to anthologies on particular themes so it was clearly an opinion she shared. Even in his own lifetime he was satirized on the public stage for his lowly origins and installed in a role that was the forerunner of the Poet Laureate by King James VI and I. His generic range is in some respects a marker of the difficulty of categorizing him as an author: he was involved in everything from poetry to plays to masques and entertainments to prose. His plays were performed in different types of playhouses and contexts, and he tried his hand at various times at comedy, tragedy and romance.

The popular figure of myth and legend suggests a heavy drinker and gourmand; Jonson's increasing bulk as he grew older occasioned comment from himself as much as anyone, and yet, and there always appears to be an 'and yet' where Jonson is concerned, he managed that aforementioned walk to Scotland. He is renowned as a man quick to argument, someone who had been tried and only narrowly acquitted for the murder of an actor in a duel in the early part of his theatrical career (he was branded with a T for 'Tyburn' on his thumb as a permanent reminder, a literary mark of some note). And yet this is also the Westminster-educated classicist, the invoker of Horace and Tacitus, Martial and Juvenal, the man who added copious new terms to the English language. Compared to Shakespeare, and, as this volume attests, this was a comparison which dogged Jonson even in his own lifetime, Jonson is frequently held up as a social documenter, the man whose work is less for 'all time' than embedded, sometimes inextricably, in its own time, its jargons and its grievances, its political pressure points and its spatially and temporally specific structures, actual and cultural. More than anyone, perhaps, he is linked to the space and site of the expanding capital itself in the late sixteenth and early seventeenth centuries. For that is another point about the Jonsonian career – that it is remarkably long, and that alone would caution against simple categorizations. Jonson wrote plays and poems during the reigns of Elizabeth I, James VI and I, and Charles I, and it would be a strange beast indeed that did not alter and change with the flow of political life.

It is, then, *all* of these Jonsons that this volume seeks to contextualize. The first part, 'Life, works and afterlife', looks, as the title suggests, at the man's life and works but from a range of perspectives. Biographical, textual and theoretical approaches to Jonson are deployed here, and his rich and varied afterlife in criticism and performance is also considered. The second part on 'Cultural and historical contexts' selects a range of themes, many of a socio-historical angle, not only to shed light on the subject matter and operations of particular plays and poems but also to examine and make visible the events and contexts that were the backbone of Jonson's writing life and experience. The aim is not to offer comprehensive surveys of the Jonsonian canon nor to offer closed-down versions of his life but rather to offer a series of vibrant interventions and discussions, sometimes operating in sharp contrast to one another, in order to emphasize the sheer plurality of our subject, in the hope that these will inspire new and newly engaged encounters with Jonson and his work on the part of readers.

NOTES

1. Edward Bond, *Bingo* in *Plays: Three* (London: Methuen, 1987).
2. See U. A. Fanthorpe, 'Jonson at Hawthornden', published in *Queuing for the Sun* (Cornwall: Peterloo Poets, 2003).

PART I

Life, works and afterlife

CHAPTER I

Tales of a life

Richard Dutton

In 1925, just to as the first two volumes of their magisterial Oxford *Ben Jonson* went press, C. H. Herford and Percy Simpson were faced with a devastating challenge to the material in those volumes which are largely concerned with Jonson's life. C. L. Stainer published an eighty-page booklet, whose title is self-explanatory: *Jonson and Drummond: Their Conversations – A Few Remarks on an 18th Century Forgery*.[1] The account left by William Drummond of his conversations with Jonson, when Jonson visited Edinburgh in the winter of 1618/19 and stayed for a time at Drummond's Hawthornden estate, has long been the cornerstone of our knowledge of Jonson's eventful life and no less colourful opinions. An edited summary of what Drummond wrote was published under the title of 'Heads of a Conversation betwixt the Famous Poet Ben Johnson, and William Drummond of Hawthornden, January 1619' in the 1711 folio of Drummond's *Works*, edited by Bishop John Sage and Thomas Ruddiman. The original document was lost after they saw it, but not before an apparently full and faithful transcript of it was made by Sir Robert Sibbald, a physician and antiquary. In 1843, that transcript (Sibbald MS.33.3.19) – much fuller and more unbuttoned than Sage and Ruddimans' version – was discovered by David Laing in the Advocates' Library of the National Library of Scotland.[2]

From the very beginning there were those who *wished* that it might have been a forgery. Opinions such as that 'Shakespeare wanted art' would hardly endear themselves to bardolators, and even Jonson's defenders feared that it reinforced a reputation for being envious, ambitious and possibly mean-spirited. Some of its frank and bawdy anecdotes, moreover, were unrepeatable in polite Victorian society. And, in the wake of notable Shakespearian forgeries by William Henry Ireland and John Payne Collier, the circumstances of the transmission of Drummond's document did leave some scope for conspiracy theories. But Stainer went completely over the top. He dubbed Sibbald's 'transcript' a clumsy forgery; he suggested that Sage and Ruddiman knew it was a forgery but rejected it in favour of concocting their own rival version, adding to it forged letters by Drayton and Jonson to Drummond (Sage was a bishop, remember); he even argued that Drummond's son, Sir William Drummond, was a consenting party to the whole business.

It fell to Percy Simpson to expose Stainer's unscholarly tissue of mendacity and so maintain the *bona fides* of the 'Life' section of the *Oxford Jonson,* which in fact were largely the work of his partner, Herford. He did this in 'The Genuineness of the Drummond "Conversations".[3] Where, for example, Stainer doubted that the 'Johnson' indicted for killing the actor Gabriel Spencer in 1598 was the poet, Simpson was able to cite the independent witness of Philip Henslowe, who in a letter records that 'gabrell' had been 'slayen in hogesden fyldes at the hands of benge[men] Jonson bricklayer'.[4] This was published in 1841, far too late for Sibbald, Sage or Ruddiman, but Stainer should have known about it before he started making such claims.

The whole business is of critical importance in the narrative Drummond tells: 'being appealed to the fields, he had killed his adversary, which had hurt him in the arm, and whose sword was ten inches longer than his; for the which he was imprisoned, and almost at the gallows. Then took he his religion by trust of a priest who visited him in prison. Thereafter he was twelve years a papist' (*Informations,* 13.186–90). This offers itself as a decisive, life-changing sequence of events. As I myself have suggested, for example, 'It is difficult not to read Jonson's religious conversion in 1598 as an act of defiance against the authority to which he had so nearly forfeited his life, in what he regarded as a matter of honour … The assertion of his authority as a writer coincides with his adoption of Roman Catholicism as an act of symbolic resistance to the overweening state.'[5] If Stainer's claims had been substantiated, this entire construction of what many would regard as the most critical years of Jonson's life would have no foundation.

As I shall go on to argue, we still need to be circumspect about the precise terms in which Jonson, Drummond, or both record such events. But it is helpful, to say the least, to have corroboration such as Henslowe's letter to testify to the factual basis of it all. And whenever we *can* corroborate Drummond in such matters, his account holds up. There are, of course, apparent untruths there: 'Next himself only Fletcher and Chapman could make a masque' (*Informations,* 3.38). There is no record of Fletcher ever writing a masque. But this is an entirely plausible slip in the context of Drummond writing things up after the event, where talk of Beaumont and Fletcher might very understandably have been confused in his memory. On biographical matters concerning Jonson, however, he has not been shown to be wrong on any significant item. Stainer, for example, tried to follow up his denial of the Spencer killing with claims that '[t]hereafter he was twelve years a papist' are belied by Jonson's own writings: 'The quarto of *Every Man In His Humour,* published in 1601, with its phrase, "Nor rigid *Roman*-catholike," shows that he was a Protestant at that time.'[6] This was a sitting duck for Simpson: 'The quarto of 1601 says nothing of the kind. Mr. Stainer does not know that he is quoting the revised text of the play first printed in the folio of 1616.'[7] Personally I would add that even in 1616 the phrase does not prove 'that he was a Protestant at that time': the catch is in the force of 'rigid'.

But enough of Stainer. Simpson's damning dismissal is accurate in all particulars: 'He is grossly ignorant of the facts of Jonson's life. He makes a parade of minute knowledge which is often erroneous, he misreads evidence, and he ignores obvious facts which tell against him. In fact, the book is a monument of misreading and perversity.'[8] Drummond was vindicated, and has continued to be so by subsequent scholarship. For example: 'He himself was posthumous born a month after his father's decease; brought up poorly, put to school by a friend (his master Camden), after taken from it, and put to another craft (I think was to be a wright or bricklayer), which he could not endure' (*Informations,* 13.180–3). The fact of a stepfather is never mentioned but might be said to be implied. Thomas Fuller, writing more than twenty years after Jonson's death and without citing his authorities, claimed 'when a little child he lived in Hartshorn Lane near Charing-cross, where his mother married a bricklayer for her second husband'.[9] In 1960, J. B. Bamborough put a very plausible name, Robert Brett, to that 'second husband', a building contractor who did in fact live in Hartshorn Lane. And, in 1988, Mark Eccles established not only that Jonson himself was a member of the Tylers and Bricklayers Company, but that he continued his quarterage payments to them until as late as 1611.[10]

So Drummond is factually correct on such matters, as far as we can tell – and as far as he chooses to commit himself. This is an instance (one of many) where we would dearly love to know exactly what Jonson told him. Drummond's 'I think' surely suggests that Jonson himself did not mention the bricklaying, which he may well have heard about from friends in London, where it was certainly no secret, as Henslowe's letter attests. The underlying tale is a very Dickensian one, of an orphaned Ben, whose talents are apparent to some, but not to his (unnamed) stepfather, and who is put to demeaning work, from which he later escapes (implicitly on the strength of his own abilities, since his earlier chance of a first-rate education was cut short). But is this tale Jonson's or Drummond's? Ian Donaldson suggests that Drummond was essentially at pains to record what he heard and saw of his famous guest:

> for the most part [he] keeps his own opinions well out of view. The title bestowed upon these notes in more recent times, *Conversations with William Drummond of Hawthornden,* is not only at variance with Drummond's own (alternative) titles, but misleading in its suggestion that the notes record a dialogue or exchange of views between the two men. The opinions noted are unvaryingly those of Jonson himself, though the narrative voice, strongly coloured by Scotticisms ... is clearly that of Drummond.[11]

But how can we tell the teller from the tale? Was someone being coy about the bricklaying, and, if so, was it the self-made Jonson (at the height of his laureate fame in 1619) or the fastidious Scots laird? The biographical tradition has largely treated the bricklaying as on a par with the work in the blacking factory of David Copperfield and indeed of Charles Dickens himself, a dark secret from which the later life was always a slightly neurotic, even Oedipal escape. Yet this may be to see it through Victorian eyes or indeed the eyes of a member of the Scots gentry who never had to work for a living. Jonson himself left no direct comment on the matter (unlike his enemies, who did indeed taunt him with it often enough). But the fact that Jonson retained his membership of the Tylers and Bricklayers Company for so long tells a rather different story and one which our recent increased understanding of citizen status, and of relations between the theatres and the livery companies, makes us better able to understand.[12] Even Henslowe's note about 'benge Jonson bricklayer', so often read as a scornful snub, may be no more than an accurate record of the actor-playwright's status in 1598, the kind of thing a successful Elizabethan businessman would want to keep track of.

What this should bring home to us is that the real worry about Drummond's *Informations* is not that they might be forgeries but that (in addition to the ongoing ambiguity of whether it is actually Drummond or Jonson speaking at any particular moment) we can only see them through modern eyes, which may not always understand what they are seeing. I want to pursue that issue in relation to two of the most widely quoted passages in Drummond, ones for which we have no corroboration elsewhere or where the corroboration we have makes reading them more difficult, not less. These are the mentions of *Sejanus* and *Eastward Ho!,* both texts that brought Jonson into confrontation with state authorities at the beginning of the most fruitful decade of his career.

'Northampton was his mortal enemy for brawling, on a St George's Day, one of his attenders; he was called before the Council for his *Sejanus,* and accused both of popery and treason by him' (*Informations,* 13.250–2). Thus Ian Donaldson reduces to intelligible modern English one of the more syntactically impenetrable passages that Sibbald transcribed.[13] Unfortunately, Sage and Ruddiman chose not to print this passage, so we do not have their separate authority for it. What, if any, is the relationship between the brawling and being called before the (Privy) Council? What, if any, is the relationship between *Sejanus* and accusations of 'popery and treason'? Is the only common factor between these two events (or three, if the accusations were not part of the Privy Council business) Northampton? Henry Howard, first Earl of Northampton, was a scion of one of the oldest noble families in England and one of the most unprincipled politicians of the Jacobean era. Son of the poet the Earl of Surrey and brother of the 4th Duke of Norfolk (who was executed for plotting on behalf of Mary, Queen of Scots), he changed his religious allegiance four times over the years, though he was widely believed to be Catholic at heart. It is often assumed (though on no authority – this is the only tangible record of their being 'mortal enem[ies]') that the real antagonism between Howard and Jonson would have been over religion: the Catholic peer turned (for now) Protestant polishing his own credentials at the expense of the Protestant-turned-Catholic playwright.

And perhaps it was. But this reading quickly glosses over the beginning of the passage, doubtless to indulge the modern taste for 'popery and treason'. There are other possibilities. When and why did this brawling take place? Throughout Elizabeth's reign Howard was in effect an outcast, sometimes directly under suspicion by the authorities and never with the real access to power that he clearly believed his lineage warranted. If Jonson, for whatever reason, engaged in a quarrel with one of his attendants – like Kent with Oswald in *King Lear* – it was reckless at that time but not exactly foolhardy. Such behaviour would hardly have been out of character with what we learn elsewhere in the *Informations,* which tell us how he fought at least three duels – how he killed an enemy in the face of both camps (13.185), killed Gabriel Spencer (13.186–8) and 'beat [Marston], and took his pistol from him' (13.216). A Freudian could have a field day with this, and not least with Jonson's determination to let Drummond know that Spencer's sword had been 10 inches longer than his own. But this also has to be seen in the context of an extremely contentious age, when matters of honour, status and manhood were often referred to the duelling fields, despite the best efforts of the authorities to stop it. Jonson may simply have stood on his dignity in some context.[14] Howard in turn would have felt the affront to the dignity of one of England's most ancient families. Following the famous tennis-court confrontation between them, Elizabeth herself told Sir Philip Sidney in no uncertain terms that he was not fit to match swords with the 17th Earl of Oxford. How much greater was the gulf between Jonson and Howard (or, in this context, even one of Howard's 'attenders', who would have worn his livery and so represented the family honour). Howard would not at that time have carried the authority of an Oxford, but he would have regarded a playwright like Jonson as an upstart nobody, beneath his notice. And he may well have nursed his resentment until he really had the authority to put him in his place.

From the moment James I came to the throne the Howard family in general were restored to royal favour. Henry was quickly appointed to the Privy Council and on 13 March 1604 was made Earl of Northampton. If Jonson engaged in that brawl after the change of reigns, it was foolhardy in the extreme: Howard carried the authority to match his prestige. And *Sejanus* perhaps gave him just the excuse he needed to exercise it. Unfortunately, we have no corroboration of the circumstances, since the Privy Council records for the period seem to have been destroyed in the Whitehall fire of 1619. We cannot even say whether it was the one (apparently disastrous) performance in 1603 that prompted the Privy Council summons, or the revised text published in 1605.[15] That is one reason we cannot say whether the charges of 'popery and treason' related to the play. They might, for example, have been occasioned by Jonson's arraignment for recusancy, in the wake of the Gunpowder Plot, in January 1606. On the other hand, it was once incomprehensible to twentieth-century readers that *Sejanus* could have troubled the authorities at all, especially in matters of religion. According to John Palmer, for instance, it had not 'the faintest analogy with anything to be observed in English contemporary laws, liberties or persons'.[16] But we are indebted to two recent pieces of scholarship by Gary Taylor and Peter Lake, which demonstrate convincingly (and to that extent yet again vindicate Drummond's *Informations*) just how the play might be coded to address matters of 'popery' and so perhaps also of 'treason'.[17] But even so, which really mattered more to Northampton, supposed 'popery and treason' or the affront to his family honour?

The question is all the more pertinent when we set it against the other passage that I want to consider. 'He was delated by S[i]r James Murray to the king for writing something against the Scots in a play, *Eastward Ho!*, and voluntarily imprisoned himself w[i]t[h] Chapman and Marston, who had written it amongst th[e]m. The report was that that they should then had their ears cut and noses' (*Informations,* 13.207–10). There then follows the melodramatic tale of a banquet following their release, attended by 'Camden, Selden and others', at which Jonson's mother produced 'lusty strong poison' which she intended to put in his drink but 'first to have drunk of it herself', if the punishment had been carried out.

In this instance there is – or at least appears to be – corroboration of the imprisonment, if not the banquet. Ten letters have survived, three from Chapman and seven from Jonson, all addressed to major figures of the Jacobean establishment (from the King and the Earl of Salisbury down), asking for help in relation to their joint imprisonment over a play.[18] There is in fact room to doubt whether these letters relate to *Eastward Ho!* No title is actually mentioned, nor is Marston. Stainer (and in this he has not been alone) wanted them to relate to the *Sejanus* business, partly on the grounds that Chapman is widely suspected to be the unnamed co-author of the original version of that play. But the *Eastward Ho!* association seems the more likely because one of Chapman's letters, that to the King, talks of his and Jonson's 'chief offences' being 'but two clauses, and both of them not our own'.[19] This seems to refer to an unnamed third author, presumably Marston. But the implication *seems* to be that Marston was not imprisoned with them. The title page of Marston's *The Fawn,* published only the next year in 1606, explicitly refers to his being out of London, and the two items together have led many to conclude that he 'contrived to avoid arrest until this uproar was over'.[20]

This, of course, contradicts the claim in the *Informations* that Jonson was imprisoned with 'Chapman *and* Marston' (my emphasis). Did Jonson's memory let him down on this? Did Drummond misunderstand? Another of these letters – Jonson's to Salisbury – shamefacedly admits that he and Chapman have been '*committed* to a vile prison',[21] which does not square very well with the *Informations* claim that he '*voluntarily* imprisoned himself' (my emphases in both quotations). It is difficult to escape the conclusion that Jonson embroidered his part in this affair, presumably to impress his Scottish host, though it is less easy to see why he should compound the self-aggrandizing 'voluntarily' with the mistake about Marston being there. Suzanne Gossett has reviewed these matters from Marston's perspective and, agreeing that he probably fled, concludes:

Marston seems to have had great difficulty developing and maintaining 'the socially sanctioned bonds among men within the institutions of the theatre'. Even Jonson, although capable of killing a fellow actor, normally honored the demands of those bonds; consider his claim that he voluntarily imprisoned himself with Chapman. Even if not true, as 'spin' it reflects an expected attitude towards colleagues.[22]

This seems more than plausible. Homosocial bonds are a constant issue in Jonson's plays and poetry, and their significance surfaces often in the *Informations:* 'Th[a]t S[i]r John Roe loved him ... He died in his arms of the pest, and he furnished his charges, £20'; 'That Sir R. Ayton loved him dearly'; 'That Chapman and Fletcher were loved of him' and so on (*Informations,* 11.113, 12.140–1; 11.120; 11.126). Co-authoring a play was doubtless a very different relationship, yet it too carried loyalties and obligations. Voluntarily imprisoning yourself alongside colleagues when the vicious penalties for seditious libel might be the outcome was not so unlike tending a friend who was dying of the plague (and paying his substantial 'charges'). And at that moment in 1619 it was more important to Jonson to project himself obeying that code, even to the extent of putting himself in the company of the absent Marston, than it was to be true to the facts.

This brings into focus the way the discussion moves to the banquet, with Jonson's male guests (Camden, Selden) and the melodramatic figure of his mother, prepared with poison for both him and herself. The implication is that for Ben to suffer his 'ears cut and nose[]' would be an intolerable shame for both of them, though conversely he himself had submitted to that risk 'voluntarily'. When William Prynne actually had his ears cropped over *Histriomastix* in 1633 he carried the mutilation as a sign of pride – to the extent that he was tried again for seditious libel in 1637, lost the rest of his ears and was branded *SL* (which he insisted meant *stigmata Laudis* – the marks of Archbishop William Laud, his nemesis). Over *Eastward Ho!* (at least in retrospect) Jonson wanted perhaps to project a similar defiance, if the worst should come to the worst. That was the true masculine way, as opposed to his mother's idea of affecting the 'antique Roman'.

Read in this way, the whole passage becomes an assertion of Jonson's manliness. I joked earlier about a possible Freudian reading of the swordplay in the *Informations,* but there is a serious side to all of this. Repeatedly in this document Jonson projects himself (with Drummond's help) in the most manly light possible, but it is a manliness whose codes we are only just beginning to understand. They are tied to questions of physical courage ('ears cut and noses', duelling) to social hierarchy (brawling with Northampton's attendant, berating Salisbury for the dining arrangements), to professional relations (as with fellow playwrights, poets and scholars), to very specific forms of misogyny ('He thought the use of a maid nothing in comparison to the wantonness of a wife, and would never have another mistress'; 'He married a wife who was a shrew yet honest. Five years he had not bedded w[i]t[h] her': *Informations,*13.219–20, 13.192–3), all centering upon the issue of honesty and honour. 'Of all styles he loved most to be named honest, and hath of that an hundred letters so naming him' (*Informations*, 18.507–8). One has to guess that they all came from men.

The issue with Drummond's *Informations* is not whether they are 'true' or not but whether we can read them with close enough attention to these early modern codes and Jonson's very specific agenda of self-projection. We may look to them to find out more about popery or patronage, censorship or literary taste. And we will find it, but only through the omnipresent perspective of Jonson's manliness.

NOTES

1. C. L. Stainer, *Jonson and Drummond: Their Conversations – A Few Remarks on an 18th Century Forgery* (Oxford: Blackwell, 1925).
2. On the modern titles used for this document, see Note 11 below.
3. Percy Simpson, 'Heads of a Conversation betwixt the Famous Poet Ben Johnson, and William Drummond of Hawthornden, January 1619', *Review of English Studies*, 2 (5) (1926): 42–50. The 'Life' appears in C. H. Herford, P. Simpson and E. Simpson (eds.), *Ben Jonson*, 11 vols. (Oxford: Oxford University Press, 1925–52).
4. Quoting from W. W. Greg's edition of the Henslowe Papers (London: A. H. Bullen, 1907), p. 48.
5. Richard Dutton, *Ben Jonson, 'Volpone' and the Gunpowder Plot* (Cambridge: Cambridge University Press, 2008), pp. 15–16, 25–6.
6. Stainer, *Jonson and Drummond: Their Conversations*, p. 29.
7. Percy Simpson 'The Genuineness of the Drummond "Conversations"', *Review of English Studies*, 2 (5) (1926): 42–50; p. 48.
8. Simpson, 'The Genuineness of the Drummond "Conversations"', p. 50.
9. Thomas Fuller, *The History of the Worthies of England* (London, 1662), 'Westminster', p. 243.
10. J. B. Bamborough, 'The Early Life of Ben Jonson', *Times Literary Supplement*, 8 April 1960, p. 225; Mark Eccles, 'Ben Jonson, "Citizen and Bricklayer"', *Notes and Queries*, 35 (ns) (1988): 44–56.
11. *Introduction to Informations to William Drummond of Hawthornden* (his own preferred title, from the cover-sheet of the Sibbald manuscript) in The Cambridge Edition of the Works of Ben Jonson, 4. *Informations* is how I shall refer to the document henceforth.
12. See, for example, David Kathman, 'Grocers, Goldsmiths, and Drapers: Freemen and Apprentices in the Elizabethan Theater', *Shakespeare Quarterly*, 55 (2004): 1–49.
13. The passage is given in the Herford and Simpson edition as follows: 'Northampton was his mortall enimie for brauling on a St Georges day one of his attenders, he was called befor the Councell for his Sejanus &

accused both of popperie and treason by him', in *Conversations with William Drummond of Hawthornden*, lines 325–7, in Herford and Simpson (eds.), *Ben Jonson*, vol. I, pp. 128–78.
14. Cf. his challenge to the Earl of Salisbury: '"My Lord", said he, "You promised I should dine with you, but I do not", for he had none of his own meat. He esteemeth only th[a]t his meat which was of his own dish' (*Informations*, 13.244–6). For a fuller insight into the duelling code of honour in Jonson's day, see the autobiography of his friend, Sir Edward Herbert, later Lord Herbert, later Lord Herbert of Cherbury. Edward Herbert, *Autobiography*, ed. J. M. Shuttleworth (Oxford: Oxford University Press, 1976).
15. I have explained at length elsewhere the compound levels of our ignorance about *Sejanus*, so I shall not repeat it here. See Richard Dutton, *Mastering the Revels: The Regulation and Censorship of English Renaissance Drama* (Basingstoke: Macmillan, 1991), pp. 10–16.
16. John Palmer, *Ben Jonson* (London: Routledge, 1934), p. 72.
17. Gary Taylor, 'Divine []sences', *Shakespeare Survey*, 54 (2001): 13–30; and Peter Lake, 'From Leicester his Commonwealth to *Sejanus his Fall*: Ben Jonson and the Politics of Roman (Catholic) Virtue', in Ethan Cagan (ed.), *Catholics and the 'Protestant Nation': Religious Politics and Identity in Early Modern England* (Manchester: Manchester University Press, 2005).
18. The letters can be found as an appendix to the Revels Plays edition of *Eastward Ho!*, edited by R. W. Van Fossen (Manchester: Manchester University Press, 1979), pp. 218–25.
19. Fossen, *Eastward Ho!*, p. 218. The 'two clauses' squares suggestively with the apparent censorship of the quarto of *Eastward Ho!* that occurred after its first imprint, when one passage in 3.3 was omitted and another was slightly revised. Even so, plenty of anti-Scottish satire survived into the second impression. See Dutton, *Mastering the Revels*, pp. 174–5.
20. MacDonald P. Jackson and Michael Neill (eds.), *The Selected Works of John Marston* (Cambridge: Cambridge University Press, 1986), pp. xiv–xv.
21. Fossen, *Eastward Ho!*, p. 221.
22. Suzanne Gossett, 'Marston, Collaboration, and *Eastward Ho!*', *Renaissance Drama*, 33 (2004): 181–200; p. 195. She cites Jeffrey Masten, *Textual Intercourses: Collaboration, Authorship, and Sexualities* (Cambridge: Cambridge University Press, 1977), p. 2. She also adds her own note: 'Jonson's career with Inigo Jones demonstrates both collaboration at its most effective and its eventual limits and collapse.'

CHAPTER 2

Jonson in the Elizabethan period

Matthew Steggle

Queen Elizabeth I died on 24 March 1603. In the months after her death, plague broke out in London, and thousands were killed by it, among them Ben Jonson's eldest son. If one were to imagine for a moment that Jonson himself, too, had died in that plague, and that all that was left of Jonson's corpus was the Elizabethan section of it as it now survives, what sort of writer would Jonson seem?

This type of counterfactual game is, of course, an intriguing and harmless one to play with any author, but it presents particular difficulties to readers of Elizabethan Jonson, since the major paradigms for thinking about Jonson's work tend to belong distinctively to the later, Jacobean, portion of his career. Most obviously, the four comedies that sustain Jonson's reputation as a dramatist in the modern theatre – *Volpone*, *The Alchemist*, *Epicene* and *Bartholomew Fair* – were all written during the reign of Elizabeth's successor King James I. As for the second part of Jonson's major cultural significance, as a writer of masques, entertainments and royal entries, this had not yet begun when Elizabeth died, and started, in fact, with James's arrival in London months after her death. By 1603, too, some of Jonson's poetry was written, but it is hard to tell exactly how much. So the canon of texts one has to work with when thinking about the Elizabethan Jonson is far from being merely a representative subset of Jonson's total output.

What is more, the most usual cliché of Jonson criticism is obviously inappropriate to his Elizabethan incarnation. We tend to imagine Jonson as a figure of metaphorical, and literal, bulk and *gravitas*, obviously learned, recognized as a giant in his field, and rather above the day-to-day business of new plays at the theatre. He is usually pictured holding court in a tavern surrounded by admirers, rather than learning his trade. But the Elizabethan Jonson was literally, and metaphorically, lean and hungry, a 'hungrie-face ... hollow-cheekt Scrag' according to one enemy, still establishing a name and an identity.[1] That identity is forged most clearly in his Elizabethan plays, and it is on these that the ensuing discussion will mainly focus.

Jonson's 1616 folio offers one narrative of an Elizabethan playwriting career. It begins with *Every Man In His Humour* (performed 1598), a city comedy set in London whose Prologue offers a manifesto for a new, fresh, realist drama rather than the creaking romances and histories currently popular. In particular, the Prologue promises:

> deeds, and language such as men do use,
> And persons such as Comedy would choose
> When she would show an image of the times,
> And sport with human follies, not with crimes.
> (Prologue, ll. 21–4)

In that play's successor, *Every Man Out of His Humour* (performed in 1599), Jonson develops this idea of comedy as a curative for human folly, based around and unified by the pseudo-medical terminology of humours. *Every Man Out of His Humour* also inaugurates a new stage genre, 'comical satire', developed further in the two subsequent 'comical satires', *Cynthia's Revels* (performed in 1600), and *Poetaster* (performed in 1601), both of which, distinctively, include long discussions of the theory and practice of moral reformation through satirical reprehension. In *Cynthia's Revels*, the scholar-satirist Crites has a mandate to 'correct, / And punish, with our laughter' given to him by no less a person than the god Mercury, present onstage as a divine warrant for his subsequent satirical humiliation of the play's fools (5.1.17–18). *Poetaster* puts on stage as a character the poet Horace, and, in a passage translated closely from the Latin of the 'real' Horace, Horace himself defends his right to use satire as an instrument of almost legal reform:

> But if they shall be sharp yet modest rhymes
> That spare men's persons, and but tax their crimes,
> Such shall in open court find current pass,
> Were Caesar judge, and with the maker's grace.
> (3.5.133–6)[2]

This programme to institute a new drama, though, involves Jonson in bruising personal feuds with other dramatists writing for the popular theatre. Indeed, *Poetaster* itself is framed as an attempt to educate the writer's less literary colleagues including Thomas Dekker:

> I at last, unwilling,
> But weary, I confess, of so much trouble,
> Thought, I would try, if shame could win upon 'em.

> And therefore chose Augustus Caesar's times,
> ...
> And by this line (although no parallel)
> I hoped at last they would sit down and blush.
> (Apologetical Dialogue, ll. 85–8, 93–4)

This project fails. As the end of Elizabeth's reign approaches, Jonson is last seen as the author-figure of the Apologetical Dialogue to *Poetaster*, retreating altogether from the rough-and-tumble world of the commercial stage:

> Leave me. There's something come into my thought,
> That must and shall be sung, high and aloof,
> Safe from the wolf's black jaw and the dull ass's hoof.
> (Apologetical Dialogue, ll. 224–6)

Instead, according to the narrative of the folio, Jonson sets out alone to develop a literary, classicizing, essentially solitary drama at whose heart are ideas of moral reformation and rescue, which is exemplified by the Jacobean comedies and to which the folio itself is testament.

The intriguing thing, however, about the folio's narrative of Jonson's Elizabethan career is that it is so obviously just that: a narrative. *Every Man In His Humour*, *Every Man Out of His Humour*, *Cynthia's Revels* and *Poetaster* all survive in Elizabethan quarto versions, all textually substantially different from those selected for publication in the folio. The passages directly quoted from Jonson so far, for instance, are all taken solely from folio-only material, which in some of those cases at least is evidently written years later than the play into which it is inserted. The very term 'comical satire' is one which first appears in the 1616 folio, as a retrospective and unifying description. The folio works hard to impose, or at least to accentuate, the narratives of dramatic strictness, classicism and a retreat from the popular. But there are other ways of reading Jonson's Elizabethan career, and what follows offers one alternative construction of that career read 'against the grain' of the version encapsulated in the folio.

The Elizabethan Jonson was both an actor and a flexible and adaptable literary professional, active in a range of genres: not just comedy, but also tragedy – it was as a tragedian that Francis Meres praised him in 1598 – and also, seemingly, history, or at least lost plays on historical subjects including *Robert II King of Scots* and *Richard Crookback*. The supposedly solitary Jonson collaborated successfully with a range of other writers, including Thomas Dekker himself. He also took part in revising existing plays, including *The Spanish Tragedy*. The dark and philosophically playful 'additions' preserved in a later quarto of that play may well be Jonson's work. Finally, and most importantly, there is a fifth surviving Jonson play from the Elizabethan era, although the folio found no space for it: *The Case is Altered,* a lively drama possibly dating from around 1597 and first printed in 1609.

One can consider as a group these five comedies – the four folio plays in their Elizabethan versions, plus *The Case is Altered*. As a group, they are varied and experimental both in setting and in plot. *The Case is Altered* and *Every Man In His Humour* are set, respectively, in Milan and Florence, seemingly in the present day; *Cynthia's Revels* takes place in the valley of Gargaphia, in Greece, at some mythological no-date; and *Poetaster* in a sharply historicized Augustan Rome. *Every Man Out of His Humour* is the most confusing of them all, set in *'Insula Fortunata'*, or 'Elysium', a place which both is, and is not, England (Induction, l. 257). Several characters refer to London, which is seemingly the capital of *Insula Fortunata,* but London itself, in this play, seems like a continent in its own right from an exotic geographical map, where a traveller may go to see the 'Ludgathians' in the Ludgate debtor's prison, or visit the 'Long Lane cannibals' of the second-hand shops near the Strand (5.3.136). And at the heart of *Insula Fortunata,* in what Revels editor Helen Ostovich describes as the central scene of the play, is *Insula Paulina,* the aisle of Saint Paul's, another entire land in itself. Asper/Macilente starts the play by mocking the idea that 'my mind to me a kingdom is' (1.1.14): but in *Every Man Out of His Humour* Jonson experiments with the idea that the stage can represent a dizzying set of separate imagined kingdoms, some of them nested within one another.[3]

Similarly, the plotting in these Elizabethan plays, like the location, is not a mere foreshadowing of the technique of the great plays but something altogether stranger. Plots are driven by young love (*Every Man In His Humour*), or long-lost children (*The Case is Altered*); both elements more familiar from Shakespeare than from Jonson's Jacobean comedies, although both also re-emerge in the Caroline plays. *Poetaster* even includes a 'sentimental' plot, the parting of the lovers Ovid and Julia, treated with seriousness and compassion. More daring still in its plotting is *Cynthia's Revels,* a play whose *dramatis personae* includes three major gods, the nymph Echo and the Evening Star. In such company, conventional comedy of intrigue is untenable, and, instead, with an inventiveness that both reflects Lyly and anticipates *Waiting for Godot,* the non-divine characters spend most of the first four acts simply waiting for things to happen. Of all of the five early plays, *Every Man Out of His Humour* is the most like the later ones in its plotting, telling a story of exhibitionism and deception among a large cast of London fools and knaves. But even *Every Man Out of His Humour* is hardly an exact precursor of the later city comedies, given its proto-Brechtian onstage audience, Mitis and Cordatus, and their friend Asper/Macilente who seems able to travel between the onstage audience and the reality of the play itself.

This treatment of place and plotting in early Jonson makes one look anew at the folio's new Prologue to *Every Man In His Humour*, refusing outlandish settings and geographical transformations, and insisting instead on 'deeds, and language, such as men do use' (Prologue, l. 21). The new Prologue to the revised play, standing first in the whole volume, is programmatic, and one of the things it looks to do is to help fit Jonson's earlier work into the later trajectory of plays such as *The Alchemist*, *Bartholomew Fair* and *Epicene*. But Jonson's early plays are profoundly diverse and innovative in their handling of place and plotting, and perhaps even profoundly anti-realist. The prologue of the folio *Every Man In His Humour* is in some ways singularly inappropriate as an introduction to Jonson's Elizabethan work.

One final extension of this argument, this idea of reading Elizabethan Jonson 'against the grain' of later Jonson, relates to the handling in these plays of the figure who dominates their imagination: Queen Elizabeth herself. By and large, in the history of Jonson criticism, Jonson has been seen as a strongly pro-monarchical writer, largely on the strength of his extensive later ties with James and with James's court. Jonson's early plays, though, and particularly *Every Man Out of His Humour* and *Cynthia's Revels,* might tell a different story about Elizabeth.

By the late 1590s, Elizabeth herself was well into her sixties, and it was evident that her reign was coming towards its end. Although, for obvious reasons, it was imprudent to discuss the succession too openly, James VI of Scotland was widely tipped as her most likely successor. In the earliest of Jonson's surviving plays, reflection on Elizabeth's mortality is appropriately muted. *The Case is Altered* is set in the aftermath of the death of a countess, as if rehearsing for the death of Elizabeth. *Every Man In His Humour* alludes, as Robert Miola has demonstrated, to plots against Elizabeth's life.[4] But *Every Man Out of His Humour* is more daring in its representation of Elizabeth's imminent death.

At the end of *Every Man Out of His Humour,* Macilente, the man consumed by envy, must be driven out of his humour along with the others: and to cure him of Envy, extraordinary means are required. Macilente sees Queen Elizabeth herself:

> Suddenly, against expectation and all steel of [Macilente's] malice, the very wonder of her presence strikes him to the earth dumb, and astonished. From whence rising and recovering heart, his passion thus utters itself:
> Macilcente: Blesséd, divine, unblemished, sacred, pure,
> Glorious, immortal, and indeed immense ...
> (5.6.78–9)

This direct representation of the Queen on stage was probably, Helen Ostovich suggests, achieved in the public theatre by having an actor representing the Queen pass across the stage. It is, first and foremost, a startlingly direct representation of the Queen, collapsing (for a moment) the distance between *Insula Fortunata* and Jonson's London. So direct, indeed, was it that the original ending appears to have got Jonson into trouble: 'many seemed not to relish it, and therefore 'twas since altered' (Appendix A, 2–3). And while, at first glance, this representation of Queen Elizabeth seems to be almost nauseating flattery – and has often been treated as such by Jonson commentators – it does not take much imagination to see more troubling notes in it. Thus, for instance, Macilente offers a prayer for the Queen:

> O Heaven, that she, whose Figure hath effected
> This change in me, may never suffer change
> In her admired and happy government.
> (5.6.99–101, Quarto readings retained)

The very prayer that that change should never happen, of course, is double-edged: it reminds the listeners of the fact that it will happen. In the folio, revised with the benefit of hindsight after the Queen's death, the phrase appears as 'suffer most late change', but the revision's explicit concession that Elizabeth *will* die is already implicit in the quarto's wording. And that note in Macilente's speech – that interest in the fact that Elizabeth's death is on the horizon, and that when it comes it will bring a major shift in power – comes back, more loudly, in the closing lines:

> Let Flattery be dumb and Envy blind
> In her dread presence; Death himself admire her,
> And may her virtues make him to forget
> The use of his inevitable hand.
> Fly from her Age: Sleep Time before her throne!
> Our strongest wall falls down when she is gone.
> (5.6.112–17, Quarto readings retained)

In effect, the last lines of the encomium of Elizabeth look forward to the time 'when she is gone'.

Similarly, in *Cynthia's Revels,* Elizabeth is figured as the moon-goddess Cynthia who, in a thinly disguised allegory of the disgrace of the Earl of Essex, has punished the impetuous Actaeon for daring to see her naked. Much of the scholarly interest in this play has focused on the treatment of Actaeon/Essex, written seemingly before the events of February 1601, when Essex launched his abortive military coup and was put to death. *Cynthia's Revels* is certainly deeply implicated in the fine details of late-Elizabethan court politics, and Jonson himself had many links to the Essex circle, as Tom Cain has explored in connection with *Poetaster*.[5] But in a wider perspective, *Cynthia's Revels* is remarkable for its interest in the temporariness of the reign of Cynthia/Elizabeth. At one point, Cynthia sees a miraculous vision of Elizabeth and comments that her glory 'Seems ignorant of what it is to wane': a double-edged phrase which again draws attention to the very possibility that it seems to deny (5.8.12). But even Cynthia herself is presented in the play as far from permanent. At one point, she is called, 'Sister of Phoebus, to whose bright orb we owe that we not complain of his absence': merely a temporary stand-in for the sun-god himself (5.9.1–2).

One possible allegorization of this imagery of moon and sun is made explicit in the folio's version of *Cynthia's Revels,* whose Preface figures Elizabeth as the 'Cynthia' of the English court, and James as its Phoebus, its sun-god. But that idea of James as a sun-god can be traced back at least as early as 1603: Jonson's own poem *A Panegyre,* written to celebrate James's accession, imagines the new king casting a thousand radiant lights in all directions. Nor would the possible reading, one surmises, have been lost on playgoers in 1601. *Cynthia's Revels,* for all that it appears to be Elizabethan panegyric, is using that panegyric to start to look to a world after the Queen.

And yet, of course, the rest of Jonson's career is dominated by memory of Elizabeth. Elizabeth returns, in refracted form, as the Fairy Queen, the last of Dol's disguises in *The Alchemist;* as is recorded in the document known as *Informations,* Jonson is still telling stories about Elizabeth when he visits William Drummond in 1618; even the Caroline plays are constantly seeking their cultural reference points in Elizabethan England, in a process that Anne Barton has described as a conscious 'Elizabethanism'.[6] The Elizabethan era defined Jonson's later career: and yet, as the case of *Cynthia's Revels* seems to suggest, Jonson's Elizabethan productions may yet be surprising in the way that they interrogate that era.

Jonson's Elizabethan dramatic output, then, need not be read solely in terms of the narrative offered by the 1616 folio, dominated by themes of solitary endeavour and reformation through satire. Instead, these plays can be seen as restless experiments in modes of representation; as calculatedly political explorations of the state of the monarchy; and as, in fact, participating widely and deeply in the theatrical and intellectual culture of their period. Jonson's five surviving early plays are part of a varied, considerable and firmly late-Elizabethan achievement.

NOTES

1. Thomas Dekker, *Satiro-mastix* (London: Edward White, 1602), D2r, L4v.
2. The quotations from *Poetaster* are tied to the Revels edition edited by Tom Cain (Manchester: Manchester University Press, 1995), as that text is forthcoming in the Cambridge University Press edition at the time of writing. All other Jonson quotations in this essay refer to the Cambridge University Press edition.
3. Ben Jonson, *Every Man Out of His Humour*, edited by Helen Ostovich, Revels Plays (Manchester: Manchester University Press, 2001).
4. Ben Jonson, *Every Man in His Humour*, edited by Robert Miola, Revels Plays (Manchester: Manchester University Press, 2000), Introduction, pp. 23–4.
5. Tom Cain, '"Satyres, that Girde and Fart at the Time": *Poetaster* and the Essex Rebellion', in J. Sanders, K. Chedgzoy and S. Wiseman (eds.), *Refashioning Ben Jonson: Gender, Politics and the Jonsonian Canon* (Basingstoke: Macmillan, 1998), pp. 48–70; see also, in the same collection, Janet Clare, 'Jonson's Comical Satires and the Art of Courtly Compliment', pp. 28–47; for a wider reassessment of Jonson's relationship with the court as a whole, Martin Butler, '"Servant, but Not Slave": Ben Jonson at the Stuart Court', *Proceedings of the British Academy*, 90 (1995): 65–93.
6. Anne Barton, 'Harking Back to Elizabeth: Ben Jonson and Caroline Nostalgia', *English Literary History* 48 (1981): 706–31.

CHAPTER 3

Jonson in the Jacobean period

Andrew McRae

It can be difficult, as readers of Jonson, to recover a sense that Jonson was anything other than Jacobean. Indeed he can seem the quintessential Jacobean author: a man whose greatest dramatic and poetic achievements span the reign of James, who gave the Jacobean court some of its finest masques and who helped his monarch to define some of the signal values of the reign. But Jonson's career stretched across three reigns, as other chapters in this volume remind us, and in some respects the association with James might be considered a matter of chance. The years of James's reign, perhaps, simply happened to be those in which Jonson reached maturity as a writer. In this context it is worth pausing to consider what it means to position Jonson as a 'Jacobean' author. What made the Jonson of the years 1603–25 – unquestionably his most productive and influential – distinctly Jacobean? In what ways did the reign of James inform his works and shape his career?

For Jonson, crucially, being a Jacobean author mattered. His works are studded with addresses and dedications to James, implicit comparisons between himself and his king, engagements with Jacobean policies and invocations of monarchical authority. In his *Epigrams,* this process begins in the fourth poem. After poems 'To the Reader', 'To My Book' and 'To My Bookseller', all of which circle anxiously around concerns about reading and interpretation, he turns attention to his nation's ultimate source of authority:

> How, best of kings, dost thou a sceptre bear!
> How, best of poets, dost thou a laurel wear!
> But two things, rare, the Fates had in thy store,
> And gave thee both, to show they could no more.
> For such a poet, while thy days were green,
> Thou wert, as chief of them are said t'have been.
> And such a prince thou art, we daily see,
> As chief of those still promise they will be.

> Whom should my muse then fly to, but the best
> Of kings for grace; of poets for my test?
>
> (*Epigrams,* 4, ll. 1–10)

This piece of panegyric is as much about Jonson as James. Overtly, it positions James, who published poetry in his youth and continued thereafter to present himself as a writer, as an ideal author and monarch. By extension, within the volume's opening narrative of a search for correct interpretation, James is also figured as an ideal reader and patron. In a world in which other readers may prove inconsistent or unreliable, James is invoked as a witness or judge, attesting to the worth of the poems, and rewarding Jonson accordingly. But there is also a characteristic edginess to the poem, as Jonson seeks to negotiate, in accord with a lifelong project, a position in the state for the professional poet. James's qualities as a poet are thus placed carefully at a distance, and the poem deftly avoids making its own judgement on the monarch's work. He is, Jonson notes, 'said t'have been' the 'chief of them'. In this context, the suggestive final word, 'test', presses upon the poem as not just an appeal for judgement but equally a desire to challenge James's supposed status, claiming in the process Jonson's desired role as the nation's pre-eminent poet.

In a manner that works outward from this brief reading of his epigram to James, this chapter aims to consider Jonson's efforts to write his way into the centre of Jacobean society. Indeed he, perhaps more than anybody else, helped to define what it meant to be 'Jacobean'; and in the process, as Richard Helgerson has argued, at a time before the official status of poet laureate had been created, he gave shape nonetheless to a 'laureate' identity.[1] The chapter aims to encompass at once the success of this strategy and also its inherent tensions, at a time when central values were increasingly fractured under the weight of political struggles.

In many respects, the epigram 'To King James' is a classic poem of patronage. When Jonson asks, rhetorically, 'Whom should my muse then fly to, but the best / Of kings for grace[?]' (*Epigrams,* 4, ll. 9–10), he implies his own appeal to James for support. Within a patronage system, of the like that shaped virtually all forms of Jacobean life, patrons and clients were bound together in unequal yet mutually beneficial relationships. A patron would provide for the client status, office and material reward. In response, a client would work towards the interests of his or her patron, either at a material level, or – as was more appropriate for poets – by promoting the patron's image and interests. At the top of this profoundly hierarchical system stood the monarch, dispensing 'grace' (a recurrent codeword in discourses of patronage) and requiring, in response, the loyal labours of his clients. As Jonson was keenly aware, his king offered a degree of authorization: the right, that is, to speak.[2]

Jonson's claims to James's 'grace' dominated his career. Most notably, he laid claim to the position of James's most-favoured poet by producing, for a number of years early in the reign, a series of the King's court masques. The masque was the quintessential literary form of the Jacobean patronage system. The entire theatrical occasion, staged for one night only and generally at huge cost, involving elaborate costumes and stage machinery as well as a lavish feast, focused attention on the masque's patron. Masques were held at different times for various courtiers and members of the royal family; indeed other chapters in this volume attend particularly to those Jonson wrote for the Queen, Anna of Denmark. But without question the most prominent of all were those staged for the King, who would sit throughout in the very centre of the hall, raised above his subjects in a manner designed to underscore his authority. The typical masque narrative, as the form developed in a manner heavily influenced by Jonson, was a simple transition from disorder to order. At its conclusion, the order within the English state would be emblematized in the form of dance, again centring attention on the King. Jonson enjoyed considerable financial rewards for his work as a writer of masques, and famously fumed when he felt not only that he was being edged out of the role but that the poetry of masquing was being overlooked in favour of its mechanics. But the greater rewards were arguably immaterial. His association with masquing, that is, enhanced the reputation he was so determined to construct for himself.

Jonson sought to reinforce this reputation in his wider creative work, which often engages supportively with matters of Jacobean policy. In the *Epigrams,* for instance, the poem directly following 'To King James' is a piece titled 'On the Union', addressing James's controversial, and eventually unsuccessful, goal of unifying his kingdoms of England and Scotland:

> When was there contract better driven by Fate?
> Or celebrated with more truth of state?
> The world the temple was, the priest a king,
> The spousèd pair two realms, the sea the ring.
> 				(*Epigrams* 5, ll. 1–4)

While this piece verges upon mere propaganda, other works are somewhat more expansive and creative in their topical concerns. For example, Jonson was interested, like James, in what might loosely be defined as the relation between social and spatial order. James spoke and wrote on several occasions about the apparently unstoppable growth of London and the evidently growing phenomenon, across the country, of geographical and social mobility. Social order in the nation, he believed, was founded upon the cohesion of local communities, within which people at all levels were held together by bonds of deference and responsibility.[3] His subjects, in other words, should know their places. For Jonson, this policy informs his influential country-house poems, 'To Penshurst' and 'To Sir Robert Wroth', with their celebrations of landlords who 'dwell' (the resonant closing word of the former) on their estates and observe traditional codes of hospitality (*The Forest* 2 and 3). It also echoes through a number of his city comedies, which repeatedly bring supposedly traditional social values into brutal collision with the newly individualistic and exploitative codes that Jonson associated with the city. Bartholomew Cokes, in *Bartholomew Fair,* for example, is primarily a figure of fun because he is a fool. Beneath this crude layer of humour, however, the audience is alerted to the fact that he is also an absentee landlord, who is failing to fulfil his social role in the country and is wasting the wealth produced from his lands in the city. Apart from his sheer idiocy, the play suggests that his fault is to identify with the rampant consumerism of the city rather than the productivity of the country.

Works such as these were therefore intended to make powerful and authoritative social comment. Throughout his career, in fact, Jonson maintained a commitment to the didactic value of his writing; in the prefatory epistle to another city-comedy, *Volpone,* he declares sententiously that 'The principal end of *poesie*' is 'to inform men, in the best reason of living' (Epistle, 81–2). In this context, satire, the dominant mode in the majority of his drama and also much of his poetry, is positioned as an essentially conservative instrument, wielded to discipline those who depart from social norms. The point, for Jonson, of placing himself at the centre of his society, and aligning himself so consistently with the authority of James, was that it enabled him to promote the impression that his values were not only right in a moral sense but were those underpinning the nation.

Jonson's claim to a position of centrality, however, was founded on assumptions that were fracturing around him. For what he tried so hard to position as statements of impeccable moral and ethical values, and what he presented as dispassionate discriminations between virtue and corruption, were also political judgements. This is true at any time; a statement that purports to determine between right and wrong is always to some extent political. But it pressed with particular urgency upon those involved in political life in the early Stuart era. Throughout the reign of James, factional struggles dominated political commentary, which, as a result, exposed the court as being riven by dissension and rivalry. In particular, the widespread circulation of libels – short, vitriolic poems, on individuals and issues – shattered myths that all involved in political life were concerned simply with providing loyal counsel to their monarch.[4] In his commonplace book, in which he recorded some of his fundamental views of his vocation, Jonson dismisses flattery and calumny as twinned corruptions of language. There can, he writes, be 'as great a vice in praising, and as frequent, as in detracting'.[5] But maintaining such a position of apparent purity, and even clinging to the authority of the king, which in theory rose above all political divisions, was becoming increasingly difficult.

The strains show in the *Epigrams*. While 'To King James' is a piece determined to fix the business of interpretation, poems on either side fret over the matter. Epigrams, he acknowledges, have not only become associated with vitriolic attacks and coded allusions to political figures; the naming of individuals, both good and bad, has been perceived as a political act. And, since many of the poems were originally written as patronage pieces, presumably presented in manuscript form to the desired patron, they are full of names, each of which threatens to situate the poet on a factional map. This became even more troubling for him when the poems came to be published. For instance, to praise Robert Cecil, Earl of Salisbury, when he was at the height of his powers, as the leading statesman of James's first decade in power, was relatively unproblematic. Contemplation of Cecil's 'virtue', Jonson writes in one, demonstrates to observers how '[t]he judgement of the king so shine[s] in thee'. Criticism of him may be dismissed merely as the expression of 'envy' (*Epigrams* 63, l. 4). But to print those poems several years later, after Cecil's death and the erosion of his reputation, sullied in particular by a searing libelling campaign, was another matter. In the printed collection, it is surely no coincidence that two poems in praise of Cecil are followed immediately by one addressed 'To My Muse', in which Jonson cagily displaces the blame for acts of flattery onto his muse:

> thou thing most abhorred
> That hast betrayed me to a worthless lord.

Even if the consequences are 'poverty', he expresses the desire thereafter only 'to write / Things manly, and not smelling parasite' (*Epigrams* 65, ll. 1–2, 12, 13–14).[6] The mere admission that he might once have been distracted from his purported commitment to truth, however, unsettles his entire poetic project.

The pervasive politicization of literature in this period influenced even that most assured mode of Jacobean rule. In 1621, Jonson accepted a commission from George Villiers, Duke of Buckingham, to write a masque to be staged at one of his own estates, before the King. Villiers was at this date merely the Marquis of Buckingham but was nearing the zenith of his meteoric rise at court, all thanks to the favour of James. Indeed, he became the supreme royal favourite of the early Stuart era, sustaining lucratively intimate relations with both James and his son, Charles I, accruing immense personal authority and in the process dragging his own family out of the obscurity of the provincial gentry. In 1628 he was assassinated: an event that became more bitterly debated than any other, in this divisive century, before the execution of Charles in 1649. So how might a poet who was so committed to the myth of social and political cohesion manage such a commission? The result, *The Gypsies Metamorphosed*, Jonson's longest masque if measured simply in terms of lines of text, has puzzled critics ever since its first production. Given the prevalence of libellous attacks on Buckingham and his family as immoral upstarts, some readers have tried hard to represent the entire production as a subtly veiled attack. While this audacious interpretation is unsustainable in many respects, there is no question that *The Gypsies Metamorphosed* lacks the assurance of Jonson's earlier masques and allows for, even if it does not invite, variant readings. One documentable fact, moreover, is that in the 1620s the masque was widely discussed and debated, circulating in manuscript texts and generating a range of responses. In particular, one libel took a song from Jonson's masque and turned it subversively inside-out, presenting to its wide readership a savage critique of the politics of favouritism.[7]

Jonson's own critique of that politics – whatever one might want to argue about *The Gypsies Metamorphosed* – actually predates the rise of Buckingham. *Sejanus His Fall*, which was first staged in the very year of James's accession, follows the narrative, largely derived from the Roman historian Tacitus, of the overreaching court favourite ultimately outwitted and brought down by his patron, the Emperor Tiberius. While this play, Jonson's first experiment in tragedy, is often seen as being engaged primarily with late-Elizabethan political crises, some have argued that it touches equally upon characteristically Jacobean anxieties, perhaps with a view to regulating the emergent political culture.[8] The play delineates an environment in which political interaction is governed by factionalism and liberty of speech is an inconceivable ideal. Those who attempt to speak or write freely, such as the historian Cordus, are ruthlessly dragged down. The claustrophobically crowded stage consistently reminds the audience of the effects of surveillance and of the ways in which words might be twisted in order to serve political ends. Arruntius, who serves more than any other character as Jonson's spokesman, asks rhetorically, 'May I think, / And not be racked? What danger is't to dream' (4.305). Drawing together a powerful strand of imagery in the play centred on hearing, he concludes that 'Nothing hath privilege 'gainst the violent ear' (4.311). 'Privilege' was a loaded word in early seventeenth-century political discourse, as contemporaries struggled to define the fraught power relations between the King and his parliament, and, ultimately, between the King and his individual subjects. For all his professed adherence to the ideological orthodoxies of James's reign, Jonson was never deluded about his world and presents here one of his era's most searching critiques of favouritism and, by implication, the absolutism upon which it depends. Though few details of the encounter survive, Jonson was in 1604 brought before the Privy Council to answer questions about the play.

The mere existence of *Sejanus* serves as a reminder of the complexity of Jonson's position as a Jacobean author. The man who began the reign producing one of the most sophisticated and daring pieces of political drama ever written, and whose social background gave him no claim whatsoever to a position at court, nonetheless managed to situate himself as the preeminent voice of Jacobean orthodoxy. Responses to this, predictably enough, vary. For some readers, the achievement is fundamentally admirable, while for others the uneasy compromises required along the way leave a sour taste in the mouth. As Jonson acknowledged himself, producing literature 'not smelling parasite' was a struggle that inevitably shadowed his ambition, right through to the end of his life. Perhaps the key lesson for readers, 400 years later, is that we remain alert to the ways in which this struggle shaped his work. To read his output across the Jacobean period is to confront most of the key individuals and issues of the time, staged in what can appear at times to be an edgy and inconsistent body of writing. Indeed, one might argue that this, above all else, is what makes him so distinctively Jacobean.

NOTES

1. Richard Helgerson, *Self-Crowned Laureates: Spenser, Jonson, Milton and the Literary System* (Berkeley, Calif.: University of California Press, 1983), pp. 101–84.
2. See esp. Linda Levy Peck, *Court Patronage and Corruption in Early Stuart England* (London: Routledge, 1990); Robert C. Evans, *Ben Jonson and the Poetics of Patronage* (Lewisburg, Pa.: Bucknell University Press, 1989).

3. See further Andrew McRae, *God Speed the Plough: The Representation of Agrarian England, 1500–1660* (Cambridge: Cambridge University Press, 1996), pp. 280–2.
4. See Andrew McRae and Alastair Bellany (eds.), 'Early Stuart Libels: An Edition of Poetry from Manuscript Sources', *Early Modern Literary Studies,* Text Series I (2005). Available online at http://purl.oclc.org/emls/texts/libels.
5. Ben Jonson, *The Complete Poems,* edited by George Parfitt (Harmondsworth: Penguin, 1975), p. 423.
6. See further Robert Wiltenburg, '"What Need Hast Thou of Me? Or of My Muse?": Jonson and Cecil, Politician and Poet', in Claude J. Summers and Ted-Larry Pebworth (eds.), *'The Muses Common-Weale': Poetry and Politics in the Seventeenth Century* (New York: Columbia University Press, 1988), pp. 34–47.
7. McRae and Bellany, 'Early Stuart Libels', L8; James Knowles, '"Songs of Baser Alloy": Jonson's *Gypsies Metamorphosed* and the Circulation of Manuscript Libels', *Huntington Library Quarterly,* 69 (2006): 153–76.
8. See especially Curtis Perry, *The Making of Jacobean Culture: James I and the Renegotiation of Elizabethan Literary Practice* (Cambridge: Cambridge University Press, 2006), pp. 99–106.

CHAPTER 4

Jonson in the Caroline period

Martin Butler

Jonson's output in the reign of Charles I has often been taken to lack the artistic focus and internal coherence that are so apparent in his earlier work. Qualities of belatedness and dislocation in his Caroline writing have suggested to critics that he was no longer at ease and was struggling to find new directions. In large measure, this impression derives from structural, economic and physical changes that were deeply affecting his life: the loss after 1631 of his status as favoured masque writer, following his final rift with Inigo Jones; the uncertain reception of his later plays, particularly the fiasco of *The New Inn*, which faced a hostile reception at its first performance and the furore prompted by the 'Ode to Himself' (which had blamed the play's failure on the audience's lack of understanding); the decline of his health, following a stroke which left him subject to a 'palsy' (probably Parkinson's Disease) and 'set round with pain' (*New Inn*, Epilogue, l. 10); and the financial troubles caused by delays to his court pension and his loss of salary as City Chronologer for non-performance of his duties. More importantly, though, Jonson's Caroline phase seems inchoate because it lacks compelling narrative logic. When he compiled his folio *Works* (1616), he projected onto his earlier writings his own authorized version of his achievements to date. Symptomatically, plans for a second volume of *Works* in 1630–1 came to nothing. Only three plays were printed, and these remained unissued until 1641, so he was unable in his lifetime to canonize his later writings in the way that he may have wanted.

In dedicating one of those three unissued plays, *Bartholomew Fair*, to 'King James of blessed memory', Jonson implicitly harked back to the previous reign as a time when he felt attuned to the world in which he lived. He had flourished under James I, whose intellectual, humanistic and peace-loving model of monarchy was close to his own political and ideological preferences. Caroline England was not necessarily a less congenial place. The new king was a man of the arts, proud of himself as a connoisseur, and ready to spend money to prove it. As prince, Charles had danced in six Jonsonian masques, and early in the reign he converted the royal cockpit into an intimate space for drama. But he was as much interested in painting as in plays and embodied a more restrained version of monarchy than his father had done. His court was notable for its order and stateliness and for qualities of decency, refinement and dignity that were potentially at odds with Jonson's robust enthusiasms and rude good health. One cannot imagine a rumbustious masque like *The Gypsies Metamorphosed* (1621) being written to celebrate the new king's relationship with the royal favourite, the Duke of Buckingham. Moreover, the reckless warmongering of Charles's early years – when he attempted to pursue campaigns against Spain and France simultaneously, then, after their dismal failure, backtracked from the European scene – left a legacy of financial shortages, constitutional anxiety and ideological polarization. After 1630, Charles kept England at peace and concentrated on rebuilding his revenue, but for all his domestic success, he could never project his desired image of a capable modernizing monarch with complete conviction. Underlying ideological disagreements meant that Caroline kingship was always hedged with elements of confrontation and controversy.

Charles's warmongering directly impacted onto Jonson, since it created the shortage of cash that provoked the poet into writing humiliating epigrams begging for his pension to be paid. In other respects, though, Jonson strove to function as a loyal servant to his master. He strenuously objected in 1628 when he was suspected of the authorship of 'Felton Commended', a poem praising the man who had assassinated Buckingham, and when, in 1629, *The New Inn* was cried down at the Blackfriars, he retorted in the 'Ode to Himself' that it was happiness enough simply to have the prospect of royal approval. If his theatre public deserted him, he would still sing 'The glories of my King', 'tuning forth the acts of his sweet reign, / And raising Charles his chariot 'bove his wain' ('Ode to Himself', ll. 52, 59–60). His epilogue for *The Magnetic Lady* (1632) makes a similar appeal to the King, and, in his panegyrical poetry from this period, he carries forward his support, celebrating the crown's domestic landmarks, such as anniversaries and births, and defending Charles from his critics. Amongst his patrons were well-placed courtiers, notably Richard Weston, Earl of Portland, who was Charles's Lord Treasurer and who, more than anyone else, was responsible for rebuilding the royal finances. *The Underwood* 78 thanks this 'learnèd lord' for approving his poems (28).

But Jonson's standing at court was complicated. It was damaged by his personal enmity towards Inigo Jones and coloured by his friendships with men whose attitudes to the court were mixed. One long-standing patron, who commissioned the entertainments at Welbeck (1633) and Bolsover (1634), was William Cavendish, Earl of Newcastle. Newcastle was a fervent royalist who in the 1640s would general the King's army, but in the 1630s he felt resentful towards the favoured courtiers who were leading the crown away from what he regarded as the good old ways of government. Another devoted friend, who held Jonson as a 'father' and helped him with monetary gifts, was Lucius Cary, Viscount Falkland. Falkland surrounded himself with a circle of poets, philosophers and intellectuals whose outlook was moderate, rationalistic and peace-loving, who were unhappy with aspects of Charles's government that seemed unconstitutional and who were hostile to the Arminian doctrines and rituals associated with Archbishop Laud. In the Long Parliament, Falkland would be one of the crown's most determined critics, though he became an equally determined supporter once Charles's authority came under threat. It is easy to see how Jonson might gravitate towards men who, while fundamentally loyal to the regime and no friends of Puritanism, nonetheless entertained reservations about Charles's kingship on intellectual and philosophical grounds.

Charles's court was further notable for the emergence of a feminocentric culture associated with his wife, Henrietta Maria, who brought with her from France codes of polite manners, moral renewal and neoplatonic woman-worship that impacted powerfully onto Whitehall's daily life and made it a sympathetic space for aristocratic women. As a former Catholic, Jonson might have been responsive to this new cultural presence. Indeed, his circle in later life contained several prominent Catholics, notably Portland (though politically he was no friend to the Queen), Sir Thomas Hawkins and Sir Kenelm Digby (who after his conversion became close to Henrietta Maria). In an epigram celebrating Prince Charles's birth, Jonson playfully addresses the Queen with 'Hail, Mary, full of grace!' (*The Underwood* 66, 1), and in another (*The Underwood* 67, 4–6) he urges her subjects to celebrate her birthday with the same bells and bonfires they were likely to use on the following day, which was the great Protestant festival, the anniversary of Elizabeth's accession.

But despite these hints of affinity Jonson seems to have had little common ground with Henrietta Maria's proselytizing Catholicism – the rash of court conversions that occurred around her were a long way from his eirenic theology – or with her cult of neoplatonic love. He came closest to reflecting on her neoplatonism in *The New Inn,* which presents the story of Lady Frampul, who rules over the emotions of her male friends rather like a court platonic. She commissions her reluctant admirer Lovel to speak for two hours in praise of love and valour and scoffingly compares him with Honoré d'Urfé, the French writer whose pastoral romance *L'Astrée* provided the literary model underpinning the salon culture which Henrietta Maria sought to import (*The New Inn*, 3.2.204). However, the discourses with which Lovel wins Lady Frampul's heart displace D'Urfé's rarified platonism with a view of love firmly resting on Aristotelian and neo-stoical foundations. His orations on the good life focus firmly on the individual's moral responsibilities rather than on erotic subordination to spiritualized female beauty, and, although the play interestingly promotes the resourceful waiting gentlewoman, Prudence, through marriage with a lord, it represents her wayward mistress as in need of emotional and moral self-discipline. And Jonson's other late plays did little to accommodate themselves to Henrietta Maria's aesthetic tastes. The refined pastoral dramas which amateur playwrights produced for her at Whitehall were at the opposite end of the theatrical scale from the ironically depicted country landscapes of *A Tale of a Tub* (1633) and *The Sad Shepherd* (1637). The prologue to *A Tale of a Tub* jokes about 'what different things / The cotes of clowns are from the courts of kings' (ll. 11–12).

Undoubtedly Jonson was capable of adjusting to the changed court climate. In 1631, in the only two masques that he wrote for Charles and Henrietta Maria, he brilliantly adapted Jacobean festival culture to the new political environment. *Love's Triumph Through Callipolis* is the first Caroline masque to present the King as virile amorist, a heroic St George valiantly combating monsters for love of his adored princess, while *Chloridia* celebrates Henrietta Maria as a beautiful nature-goddess in a device that recreates the *ballets du cour* she knew from Paris. Both of these were significant new departures: they revised Jacobean masque form in the direction of a romantic dialogue between monarch and consort and created the enduring images of the couple as, respectively, a triumphant knight and a beauty whose attractions were both spiritual and sensual. All subsequent masque poets were directly indebted to these new emphases. But Jonson's falling-out with Inigo Jones over artistic ownership of the masques shattered his prospects for future commissions, and Jones's stranglehold over masque production marked a shift in court festival towards ceremonial and away from satire which matched broader changes in Whitehall's underlying aesthetic. Jones preferred to work with bland compliant poets such as Aurelian Townshend and William Davenant, so his appropriation of responsibility for the masques was decisive for Jonson's future. Jonson took his revenge in the characters of Vitruvius Hoop in *A Tale of a Tub* and Iniquo Vitruvius in the Bolsover entertainment, who are small craftsmen with absurdly pompous and overinflated egos. It was, though, already apparent in the

'Expostulation with Inigo Jones' (1631) – with its attack on the architect's 'shows, mighty shows', 'spectacles of state' and 'true court hieroglyphics' (39, 42–3) – that this was a collaboration which had run into the sand.

Behind these personal antagonisms were long-term cultural changes that were working to transform the situation of the court poet. Their impact on Jonson is well seen in his panegyrical verse, not least because his Caroline poems return obsessively to the problem of how to praise a king who no longer seems able to command his subjects' unqualified respect. A representative example is *The Underwood* 64, an epigram from 1629 celebrating the fourth anniversary of the accession. This confronts what for the poet is the puzzling gap between Charles's self-evident virtues and the absence of public enthusiasm for him:

> How happy were the subject, if he knew,
> Most pious king, but his own good in you!
> How many times 'Live long, Charles' would he say,
> If he but weighed the blessings of this day?
> And as it turns our joyful year about
> For safety of such majesty cry out?
> Indeed, when had Great Britain greater cause
> Than now, to love the sovereign and the laws?
> When you that reign are her example grown,
> And what are bounds to her, you make your own?
> ('To Our Great and Good k[ing] Charles', ll. 1–10)

This is less a panegyric to the King than an attempt to instil in the wider readership a sense of public confidence that, perplexingly, will not materialize by and of itself. The lines point up Charles's piety, ethical 'example' and respect for law (Britain's 'bounds'), but they remain double-edged since they dwell on the subjects' reluctance to acknowledge those qualities which to the poet seem so obvious. A disabling tension emerges between Jonson's assertions of royal competence and Charles's inability to attract the respect that ought to be his due:

> O times! O manners! Surfeit bred of ease,
> The truly epidemical disease!
> 'Tis not alone the merchant, but the clown
> Is bankrupt turned; the cassock, cloak, and gown
> Are lost upon account; and none will know
> How much to heaven for thee, great Charles, they owe!
> (ll. 17–22)

Jonson attributes this popular ingratitude to a 'surfeit', a sickness bred by excessive prosperity, but his metaphor cannot dispel the contradiction between Charles's dignified image and his subjects' refusal to credit it. Reluctant to blame the monarch, Jonson censures the subjects for their inability to count their blessings, but there is a double bind at work here, since the more strongly the poet criticizes the subjects' recalcitrance, the more strained his protestations sound. If Charles's goodness really were incontestable, his poem would not have to be written. Jonson's honesty and directness are impressive, but it is difficult not to feel that the poem is bedevilled by polarizations within the political culture that would become increasingly disabling for contemporary panegyric. The authoritative kingship that Jonson wished to associate with Charles could not be represented without also acknowledging the erosion of trust that was the main ideological legacy of the 1620s.

Jonson was, then, caught between his loyalty to a monarch whose authority was diminished and whose political culture seemed increasingly divisive, and a theatre-going public whose attitude to his new plays was often less than enthusiastic. In his remaining works – *The New Inn, The Magnetic Lady, A Tale of a Tub,* and *The Sad Shepherd* – Jonson responded to this unprecedented situation by creating plots which are ostensibly devoid of political issues but which nonetheless resonated with the concerns of the moment. These four plays all focus on specific and bounded localities, being set in spaces which are historically or geographically distanced. They are inhabited by insular, parochial or marginalized groups whose affairs seem innocent and even trivial, but they implicitly take up topics which address the social value and life of the encompassing community.

Two of these plays have localized urban settings: *The New Inn,* confined to an inn in Hertfordshire where Lady Frampul plays love-games with her family of followers, and *The Magnetic Lady,* set in the London house where the rich city widow Lady Loadstone draws together potential suitors for her niece. *The New Inn* seems very much in step with the future directions of Caroline theatre: its two central orations deal with those characteristic cavalier themes, love and honour. However, its hero, Lovel, is not a conventional cavalier but a melancholy gentleman alienated from the world around him. He strives to reconcile his hidden but forceful emotions with the demands of ethical discipline and eventually articulates an intellectualized code of private heroism and self-control which schools the unpredictably self-indulgent Lady Frampul and becomes the model for the aristocratic society which he joins. In *The Magnetic Lady,* the objects of satire are the avaricious city businessman Sir Moth Interest, the frivolous courtier Sir Diaphanous Silkworm, the secretive court politician Bias, and the self-serving lawyer Practice. All these have designs on the play's heiress, but they are defeated by Compass and Ironside, independent gentlemen who embody, respectively, qualities of easy scholarly wit and bluff military courage. The play further mocks its puritanically minded city women but also juxtaposes them with Parson Palate, the parish priest whose manners and ornate vestments exemplify the social ambitions and ceremonial excesses of the Laudian church. Without ever moving into explicit political allegory, this seemingly inconsequential plot deftly sketches a society where personal and public humours alike are in need of careful amelioration.

The final two plays move into provincial settings and make what for Jonson were innovative literary experiments. *A Tale of a Tub* is set in a group of Middlesex villages in the 1550s and follows the farcical misadventures surrounding the wedding of Audrey, daughter of the parish constable Toby Turf. Her hand is promised to a village craftsman, but she is pursued by powerful local rivals – the squire and the magistrate, abetted by the tricksy self-serving vicar – whose intricately counter-plotted devices send the constable's men on a series of wild-goose chases through the countryside, leaving Audrey to be finally if unexpectedly netted by a gentleman usher working for the squire's mother. The play's mid-Tudor setting, literary pastiche and trivial plot ensure that it remains charmingly distanced from contemporary events, but it still has underlying political purchase. Jonson's minutely detailed depiction of the hierarchy of parish officialdom makes capital out of Charles's drive to tighten up local administration, and his focus on the tiresomeness of village business – for Audrey's wedding banquet is endlessly deferred by fake crime reports and unexpected commands from Whitehall – echo the tensions which the Caroline magistracy faced, both within local parishes and between centre and localities. Finally, at the time of his death, Jonson was working on a pastoral play, *The Sad Shepherd,* which seems (as far as we can tell from the unfinished text) equally focused on questions of collective identity. The play's setting in Sherwood Forest seems safely nostalgic and fanciful – populated as it is by Robin Hood, a Spenserian witch and various lovelorn shepherds and shepherdesses – but this world is implicitly at odds with itself. The inner lives of the shepherds are turbulently emotional, while on the edge of the forest lives the witch Maudlin, her socially ambitious daughter and her upwardly mobile son (who proudly enumerates his rents, herds and pastures). Robin promotes an ethos of feasting and gift-giving amongst his family, but it is challenged by these outsiders, whose envy and coarseness is a displaced echo of the puritanical hostility towards licensed games voiced by 'The sourer sort / Of shepherds [who] now disclaim in all such sport, / And say our flocks the while are poorly fed / When with such vanities the swains are fed' (1.4.18–21). Jonson by no means accepts the witch's demonization at face value, but his play clearly acknowledges the ways in which an ethos of loyal social amity (most conspicuously announced in the 'Book of Sports' promulgated by Charles in 1632) was struggling to contain social and economic forces that were working to reshape the wider political culture.

In *Ben Jonson, Dramatist,* Anne Barton rather beautifully explicates *The Sad Shepherd* as an act of Jonsonian nostalgia, in which the playwright reached back to reconnect with a literary past from which in his earlier career he had detached himself.[1] But in the 1630s nostalgia for earlier times was also part of a wider process of political reassessment, which articulated competing and ultimately incompatible models of the social fabric. The various imagined communities of Jonson's late plays display a writer striving to locate himself within these debates and looking for forms of social consensus which – as the plots seem to acknowledge even as they advance them – were increasingly under threat from extreme positions adopted both by the court and by the court's critics. It is a measure of Jonson's creative energies that, despite these unpropitious circumstances, his unparalleled inventiveness and double-edged optimism remain in evidence to the very last moments of his career.

NOTES

1. Anne Barton, *Ben Jonson, Dramatist* (Cambridge: Cambridge University Press, 1984), pp. 338–51.

CHAPTER 5

Genre

Katharine Eisaman Maus

The title page of Jonson's 1616 folio *Works* presents five figures standing in a classical frieze: Tragedy, Comedy, Satire, Pastoral and Tragicomedy (see Figure 5.1). Each figure is labelled in Latin and appropriately attired. Tragedy, for instance, is outfitted with a crown and sceptre, suggesting tragedy's focus on royal characters, and wears buskins, the distinctive footwear of tragic actors on the classical stage. Pastoral is rustically clad and equipped with a shepherd's hook. Satire is a satyr with goat legs and a panpipe. Tragicomedy combines Tragedy's regalia with the informal dress and bare feet of Comedy.

Jonson's title page is only one manifestation of an almost reflexive Renaissance habit of subdividing literary territory by genre. Julius Caesar Scaliger devotes the first book of his immense 1560 overview, *Poetices libri septem* (*Poetics in Seven Books*), to chapters on a wide variety of 'kinds', from tragedy and comedy to Latin satiric plays, dirges and epithalamia, songs of good cheer and foreboding, rowing songs, proverbs. In *The Arte of English Poesie* (1589), George Puttenham, like Scaliger, spends most of his first book on a 'Division of Poetic Forms as Derived from the Greeks and the Romans' with descriptions of hymn, tragedy, comedy, satire, pastoral eclogue, elegy, epigram and so on. Similarly, Sir Philip Sidney, writing *The Defence of Poetry* around 1580, distinguishes hymns and philosophical or scientific works from fictional genres and subdivides the last category into pastoral, elegy, comedy, tragedy, lyric and heroic poetry.

Such lists – even Scaliger's – are not meant to be exhaustive, and their criteria are heterogeneous. In some cases, as Sidney notes, the subject matter of literary works, 'The matter they deal with', determines their genre; in other cases, 'a sort of verse', that is, stylistic or technical features, distinguish one genre from another. In other words, Renaissance genres are not rigid categories or lists of rules. Rather, genres provide rough templates for the aims of writers and the expectation of audiences. Taken together, the various genres deal with the multifarious forms of human

Figure 5.1 Frontispiece to the 1616 folio *Works*.

experience and endeavour: tragedy with the fall of princes and nobles; epic with the adventures of heroes; comedy with the interactions of ordinary people, often in urban settings; pastoral with the lives of shepherds. Commentators attribute etymologies and origin stories, sometimes fanciful ones, to the different genres, asserting that each genre captures the modus vivendi of a particular juncture in human development. The crudeness and aggression of satire is laid at the cloven feet of the satyrs who were allegedly its first practitioners, while pastoral exemplifies the simple, uncorrupted tastes of the shepherds who supposedly invented it. Genre thus works as a filtering device, focusing on some phenomena and implicitly excluding others. The way tragic characters speak and the values they represent are different from comic or pastoral speech patterns and values. The kinds of things that happen in satire are different from the kinds of things that happen in romance. Different genres accept different reality principles as axiomatic.

Consequently, genre is closely associated with the concept of 'decorum' or propriety. In modern parlance, the word 'propriety' seems to denote something primly polite, but in Renaissance literary usage, decorum is relativistic and context-dependent. Unity of time and place might be desirable in a play, but not in an epic. Obscene humour might be suitable in a comedy or a satire but inappropriate in an elegy. Nonetheless, the decorum of different genres remains hard to pin down exactly, both because distinctions between genres are hardly clear-cut and because hybrid forms are welcomed – 'If severed they be good', Sidney opines, 'the conjunction cannot be hurtful.' In romantic comedy, the main characters are often highborn, as in tragedy, but the plot deals mainly with courtship and marriage, not wars or affairs of state. Tragicomedies include distressing events, even deaths, but the ending is typically joyful. In other words, the rules of genre, and the conventions of decorum that accompany them, often seem honoured as much in the breach as the observance.

Jonson is a writer of enormous generic range, producing over the course of his career satire, comedy, tragedy, romance, masque, epigram, ode, hymn, elegy, epode, song, pastoral dialogue, sonnet, epithalamion and verse epistle. He participates self-consciously in the tradition I have just been outlining. Often, especially in the late collection *The Underwood* (published posthumously in 1640 but containing poems that span over twenty years), he specifies the genre of a poem in its title, calling it 'Song', 'Elegy', 'Epitaph' or 'Epistle'. In the prefaces and prologues to his plays, he likewise draws attention to generic concerns, carefully aligning his practice with classical precept: while comedy, he writes on the authority of Aristotle, 'sport[s] with human follies, not with crimes' (*Every Man In His Humour,* Folio, Prologue, l. 24), tragedy is characterized by 'truth of argument, dignity of persons, gravity and height of elocution, fullness and frequency of sentence' (*Sejanus,* Preface 'To the Readers', ll. 14–15). Richard Dutton writes, 'There is a demonstrable connection between Jonson's sense of his place as an author within the state (the laws of the land) and his respect for the formal "laws" of literature.'[1] The same respect for 'best critics' sometimes leads Jonson to defend an unusual feature of one of his works (for instance, the unhappy ending in *Volpone*) by citing its classical precedents, where a modern reader might rather value its novelty.

Yet Jonson's obedience to the rules of genre is always pragmatic and provisional. 'The laws of time, place, persons he observeth', he writes of himself in the prologue to *Volpone*: 'From no needful rule he swerveth' (ll. 31–2). Although rules are important, what constitutes a 'needful rule', and what can safely be ignored, is a matter of authorial discretion. 'I see not then', Jonson writes in *Every Man Out of His Humour*, 'but we should enjoy the same *licentia*, or free power, to illustrate and heighten our invention as [classical authors] did; and not be tied to ... strict and regular forms' (Induction, 252–4). To his friend William Drummond, Jonson deplores the Petrarchan sonnet, which he likens to 'that tyrant's bed, where some who were too short were racked, others too long cut short' (*Informations*, 4.43–4).

Throughout his career, Jonson restlessly experiments with genre. He pioneers humours comedy, London satiric comedy and the classical epigram in English. He develops the court masque into a major literary form. 'To Penshurst', his English adaptation of the Latin paean to rural life, spawns a host of imitators that eventually constitute a sub-genre of their own, the country house or estate poem. He combines genres in innovative ways. The early 'comical satires' bring some of the techniques of verse satire, banned by the Bishop of London in 1599, into a theatrical format, while several later comedies – *The Devil is an Ass*, *The Staple of News* and *The Magnetic Lady* – blend conventions of allegorical medieval drama with those of city comedy. Late in life, too, Jonson manifests an unexpected interest in romance, pastoral and the English history play, as evidenced by *The New Inn* and the fragmentary *The Sad Shepherd* and *Mortimer His Fall*.

Jonson is one of the first writers in England to support himself wholly by the pen, and undoubtedly his generic versatility reflects the fact that someone in his position needs to be a jack-of-all-literary-trades. Some of his particular generic enthusiasms make practical sense, too: for instance, short verse forms are better suited than long ones for cultivating a number of patrons simultaneously. Yet it is impossible to reduce Jonson's inventiveness to mere expediency. His propensity for generic experimentation often far exceeds what the occasion seems to require. For instance, Jonson conceivably writes his beautiful poem on the early death of Henry Morison at the behest of Morison's affluent friend, Lucius Cary. Yet the bid for patronage, if in fact that is what the poem constitutes, hardly demands what Jonson undertakes, an ambitious translation of the conventions of Pindaric ode from Greek into English. In fact, as a way of making a living, constantly attempting new things is riskier than simply repeating a tried-and-true formula. Many of Jonson's innovations are poorly received. His classically regular tragedies and several of the late comedies are controversial flops, and so, apparently, are some of the more audacious moments in his earlier works – the appearance of Elizabeth I onstage in *Every Man Out of His Humour*, the armed first-person prologue to *Poetaster* and its 'apologetical dialogue' afterward, the startling conclusion to *Epicene*.

The variety of Jonson's different generic enterprises, and the relativistic way in which those enterprises determine what is decorous in a particular situation, make him harder to pin down than some critics have acknowledged. Of course, there can be good intellectual reasons for restricting the purview of one's scholarship to one or two of the many genres in which Jonson worked. Yet that restriction has sometimes had the effect of misrepresenting generic imperatives as psychic symptoms, manifesting themselves helplessly in his works. For instance, in an influential psychoanalytic study, Edmund Wilson maintained that Jonson was an 'anal' personality: a conclusion that seems borne out by, say, the opening of *The Alchemist* – 'I fart at thee!' (1.1.1) or by the entirety of 'On the Famous Voyage', a mock-heroic tour through the London sewer.[2] Yet Jonson's scatological vein is a sometimes thing, manifest in the comedies, anti-masques and satiric poems but not in the idealizing works, and thus probably a result of the way Jonson construes the decorum of those genres. It is still possible, of course, to assert that Jonson's comedy and satire are more vital than his epideictic verse precisely because they successfully tap into what Bruce Boehrer calls his 'preoccupation with excretory processes'; thus Boehrer argues, convincingly, that Jonson is 'a poet who was – and I mean this in the best possible sense – something of a lunatic'.[3] Yet these claims need to be made in a nuanced, conditional way and historicized with reference to the literary precedents Jonson found in Latin satire and epigram, which were outrageous along similar lines.

Given this caveat, how can genre help us understand what Jonson is up to, either in a particular work or over the course of his career? A couple of issues surface repeatedly across a wide swathe of his oeuvre. One concern that pervades Jonson's thinking about genre is the way in which literary form might provide a way to reconcile the apparently competing pleasures of order and heterogeneity. In his prefaces and prologues to his plays, he excoriates random, formless drama. 'There is a great difference', he writes in the preface to *The Alchemist*:

between those that, to gain the opinion of copy [copiousness], utter all they can, however unfitly, and those that use election and a mean. For it is only the disease of the unskilful to think rude things greater than polished, or scattered more numerous than composed. ('To the Reader', ll. 23–6)

The induction to *Bartholomew Fair* features an ignorant stagehand who complains that 'The Master-poet' has omitted many of the Fair's attractions: a 'sword-and-buckler man' (Induction, l. 11) a tooth-puller, an amazing trick monkey. The literate Bookkeeper, or prompter, a mouthpiece for Jonson, reproves the Stage Keeper for this impertinent critique.

And yet, as the Bookkeeper admits, *Bartholomew Fair* is hardly a paragon of elegant theatrical minimalism. Although Jonson seems to champion disciplined unity, he stuffs his plays full of characters and incidents; the comedies are generally funny because multiple plotlines and people, each pursuing an apparently independent trajectory, unexpectedly collide amid mounting noise and chaos. Jonson wants us to know that the effect of confusion is achieved via careful selectivity. He refuses to insert a 'servant-monster' like Shakespeare's Caliban into *Bartholomew Fair*, for instance, but points out in compensation that the play does contain a puppet-show, which the author considers to be within the bounds of plausibility and decorum. Some of Jonson's poetry of praise manifests a similar pattern of wide, yet circumscribed, inclusion. 'Inviting a Friend to Supper' dwells on what Jonson is *not* able to serve his guest but eventually details an ample feast. Jonson begins 'To Penshurst' by listing what Penshurst lacks – a row of pillars, a gold roof, a gaudy lantern, an ostentatious staircase. Yet the poem goes on to detail the estate's fabulous abundance and variety.

Jonson is aiming, in other words, at an effect of contained complexity. When, at Queen Anna's request, Jonson begins to supplement the court masque with a prefatory anti-masque, he designs it as 'a foil or false masque ... a spectacle of strangeness, producing multiplicity of gesture, and not unaptly sorting with the current and whole fall of the device'.[4] In other words, the anti-masque delights by its simultaneous contrast with and resemblance to the masque proper, by a strangeness that nonetheless ultimately yields to enlightenment, by a multiplicity that is tamed and made to signify. Similarly, when Jonson gathers his very heterogeneous non-dramatic verse in the 1616 folio, he arranges the epigrams and other short poems into groups modelled on the classical verse collection, or *silva*. Jonson translates and plays upon the classical generic term (*silva* is Latin for 'woods') in *The Forest* and *The Underwood*, as well as in his commonplace book *Timber; or, Discoveries*. The pleasure of the *silva* is supposed to lie in its variety: it contains different kinds of poems just as a forest is supposed to contain more than one kind of tree. Nonetheless, the *silva* is not endlessly miscellaneous. Artful juxtaposition and sequencing makes such a collection more than the sum of its parts. This is the widely admired aesthetic ideal of *concordia discors,* familiar to Renaissance writers from classical philosophers and poets, who argued that the cosmos itself is composed of parts that seem various or even incompatible but that may be reconciled at a higher level.

Generic guidelines and the rules of decorum, then, provide Jonson with the tools for deciding what to include and what to exclude. In addition, Jonson often uses concepts of genre to mediate between the particular and the universal. Much of his work was occasional. The masques and entertainments were written on commission, to be performed once or twice at a wedding or at Christmas festivities by Jacobean courtiers. Patronage poetry sought support from particular friends and social superiors – the Earl of Pembroke, Lady Mary Wroth, the Countess of Montgomery, Robert Sidney. The comical satires, written during the War of the Theatres, respond to topical incitements, and several critics have suggested the same about the tragedies, linking *Sejanus* with the unsettling transition from Elizabeth to James and *Catiline* with the Gunpowder Plot.[5] Plays such as *Epicene, The Alchemist, Bartholomew Fair, The Devil is an Ass, The Staple of News* and *The Magnetic Lady* feature an elaborately depicted contemporary London setting, full of slang and packed with references to passing fashions and current events. These up-to-the-minute renderings are presumably a source of pleasure for the original audiences, constituting them as in-groups able to appreciate the representation of the immediate surroundings and suggesting that London life, in all its vitality, cannot properly be captured in terms designed for previous ages or other locations. 'No country's mirth is better than our own', Jonson boasts mock-jingoistically in the prologue to *The Alchemist*:

> No clime breeds better matter for your whore
> Bawd, squire, impostor, many persons more.
>
> (ll. 6–8)

Indeed, one of the jokes in *The Devil is an Ass* is the disorientation of the old-fashioned morality-play devil, Pug; sent from Hell to tempt London residents into sin, he is by turns baffled and horrified by modern depravity.

How is Jonson to reconcile his attraction to such ephemeral materials with his ambition to create enduring works of art? In the preface to *Hymenaei* he writes of court entertainments that: 'though their voice be taught to sound to present occasions, their sense or doth or should always lay hold on more removed mysteries' (ll. 15–17).[6] Hundreds of years hence, after the urgency of the 'present occasion' has faded, the 'more removed mystery' might, Jonson hopes, remain valuable for the reader and the guarantee of Jonson's literary immortality. Often, for Jonson, the conventions of genre seem to provide a way to situate the singular historical moment in supposedly permanent patterns of significance. *Volpone* may speak to the contemporary phenomenon of the explosion of consumer goods in early modern Europe, but its plot and character-types derive from Lucian, Petronius and Juvenal; *Epicene* owes much to Libanius and Plautus. In *Bartholomew Fair,* Jonson parodies the making-contemporary that he himself traffics in, as the puppetmaster Leatherhead recasts the story of Hero and Leander into contemporary terms: 'As, for the Hellespont, I imagine our Thames here; and then Leander I make a dyer's son about Puddle Wharf, and Hero a wench o' the Bankside, who, going over one morning to old Fish Street, Leander spies her land at Trig Stairs and falls in love with her' (5.3.93–6). The absurdity of Leatherhead's translation is evident, but there is a serious point as well: that some plots and character types are hardy perennials, taking much the same form in ancient Greece or Rome as they do in England in the 1600s.

In the past twenty-five years or so, many scholars have shied away on ethical and political grounds from universalizing language and from stereotypes, and, in consequence, genre criticism, which often trades in both, has fallen into abeyance. Jonson, though, sees generic conventions as enabling his creativity, not constricting it. The title-page engraving to the folio *Works,* with which this chapter began, portrays Comedy, Tragedy, Satire, Pastoral and Tragicomedy as monumental components of an elaborate architectural composition, tying Jonson's works to a glorious classical past and providing patterns for future artistic endeavour. Yet the genres are not statues. They step out of their architectural niches, peer at one another around the columns and pediments. There is no contradiction, for Jonson, in representing genres as simultaneously inherited and contemporary, universal and local, architectonic and vigorously alive.

NOTES

1. Richard Dutton, *Ben Jonson, Authority, Criticism* (New York: Palgrave Macmillan, 1996), p. 105.
2. The classic articulation of this thesis is Edmund Wilson's famous essay, 'Morose Ben Jonson', *The Triple Thinkers: Twelve Essays on Literary Subjects* (New York: Oxford University Press, 1948), pp. 213–22.

3. Bruce Boehrer, *The Fury of Men's Gullets: Ben Jonson and the Digestive Canal* (Philadelphia, Pa.: University of Pennsylvania Press, 1997), pp. 14, 205.
4. *The Masque of Queens,* ll. 12–19. The edition cited is that from *The Complete Masques,* edited by Stephen Orgel (New Haven, Conn.: Yale University Press, 1969).
5. See, *inter alia,* Jonathan Goldberg, *James I and the Politics of Literature* (Baltimore, Md.: Johns Hopkins University Press, 1983); Curtis Perry, *The Making of Jacobean Culture: James I and the Renegotiation of Elizabethan Literary Practice* (Cambridge University Press, 1997); and B. N. De Luna, *Jonson's Romish Plot: A Study of Catiline in its Historical Context* (Oxford: Clarendon, 1967).
6. *Hymenaei,* in *The Complete Masques,* edited by Stephen Orgel (New Haven, Conn.: Yale University Press, 1969).

CHAPTER 6

Friends, collaborators and rivals
Michelle O'Callaghan

Literary sociability took a variety of forms in the early modern period – coteries and clubs, collaborative ventures in verse and on the stage, friendships and even rivalries. It was one of the defining material contexts, alongside patronage, in which literary texts were produced. Recent work on collaborative practices in the theatre has demonstrated how the study of writing arrangements between men, and the institutions and cultures within which they worked, is integral to our understanding of early modern cultural and creative practices. Ben Jonson plays a key role in early modern cultures of conviviality. His name is identified by contemporaries and subsequent generations with the companies of wits who frequented the Mermaid tavern and later the Apollo Room. Jonson, himself, frequently asserted that wine and good company were the necessary stimulants for creativity. And, he is the author, and recipient, of verse epistles on friendship that helped to shape the genre. Yet, as William Drummond concluded, Jonson was also a notoriously belligerent and difficult character: 'He is a great lover and praiser of himself, a contemner and scorner of others, given rather to lose a friend than a jest, jealous of every word and action of those about him (especially after drink, which is one of the elements in which he liveth)' (*Informations,* 19.554–7). Jonson's career is punctuated by his violent rivalries with Inigo Jones and his fellow dramatists, Thomas Dekker and John Marston, which generated numerous vitriolic exchanges of fire in verse and plays.

It is telling that Jonson's most bitter rivalries were with those with whom he collaborated. If friendship posits an idealized affinity, then Jonson's rivalries suggest that proximity also generates aggression. Robert C. Evans argues that this dynamic between friendship and rivalry is integral to the power politics of early modern patronage culture, dominated by the need to form alliances and to compete for access and status.[1] Rivalries could divide communities into factions, mirroring the wider factionalism of early modern political culture. There is a class dimension to Jonson's jealousies as well as his friendships. Jonson was a labouring man turned 'gentle' poet. The early modern discourses of gentility, which Jonson drew on to negotiate this transformation, were riven by social contradictions: on the one hand, they emphasized civil behaviour and friendship between gentlemen, and, on the other, they continued to reserve a place for the jealousies of an older honour culture, which advocated the use of violence to defend one's reputation.

The interdependency of literary topoi and social practices is foregrounded in the poetry of friendship. Although it was not simply a transparent medium in which actual friendships had their expression, writers employed the vocabulary of friendship to negotiate and idealize social networks. Jonson, along with his fellow Renaissance writers, inherited a complex discourse of friendship from classical authors. Cicero's seminal treatise, *On Friendship*, set out a key distinction between the common 'friendships of ordinary folk' and 'true and perfect friendship', distinguished by its rarity and exemplarity.[2] This class distinction was at the heart of the ideal of friendship promoted in the Renaissance. A Ciceronian language of friendship was integral to fashioning a masculine, gentlemanly self in the Renaissance because it posited on an idealizing and exclusive affinity with other men of quality. It thus held particular attractions to a writer like Jonson, a self-made author whose labouring past as a bricklayer was often used to mock him. Jonson renegotiated the class basis of Renaissance friendship to fashion an ideal homosocial community that rests on the premise that integrity does not derive from social status but from learning and the cultivation of a better self.

'For the man who keeps his eye on a true friend', Cicero wrote, 'keeps it, so to speak, on a model of himself.' The exemplary friend is a man's double in the sense that he is the other, ideal self.[3] We can see this projection of the friend as one's better self in the opening address to 'An Epistle to Master John Selden' (*The Underwood*, l. 14):

> I know to whom I write; here, I am sure,
> Though I am short, I cannot be obscure.
>
> (ll. 1–2)

Such perfect knowledge rests on something more than an identification between the speaker and his addressee; the friend, Selden, is not simply Jonson's double, but his exemplar, the projection of his ideal centred self – only in Selden, 'I am sure.' Yet, even such an ideal friendship is haunted by the spectre of friendship's other, flattery. Jonson candidly admits that 'I have too oft preferred / Men past their terms, and praised some names too much' (ll. 20–1). Here, Jonson is drawing on another classical text on friendship, Plutarch's 'How to Tell a Flatterer from a Friend', an essay that Jonson returns to again and again in his epistles to friends. Flattery focuses attention on the problems posed by epideictic poetry, in particular, how to produce sincerity as a rhetorical affect within the forms of praise and ensure that it is not undermined through this very process. One solution Jonson proposed to this problem was brevity, which he equated with speaking plainly and honestly. The opening lines of his epistle to Selden are a study in brevity. The repetition (*anaphora*) across the lines creates a set of ongoing correspondences. 'I am short', starkly exemplified in the monosyllables that dominate these lines, is equated with ethical certainty, 'I am sure.' There is a positive avoidance of the forms of amplification. The rhetorical effect is understatement, that Jonson has not 'praised too much', and yet the repetition, which structures the epistle, artfully extends Jonson's praise of his friend. Brevity assumes shared knowledge and, as such, projects an exemplary and exclusive community of friends that hold key values in common – they have need for only few words, since they think the same.

The language of friendship, with its idealized affinities, enabled poets both to critique and to posit an alternative to the dependency of patronage culture. Jonson's 'Epistle to a Friend' (*The Underwood*, l. 17) counterpoints the sincere trust of the friend with the fickleness of patrons, the 'great names' who 'have broke with me, / And their words too' (ll. 8–9). Yet, the epistle also asks the friend not to call in Jonson's debt and, in fact, demonstrates the way in which friendship has its own economy of obligations that was part of a culture of credit in the period. Dependency was not only hierarchical, as in the patron–client relationship, but was also a feature of relations amongst those of similar social status. 'Trust' was central to these transactions; hence the value Jonson places on this term in his friendship epistles. Jonson was financially indebted to his friends throughout his career – this situation was exacerbated once he became estranged from the court in the second half of the 1620s and in the 1630s. Such dependency makes its presence felt in his friendship epistles, many of which belong to Jonson's later years; as David Riggs notes, whereas the word 'friend' hardly ever appears in the *Epigrams* (1616), it is prominent in *The Underwood* (published posthumously in 1640).[4]

A number of Jonson's key friendships were first formed when he was a boy at Westminster School, including those with its master, the famed humanist scholar, William Camden, and his schoolfellows, Hugh Holland and Robert Cotton and John Hoskyns, who was briefly at the school. Sir Robert Cotton's library subsequently became a meeting place for his former schoolfriends and other poets and antiquaries, including Jonson,

Holland, Selden and John Donne. Many of these men had attended the Inns of Court, a site of gentlemanly association in London. Jonson declared his own alliance with the Inns, 'The Noblest Nurseries of Humanity, and Liberty, in the Kingdom', in his 1616 folio dedication of *Every Man Out of His Humour*. These friendships were formative in a social as well as intellectual sense. Jonson would reputedly say of John Hoskyns, when Hoskyn's son, Benedict, asked the poet to adopt him as his son, that he 'dare not, 'tis honour enough for me to be your Brother. I was your Fathers sonne; and 'twas He that polished me'.[5] Polish, here, carries both the sense of intellectual refinement and to 'free from roughness, rudeness, or coarseness; to imbue with culture or refinement.'[6]

The late sixteenth and early seventeenth centuries saw the emergence of a culture of clubbing at fashionable London taverns, such as the Mitre and Mermaid on Bread Street, that owed much to the homosociality of the Inns. Francis Beaumont's epistle to Jonson, which celebrates the company that frequented the Mermaid, 'when there hath been thrown / Wit able enough to justify the Town', is the earliest recorded usage of 'town' in its modern sense as a synonym for fashionable society. At the same time, the term 'wits' takes on a specific social meaning to refer to a particular milieu that lived and socialized in the West End of London. Jonson not only took part in these sociable tavern gatherings but also put companies of wits on stage in *Epicene* (1609).[7] His fashioning of a 'clubbable' persona in his satiric epigrams culminates in the gloriously vulgar mock-heroic poem, 'On the Famous Voyage', whose protagonists, 'At Bread Street's Mermaid, having dined, and merry, / Proposed to go to Holborn in a wherry' (*Epigrams*, 133, ll. 37–8).

Jonson and Donne not only had many friends in common at this time but appear to have been particularly close. Their literary friendship gives a view to creative practices among fellow poets within this environment. Jonson sent a copy of his unpublished *Epigrams* to Donne with an epigram requesting that he 'Read all I send; and, if I find but one / Marked by thy hand ... / My title's sealed' (*Epigrams*, 96, ll. 7–9). Jonson sent another epigram to Lucy Harington, Countess of Bedford, their mutual patron, with the manuscript book of Donne's 'Satires', which she had requested (*Epigram*, 94). Friendship here coexisted seemingly amicably with the competitive world of patronage. It was not only through the exchange of verse in manuscript that writers could express their affinities. The dedicatory and commendatory poems prefacing the printed book provided a mechanism for crediting the author's literary friendships. Jonson invited the reader to witness the 'voluntary labours of his friends' in the commendatory verses placed by George Chapman, John Marston, Hugh Holland

and William Strachey, at the front of his *Sejanus* (1605). The sociable uses the book's preliminary matter could be put to is taken to new heights in *Coryats Crudities* (1611). Thomas Coryate's account of his European travels is prefaced by around 160 pages of mock-'Panegyricke Verses', dedicatory epistles and other material. Jonson took a leading role in orchestrating this gathering of the wits, which included a number of his friends and associates – Donne, Hoskyns, Holland, Martin, Cotton and Inigo Jones.

Coryats Crudities was the product of an elite coterie in which professional writers were in the minority. While Jonson advertised his collaboration with these gentlemen wits, he did not acknowledge his paternity of plays written in collaboration with fellow playwrights in his *Works*. Jonson may have praised 'so happy a genius' who 'had a good share in writing' *Sejanus*, but he carefully excised this 'second hand' when he published the play in 1605. His refusal to acknowledge that collaboration played a part in his work for the stage resulted from his claim to a proprietary author-function that insists possessively on the singularity of authorship. Even so, collaboration was part of the theatre's working practices, and Jonson did work as part of a writing team, particularly at the start of his career on the stage. Many of these details are available because two of his collaborative plays ran foul of the authorities. *The Isle of Dogs* (1597) caused such offence that Jonson was imprisoned along with the actors in the play, Gabriel Spencer and Robert Shaa, while the lodgings of one of his co-writers, Thomas Nashe, were searched. Following his release in late 1597, Jonson worked for Philip Henslowe and the Admiral's Men at the Rose Theatre as part of a team of writers that included Henry Chettle and Thomas Dekker. Eight years later, *Eastward Ho!* (1605), co-written with Chapman and Marston, once again landed Jonson in prison, this time for its satire on the Scottish courtiers of the new English king, James I.

This was the year in which Jonson began his fraught, yet long and fruitful, partnership with Inigo Jones. Although the two worked closely together on the production of elaborate masques for the Stuart court, Jonson insisted on a clear division between the poet, responsible for the soul of the masque, and the architect, whose skill was confined to the mechanical body. Hence, Jonson prioritized hearing the words of the poet over seeing the spectacle. As these aesthetic differences suggest, this apparently successful partnership was also a source of fierce rivalry. Jonson's rivals tended to be those men with whom he had worked closely – in the case of Jones, the two were part of the same social network and shared close friends, including Donne, Holland and Sir Henry Goodyere, who attempted to end the conflict by gently calling Jonson to account over his satiric impersonation of Jones in the puppet-master of *Bartholomew Fair* (1614). Rivalry, Evans notes, is 'friendship's dark opposite', and is the function of a status society, driven by the need to compete and to maintain face. If friendship posits an ideal affinity, then rivalry experiences similitude as a negative, threatening force and uses aggression to assert difference.[8]

Jonson's rivalries were certainly bitter, and they were often violent. In 1598, Jonson killed Gabriel Spencer, a fellow actor with whom he had worked over the previous three years, in a sword fight that he later insisted was a duel. Given that the duel was part of a gentlemanly culture not open to commoners, Jonson was implicitly claiming his own part in this elite honour culture. A few years later, Jonson's quarrel with Marston turned violent – Jonson boasted that he 'beat Marston, and took his Pistol from him' (*Informations* 11, 117). In this case, physical violence was also channelled into flyting, a form of versified duelling which used the satiric epigram as its weapon. The quarrel between Marston and Jonson was part of the so-called 'War of the Theatres' that was played out on and off the stage from 1599 to around 1601. Jonson had taken offence at Marston's perceived presumption in personating him on stage in 'Chrisoganus', a character in *Historiomastix* (1599), and retaliated with swipes at Marston in *Every Man Out of His Humour* (1599) and a full-scale attack in his *Poetaster* (1601). Dekker hit back with his *Satiromastix* (1601) and Marston with *What You Will* (1601). This 'War' was more than 'a personal feud between dramatists' and more than 'an argument between poets and about poetry'.[9] Issues of status and precedence cannot be separated from aesthetic concerns in these professional rivalries. Jonson sought to distinguish himself amongst his contemporary dramatists by adopting the term 'poet' and scorning the mere 'playwright'. The rival 'playwright' in the *Epigrams* functions to assert difference; his affinities with the 'poet' Jonson are often cast in terms of a false, debased emulation, hence in one epigram the rival is charged with both flattery and plagiarism (*Epigrams*, 100).

The late Elizabethan 'War of the Theatres' coincided with the intense factionalism of Elizabeth's last years. The early 1620s, when Jonson assembled his own company of wits, the 'Sons of Ben', at the Apollo Room, in the Devil and St Dunstan tavern on Fleet Street, were similarly fractious. War had broken out following the invasion of Bohemia, the principality of James's son-in-law, Frederick. Returning soldiers formed roistering fraternities – the 'Tityre-tus', the 'Order of the Bugle', the 'Order of the Blue' and, later, the 'Order of the Fancy'.[10] This is the context for the rivalry in 'An Epistle Answering to One that Asked to be Sealed of the Tribe of Ben' (*The Underwood* 47), in which Jonson's company is set

Figure 6.1 Bust of Apollo, from the Apollo Room, Fleet Street.

against 'The covey of wits' (l. 22). Presented as a speech delivered to an initiate, Jonson strengthens the ritualistic aspect of conviviality in this epistle so that friendship becomes tribal. Jonson's formation of the 'Sons of Ben', in part, is a response to the competition. The Apollo Room was, itself, a ceremonial space, graced by a bust of Apollo and verses over the door that welcomed 'all who lead or follow / To the oracle of Apollo' (see Figures 6.1 and 6.2). Those 'adopted' by Jonson include Lucius Cary, Viscount Falkland, James Howell, William Cartwright, Thomas Randolph, Richard Lovelace, Robert Herrick and Jonson's protégé, Richard Brome. Patronage and friendship coalesce in Jonson's relationship to a number of his 'sons', particularly Cary. The patriarchal premise of this company is a deft response to such dependency. The equivalence it introduces between the son and the friend endows friendship with the consanguinity of kinship. The effect is to intensify affinity and to naturalize dependency, both

> Welcome all who lead, or follow,
> To the Oracle of Apollo.
> Here he speaks out of his Pottle,
> Or the Tripos, his Tower Bottle
> All his Answers are Divine,
> Truth itself doth flow in Wine.
> Hang up all the poor Hop-Drinkers,
> Cries Old Sym, the King of Skinkers;
> He that half of Life abuses,
> That sits watering with the Muses.
> Those dull Girls, no good can mean us;
> Wine it is the Milk of Venus,
> And the Poets Horse accounted,
> Ply it, and you all are mounted;
> 'Tis the true Phoebian Liquor,
> Cheers the Brains, makes Wit the Quicker,
> Pays all Debts, cures all Diseases,
> And at once three Senses pleases.
> Welcome all, who lead or follow,
> To the Oracle of Apollo.
> O rare Ben Johnson!

Figure 6.2 Verses over the door in the Apollo Room, Fleet Street.

social and literary. This patrilineal mode of textual sociability places the father-author at the head of the processes of literary transmission, giving material as well as poetic expression to Jonson's legacy.

Factionalism continued throughout the 1630s. Jonson's 'son', the playwright Richard Brome, was attacked on stage in a second 'War of the Theatres'. Clubs were organized at taverns and assembled at theatres to mock and disrupt plays by rivals. This period witnessed renewed antagonism between Jonson and Jones. The two had successfully collaborated on the court masque, *Love's Triumph through Callipolis;* however, Jones had taken offence over an issue of precedence – when Jonson published the masque in 1631, he put his name first on the title page. Jonson then ridiculed Jones in a series of satiric epistles; Jones and his supporters responded by jeering *The Magnetic Lady* off the stage in 1632. Jonson retaliated by satirically personating Jones in the figure of In-and-In Medley in *A Tale of a Tub* (1633).[11] The quarrel caused more damage to Jonson than it did to Jones. Jonson had taken not only the laughter of ridicule beyond its accepted limits in his attacks but had also became his own flatterer, indulging in the defensive language of self-praise and, in the process, deforming his own reputation.

In the memorial volume, *Jonsonus Virbius* (1638), Jonson's 'sons' and other admirers, headed by Lucius Cary, clubbed together to monumentalize the memory of Father Ben that was, as they note, already enshrined in his *Works* (1616). And yet the volume is not simply celebratory; instead, it is remarkably defensive, with many of those assembled devoting considerable energy in their poems to answering Jonson's critics. It is a reminder that Jonson was responsible for both reviving classical literary forms of conviviality, which advocated civilized moderation, and for vicious, intemperate personal satire. To return to the words of Drummond, tellingly paraphrasing Quintilian's description of the scurrilous wit, Jonson was 'given rather to lose a friend than a jest'.

NOTES

1. Robert C. Evans, *Ben Jonson and the Poetics of Patronage* (London and Toronto: Associated University Presses, 1989), pp. 9–10.
2. Cicero, *De Amicitia*, cited in Jacques Derrida, *The Politics of Friendship*, translated by George Collins, 2nd edn (London and New York: Verso, 2005), pp. 3–4.
3. Derrida, *The Politics of Friendship*, pp. 3–4.
4. David Riggs, *Ben Jonson: A Life* (Cambridge, Mass.: Harvard University Press, 1989), p. 283.
5. Quoted in Riggs, *Ben Jonson*, pp. 56–7.
6. *Oxford English Dictionary*, 2.
7. Michelle O'Callaghan, *The English Wits: Literature and Sociability in Early Modern England* (Cambridge: Cambridge University Press, 2007), pp. 1–2, 44–9.
8. Evans, *Ben Jonson and the Poetics of Patronage*, p. 156.
9. Matthew Steggle, *Wars of the Theatres: The Poetics of Personation in the Age of Jonson*, ELS Monograph Series, No. 75 (Victoria: University of Victoria Press, 1998), p. 21.
10. Timothy Raylor, *Cavaliers, Clubs, and Literary Culture: Sir John Mennes, James Smith, and the Order of the Fancy* (London and Toronto: Associated University Presses, 1994).
11. Riggs, *Ben Jonson*, p. 337.

CHAPTER 7

Jonson and Shakespeare

Mark Robson

> One could wonder, moreover, if one might not discover fascinating secrets if one subjected a text, a discourse, a book to a spectral analysis ... of all the uses of 'and' ... And each writer, and each poet, and each orator, and each speaking subject, even each proposition can put to work a different 'and'.[1]

And so it begins with 'and'. Not out of a sense that this is the easiest place from which to start: the surface complexity of the proper names that surround the 'and' in a phrase such as 'Jonson and Shakespeare' might suggest that all the effort needs to be expended on them, but this complexity has to be read as an acknowledgement that we already know these two, that these names come to us already freighted, all too obviously sweating under bag and baggage. Analysing 'and' in such a phrase stems from a recognition that there is nothing natural about this conjunction, however expected it has become. Ben Jonson and those texts which bear his name have always had one context before all others (assuming for a moment that a spatio-temporal relation of contexts makes sense), and this context goes under the name of William Shakespeare. And as Ian Donaldson has argued, the construction of this context is perhaps initiated in the seventeenth century by Jonson himself, most markedly in the reference to 'The tother youth' in *Epicene* (2.2.87).[2]

Derrida's evocation of a spectral analysis of the 'and' and its uses refers to the chemical analysis of substances, but doesn't it also conjure a ghost? Certainly Jonson – and Jonson studies – has always been haunted by Shakespeare. The phrase 'Jonson and Shakespeare' already encompasses something of that other frame for this discussion, *Ben Jonson in Context*. In other words, to say *Ben Jonson in Context* is the same as saying Jonson and Context, and the meaning given to this particular 'Jonson and ...' is part of a sequence of other possible variations of the form 'Jonson and X'. X marks a point of indecision or imprecision but it also locates a chiasmatic interaction, an always possible reversibility of the relation. What, then, does it mean to employ the 'and' in this way to conjoin Jonson and Shakespeare, once more, in the context of *Ben Jonson in Context*? And doesn't this 'once more' amplify the central problem, gesturing towards an intertextual and metacritical series of discussions of 'Jonson and Shakespeare' that could never be fully accounted for?

Thinking the 'and' leads us in at least two directions at once, depending on the logic that allows the 'and' to operate. One form of this logic would suggest that the 'and' links two terms in a series, and that therefore this series could be continued beyond the present pair (Jonson and Shakespeare and Marlowe and Fletcher and …). This is that serial logic that so often ends in 'and so on', et cetera, etc., with the implication that the elements in the series are in the same category, and that this category is capable of substantial if not infinite extension. These lists thus end with a silent 'and', poised yet unremarked, waiting at the end of a sequence that it refuses to allow to end. But there is also an alternative logic that uses 'and' to draw together items sufficiently dissimilar to not normally be thought of as belonging to the same category. The 'and' produces an effect of doubling; either we have two of the same kind of thing, or else we have two things distinguished from each other by comparison (where the 'com-' marks the 'with' of co-presence that 'and' always conjures). Sameness and difference inhabit the operations of the 'same' word, and this is observable even within the 'same' example, dependent on the categories at work. To use the pair 'apples and oranges' could be a demonstration of sameness, if the category is fruit. The similarity becomes apparent by adding a third term, say, Westminster Abbey, or Napoleon. But idiomatically 'apples and oranges' indicates dissimilarity, linking two terms in order to distinguish them. Deciding whether 'and' implies similarity or difference is thus only possible by reference to a context, let us say at the very least to a sense of the categories or concepts in play. In this sense, 'and' makes apparent a determination by context that is both necessary and necessarily insufficient – demanded but never fully supplied since it can never be certain that the series has ended – and context is thus never fully determinative.

Jonson uses both of these versions of 'and', sometimes in the same text. The 'Ode to Himself' that followed the supposed failure of *The New Inn* when first performed at the Blackfriars Theatre in 1629, begins with 'Come, leave the loathèd stage, / And the more loathsome age' (ll. 1–2).[3] The 'And' works with the rhyme to draw together the theatre and the world – we might want to think about this as Jonson's context and its context – suggesting that each is as bad as the other for its failure to recognise his 'wit'. This failure is attributed to 'pride and impudence' in faction (l. 3), where 'pride' relates to a sense of self that is not in keeping with a particular situation or course of action (context) and 'impudence' suggests a shamelessness, immodesty or arrogance that similarly puts a distance between the judge and that being judged (context as decorum). This breach of context comes through combination, through pride and impudence. Later, he tells himself to 'Leave things so prostitute, / And take the Alcaic lute' (ll. 41–2). The 'And' this time works to differentiate between commercial theatre-poetry and the purity of a poetic form that supposedly escapes such considerations. But this escape is only possible if it is also possible to leave the age with which the stage has already been aligned; Jonson's persona seeks a temporal dislocation that makes the Alcaic archaic, and that thus announces a desire to transcend the determinative effects of a present context. (Of course, this poem contains the less than flattering comment on *Pericles* as a mouldy tale and so becomes part of the context for any discussion of the relation of Jonson to Shakespeare.) Breach of context is both condemned and desired.

Jonson here employs an entirely expected range of possibilities for the 'and'. Is a more idiomatic use of 'and' possible? There does appear to be a different relation to the idea of entitling texts around the 'and'. Jonson generally avoids doing so, although he has that 'or' in *Volpone; or, The Fox* that in fact marks an 'and'. Since Volpone is both Volpone and the Fox, the 'or' in fact marks a place of translation, or rather the movement of translation between places, in so far as the origin of the name in the Latin *vulpes* already tells some of its readers that there is a fox present. Jonson divides his audience according to linguistic competence (just as his remarks on Shakespeare's linguistic limitations – the small Latin and less Greek – have become one of the most prominent aspects of his poetic epitaph). Elsewhere, Jonson's work offers *Timber; or, Discoveries* and *Epicene; or, The Silent Woman,* both of which enact a similar doubling or translation-within-a-language that makes an 'and' of an 'or', since each text effectively carries two titles. Jonson doubles by division. Shakespeare, on the other hand, repeatedly employs 'and' to link characters in titles, producing double-acts as couples: *Antony and Cleopatra, Troilus and Cressida, Venus and Adonis, Romeo and Juliet.* (Perhaps also those other pairs, *The Two Noble Kinsmen* and *The Two Gentlemen of Verona,* which enact another kind of doubling or coupling. And what of *The Comedy of Errors?* And so on. There are at least a couple of books to be written on 'Shakespeare and And'.) The 'ands' in these titles mark the place of a problem: they cannot be read as meaningful in themselves, if by that is meant any notion that the relations marked by the 'and' are by virtue of that mark the same, and that the 'and' does more than open a space for the meaning produced by the conjunction of the elements brought together. The contextual indicator par excellence is characterless without the proper names that determine it. The difficulty, as Derrida suggests, lies in the theatricality of the 'and' itself and its connections to and of proper names:

Romeo *and* Juliet, the conjunction of two desires that are aphoristic but held together [*tenu ensemble*], maintained in the dislocated now [*maintenus dans le maintenant*] of a love or a promise. A promise in their name, but across and beyond their given name, the promise of another name, its request rather: 'O be some other name ...' (II. ii. 42). The *and* of this conjunction, the theater of this 'and', has often been presented, represented as the scene of a fortuitous contretemps, of aleatory anachrony.[4]

It is the power of the 'and' that holds and holds open this theatre of co-presence, with that which is present – as always in Derrida – held in a spatio-temporal here and now (*tenu ... maintenus ... maintenant*) always already structured by *différance*. The countertime of the contretemps hinges on the simultaneity of the 'and'; that is, it depends on the ability of time to be something other than singular and to be opened to anachrony. It is the point at which theatre is opened, Derrida suggests, since this is not an opening that can be limited to a single moment, nor even to time as a logic of serial succession (and then ... and then ...). No theatrical text's performability is ever exhausted by a given performance. Or its context.

A key aspect of this variation in the status of the 'and' is that in the case of Shakespeare's couples it becomes a question of character-and/as-name. The dog-eared contrast between the 'roundness' of Shakespeare's characters and the relative flatness of Jonson's may therefore be remarked in this use of the and/or through two different forms of doubling (division/multiplication). But is this quite it? Shakespeare's coupled characters attain their supposed depth because they are seen in relation. In contrast, Jonson's use of the 'or' as double marks a linguistic multiplication: the names Volpone or Epicene flaunt a Latinity that seemingly demands a glossing in English so that the doubled titles enact a poly-linguistic, quasi-tautologous stuttering, saying what may be (but never quite is) the same thing twice and thus revealing that species of linguistic difference that means that 'equivalent' words in different languages retain and enact their differences. Jonson's texts point towards a materiality of language papered over in recent years in an emphasis on archival materiality (understood as physical objects: manuscript, printed book, modern edition, hypertext and so on).[5] The term 'materiality' masks the term 'materiality'. Jonson, however, is interested in the characters of his plays, but by this we have to think literally of the letters from which they are formed as much as of the more usual sense of personae on a stage.

T. S. Eliot provides one of the most intriguing comparisons of the two poets, both focusing on the surface/depth problem to distinguish them and relating it to different approaches to character: 'The characters of Shakespeare are such as might exist in different circumstances than those in which Shakespeare sets them.'[6] In other words, what makes Shakespeare's characters superior to those of other writers – and particularly to those of Jonson – is their ability to be imagined out of context (which always means, of course, in another context). By contrast, 'Volpone's life', Eliot continues, 'is bounded by the scene in which it is played ... the life of the character is inseparable from the life of the drama. This is not dependence upon a background, or upon a substratum of fact.'[7] For Eliot, the crucial distinction rests in the difference between the worlds that the playwrights' characters inhabit. It is possible to imagine Shakespeare's characters living in 'our' world, or at least, in a world that is not that of the plays in which they occur. Jonson creates his own world, and his characters operate within its confines, that is, within a world that is never other than fictional and that frequently flaunts an artful 'flatness'. In thus appearing to lack the third dimension so often attributed to Shakespeare's characters, says Eliot, Jonson's plays seem consequently to lack world. The flatness of Jonson's fictional worlds leads to the impression of flatness in the characters. But Eliot specifies this clearly: 'We cannot call a man's work superficial when it is the creation of a world; a man cannot be accused of dealing superficially with the world which he himself has created; the superficies is the world.'[8] Jonson does not fail to achieve a third dimension but is instead aiming for something else.[9] In fact, Eliot sees Jonson's satire as fundamentally performative; it creates its object rather than 'hitting' an object already existent in the world.[10] The internal logic of the plays is thus not that of the world, but it 'illuminates the actual world' through anamorphosis.[11]

Might Eliot's reading itself illuminate some of the difficulties that New Historicists seem to have in dealing with Jonson? Crucial to the New-Historicist mode is an anthropologically inflected form of 'thick' description resting on an opposition of surface to depth. 'Historical' depth is favoured over the supposed 'thinness' of formalist readings only thought to scratch the surface of a life-world. There is, then, in Eliot's insistence on the surfaces-without-superficiality of Jonson's work, a clue to the relative neglect of Jonson within New Historicism in favour of Shakespeare.

In Stephen Greenblatt's early essay on *Volpone*, which remains his sole engagement with Jonson's work beyond a handful of footnotes, an Eliot-like contrast between Shakespearian depth and Jonsonian surface animates his reading: 'Profusion in Shakespeare creates, in Yeats's expressive phrase, "The emotion of multitude", the sense that the whole cosmos is involved in the action of the play. In Volpone, instead of the emotion of multitude we have precisely the avoidance of depth in a vertiginous swirl of words.'[12]

Despite this avoidance, Greenblatt repeatedly searches for something behind the surface of those words: 'in silence lurks the hidden meaning of the words'; 'deadness has all along been lurking just beneath the glittering surface ... We suddenly glimpse the dark thing which lay hidden'; he cites Burckhardt on the 'veil' which 'melted into air' in the move towards modern self-consciousness that Greenblatt recasts as self-fashioning; behind the play's disguises, masks and role-playing is emptiness, hollowness, the void; there is the 'buried suggestion' of impotence; 'beneath the masquerade, time is secretly at work'; he invokes 'our latent perception'.[13] Greenblatt's reading here is relentlessly structured around a hidden/revealed, latent/manifest model; all surfaces are to be penetrated because there must be something behind them even if the text seems at pains to deny it. So what lies behind the swirl of words? Critic and text are divided: Greenblatt supplies a series of socio-historical markers but also contends that only emptiness lies behind the glittering surface. Greenblatt thus seeks to impose a context for the play that it seems determined to renounce. The vertigo induced by Jonson's swirl of words is that of the historicist critic, faced with a monadic 'lack' of world that equates to a lack of Shakespearian multitude and thus driven to make either depthlessness or the void ethnologically full. To conceive of Will in the world is a less dizzying task, but it reveals a fundamentally romantic sensibility (for which Greenblatt's recourse to Yeats is only one of many signs) that itself demands a constitutive anachrony to read early modern texts.[14] Jonson's words lead Greenblatt to the edge of the abyss because of their refusal to give access to an object susceptible to thick description other than in a negative mode. Greenblatt's reading is thus the same as Eliot's in its insistence that the play invites anamorphotic reading, even if he draws wholly different conclusions from this insight. Jonson is not Shakespeare, and it is not obvious that a critical mode primarily attuned to Shakespeare offers the best chance of reading Jonson.

Telegraphically put, in critical terms the 'and' in 'Jonson and Shakespeare' indicates not equivalence but co-dependency. Jonson may always be defined by a certain vision of Shakespeare, but that 'Shakespeare' is itself the product of a comparison with Jonson. This is not an opposition so much as a process of redefinition that hinges upon the crux marked less by the proper names themselves than by their conjunction in the co-presence of an 'and'. And what is consequently at stake in this process is an articulation of word and world, an articulation that might properly be thought of as the burden of the aesthetic but that calls for a criticism opened by and open to Jonson's performativities.

NOTES

1. Jacques Derrida, 'Et cetera ... (and so on, und so weiter, and so forth, et ainsi de suite, und so überall, etc.)', in *Jacques Derrida*, ed. Marie-Louise Mallet and Ginette Michaud (Paris: L'Herne, 2004), pp. 21–34, p. 24; 'Et Cetera ... (and so on, und so weiter, and so forth, et ainsi de suite, und so überall, etc.), trans. Geoffrey Bennington, in Nicholas Royle (ed.), *Deconstructions: A User's Guide* (Basingstoke: Palgrave, 2000), pp. 282–305, 287–8 (translation modified).
2. See Ian Donaldson, 'Jonson and the Tother Youth', in *Jonson's Magic Houses: Essays in Interpretation* (Oxford: Oxford University Press, 1997), pp. 6–25.
3. While there is only slight evidence of this failure – and almost all of what there is comes from Jonson's texts – it has been claimed that *The New Inn* received only a single performance and that this was perhaps not completed. Certainly the second epilogue written in defence of the poet mentions a hissing audience, and 'The Dedication, To the Reader' complains of audience members who understand nothing of the play and are simply present 'To see, and to be seen'.
4. Jacques Derrida, 'L'aphorisme à contretemps', *Psyché: Inventions de l'autre II* (Paris: Galilée, 2003), pp. 131–44; p. 133; 'Aphorism Countertime', trans. Nicholas Royle, in *Psyche: Inventions of the Other,* vol. II, edited by Peggy Kamuf and Elizabeth Rottenberg (Stanford, Calif.: Stanford University Press, 2008), pp. 127–42; p. 130.
5. There is only space here to indicate the gulf between materiality in, for example, Paul de Man's late essays and a 'new materialism' that often becomes (to paraphrase Simon Jarvis) a mute pointing at things. Please see my *The Sense of Early Modern Writing: Rhetoric, Poetics, Aesthetics* (Manchester: Manchester University Press, 2006), Chapter 4.
6. T. S. Eliot, *The Sacred Wood: Essays on Poetry and Criticism* (London: Methuen, 1960), p. 112.
7. Eliot, *The Sacred Wood*, p. 112.
8. Eliot, *The Sacred Wood*, p. 116.
9. Eliot, *The Sacred Wood*, p. 121.
10. Eliot, *The Sacred Wood*, p. 120. See James Loxley and Mark Robson, *Shakespeare, Jonson and the Claims of the Performative* (London and New York: Routledge, forthcoming).

11. Eliot, *The Sacred Wood*, p. 117.
12. Stephen J. Greenblatt, 'The False Ending in *Volpone*', *Journal of Germanic and English Philology*, 75 (1976): 90–104; p. 91.
13. Greenblatt, 'The False Ending in *Volpone*', pp. 91, 93, 94, 93–100, 97, 98 and 100.
14. On New Historicism's romanticism, see Mark Robson, *Stephen Greenblatt* (London and New York: Routledge, 2007).

CHAPTER 8

Editions and editors

Eugene Giddens

Ben Jonson's most famous book is undoubtedly his folio *Works* of 1616, but the story of Jonson in print begins with the 1600 publication of *Every Man Out of His Humour* and continues with major editions in progress. Jonson is traditionally seen as the Renaissance dramatist most interested in his own print reputation. Although his overall canon discloses varying degrees of authorial oversight, Jonson was for the most part his own editor. Therefore, any consideration of editions and editors must begin with the author himself, especially as subsequent editions have been less radical in altering Jonson than his contemporaries. Editors since the eighteenth century have felt few qualms about radically recasting Shakespeare, changing his characters' names, emending his words, rearranging his lines. No such tradition exists for most of Jonson's canon. The editorial history of Jonson has been a conservative one, yet there is a rich vein of subsequent publication, in editions both unthinkingly derivative and highly innovative.

JONSON'S SELF-EDITING

Ten quartos of Jonson's plays were published before the folio *Works* of 1616. Although it is axiomatic to say that Jonson took a heavy interest in the publication of his own works, it is probably more true to say that Jonson's print authority becomes increasingly stamped upon his works as his career matures. His earliest printed work is the 1600 *Every Man Out of His Humour*, published by William Holme. That edition is said to be 'composed by the author B.I.' on the title page, suggesting a minimal authorial presence. Yet it also claims to contain 'more than hath been publicly spoken or acted', heightening Jonson's authority. Furthermore, the play's most recent editor, Helen Ostovich, notes that the text shows signs of 'authorial involvement in reading proofs'.[1] So Jonson was present in the print shop from the very beginning of his publishing career. Jonson's 1601 publications include two quarto editions, *Every Man In His Humour* and

Cynthia's Revels, published by Walter Burre. The distinction that is drawn on the title pages between the 1601 *Every Man In His Humour* being 'publicly acted' and the 1601 *Cynthia's Revels* being 'privately acted' seems tellingly Jonsonian. Most plays of the time simply disclosed the acting company and theatre, without describing the nature of the original audiences. What is un-Jonsonian about these three earliest quartos is a lack of direct authorial address to the reader. Such an address is also absent from the 1602 *Poetaster.*

It could be said that 'editions' of Jonson effectively begin with the 1605 quarto of *Sejanus,* a text that marks Jonson's first serious attempt to establish his authority as an author and editor of printed poetry. Jonson surrounds this play with paratextual information that serves to reinforce his presence. *Sejanus* is Jonson's first play to include a dedication 'To the Readers', the author's critical introduction to his own text. His address defensively takes pains to justify the play in the light of classical precedent, saying that he could not reconcile previous poetic ideas with 'any popular delight' (¶2). *Sejanus* offers two further textual innovations, at least as far as Jonson's career is concerned. The quarto prints dedicatory poems from eight other poets, including George Chapman, Hugh Holland and John Marston. None of Jonson's first four play quartos was so celebrated. *Sejanus* also offers an 'Argument' or plot summary, again Jonson's first, to assist the understanding of the reader. But the biggest Jonsonian innovation – and this is something unheard-of for a stage play – was the inclusion of an extensive scholarly apparatus. The first page of the play alone has nine marginal notes concerning classical sources. In fact, every page of the play except two (D4v, G1) has marginal notes, and some of them are so extensive as to continue beyond the margin and wrap around the bottom of the text itself (B3, C2v). This editorial apparatus makes the play more a product of scholarship than a collaborative work of theatre. The title page is in keeping with this interpretation. Unusually, it does not mention the theatrical troupe who performed the play, in an age when the author's name was frequently left off in favour of the acting company's.

Volpone (1607) comes next in Jonson's play publication history. It continues some of the innovations of his earlier works by stripping out any mention of the acting company and including several dedicatory verses by other poets. *The Case is Altered* (1609), however, shows none of the signs of textual authority that Jonson had steadily accumulated in his earlier publications, probably because Jonson did not wish to see it printed at all.

The Alchemist of 1612 is the final play quarto to be published before the substantive first folio of 1616. Along the way, however, it is important to consider two developments that reflect Jonson's changing relationship to his readers. *The Alchemist* has Jonson seeking aristocratic patronage, from Mary, Lady Wroth, and he begins to take a more assertive relation to his readers. Jonson's infamous statement, 'To the Reader', manages to insult both readers and playgoers at once:

To the Reader
    If thou beest more thou art an Understander, and then I trust thee. If thou art one that tak'st up, and but a Pretender, beware at what hands thou receiv'st thy commoditie. For thou wert never more fair in the way to be cozened (then in this Age, in Poetry, especially in Playes: wherein, now, the Concupiscence of Jigges; and Daunces so raigneth, as to runne away from Nature and be afraid of her, is the onely point of art that tickles the Spectators.

(sig. A3r)

Jonson here outlines a hierarchy of those who might encounter his work — Understander, Reader, Pretender and Spectator — and thereby classifies his audience according to how favourably they receive him. The ultimate understander is of course an aristocrat like Lady Wroth who might offer economic support to the poet. Such dedications to patrons will frame the plays of his 1616 folio.

Over the course of his career, Jonson becomes increasingly 'present' in his texts. For many of his works, he read his own proofs in the printing house, something that Shakespeare, for instance, never seems to have done. Although the folio of 1616 is taken to be Jonson's most powerful statement in shaping his textual reputation — he is the first public dramatist to call his plays 'works' — the quartos that he edited for the press build up to that more substantive edition.

At 1,015 folio pages, Jonson's 1616 *Works* made a statement that few poets and no dramatists of his time could rival. Importantly for subsequent editorial history, Jonson's involvement in the production of the folio was heavy, though he seems to have taken more care over certain parts than others. David Gants's very thorough collation has shown that extensive corrections were made to most sheets.[2] These corrections often concern small matters of spelling and punctuation that printers of the period would generally ignore. These punctuation changes are important when considering Jonson, because, as John Jowett notes, even of his quartos, Jonson's 'punctuation painstakingly etches out the various nuances of phrasing, and as such works upon the text so as to stabilize its interpretation'.[3] There can be little doubt that many of the folio corrections resulted from Jonson's presence as proofreader, although the extent to which Jonson oversaw all sections of the *Works* is not fully known. To further complicate the issue of correction, many pages in the folio were entirely reset, in part because large-paper, presentation pages of the works were printed before normal folio-sized copies.[4] The result is that, though many copies of the folio *Works* are known to survive today, editors must compare a large proportion of them to determine which readings are the corrected ones.

More problematic still is the fact that Jonson revised his plays for publication in the folio. *Every Man In His Humour* offers the most complex example of an altered text. Jonson transposed the Italian setting and character names of the quarto to Elizabethan London for the folio. Unlike *Hamlet,* these two very different versions of the play cannot be 'conflated' effectively. Fairly substantive changes are also made to Jonson's other early plays *Every Man Out of His Humour* and *Cynthia's Revels,* and more minor changes affect all of the work he had published previously (including some masques and entertainments). Perhaps most strangely of all, considering the care that Jonson took over the 1605 quarto, *Sejanus* in the folio loses its marginal notes and preliminary poems.

JONSON'S SUBSEQUENT EDITORS

Roughly half of this chapter has been taken up with the original publication of Jonson's works, because Jonson as an author presents some unusual, occasionally unique, problems for subsequent editors. To summarize:

1. Jonson had most of his plays printed soon after their first performances.
2. He was heavily involved in the print publication of his most canonical works, and in some cases directly shaped spelling and punctuation.
3. He reshaped his works specifically for print, and revised them for later printings.
4. He included his own editorial apparatuses, dedications, introductions, plot summaries, glosses and commentaries for many of his works.

All of these points make Jonson's texts more 'authoritative' than typical printed plays from the period. Most editors of Renaissance drama face texts with poorly ascribed speeches, missing or incomplete cast lists, misreadings, dropped lines, mistaken scene divisions, faulty stage directions and other errors to correct. Many readers are surprised to learn just how many alterations need to be made, for instance, to the original printing of Shakespeare's *The Comedy of Errors* in producing a modern edition. Of course that play was published thirty years after its first performance, and seven years after Shakespeare's death, so the author had a distant relation to its reception. Since Jonson took such care in seeing that his work was carefully printed, his texts have seemed to require a different editorial approach from that applied to Shakespeare.

Subsequent editors have had to find ways of coping with Jonson's overbearing presence in the re-creation of his works. The first 'editor' of Jonson was the printer of the 1640–1 folio, which was largely produced in the years following Jonson's death in 1637.[5] That printer, John Dawson Jr., closely followed the 1616 folio for the first volume, but Volumes II and III contained new work, or work written after 1616. Dawson deliberately replicated the kind of textual authority that Jonson established in his lifetime by imitating the style and format of the 1616 folio. He was able to do so because Jonson's manuscripts were in good condition and were put together, almost certainly by the author, with an eye towards print publication. For instance, Jonson's two unfinished plays, *Mortimer* and *The Sad Shepherd,* both contain 'Arguments', which Jonson included in earlier plays to help the reader follow the plots. The third folio of 1692 largely reprints from the 1640–1 folios, but it does correct a few earlier misprints, and, as such, it is rigorously compared to earlier editions by responsible editors.

Although Peter Whalley's seven-volume edition of the *Works* from 1756 offers some significant corrections, the most admirable subsequent edition of Jonson is that of William Gifford, published in nine volumes (London, 1816). Gifford does not occupy a place in history as one of literature's great editors, but that might be largely because he never, unlike more famous contemporaries Edmund Malone and Alexander Dyce, edited Shakespeare. Gifford modernized (at least in terms of 1816) Jonson's spelling and punctuation fairly freely. He was also willing to emend the sense of passages he deemed faulty. For instance, the 1641 folio copy of *The Sad Shepherd* at 1.4.17 reads: 'Such were the Rites, the youthfull *Iune* allow.' Gifford's 'Such are the rites the youthful June allow' is recognizably modernized in the use of spelling, capitalization and roman type. But Gifford also changes 'were' to 'are' in his edition on the basis that the following line repeats the word 'were' in the folio. Although Gifford emends more freely than editors would today (for instance, he changes "em' to 'one' without noting the change), he generally acknowledges where his readings differ from those found in his copy-text. Therefore he can be said to be the first editor to provide what we might recognize today as a genuinely scholarly apparatus. He offers a fairly full commentary – in places his text resembles a modern Arden Shakespeare edition in terms of the space devoted to notes. Gifford also ignores Jonson's classical scene divisions (when several characters enter) and divides the play into more Shakespearian scenes (when the stage is completely cleared). In this practice he is a more radical editor than any of those who follow.

Clearly Gifford's most important contribution to Jonson studies is the inclusion of additional stage directions. Jonson quite deliberately kept the stage directions in his plays to a minimum. His folio entry directions, in an attempt to resemble classical models, do not even contain the word 'enter', relying instead on simple lists of character names. Jonson also typically includes no exit directions or other indications of the action in his folios. (That his quartos often have a fuller indication of stage business suggests that the folio omissions were deliberate on Jonson's part.) To make the plays suitable for a dramatic performance or even for a reader's full understanding, stage directions must be added. Gifford added most of the exit directions required in Jonson (and in sensible places). He also added many other directions needed by the action. Later editors typically replicate these directions with slight revisions, so Gifford was pioneering in this respect.

The next attempt at a *Complete Works* is probably the most ambitious. *Ben Jonson,* edited by C. H. Herford, Percy Simpson and Evelyn M. Simpson has been the standard edition for over fifty years.[6] No other work has had more impact upon the course of Jonson studies. But at eleven very large volumes, and published over three decades, the 'Oxford Jonson' is also both unwieldy and difficult to navigate. Material relating to a single work often spreads over several volumes, and there is little cross-referencing to assist the reader. Just about everything that was known about Jonson by 1952 is contained in the edition, but several volumes might need to be consulted to find a specific piece of information.

Scholars frequently refer to the Oxford Jonson as 'monumental' because of the weight of the editors' learning. Although it is true that the depth and range of the research into such issues as sources and Jonson's life is impressive, the volume has for some time seemed dated and, more importantly, made Jonson seem dated to scholars and students. Yet the editorial policy of the Oxford Jonson is perfectly in keeping with Jonson's own attempts to shape his authorial identity, especially his placement of learning above accessibility. (The Oxford editors do not translate Latin or Greek.) The text is set in original spelling and punctuation and, in fact, attempts to replicate the type of the 1616 folio. The Oxford editors generally choose the folio editions of plays and masques above their quarto counterparts, so that the textual Jonson – as detached as possible from the stage – comes to the fore. Both of these decisions have led to a fairly alien dramatist, especially when compared to Shakespeare. Shakespeare is typically read in modernized spelling and punctuation and with a long history of editorially added stage directions. These conditions greatly assist the student reader, and even scholars favour modernized editions as their working copies. Herford and the Simpsons can be understood to take a fairly sophisticated approach to issues of old spelling and punctuation – they are in fact willing to change both quite radically, despite their conservative editorial policy. They, like Gifford, change 'were' to 'are' in *The Sad Shepherd* (1.4.17), yet they retain other Jonsonian spelling, capitalization and italics in the line: 'Such are the Rites, the youthfull *Iune* allow'. The Oxford editors also offer a thorough collation of all changes, and they checked multiple copies (typically around ten) of early editions for variants and corrections. As an old-spelling edition, the Oxford Jonson is superb. The trouble is that an old-spelling edition is radically out of keeping with the preferences of modern readers and scholars, even if it seems more true to Jonson's intentions.

Some of the most important recent editorial work on Jonson has come in the Revels series of plays, published by Manchester University Press, which by its nature cannot offer a complete edition of Jonson's works, as it does not concern itself with prose and poetry. That series deserves to be lauded for editorial excellence. Even though several different editors (and somewhat different editorial styles) have produced the individual editions, they are all of the highest quality. They tend to have collated more thoroughly than the Oxford editors, offer more substantial commentary (and gloss for meaning), modernize spelling and punctuation and fully discuss stage business. I suspect that more scholars would cite these editions if the series provided a complete Jonson. (Scholars who write on Jonson tend to quote widely from his canon and therefore for convenience continue to rely on the Oxford edition.)

The final complete edition I will consider has not been published at time of writing, though it is planned for release in the very near future. The Cambridge Edition of the Works of Ben Jonson, edited by David Bevington, Martin Butler and Ian Donaldson, aims to update the Oxford Jonson in the light of recent scholarship (and we now know much more about Jonson's texts than the Oxford editors did). More significantly, the editorial policy of the 'Cambridge Jonson' radically departs from that of the Oxford edition, bringing Jonson to readers in a way more in keeping with how they encounter Shakespeare and other Renaissance dramatists. Spelling and punctuation will be fully modernized, and necessary stage directions will be supplied. Instead of taking a blanket policy in favour of the folio, the Cambridge Jonson will either edit both folio and quarto versions or select the copy-text on a case-by-case basis.[7] Although Jonson's classical scene divisions will be retained, in most other respects the Cambridge Jonson will depart from the work of Herford and the Simpsons. Importantly, the Cambridge Jonson's electronic edition will supply full hypertexts of Jonson in both modernized and original spelling. The electronic edition will also include supplementary material relating to Jonson's life, the performance history of his plays and masques, his library and manuscripts. The Cambridge edition will certainly present a very different Jonson, one who will paradoxically become less 'Jonsonian' and more in keeping with other great dramatists from the period.

NOTES

1. *Every Man Out of His Humour,* ed. Helen Ostovich, Revels Series (Manchester: Manchester University Press, 2001), p. 3.
2. Printers in this period did not dispose of 'uncorrected' sheets, so many of these survive in copies of the *Works*. See David Gants, 'A Descriptive Bibliography of *The Workes* of Benjamin Jonson', Ph.D. dissertation, University of Virginia, 1997.
3. John Jowett, 'Jonson's Authorization of Type in *Sejanus* and Other Early Quartos', *Studies in Bibliography* 44 (1991): 254–65; p. 257.
4. See Johann Gerritsen, 'Stansby and Jonson Produce a Folio: A Preliminary Account', *English Studies*, 40 (1959): 52–5.
5. An aborted attempt to produce a second folio was conducted in 1631, but Jonson became dissatisfied with the standard of printing, and abandoned the project.
6. C. H. Herford, Percy Simpson and Evelyn M. Simpson (eds.), *Ben Jonson,* 11 vols. (Oxford: Clarendon Press, 1925–52).
7. See the pieces by Martin Butler and David Bevington in Martin Butler (ed.), *Re-Presenting Ben Jonson: Text, History, Performance* (Basingstoke: Macmillan, 1999) for more information on the rationale of the Cambridge Jonson.

CHAPTER 9

Critical reception

James Loxley

Six months after Jonson's death, a volume of elegiac tributes by friends, followers and admirers appeared in print. Entitled *Jonsonus Virbius,* the collection was both a recognition of Jonson's eminence and an early attempt to establish the terms in which the Jonsonian inheritance would be assumed or assimilated. Thomas May, whose translation of Lucan's *Pharsalia* had been praised by Jonson, speaks of the 'feare' that those inheritors might experience when confronted by the need to write of, and after, this 'King of English Poetry'.[1] Another contributor, Sidney Godolphin, demonstrated nothing of this nervousness in offering a succinct and elegantly summative account of the departed poet:

> The *Muses* fairest *light* in no darke time,
> The *Wonder* of a *learned Age;* the *Line*
> Which none can passe; the most *proportion'd Witt,*
> To Nature, the *best Judge* of what was fit;
> The *deepest, plainest, highest, cleerest* PEN;
> The *Voice* most eccho'd by *consenting Men,*
> The *Soule* which answer'd best to all well said
> By others, and which most *requitall* made,
> Tun'd to the *highest Key* of *ancient* ROME,
> Returning all *her Musique* with *his owne,*
> In *whom* with *Nature, Studie* claim'd a part,
> And yet *who* to *himselfe* ow'd all his *Art:*
> Heere lies BEN: JOHNSON, every *Age* will looke
> With *sorrow* here, with *wonder* on *his* BOOKE.[2]

Godolphin's poem invokes the evaluative vocabulary through which Jonson had repeatedly urged that his work, and that of others, should be assessed. Learning and wit are constitutive qualities of poetry, and the good poet shows too the judgement to reach the right balance of such qualities in his work. His writing is profound, his style appropriately lofty yet also clear and plain, eschewing the kinds of obscurities that would limit its reach and appeal. A poet who writes like this takes his social responsibilities seriously, judiciously affirming and amplifying these same qualities when they can be detected in others. He also reflects and revives the virtues of classical Rome. Yet this kind of reverence for the classics does not make him a slavish imitator: instead, his assumption of a classical inheritance actually makes him free of such debilitating dependence on others, an inheritor in fact of a classical ideal of artistic power and freedom in which the great Roman authors, in particular, can be seen to have invested. This is what classical art teaches, and the more faithful a writer is to its model the greater his capacity for autonomous creation, for – a weighty term, this – *integrity*. It is Jonson who has brought such an ideal into the modern world, establishing a respectable and stable place for poetry within the potentially corrupting modern world, defining and sustaining the forms of selfhood and collectivity that such a proper art requires.

Such exemplarity obviously makes of Jonson a master and a teacher of the poets charged with the important task of succeeding him, and many of his elegists dwell on this educative role. Yet Jonson has not only taught his followers how to write, or how to be a writer in not always commodious circumstances; more broadly and fundamentally, he has taught an age how to read. For some elegists this too is a matter of setting an example, as when Lucius Cary, another recipient of Jonson's praise, remarks on the range and scrupulosity of his reading:

> His *Learning* such, no *Author* old nor new,
> Escapt his reading that deserv'd his view,
> And such his *Judgement,* so exact his *Test,*
> Of what was best in *Bookes,* as what *bookes* best …[3]

Others, though, focus more on the ways in which Jonson's work requires a certain kind of response from them as readers or spectators. Henry King insists that English speakers can appreciate the strengths of their language 'by studying Johnson', while Jasper Mayne suggests that the audiences for Jonson's plays are 'made Judges' by the experience.[4] For Richard West, a comparison with his contemporaries serves to clarify what happens to Jonson's readers in their encounters with his works:

> *Shakespeare* may make *griefe* merry, *Beaumonts* stile
> Ravish and melt anger into a smile;
> In winter *nights,* or after *meales* they be,
> I must confesse very good companie:
> But *thou* exact'st our best houres industrie;
> Wee may read *them;* we ought to studie *thee:*
> Thy *Scænes* are *precepts,* every *verse* doth give
> Counsell, and teach us not to *laugh,* but *live.*[5]

Thus Jonson demands to be read, West suggests, 'as Classick Authors', or as William Cartwright puts it:

> *Thy verse* came season'd hence, and would not give;
> Borne not to feed the Authour, but to *live:*
> Whence mong the choycer Judges rise a strife,
> To make *thee* read as Classick in *thy life.*[6]

For the contributors of *Jonsonus Virbius,* then, a crucial part of Jonson's achievement was that his writing required a mode of readerly care and attention that his contemporaries usually accorded only to classical literature. Recognizing Jonson's classicism meant reading him as one would the classics, judiciously, studiously, as a vital part of the advancement of one's own learning.

Such a distanced, scholarly, rational mode of reading, a mode that prizes judiciousness, can accurately be described as critical. Jonson's early readers were undoubtedly aware of the extent to which his work licensed or demanded a reflective care in the form of criticism rather than more immediate, on the pulse or off the cuff, responses. This is something that Jonson had taught them, insisting throughout his work in a range of different ways on the essential role of a proper, critical reception in the healthy functioning of poetry. In his followers and commenders such care necessarily went hand in hand with praise: Jonson's work provided the evaluative terms through which it should itself be judged, and therefore could be seen as doubly exemplary. Where they acknowledge, again following Jonson, that his work had not always met with approbation, it is assumed or asserted that unfavourable responses were only failures or the absence of critical judgement rather than its proper exercise. As the years passed, though, the terms of criticism were themselves developed and transformed, and Jonson's example became sufficiently distant in time to make a different kind of distancing judgement much more likely. Keen, like his predecessor, to define the taste of an age, John Dryden re-evaluated Jonson's work a number of times, seeking to characterize and assess his place and significance according to poetic standards that were now not simply Jonson's own.

The comparison with his contemporaries also ceased, at least in one regard, to work to Jonson's credit. As Mark Robson indicates elsewhere in this volume, Jonson's reputation became inextricably tied to that of Shakespeare; as the latter's inverse, though, his stature necessarily shrank as Shakespeare's grew throughout the eighteenth century. While Romanticism could then find in Shakespeare's work sufficient kinship to its own aesthetic principles, no such family resemblance was visible in Jonson. Even Jonson's insistence on scholarly care, and his sense of what constituted proper critical reading, came to count against him. His laborious, mechanical work appeared to set itself against nature and the creative forces of spirit and genius, and Jonsonian poetics now looked alien to readers grown accustomed to reading poetry under the rubric of a fully aestheticized, rather than rhetorical, conception of literary art. The seeming grotesques populating his plays could only painfully be compared to the characters that Shakespeare had summoned from his more profound imagination. Where the latter's characters 'possessed some of the mysteriousness of real people', affirming the nobility of the human, Jonson's 'were not individuals, but blueprints of types, or else, on the contrary, they were so frantically individual, so rampantly eccentric, that they ceased to seem human altogether'.[7] Besmirched by decades of prejudiced comment, Jonson's own character was also firmly assumed to have been as warped and unbalanced as that of one of those grotesques. Despite the exemplary efforts of William Gifford, his early nineteenth-century editor, little of Jonson's work was commonly judged readable during the subsequent decades except the few lyric pieces and fragments included in Palgrave's *Golden Treasury* and the fanciful confections of the masques. The rest of his writing could be characterized as coarse, or quaint, and the strange combination of qualities posited by such polarized judgements was a source of puzzlement. As D. H. Craig has put it, he appeared to be 'a writer who could not be resolved into a single identity: he was a leviathan, massive and unwieldy, yet he was also a poet of elegance and grace.'[8]

Although Jonson was notably praised by Algernon Swinburne in the late nineteenth century as supreme among 'the giants of energy and invention', his reputation was most significantly remade when modernism, and the growing influence of academic literary study, managed to effect a profound change in the terms of criticism once again.[9] In an important essay, T. S. Eliot proclaimed anew Jonson's readability – but only by insisting on a definition of reading that departed finally from Romantic assumptions. Claiming that no one since Dryden had managed to write 'a living criticism of Jonson's work', he attempted to rediscover that kind of critical response in acknowledging both Jonson's distinctive qualities and the reasons for his neglect. Jonson writes a 'poetry of the surface', but this does not mean that his work is superficial or immediately accessible to 'the lazy reader'. On the contrary:

No swarms of inarticulate feelings are aroused. The immediate appeal of Jonson is to the mind; his emotional tone is not in the single verse, but in the design of the whole. But not many people are capable of discovering for themselves the beauty which is found only after labour.[10]

Jonson's poetry therefore 'requires study', which is itself defined as 'intelligent saturation in his work as a whole'.[11] His writing rewards a proper, deliberate appreciation of its qualities, an appreciation that arises in the conscious and judicious experience of the total work.

Eliot's account of Jonson thus suggests that it is not the work but its readers that have had the problem. Jonson is readable, but only if approached correctly, and his writing will not render the kinds of satisfaction offered by others. From one standpoint, this is a pleasantly pluralist argument that a poetry of the surface has attractions merely different from, rather than inferior to, those of depth; but its pejorative references to 'lazy' readers, and the implicit high value it places on intelligence and study, is also a resurrection of a more Jonsonian account of artistic and aesthetic value. It both recalls and revives the kind of readerly posture demanded by Jonson himself and promulgated by his early admirers. Following Eliot, and chiming with the development in academic criticism of a serious, studious interest in the formal features of literature, the new reception of Jonson began to focus on the exemplary craft and artistry of his work. *Volpone*, for example, became a focus for sustained engagement with the intricacies and effects of Jonsonian plotting, and his other major plays were subject to similar attentions.[12] The Jonsonian masque was also subject to renewed consideration as a critically respectable, specifically *literary* form, and the properties and dynamics of his non-dramatic verse were set out in the kind of detail that only close and careful textual analysis could disclose to the reader.[13]

Yet when such critical formalism ceded place in the 1970s and 1980s to more radical reimaginings of literary textuality, and therefore of what reading was held to consist in, and what criticism could now be, the critical encounter with Jonson's writings did not feature significantly in the debates. However, for Stanley Fish – to some extent a sympathizer of such reimaginings – Jonson's non-dramatic verse could indeed be read as engaging with the conditions of textual representation in a manner that could usefully be illuminated by the concerns of contemporary theory.[14] In Fish's account, Jonson's poems of praise are self-denying, if not self-consuming, artefacts: in their attempts to know their objects they seek to overcome the medium of representation through which, and only through which, they could know them. Such poems imagine an immediacy in which virtue does not need to be represented, in which it merely presents itself, and is recognized at once by those who apprehend it. This is an impossible vision of poetry as the embodiment of 'epistemological immediacy and ontological self-sufficiency', as Fish puts it, the kind of secure and closed relations of a 'community of the same' in which an authorial self finds its work and its medium gloriously, if problematically, superfluous.[15]

Yet Fish's account of Jonson's awkward reflexivity concludes by explaining the poetry's peculiar features not through a theory of textuality or representation but in an account of its author's social location. Jonson was an 'outsider', forced to 'rely on others for favour and recognition'; his vision of 'an elect fellowship' for which he could be the speaking centre was a compensatory fantasy designed to deflect an awareness of social marginality.[16] For Fish, then, even the deconstructive tendencies in Jonson's writing were actually open to explanation in terms of its historical moment. He shared this sense of the interlocking axes of textual and historical accounting with Jonathan Goldberg, whose *James I and the Politics of Literature* (1983) sought to disclose the relation of Jonson's writing to the representational strategies of his primary royal patron through a not dissimilar deployment of the concepts and terminology of post-structuralist theory.[17] In making this move towards historical explanation, Goldberg and Fish were rejoining a strong current of historicist or contextualist criticism that reached back at least as far as L. C. Knights.[18] This critical mode, seeking to locate texts in the explanatory context of their moment of first production and circulation, could also be traced to such sources as the scrupulous historical account of the Jonsonian masque offered by D. J. Gordon in important essays of the 1940s, but it became the dominant trend in the critical reception of Jonson from the later 1980s onwards.[19]

As the examples of Fish and Goldberg show, this development of a historicist horizon for Jonson criticism did not preclude a continuing engagement with the intellectual challenges and stimulants of literary theory. The historical imaginations and vocabulary of Marx, Bakhtin and Foucault have certainly influenced the ways in which Jonson's works have been read, and more recently the development in post-colonial theory of a critical sensitivity to issues of racial, national and cultural identity have left a particular mark on the reading of the masques.[20] Perhaps the most fundamental impression, though, has been made by a feminist criticism alert both to early modern discourses of gender and sexuality and to more recent critical assumptions that stand in need of correction. While some critics have suggested that plays such as *Epicene* are marked by a pervasive misogyny, others have argued instead that Jonson's drama offers a more complex engagement with the ways in which gender and sexual identities are configured.[21] Attention paid to the plays' performance on the all-male stages of early modern commercial theatre, to the participation of women in the masques performed at court, and to the importance for Jonson of female patrons, has also helped to fill out and diversify the picture of gendered discourses and relations in and around Jonson's writing.[22]

Other forms of historicist criticism have not been informed to quite the same degree by contemporary political-theoretical concerns. Instead, they have sought to illuminate Jonson's work through a more fundamental reliance on the methods and resources of mainstream empirical history and bibliographical scholarship. In particular, there has been an invigorating reliance on the hitherto under-acknowledged evidence of the archive, and on the fruits of historians' archival research, which has both developed and challenged the claims of a precedent literary history.[23] This form of enquiry has transformed critical views of the masques in particular, even to the extent of recovering lost texts.[24] While earlier generations saw them as fanciful *jeux-d'esprit,* and critics such as Stephen Orgel and Jonathan Goldberg emphasized the extent to which they could be seen as part of the representational strategies of an absolutist monarchy, subsequent work has brought a more heavily populated arena of historical actors into view.[25] The masques have consequently been seen as involved in a more intimate fashion with the day-to-day political jostlings of the Stuart court and country, and therefore as more thoroughly webbed into, and explained with reference to, the detailed narratives of political history.[26] Our views of the rest of Jonson's work have also been transformed by the dominance of this same critical orientation, especially because it has reinvigorated a more rhetorical view of his art. Detailed contextualization of this nature demands an account of his writing which presumes its instrumentality and focuses on its purposes in the moments of its production and circulation; a criticism operating from such a standpoint also finds that its own conceptions of the nature and function of writing can resonate with some of Jonson's reflections on the ideals and perils of authorship.[27]

This historicist effort is clearly a different form of reading from the 'intelligent saturation' or the 'living criticism' of which Eliot wrote: it presumes a different understanding both of criticism and of its objects. It could be argued that it is more clearly descended from the attitudes of the unnamed 'industrious readers' he describes condescendingly as 'those whose interest was historical and curious, and who thought that in discovering the historical and curious interest' of Jonson's work 'they had discovered the artistic value as well'.[28] In truth, contemporary criticism is much more sceptical than Eliot was of any singular notion of 'artistic value', and is often animated by the conviction that the artistic and historical are to be drawn into a critically productive relation as well as distinguished from each other. Its habituation within the academy, too, ensures that its exigencies are not quite those of Eliot's time and milieu. But the porosity of its boundaries and the roving eyes of its inhabitants are among the chief characteristics, perhaps the strengths, of the literary academy, and there is another important aspect to the current critical reception of Jonson within existing institutional frameworks that attempts to do justice to the contemporary experience of his plays in the theatre rather than, or in addition to, the cornucopian absorptions of the archive or library and the historical imagination that they feed. The most obviously 'living' criticism of Jonson today is perhaps that which witnesses to the power and effects of his plays in performance.

In a very influential book, Jonas Barish argued that Jonson was torn between a skilled delight in the resources and powers of theatricality and a moralistic suspicion of its painted pageantry.[29] The antagonism of which Barish wrote was in some ways reflected in the literary critical tendency to downplay the plays' status as performance texts, a tendency shared by New Critical close readers and historically minded scholars alike, and assisted by the sometimes only fitful presence of Jonson's plays in the modern repertory. Anne Barton's 1984 book *Ben Jonson: Dramatist* forcefully reasserted the centrality of theatre to critical accounts of his work, and a striking feature of Peter Womack's *Ben Jonson* was its capacity to place the plays in the speculative space and time of imagined performance.[30] Since then, critics including Richard Cave and Brian Woolland have led efforts to develop an account of Jonsonian theatricality that grows not only from the history of its staging conditions but also out of the insights derived from rehearsing, performing and watching his plays today.[31] Historicist critics can find themselves in fruitful dialogue with champions such as the playwright Peter Barnes, who suggested that 'it is helpful when writing about Jonson if you have worked in some capacity on an actual Jonson production, in a theatre, in front of an audience.'[32] Shakespeare, of course, has long had such theatrical champions, and his ubiquitous presence on the stages of the world has meant that criticism has never been able to forget his theatricality, even when it would have liked to do so. Jonson has not been so lucky, and for critics like Barnes this makes the issue particularly pressing. It is not just that the plays in performance allow us to witness another aspect of Jonson's achievement; in fact, the plays can *only* properly be understood and appreciated in performance. As Barnes puts it, in a suitably vivid simile, 'on stage his seemingly heavy, clotted verse and prose unfolds like beautiful Japanese paper flowers in water'.[33] Without the phenomenality of performance we are unable to see something absolutely essential to his work. However discerning our readerly attentions, however scrupulous our historical scholarship, we will still fail to recognize the Jonsonian word in its true guise, as a germinal potentiality always ready to be actualized as theatre.

Such an urgent insistence on the critical importance of performance is a challenge to other schools of criticism, just as they in turn offer challenges to the necessary limitations of their fellows and rivals. We should perhaps not look to resolve the salutary tensions between them into the triumph of one perspective or another, just as we should not assume that the productivity of any individual stance is completely exhausted, however untimely it can come to seem. Though Jonson would not recognize it as such, this tension within and between forms of criticism is also a kind of readerly fidelity: it testifies to the ongoing, undiminished demand for proper attention that he addressed to all those who found themselves in the presence of his words. It is a sometimes attenuated, involuted but unignorable part of the inheritance that Jonson bequeathed to us, his audience, readers and followers.

NOTES

1. Thomas May, 'An Elegie Upon Benjamin Johnson', in Brian Duppa (ed.), *Jonsonus Virbius* (London, 1638), p. 21.
2. Sidney Godolphin, 'The Muses Fairest Light [...]', in Brian Duppa (ed.), *Jonsonus Virbius* (London, 1638), p. 27.
3. Lucius Cary, Viscount Falkland, 'An Eglogue on the Death of Ben Johnson', in Brian Duppa (ed.), *Jonsonus Virbius* (London, 1638), p. 4.
4. Henry King, 'Upon Ben. Johnson', and Jasper Mayne 'To the Memory of Ben. Johnson', in Brian Duppa (ed.), *Jonsonus Virbius* (London, 1638), pp. 17, 32.
5. Richard West, 'On Mr. Ben. Johnson', in Brian Duppa (ed.), *Jonsonus Virbius* (London, 1638), p. 56.
6. West, 'Ben. Johnson', p. 57; William Cartwright, 'In the Memory of the Most Worthy Benjamin Johnson', in Brian Duppa (ed.), *Jonsonus Virbius* (London, 1638), p. 37.
7. Jonas Barish (ed.), *Ben Jonson: A Collection of Critical Essays* (Englewood Cliffs, NJ: Prentice Hall, 1963), p. 7.
8. D. H. Craig (ed.), *Ben Jonson: The Critical Heritage* (London: Routledge, 1989), pp. 34–5.

9. Algernon Swinburne, *A Study of Ben Jonson* (London: Chatto & Windus, 1889), p. 3.
10. T. S. Eliot, 'Ben Jonson', in Jonas Barish (ed.), *Ben Jonson: A Collection of Critical Essays* (Englewood Cliffs, NJ: Prentice Hall, 1963), pp. 14–15.
11. Eliot, 'Ben Jonson', p. 15.
12. See, for example, Jonas Barish, 'The Double Plot in *Volpone*', in Jonas Barish (ed.), *Ben Jonson: A Collection of Critical Essays* (Englewood Cliffs, NJ: Prentice Hall, 1963), pp. 93–105, and Stephen Greenblatt, 'The False Ending in *Volpone*', *Journal of English and Germanic Philology*, 75 (1976): 90–104.
13. Dolora Cunningham, 'The Jonsonian Masque as a Literary Form', in Jonas Barish (ed.), *Ben Jonson: A Collection of Critical Essays* (Englewood Cliffs, NJ: Prentice Hall, 1963), pp. 160–74; Wesley Trimpi, *Ben Jonson's Poems: A Study of the Plain Style* (Stanford, Calif.: Stanford University Press, 1962).
14. Stanley Fish, 'Authors-Readers: Jonson's Community of the Same', *Representations*, 7 (1984): 26–58.
15. Fish, 'Authors-Readers', p. 35.
16. Fish, 'Authors-Readers', p. 57.
17. Jonathan Goldberg, *James I and the Politics of Literature* (Stanford, Calif.: Stanford University Press, 1989).
18. L. C. Knights, *Drama and Society in the Age of Jonson* (London: Chatto & Windus, 1937).
19. See D. J. Gordon, *The Renaissance Imagination,* ed. Stephen Orgel (Berkeley, Calif.: University of California Press, 1975).
20. See, for example, Don Wayne, *Penshurst: The Semiotics of Place and the Poetics of History* (London: Methuen, 1984); Peter Womack, *Ben Jonson* (Oxford: Basil Blackwell, 1986); Richard Burt, *Licensed by Authority: Ben Jonson and the Discourses of Censorship* (Ithaca, NY: Cornell University Press, 1993); Kim Hall, *Things of Darkness: Economies of Race and Gender in Early Modern England* (Ithaca, NY: Cornell University Press, 1995); Yumna Siddiqi, 'Dark Incontinents: The Discourses of Race and Gender in Three Renaissance Masques', *Renaissance Drama*, 23 (1992): 139–64; James Smith, 'Effaced History: Facing the Colonial Contexts of Ben Jonson's Irish Masque at Court', *English Literary History*, 65 (1998): 297–321; Rebecca Bach, 'Ben Jonson's "Civil Savages"', *Studies in English Literature*, 37 (1997): 277–93.
21. See, for example, Karen Newman, *Fashioning Femininity and English Renaissance Drama* (Chicago, Ill.: Chicago University Press, 1991); Helen Ostovich, 'Mistress and Maid: Women's Friendship in *The New Inn*', *The Ben Jonson Journal*, 4 (1997): 1–26; and 'Hell for Lovers: Shades of Adultery in *The Devil is an Ass*', in Julie Sanders, Kate Chedgzoy and Susan Wiseman (eds.), *Refashioning Ben Jonson: Gender, Politics and the Jonsonian Canon* (Basingstoke: Macmillan, 1998), pp. 155–82.
22. See, for example, Laura Levine, *Men in Women's Clothing: Anti-Theatricality and Effeminization, 1579–1642* (Cambridge: Cambridge University Press, 1994); Sanders *et al.*, *Refashioning Ben Jonson*; Clare McManus, *Women on*

the Renaissance Stage: Anna of Denmark and Female Masquing in the Stuart Court (1590–1619) (Manchester: Manchester University Press, 2002).
23. Mark Bland, 'Ben Jonson and the Legacies of the Past', *Huntington Library Quarterly*, 67 (2004): 371–400.
24. James Knowles, 'Jonson's *Entertainment at Britain's Burse*', in Martin Butler (ed.), *Re-Presenting Ben Jonson: Text, History and Performance* (Basingstoke: Macmillan, 1999), pp. 114–51.
25. Jonathan Goldberg, *James I and the Politics of Literature* (Baltimore, Md.: Johns Hopkins University Press, 1983); Stephen Orgel, *The Illusion of Power: Political Theatre in the English Renaissance* (Berkeley, Calif.: University of California Press, 1975).
26. David Bevington and Peter Holbrook (eds.), *The Politics of the Stuart Court Masque* (Cambridge: Cambridge University Press, 1998).
27. Richard Helgerson, *Self-Crowned Laureates: Spenser, Jonson, Milton and the Literary System* (Berkeley, Calif.: University of California Press, 1983); Richard Dutton, *Ben Jonson: Authority: Criticism* (Basingstoke: Macmillan, 1996); Robert Evans, *Ben Jonson and the Poetics of Patronage* (Lewisburg, Pa.: Bucknell University Press, 1989); Joseph Loewenstein, *Ben Jonson and Possessive Authorship* (Cambridge: Cambridge University Press, 2002).
28. Eliot, 'Ben Jonson', p. 15.
29. Jonas Barish, *The Anti-Theatrical Prejudice* (Berkeley, Calif.: University of California Press, 1981).
30. Anne Barton, *Ben Jonson: Dramatist* (Cambridge: Cambridge University Press, 1984).
31. Richard Cave, *Ben Jonson* (Basingstoke: Macmillan, 1991); Richard Cave, Elizabeth Schafer and Brian Woolland (eds.), *Ben Jonson and Theatre: Performance, Practice and Theory* (London: Routledge, 1999); Brian Woolland (ed.), *Jonsonians: Living Traditions* (Aldershot: Ashgate, 2003); Sean McEvoy, *Ben Jonson: Renaissance Dramatist* (Edinburgh: Edinburgh University Press, 2008).
32. Peter Barnes, '*Bartholomew Fair*: All the Fun of the Fair', in Brian Woolland (ed.), *Jonsonians: Living Traditions* (Aldershot: Ashgate, 2003), p. 47.
33. Barnes, '*Bartholomew Fair*', p. 46.

CHAPTER 10

Performance afterlives

Lois Potter

When the restored Stuart monarchy officially re-established the theatre in 1660, Jonson – former poet laureate, eulogist of many aristocrats and anti-Puritan satirist – had a particularly obvious claim to be performed. His *Epicene* may in fact have been the first genuine Restoration revival, since it was put on in June 1660, only a month after Charles II's return. In November the King saw it at the Cockpit Theatre in Whitehall as part of an entertainment sponsored by General Monk, the main power behind the restoration. It was for this occasion that Sir John Denham wrote the famous prologue linking theatre to the monarchy: 'They that would have no KING, would have no Play.'[1] He must have felt that the dramatist would have thoroughly agreed with this sentiment.

At the same time, Jonson was already being thought of as difficult to perform. Though he is often called a literary dramatist, annotating his plays for publication and surrounding them with epistles and epilogues, what worried critics then as later was his close relation to the theatre of his own time. The 'Prologue to the Revived *Alchemist*', dated 1660 though probably slightly later, shows how thoroughly he had succeeded in convincing actors and spectators that he was the only possessor of the philosopher's stone: the secret of speaking his lines correctly. The imagined speaker here is a spectator who remembers pre-war productions and who has just seen the play announced in a playbill:

> *The* ALCHEMIST? What! are the Fellows mad?
> Who shall *Doll Common* Act? Their tender Tibs
> Have neither Lungs, nor Confidence, nor Ribs.
> Who *Face* and *Subtle?* Parts, all Air and Fire:
> They, whom the *Authour* did Himself inspire,
> Taught, Line by Line, each Title, Accent, Word,
> Ne're reach'd His Height; all after, more absurd,
> Shadows of fainter Shadows.[2]

The speaker clearly knows that Jonson had been closely involved with the production of his plays and fears that, since even the actors taught personally by him failed to bring out his full potential, their successors have even less hope of doing so. (Perhaps he had been talking to the Duke of Newcastle, who had known Jonson personally and described him as the best reader he ever heard.)[3]

This prologue also hints at the other great problem of Jonson's plays, summed up in the epilogue that Nell Gwyn spoke at a 1668 court performance of *Catiline*:

> His lofty Pen,
> How e're we like it, doubtless Wrote to Men.

Love is not a major theme in Jonson, and many of his women's roles are small and unrewarding. At the other extreme, though, as with Doll Common, they require raucous impudence and energy that was hard to find in 'tender Tibs' like the largely untrained actresses of the early Restoration. Within a few years there would be genuinely skilled female comedians to tackle such characters, but the lack of 'female interest' continued to be a criticism of Jonson.

It may be that *Epicene* was chosen for an early performance because it lent itself particularly well to the traditional all-male companies that had resumed acting in the last years of the Commonwealth. In January 1661 Samuel Pepys saw Edward Kynaston, a famous boy actress before the war, play Epicene, and admired how well he looked in both male and female dress (7 January 1661). Seeing the play again on 1 June 1664, he liked it less, but did not connect his reaction with the fact that a woman was now playing the role. Such casting seems an obvious mistake, likely to make an audience feel cheated rather than surprised at the end, but audiences expected to see their favourite actresses in major roles, and Epicene offered one of the few good opportunities for a woman to display a range of moods, from the subdued and obedient creature of her first scene to the virago who makes Morose eager for divorce at any price. Besides, enthusiastic theatregoers normally went to the same play many times, so the surprise factor was less important than it would later become.

Political and topical considerations motivated the performances of two other plays. One was the tragedy *Catiline*. Because it depicts republican revolutionaries as bloodthirsty maniacs and untrustworthy womanizers, it had been widely quoted in royalist literature of the 1640s and 1650s. The revival of 1668 benefited from a generous donation from Charles II to buy scarlet robes for the senate scene, and from scandalous advance publicity when a court lady discovered that the actress playing Sempronia planned to impersonate her. The company also seems to have introduced fight scenes in an effort to liven up the text. Though intelligent critics like Samuel Pepys had recognized the play's untheatrical nature from the start, it continued to be revived, probably because of the King's support. After the Revolution of 1688 and the triumph of a less absolutist ideology, it quickly disappeared; it has since been given only by amateur groups.

Early revivals of *Bartholomew Fair* (which was onstage as early as 1661) were equally topical, featuring caricatures of well-known Puritan preachers. The puppet show was omitted at first and not always given later – possibly because of its satiric targets and the indecency of the language but perhaps also because of the technical difficulty of making a squeaky-voiced puppeteer and small puppets audible and visible in a larger theatre. The play was often revived in late August and performed at the Fair itself, probably in a shortened version. Unfortunately, the association between Fair and *Fair* was fatal to the play, once the London authorities set about cleaning up the notoriously rowdy event. After 1731, when they finally prohibited theatrical performances at the Fair, it dropped out of the repertory.[4]

Robert Gale Noyes's *Ben Jonson on the English Stage,* which gives tables of Jonson performances, shows that, although the early eighteenth-century theatre repertory included only three of his plays – *Volpone, Epicene* and *The Alchemist* – they were frequently seen; in January 1734, for example, all three were given in a single month at the Haymarket Theatre.[5] They were apparently unadapted, though probably cut and expurgated, as part of a backlash against the amoral culture of Restoration England and the excessively explicit depictions of vice in satiric drama. But Jonson sometimes achieved accidental topicality, as when *The Alchemist* was revived in 1721 just after the South Sea Bubble, with a prologue suggesting that Face and Subtle were amateurs compared to such figures as the financier John Law, who was present in the audience. However, the eighteenth-century preference for lovable comic characters made the plays increasingly hard to perform. Curiously, most of the comments on eighteenth-century *Volpone*s focus on the character of Corbaccio, who seems to have attracted enough sympathy to make critics feel that his natural infirmities should not have been ridiculed.

David Garrick's success in reviving Jonson during his management of the Theatre Royal, Drury Lane (1746–76) was partly due to his ability to make the characters more lovable. In fact, Garrick, famous as an admirer of Shakespeare, adapted Jonson to make him as much like Shakespeare as possible. When he restored *Every Man In His Humour* to the theatre in 1751, the Prologue reminded its audience that Shakespeare himself had acted in it. Garrick carefully removed not only topical and erudite references but also whatever he considered too 'low' for his audience, such as most of the scenes involving Cob and Tib. Moreover, he 'improved' his own role as the jealous husband Kitely. Kitely's name in the first version of the play, Thorello, has sometimes been considered the source for Othello's. Garrick was in turn influenced by *Othello* when he added a scene between a frantic Kitely and his loyal servant Cash, who fears that someone has poisoned his master's 'generous Mind' with jealousy. The great actor was thus able to show the rapidly changing moods that were his specialty – and perhaps also to compensate for the fact that Othello was the only tragic role in which he had never succeeded.

Garrick's version of *The Alchemist* also created extra opportunities for his own character, Abel Drugger. Even though Drugger is as greedy as the other dupes in the play, the modest nature of his ambitions makes him the only one who can be played with real sympathy. Garrick's one major change was to have Drugger rather than Kastril lead the attack on Surly, whom he threatened with his fists. The audience loved this unexpected display of belligerence from the meek little tradesman, and other plays built round Abel Drugger, particularly Francis Gentleman's *The Tobacconist*, were still being performed as late as 1816. As Noyes says, 'The history of *The Alchemist* was virtually the history of the rôle of Abel Drugger.'[6] As late as 1947, in John Burrell's production at the Old Vic, Alec Guinness gave a funny and touching performance that apparently stole every scene he was in.[7] Though the prologue to *Every Man In His Humour* made a claim for Jonson's universality – 'Nature was Nature then, and still survives' (sig. A2) – both of Garrick's revivals dressed the actors in Elizabethan costume. His choice was unusual, in a period when contemporary dress was the norm. Though it may have suggested that the plays' interest was largely historical, it can also be seen as the beginning of a concern for 'authentic' performance. Authenticity was again invoked 25 years later when the young Sarah Siddons played Epicene in George Colman's adaptation. She was praised for her performance in this 'spirited role' but, according to the *Public Advertiser* for 18 January 1776, 'many admirers of Ben Jonson have expressed a Desire to see the Silent Woman performed as the Author originally intended it' – and thus the great actress was replaced by a young man only a few days after the first night.

Garrick's influence on Jonson's theatrical history was long-lasting. Though he produced an adaptation of *Eastward Ho!* in 1751, it was unsuccessful, and he never revived *Volpone,* though he had thought of doing so. As a result, both plays disappeared from the repertory for the whole of the nineteenth century. Moreover, his enormous personal popularity meant that the roles in which he appeared inevitably became the starring ones and the plays were revived only when another star – usually the leading tragedian of the company – wanted to play them. Thus, George Frederick Cooke played Kitely in 1801; William Macready and Edmund Kean played him in 1816; all three had been famous as both Othello and Iago. Kean also starred in 1815 in a shortened version of *The Alchemist* focusing mainly on Abel Drugger, but most tragedians took little interest in comic roles unless they had 'heroic' or sympathetic qualities. There was one brilliant exception to the nineteenth century's almost total neglect of Jonson: to raise money for various charitable causes, between 1845 and 1848 a company of gifted amateurs gave a short series of performances of *Every Man In His Humour* (in the Garrick adaptation). The cast included Charles Dickens as a hilarious Bobadil.

At the end of the century, as Britain and America finally caught up with the German interest in Elizabethan staging, Jonson's embeddedness in the theatre of his time, once a limitation, made him an obvious candidate for revival (though he still needed extensive expurgating). There were new scholarly contexts for his work: the American Academy of Dramatic Art presented an adaptation of *Epicene* as *The Silent Woman* in 1895, and William Poel began his series of Jonson revivals for the Elizabethan Stage Society in 1898 with – surprisingly – *The Sad Shepherd,* Jonson's unfinished pastoral, as completed by Francis Godolphin Waldron in 1783. This continuation, heavily influenced by John Hilton's *Comus,* ends with the repentance of Maudlin and her children. Poel followed it with *The Alchemist* in 1899. Frank Benson, who inaugurated England's Stratford-upon-Avon Festival with his popular productions of Shakespeare, also performed *Every Man In His Humour* at Stratford in 1903, presumably because of the Shakespeare connection. Poel was equally inclined to perform Jonson with Shakespeare in mind. In 1916, the year commemorating the 300th anniversary of Shakespeare's death, he celebrated Shakespeare's birthday by reviving *Poetaster* in a hall on the site of the old Blackfriars Theatre, with young actors who might somewhat resemble the boys' company that originally played it. Because Poel took the praise of Virgil in the final act to refer to Shakespeare, the actor who played Virgil was made up to look as much like Shakespeare as possible. When he revived *Sejanus* in 1928 Arruntius was made up as Ben Jonson and Cremutius Cordus, the historian who praised Brutus and Cassius, as Shakespeare. The appearance in

1925 of the first volumes of the Herford and Simpsons' *Ben Jonson* inspired a number of academic productions and aroused Sir Edward Elgar's interest in writing a Jonson-based opera: his projected but never finished *The Spanish Lady* (based on *The Devil is an Ass*) would have created a happy ending too by making Frances the ward rather than wife of Fitzdottrel and thus able to marry Wittipol.

Volpone was the first play to regain something like its original esteem and popularity, though, ironically, this happened through a German adaptation. Perhaps because it is the least topical of Jonson's plays, it has always been the most successful in translation. Most translators have, however, felt obliged to deal with its perceived problems: the apparently extraneous characters like the Would-Bes and Volpone's three servants, the lack of love interest and the almost shockingly dark ending. As early as 1793, Ludwig Tieck had written a German adaptation that solved the last two problems by making Celia Corvino's ward rather than his wife, so that the play could end happily with her marriage to Bonario. By contrast, as its title indicates, there is no romance in Stefan Zweig's *Volpone: A Loveless Comedy* (1926). In fact, Celia and Bonario (renamed Colomba and Leone to incorporate them into the bestiary as a dove and lion) are such fools that no one could care about them. Zweig did however lighten the ending somewhat. Instead of being sent to the galleys, Mosca in this version was left triumphant, tossing Volpone's gold into the air and planning to liberate it from its confines. The play was a huge success at its premiere in the Vienna Burgtheater and, in Ruth Langer's translation (1928), went on to be a success in the English and American professional theatre as well. (Ironically, a production of the original play in the same year by the Theater Guild, with Alfred Lunt as Mosca, was reported to the New York District Attorney's office as morally objectionable.) Jules Romains' French version (1928), which adapts Zweig rather than Jonson, forms the basis of Maurice Tourneur's classic film (1941), with Harry Baur (Volpone) and Louis Jouvet (Mosca). This script includes an opening sequence to explain the motives behind Volpone's deception: his friends refuse to help him when his ships are reported lost at sea; he is thrown into prison, where he meets Mosca. When he learns that his ships are safe after all, he resolves to take revenge on his false friends.

The original play has remained a vehicle for star actors such as Donald Wolfit, Ralph Richardson, Paul Scofield and Michael Gambon, and the universality of its satire on human greed has led to numerous relocations of the story. Barney Simon used it as the basis for *Phiri* (1971), an 'African jazz musical' performed in South African townships and in Johannesburg.

Foxy (1962), a Broadway musical by Johnny Mercer, is set in the Alaskan Gold Rush. Larry Gelbart's stage play *Sly Fox* (1977, revived in 2004) features another Gold Rush era, that of San Francisco. Influenced by Zweig, and also by the unabashedly greedy characters created by Groucho Marx, it contrasts Foxwell J. Sly (Volpone), who wants to hang onto his money, with Simon Able (Mosca), who is eager to spend it. The film of *The Honeypot* (1967) starred Rex Harrison as a twentieth-century millionaire who is inspired by *Volpone* to test the loyalty of his three mistresses. The Internet Movie Database (IMDB.com) records a surprising number of adaptations since 1960, on US, German, Hungarian, Austrian and French television.

In the eighteenth century, most critics had no doubt that Jonson's best plays were *Volpone*, *The Alchemist* and *Epicene*. By the end of the twentieth century, *Bartholomew Fair* was regarded as more important than *Epicene*. Since excess is part of its essence – it is long and has an enormous cast – it was rediscovered only when the establishment of repertory theatres, university drama departments and theatre festivals created the right performance conditions. The play made it possible to see Jonson not as the defender of Stuart absolutism but as a working-class dramatist, the creator of carnivalesque English comedy and a precursor of Bertolt Brecht's epic theatre. In 1978, both Marxist director Michael Bogdanov and playwright Peter Barnes directed *Bartholomew Fair,* the first as an example of 'capitalist corruption' and the second with emphasis on the fairground as a world that reconciled the classes.[8] The play has been reset in both the Victorian and modern periods and used for topical satire on authority – most strikingly in a French Canadian version of 1994, where the puppets break free of their play and, invoking the spirit of the Fair, cry '*Vos marionnettes en liberté! Le théâtre en liberté!*'[9]

Epicene, conversely, has suffered from problems with the casting of the title character. Keeping the secret from the audience often seems more trouble than it is worth and can be unfair to the actor, whose name is often changed in the programme to conceal his gender. All-male and all-female productions have been the most successful ways of exploiting contemporary interest in 'gender construction' and the increasing use of cross-gender casting has somewhat rescued Jonson from his reputation as a playwright unfriendly both to women and to women actors. Volpone in 1996, at the Shakespeare theatre in Washington, DC, featured comic actress Pat Carroll in the title role; there have also been female Moscas.[10]

Jonson has adapted easily to musical theatre, with its tradition of cross-gendered casting. *Epicene*'s emphasis on different kinds of noise and silence is an obvious gift to a composer. Mark Lothar adapted it as a two-act opera, *Lord Spleen* (1930). Richard Strauss (who had earlier thought of an operatic *Volpone*) composed the music for a libretto by Stefan Zweig, which premiered in 1935 as *Die Schweigsame Frau*. In this genial version, set in the eighteenth century, Morose is a basically kind man whose hatred of noise results from an explosion during his years as a sea captain. He rejects his nephew for becoming the lead tenor in an opera company; the entire company, led by the nephew's wife, undertake a series of impersonations intended to convert him. George Antheil's operatic *Volpone* (1953) is based on the Zweig and Romains version. A well-reviewed 'chamber opera', *Volpone* (libretto Mark Campbell, composer John Musto), which premiered in Vienna, Virginia, in 2004, created romance between Bonario and Celia and added new female roles: Bonario's mother, rather than his father, disinherits him, and Mosca's long-lost mother, in an un-Jonsonian happy ending, escapes from Venice with him and Volpone.

The history of Jonson's plays in the theatre is exemplified by the illustrations to this chapter, from productions of *The Alchemist* 200 years apart. In Zoffany's portrait of Garrick as Abel Drugger (see Figure 10.1), it is hard to tell whether we are seeing Face and Subtle laughing at Drugger's simplicity or two actors stepping out of character to register their delight at Garrick's performance in a role so different from his actual sophisticated self. By contrast, the photograph of the production given in 1977 at The Other Place, Stratford, and again at the Aldwych Theatre, London (see Figure 10.2), emphasizes the ensemble playing required when the dupes of Subtle and Face, each for his own reason, unite to prevent Surly from rescuing them from their own folly. Both productions used a sort of Jacobean costume, but this would have been unusual in Garrick's time, when most actors wore contemporary dress, whereas it is now the norm for Jonson's plays and modern dress until recently was controversial – as when Joan Littlewood updated the plays in the 1940s,[11] and Tyrone Guthrie (Old Vic, 1962) gave Surly, in his Spanish disguise, the white suit and sombrero of a rich Latin American.[12] In 1977, it was the occasional textual modernizations by Peter Barnes (like changing 'familiar' to 'fairy spirit') that inspired one critic's protests.[13] By the time of Sam Mendes' 1991 revival, with Subtle advertising his wonderful cures via before and after versions of Holbein's portrait of Henry VIII, no one minded at all, and Nicholas Hytner's 2006

Figure 10.1 David Garrick with William Burton and John Palmer in *The Alchemist* by Ben Jonson, 1770, by Johann Zoffany (1733–1810).

National Theatre (London) production, which, like Guthrie's, dressed Subtle as an Indian guru, was highly praised for its topicality.

The success of the major plays has led to fresh consideration of the others. *Every Man In His Humour,* the first of a brilliant series at the Swan Theatre, Stratford (1986), drew attention to the wonderful acting roles in Jonson. Even *The New Inn,* supposedly undramatic, was a success in John Caird's sympathetic 1987 revival. *The Devil is an Ass* now hovers on the edge of the canon, while 'dotages' like *The Staple of News* and *The Magnetic Lady* have been well received in university productions, usually with non-historical costumes and cross-gender, multi-racial casting.[14] Small-scale Jonson, given before a sympathetic academic audience, is probably best able to bring out his verbal brilliance. Yet Gregory

Figure 10.2 1977 Royal Shakespeare Company production of *The Alchemist* (dir. Trevor Nunn), featuring Ian McKellen (far left) as Face.

Doran's sumptuous and terrifying *Sejanus* (2005) – part of a 'Jacobean season' at the Swan – suggested that even Jonson's tragedies might benefit from the resources of a major professional theatre. Like the Restoration adapters of *Catiline*, Doran added explicit glimpses of corruption that is only described in the text, such as Sejanus's sodomizing of the slave he has hired to poison Drusus. He also cut heavily – probably a necessity with any Jonson revival. Above all, he got the actors to tread the fine line between serious and comic that has puzzled many readers of Jonson's tragedies. This balance is equally important for the comedies, even if some critics will always complain that the director doesn't make them dark enough.

NOTES

1. C. H. Herford, Percy Simpson and Evelyn Simpson (eds.), *Ben Jonson*, 11 vols. (Oxford: Clarendon Press, 1950), vol. IX: p. 209. Much of the information in this chapter comes either from this source or from Noyes's book, cited in n. 5.
2. From broadside 'Prologue to the Revived Alchemist', Worcester College, Oxford, published by C. H. Wilkinson in *Oxford Bibliographic Society Papers* (vol. 1, pp. 281–2) and reprinted in Herford et al., *Ben Jonson*, vol. IX, pp. 227–8. Wilkinson's dating of 1660 seems too early, given that women began to act only later that year.

3. From CCXI. *Sociable Letters*, 1674, letter clxxiii, pp. 362–3. Quoted in Herford et al., *Ben Jonson*, vol. XI, p. 510.
4. Along with the stage histories already mentioned, Frances Teague, *The Curious History of Bartholomew Fair* (Lewisburg, Pa.: Bucknell University Press; London and Toronto: Associated University Presses, 1985) analyses performances up to the 1980s.
5. Robert Gale Noyes, *Ben Jonson on the English Stage, 1660–1776* (Cambridge, Mass.: Harvard University Press, 1935), p. 325.
6. Noyes, *Ben Jonson on the English Stage*, p. 103.
7. See the review by Kenneth Tynan in *He That Plays the King* (1950), pp. 92–4, reprinted in R. V. Holdsworth (ed.), *Jonson, 'Every Man In His Humour' and 'The Alchemist': A Casebook* (Basingstoke: Macmillan, 1978), pp. 224–6.
8. Teague, *Curious History*, pp. 132–7.
9. *La Foire de la Saint-Barthélemy*, translated and adapted by Antonine Maillet (Ottowa: Leméac, 1994). Théâtre du Rideau Vert, Montreal, 26 April 1994, dir. Guillermo de Andrea.
10. For Pat Carroll's *Volpone*, see www.shakespearedc.org. For a New Zealand *Volpone* with a female Mosca, see www.thebacchanals.net/plays/trilogy.
11. See the discussion of Littlewood's important contribution to Jonson revivals in Elizabeth Schafer, 'Daughters of Ben', in Richard Cave, Elizabeth Schafer and Brian Woolland (eds.), *Ben Jonson and Theatre: Performance, Practice, and Theory* (London: Routledge, 1999), pp. 155–80.
12. See Bamber Gascoigne's review, reprinted in R. V. Holdsworth (ed.), *Jonson, 'Every Man in His Humour' and 'The Alchemist': A Casebook* (Basingstoke: Macmillan, 1978), pp. 227–8.
13. Bernard Levin, 'How to Devalue the Philosopher's Stone', *Sunday Times*, 18 December 1977.
14. For reviews of many of these productions, see the *Ben Jonson Journal*.

PART II
Cultural and historical contexts

CHAPTER 11

London and urban space

Adam Zucker

> The city, as one finds it in history, is the point of maximum concentration for the power and culture of a community. It is the place where the diffused rays of many separate beams of life fall into focus, with gains in both social effectiveness and significance. The city is the form and symbol of an integrated social relationship: it is the seat of the temple, the market, the hall of justice, the academy of learning. Here in the city the goods of civilization are multiplied and manifolded; here is where human experience is transformed into viable signs, symbols, patterns of conduct, systems of order. Here is where the issues of civilization are focused: here, too, ritual passes on occasion into the active drama of a fully differentiated and self-conscious society.
>
> Louis Mumford[1]

Perhaps no other English author of the early seventeenth century was more attuned than Ben Jonson to the ways in which London and urban space more generally could function as 'the form and symbol of an integrated social relationship'. Perhaps no other saw with such clarity the complex scenarios through which a city becomes a site of compression and of multiplication, a matrix where, as an idealistic Mumford points out, moral, commercial, legal and educational relations can converge into a unifying field of cohesive community. And perhaps no other took such bitter pleasure in pointing out the contemporary failures and fault-lines in this cohesive, communal space: the conflicting social possibilities, the degrading competitions over status or wealth and the deep injustices that accompanied the diversification and diffusion of commerce and civility in London and Westminster.[2] Jonson was not the first to use drama, poetry and other art forms to investigate the spatial facts of urban dynamism and diversity, nor would he be the last. But his engagement with the city that was his lifelong home marks off a decidedly influential iteration of a long-standing pattern in literary and artistic expression in early modern England and, indeed, all over the world.

Jonson's engagement with urban space took place on two basic levels: first, he repeatedly represented or made reference to different kinds of city sites in his poetry and drama; second, he laid out sets of directions for the active manipulation of urban space, in so far as he wrote plays, masques and pageants meant to be performed in and around London. Urban space, in other words, was both the subject and the object of much of his work – both his medium and, frequently, his imagined setting.[3] Our current understanding of the tenor of this doubled take on the city in Jonson's writing is grounded in the rich work being done by historians of London such as Vanessa Harding, Ian Archer, John Schofield and Julia Merritt.[4] Much of the discussion that follows has been shaped by their discoveries.

By all accounts, Jonson's London was a city in flux. By the time Jonson was born in 1572, London had begun its slow, steady transformation from a large, but by no means unusual walled medieval town into a sprawling centre for a nation's interpenetrating political and economic networks. Over the course of the sixteenth and early seventeenth centuries, government by the royal court and its associated administrative bodies became increasingly centralized in Westminster and Greenwich. The great London-based merchant-trading companies began to draw capital and commerce towards themselves and their city, consolidating its importance as a point of access for trade in the commonwealth and beyond. By James I's reign, England's gentry had begun to spend months on end in London's growing, fashionable suburbs, attracted by the seasonal rhythms of the law courts, by the goods and services increasingly available in shops and marketplaces for luxury commodities like the New Exchange and by the city's notorious entertainments, from its theatres and bear-baiting arenas to its taverns and brothels. Poorer labourers and artisans were drawn as well to the economic possibilities offered by London's role as a centre for informal commerce and production, such as the buying and selling of victuals, the trade in second-hand clothing and other petty wares and the rudimentary manufacturing and service industries like pin-making, starching and stocking-knitting, that catered to the wealthier consumers of London.

Historical demography can give us a sense for the effect of these developments in Jonson's day: according to some estimates, the population of London and its suburbs nearly doubled between 1548 and 1600 from 120,000 residents to 200,000, then doubled again to over 400,000 by 1650.[5] We should not underestimate how surprising all this seemed to long-time city-dwellers, like Jonson himself. One of his contemporaries, the urban chronicler Edmund Howes, was nothing less than flabbergasted by the changes that occurred in London between 1565 and 1615:

> the unmeasurable and uncomparable encrease of all which commodities coming into this city, & the increase of howses, and Inhabitants, within the compasse and tearme of fifty yeeres, is such and so great, as were there not now two third parts, of the people yet living, having beene eye witnes of the premises, and the bookes of the custome howse, which remain extant, the truth, and difference of all things afore mentioned were not to be Iustified, and beeleeved.[6]

There were many writers – poets, dramatists, satirists, ballad-makers and others – who shared Howes's bewilderment and fascination with the expansion of the city and who attempted to make logical and aesthetic sense of its transformation.[7] Some, like the epigrammist Thomas Freeman, joked about it: in 'London's Progress', he wonders whether suburbs that at the time seemed impossibly distant from one another might some day be connected ('Hoggesdon will to Hygate ere't be long', he predicts).[8] Some, like John Stow, looked back wistfully: his famous guide to the city, *A Survey of London* (1598), is shaped by his nostalgia for the simpler, more neighbourly London he knew in his youth. And some turned to legal forms of writing in an effort to achieve practical control over urban space. The large numbers of new homes being built in and around London and the practice of subdividing older buildings to create more – and often more decrepit – housing drew the attention of Elizabeth, James and Charles: each issued multiple proclamations over the course of his or her reign attempting to restrict the kinds of building being done in and around the city. None of these seems to have had any effect. City surveyors – including Jonson's collaborator and eventual rival Inigo Jones – were sent out to police new construction and to issue fines against those who attempted to build without permission, but London simply continued its explosive growth.

Over the course of Jonson's life, then, the quality of urban space in London was partially understood in terms of its rapid expansion, its ungovernable 'increase', and its mounting density. This, at least, would have been the long view. On a day-to-day basis, early modern Londoners would have been equally likely to experience the space of their city as a fairly stable built environment, as a series of interconnected neighbourhoods and parishes, streets and lanes, landmarks and reference points, each of which carried different associations and purposes for those who oriented their lives in relation to them. Indeed, even as John Stow looks back at a vanished London in *A Survey* – at the garden plots in Portsoken Ward that have taken the place of old drainage ditches he remembers, or at the ongoing attempts to repair the repeatedly defaced West Cheap cross in the centre of the City – each of his local histories sets out stabilizing urban knowledge that exists alongside of, and functions in collaboration with, his narratives of transition and spatial transformation. Jonson's work as a playwright and a poet bears signs of a similar combination. With precision and with a native's perspective, he calls up scenarios of local settlement and immediate knowledge that interact with the broader conception in the period that London's growth and diversification over time put stress on and even threatened to undo the social fabric of the city.

Jonson has been called the first West End dramatist, and with good reason.[9] *The Alchemist, Epicene, Bartholomew Fair, The Devil is an Ass, The Staple of News,* and *A Tale of a Tub* are all set within several miles of one another in the northern and western edges of the City of London and the area between the City walls and Westminster. Though a few of his other plays contain scenes set in the central and eastern districts of the City proper – the folio version of *Every Man In His Humour* and the collaborative *Eastward Ho!,* for example – Jonson, like the Caroline and Restoration playwrights who would look to him as a model, was fascinated with the urbane, self-regarding society finding its place in London's fashionable suburban districts. *Epicene* (1609), more than any other play by Jonson, embodies this pattern. Nearly every scene takes place in private households on or near the Strand, which was then the main thoroughfare connecting the commercial centre of London with the political complex at Westminster. By the middle of the sixteenth century, the Strand was lined with large, and sometimes enormous, homes for England's wealthiest families; by the time *Epicene* was written, some of those homes had been subdivided and rented out to the rural gentry who had begun to converge on London. By the 1630s, land near the Strand had been built up with some of London's first purposefully planned public squares and expensive housing developments, such as Lincoln's Inn Fields and the Covent Garden piazza. But as Julia Merritt has recently pointed out, it would be a mistake to imagine that the West End was exclusively an elite space in the earlier decades of the seventeenth century. It was home to some of early modern London's most noisome industries (leather-tanning, brewing and meat-butchering among them), and poor labourers lived all around the area of the Strand in dilapidated tenements. This basic fact of West End space is all but invisible in *Epicene.* The cast of characters is limited to the upper echelon of London society, and Jonson's depiction of the neighbourhood is coloured accordingly. Truewit, Clerimont and Dauphine, the play's three heroes, lounge about in Clerimont's home gossiping and scheming; Sir Amorous La Foole is described leaning out of the window of his apartment on the Strand to invite passers-by to parties he's throwing; and the members of the community of flirtatious, witty (and, in Jonson's eyes, contemptible) women known as the Collegiates make use of their own homes 'in Town' for clandestine assignations with their lovers. Urban space in *Epicene* is staged in terms of these leisurely applications of private homes and the motions between them.

Jonson rarely permits this kind of basic spatial patterning to remain separate in his comedies from his interest in critiquing the social pretensions and moral failings of urban life. Though everyone in *Epicene* uses the West End in structurally similar ways, and though a firm sense of social exclusivity is the result of this similarity, it becomes clear over the course of the play that while characters like Truewit have mastered urban space, others have been mastered by it. Jonson reserves his sharpest satire for two characters, Mistress Otter and Morose, who are dominated by the practical diversity of the city. Mistress Otter, a china-seller whose hopes for social advancement hinge on distancing herself from the *de classé* tastes of her husband, describes a dream (or perhaps a series of actual events – the wording is ambiguous) in which her clothes are repeatedly attacked by the city itself: her black satin gown is burned at a friend's house; her starched collar covered in candle wax at a court masque; her red doublet 'dashed' by a 'brewer's horse' as she rides by in a coach (3.2.60–1). The mundane materials of urban space – emblems for the crass economic relations that taint Mistress Otter in the eyes of wealthier characters – degrade everything that touches them.

Morose, on the other hand, whose desire to disinherit his nephew Dauphine makes him the villain of the play, is castigated for his attempts to carve out a perfectly silent, isolated space for himself, a space somehow both inside of but detached from the aural landscape of the city as a whole. Ringing church bells, the cries of hawkers passing by on the street and the hubbub of 'citations, appellations, allegations, certificates, attachments, intergatories, references, convictions, and afflictions' that make up the scene at the law courts all horrify him (4.7.13–14). To protect himself, Morose creates a sonically hermetic room with 'double walls and treble ceilings' (1.1.146–7) and insists that his servants communicate through gestures, rather than through speech. Needless to say, his plan fails. If one of the fundamental jokes of *Epicene* is that there is no such thing as its eponymous silent woman, this joke is mirrored by the sense in the play that there can be no such thing as a silent space in the city. Morose's sanctum is invaded first by the loquacious Truewit, then by a rowdy wedding party including his suddenly talkative wife, and by the end of the play he is a defeated man, willingly participating in noisy debates over his own sexual and mental competence as he attempts to annul his marriage. Morose's social failures are staged as spatial failures: isolation and separation are not a viable option in Jonson's vision of the West End.[10]

Spatial particularity and pressures on the same are crucial features of two of Jonson's other most famous comedies: *The Alchemist,* which takes place entirely in and around Lovewit's house in the Blackfriars precinct (Jonson himself lived in the same neighbourhood around the time the play was written); and *Bartholomew Fair,* which, with the exception of the first act, is set in the Smithfield grounds of a yearly cloth market. Jonson's interest in classical theories of art and drama are on display in both of these plays – their spatial compression helps them adhere to the Aristotelian unity of place in a way that few early modern English comedies ever did. They also provide the best evidence of Jonson's ability to stage the ways in which urban space is shaped both by settled knowledge and by the competitive, shifting pressures of city life generated by economic need and common human desires. The simple spatial premise of *The Alchemist* is a case in point. Face, the servant of a wealthy gentleman who has left him behind to look after his home in London during a plague outbreak, joins forces with two grifters, Subtle and Dol; the three use Lovewit's house as the setting for a number of interrelated scams. The unity of setting stands in sharp contrast to the multiple uses to which the house is put. False horoscopes are drawn up. Ludicrous magical formulae for keeping flies away from tobacco are spelled out. An impossible Queen of Fairies materializes for a literal shakedown. Sexual assignations are promised and postponed. And, of course, a complicated conglomeration of beakers, bellows and pipes is somewhere always on the verge of creating the Philosopher's Stone for a client. The effect is one of intense urban density. A single house – and even a single room – draws together a tobacconist, a law-clerk who thinks of himself as a rakish gambler, a wealthy gourmand, two Puritans and a naive rural arriviste bearing his sister on his arm. Each of them finds themselves caught in the vortex of their own desires for profit, for sex, for the power to transform iron into gold; each of them, in turn, hands over something of value for the privilege of being duped.

It is no accident that this house and its crowded room are located by Jonson in the Blackfriars neighbourhood, the liberty within the western wall of London that had once housed an order of monks but that had become by James's reign a rather well-to-do neighbourhood famous for its feather-sellers, its concentration of skilled portrait painters and, of course, its indoor theatre, soon to be, if not already, occupied by the King's Men around the time *The Alchemist* was first performed. Like several other former and current ecclesiastical properties in and around the city, the Blackfriars area was known as a 'liberty' because it did not fall under the legal jurisdiction of London's aldermanic establishment. More and less illicit forms of commerce – paying for plays, for example, but also prostitution and unregulated victualling or ale-selling – often found homes in London's liberties. By placing Lovewit's house in the midst of one, Jonson transforms a single dense space – a crowded room full of diverse people paying for the privilege of watching imaginary, pleasurable acts – into an analogue for the theatre and for the city more generally. As the clamouring customers in *The Alchemist* struggle for their all-too-similar satisfactions, urban space and theatrical space reflect back upon one another, shimmering with comic energy: Jonson underscores the ways in which multiplicity and particularity collaborate to produce the spectacular social and economic exchanges of London life.

Jonson's dramatic exploration of the dynamism of urban space reached a peak of sorts in 1614, when *Bartholomew Fair* was first performed at the Hope Theatre on the south bank of the Thames and then at Whitehall, before the court. Forgoing his sometimes oblique satire of the more mundane elements of consumption and exchange, Jonson takes us on a headlong tour of one of early modern London's most famous market fairs. Since at least 1123, Bartholomew Fair had been held each August near the church of St Bartholomew in Smithfield.[11] Though it was originally intended to serve as an annual opportunity for cloth merchants to display and sell their wares, by Jonson's time the fair had become a celebration of lighter forms of commerce. Puppets, gingerbread babies, beer, pie and, of course, freshly roasted pigs drew entertainment-seekers from around the city who had little interest in the going rate for a yard of buckram. Jonson takes full advantage of the wide appeal of the space of the fair to stage once more the ways in which diverse city types can be drawn together by the promise of profit and pleasurable consumption. Rather than anchoring the narrative around a small group of controlling figures and a single room, Jonson sets his characters free to roam from booth to booth. As a result, a kind of socio-spatial expansiveness pervades *Bartholomew Fair,* despite its locational specificity. Accidental encounters in the loud crowd push the plot forward, while the play's characters interact like ball-bearings in a pinball machine: always moving in seemingly random ways but eventually settling into unsurprising places. As Bartholomew Fair becomes *Bartholomew Fair,* Smithfield is staged as the matrix for a typically Jonsonian process of encounter and exchange, profit and punishment: the play's oaf, Bartholomew Cokes, is gulled of his wife-to-be and her dowry; the foolish Justice Overdo ends up locked in his own stocks; the witty gallants Quarlous and Winwife achieve the social and economic rewards associated with marriage. Urban space once more becomes comic space, a space of communal consolidation shot through with the ever-present possibility for degradation and loss.

There are any number of other plays and poems by Jonson that add nuance to this introduction to his encounters with urban space. The satirical poem 'On the Famous Voyage' describes a disgustingly odiferous trip by wherry along the sewage-filled Fleet ditch to Holborn. *The Staple of News* imagines the city as an interconnected set of nodal points and channels for the transmission of news and gossip. Even plays that are not set in London itself offer rich perspectives on the meanings and functions of urban space for Jonson: *Sejanus* contains a tableau of populist violence in the streets of Rome in which the play's eponymous consul is torn to pieces by the city's denizens; and *Volpone* imagines a world of Venetian balconies and squares where Volpone attempts to seduce Celia with a mountebank act performed below her window. But it seems fitting to end this discussion with Jonson's most elaborate intervention in and reproduction of urban space itself: the triumphal arch he designed for the coronation procession of King James through London in 1604. The arch was topped with a model of the City's skyline and supported by columns replete with a series of allegorical figures meant to represent the guiding spirits of London, 'Bouleutes ... the councell of the citie'; Polemius, 'The warlike force of the citie'; and 'Tamesis, the river' among them.[12] Jonson's description of the arch reveals his affection for the city – realism and glorification, he suggests, are in some ways identical registers. In his own words, the arch 'not onely labored the expression of state and magnificence (as proper to a triumphall Arch) but the very site, fabricke, strength, policie, dignitie, and affections of the Citie were all laid downe to life' (sig. 4B4v) Jonson goes on to offer a critique of his project in terms that, with their emphasis on the aesthetics of urban communality, echo those of Mumford:

> The nature and propertie of these Deuices being, to present alwaies some one entire bodie, or figure, consisting of distinct members, and each of those expressing it selfe, in the[ir] owne actiue spheare, yet all, with that generall harmonie so connexed, and disposed, as no one little part can be missing to the illustration of the whole. (sig. 4B4v)

We see here Jonson's fantasy of an entirely unified representation of London, one that puts 'distinct members' in a series of spaces – each in their 'owne active spheare' – so as to create a frame of formal harmony that could not exist without every one of those members. The whole of the city balances above a network of individual figures; the figures themselves lack purpose without the spatial arrangement produced by the city-topped arch. We could do worse than to understand Jonson's engagements with urban space in terms of his own sense of the mutual relation between part and whole: each play, each poem, each snide or satirical epigram an individual figure; each one standing alone and acting in semantic collaboration with the others; each creating meaning for early modern London and for urban space more generally; and each in turn made meaningful and beautiful by our own experiences of city life, experiences that Jonson's work continues to illuminate even to this day.

NOTES

1. Louis Mumford, *The Culture of Cities* (New York: Harcourt, Brace, 1938), p. 3.
2. For the sake of brevity, and in order to encompass the general scope of Jonson's interest in urban space, I will use the words 'city' and 'London' in ways that would likely have seemed inaccurate to Jonson and his contemporaries. The City of London in Jonson's day had discrete boundaries roughly (though not entirely) defined by the wards within and immediately bordering its medieval walls. Westminster was a separate corporate entity, and the areas to the north and west of London itself were administered not by the City's Lord Mayor and the aldermanic courts but by Middlesex county justices and other crown authorities. That said, Jonson tended to integrate these different cities and outlying areas into facets of a larger social totality, and the term 'urban space' accurately identifies this totality as such. When I wish to refer to the precise administrative unit of early modern London, I will use the capitalized 'City'. Otherwise, the terms 'city' and 'London' refer here to a broader area, including the parts of Middlesex that Jonson deals with in his work.
3. There are several excellent studies of Jonson's engagement with London and urban space. See, for example, Fran C. Chalfant, *Ben Jonson's London* (Athens, Ga.: University of Georgia Press, 1978); Jonathan Haynes, *The Social Relations of Jonson's Theater* (Cambridge: Cambridge University Press, 1992); Janette Dillon, *Theatre, Court and City, 1595–1610* (Cambridge: Cambridge University Press, 2000), pp. 109–36; James Mardock, *Our Scene is London: Ben Jonson's City and the Space of the Author* (New York and London: Routledge, 2008); and Henry Turner, *The Elizabethan Stage* (Oxford: Oxford University Press, 2006), pp. 133–52, 244–78.
4. Vanessa Harding, 'The Population of London, 1550–1700: A Review of the Published Evidence', *London Journal*, 15 (1990): 111–28 and 'The Changing Shape of Seventeenth-Century London', in J. F. Merritt (ed.), *Imagining Early Modern London* (Cambridge: Cambridge University Press, 2001), pp. 117–43; Ian Archer, *The Pursuit of Stability: Social Relations in Early Modern London*

(Cambridge: Cambridge University Press, 1991); J. F. Merritt, *The Social World of Early Modern Westminster: Abbey, Court and Community, 1525–1640* (Manchester: Manchester University Press, 2005). Other work on the history of Jonson's London includes Norman G. Brett-James, *The Growth of Stuart London* (London: George Allen & Unwin, 1935); A. L. Beier and R. Finlay (eds.), *London, 1500–1700: The Making of a Metropolis* (Harlow: Longmans, 1986); and Lena Cowen Orlin (ed.) *Material London, ca. 1600* (Philadelphia, Pa.: University of Pennsylvania Press, 2001).
5. Harding, 'The Population of London', p. 112.
6. Citation taken from Howes's additions to John Stow's *Annales, or A Generall Chronicle of England* (London, 1615), 4D2r.
7. See Lawrence Manley, *Literature and Culture in Early Modern England* (Cambridge: Cambridge University Press, 1995).
8. Thomas Freeman, *Rub, and a Great Cast* (London, 1614), B3r.
9. Emrys Jones, 'The First West End Comedy', *Proceedings of the British Academy*, 68 (1982): 215–58.
10. On the spatial register of *Epicene*, see Adam Zucker, 'The Social Logic of Ben Jonson's *Epicoene*', *Renaissance Drama*, 33 (2004): 37–62, and Mimi Yiu, 'Sounding the Space between Men: Choric and Choral Cities in Ben Jonson's *Epicoene; or, The Silent Woman*', *PMLA*, 122 (1) (2007): 72–88.
11. On the history of the market, see E. A Webb, 'Bartholomew Fair', in *The Records of St Bartholomew's priory [and] St Bartholomew the Great, West Smithfield*, vol. 1 (Oxford: Oxford University Press, 1921), pp. 298–317.
12. Part of the 'Kings Entertainment', in *Works* (London, 1616), 4B2v–3r.

CHAPTER 12

The Globe Theatre and the open-air amphitheatres

Tiffany Stern

In the 1650s, after all theatres had long been closed, it was a specific round playhouse that sprung to Aston Cockain's mind when thinking of Jonson: he maintained that the mere performance of a Jonson play would be able to 'Create the Globe anew, and people it, / By those that flock to surfeit on his wit'.[1] Robert Herrick, poet and self-styled 'son of Ben', had a bleaker outlook. Mourning the death of Jonson, he bemoaned the fact that the 'cirque' – the round theatre – had for ever been 'prophan'd' by Jonson's demise: 'No clap of hands, or shout' would 'crack the Play-house sides' any more now, he lamented.[2] What both poets share, as they evaluate Jonson's life, is a sense that public round theatres – not private square ones – are the playwright's quintessential home.

This should come as no surprise, for Jonson was intimately familiar with most of the round theatres of London. Unlike Shakespeare, a 'fixed' playwright writing for his company's single amphitheatre (first the Theatre, then the Globe), Jonson was an 'unattached' writer, ready to have his plays put on by whatever company bought them and in whatever space was to hand. During his lifetime, his dramas were performed in five different round playhouses, so his sense of theatrical possibility was repeatedly challenged and shaped by amphitheatrical space: his *Every Man In His Humour* was mounted in the Curtain by the Lord Chamberlain's Men; his lost *Isle of Dogs* (with Thomas Nashe) was performed by Pembroke's Men at the Swan; his lost series of plays *Hot Anger Soon Cold* (with Henry Porter and Henry Chettle), *Page of Plymouth* (with Dekker), *Robert II; or, The Scot's Tragedy* (with Chettle, Dekker '& other jentellman'), and *Richard Crookback* were all produced by the Admirals' Men at the Rose; *Bartholomew Fair* was put on in the Hope by the Lady Elizabeth's Servants; and *Every Man Out of His Humour*, *Volpone*, *Sejanus* and even *The Alchemist* (though it was obviously intended for the Blackfriars), were Chamberlain's/King's Men plays first staged at the Globe.

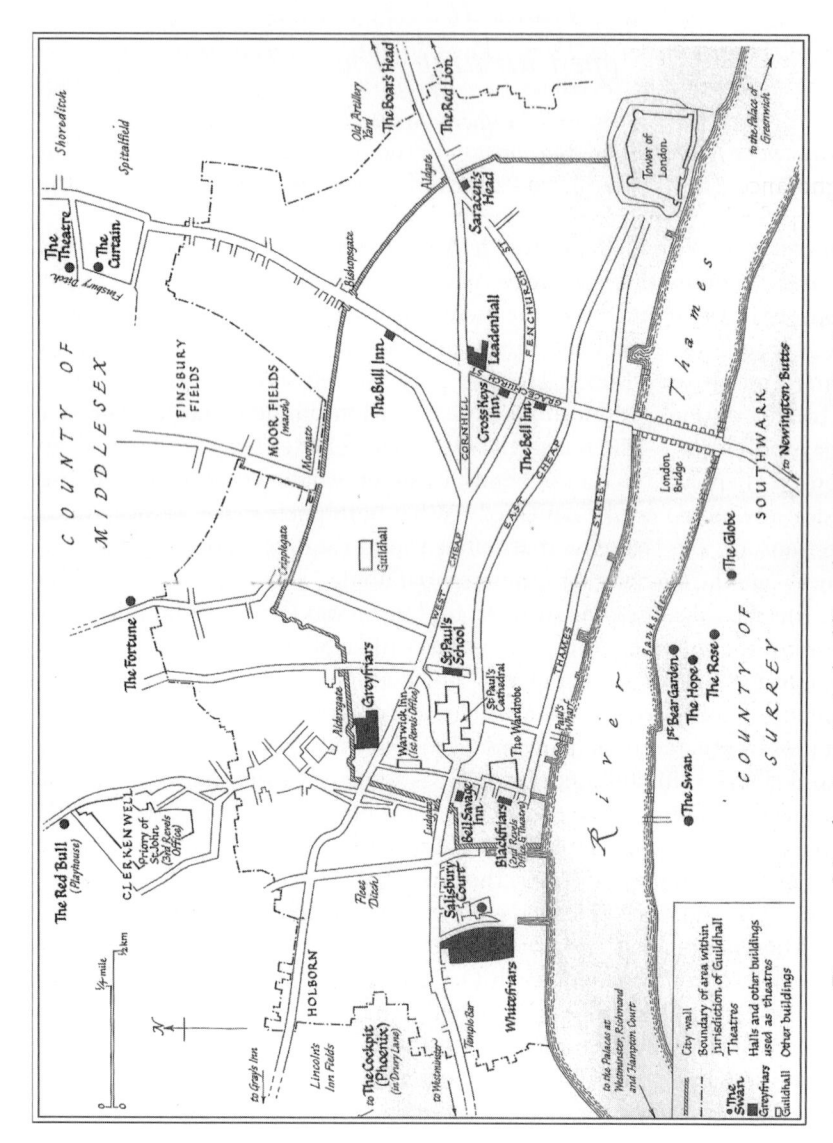

Figure 12.1 Map showing principal public and private theatres in London, c. 1560–1640.

In the circumstances, it may seem surprising that Jonson is usually written about in the context of indoor private theatres rather than outdoor public ones. But the reason is traceable to Jonson himself: despite writing so regularly and so well for amphitheatres, Jonson distrusted them. He has Asper in *Every Man Out of His Humour* suspect the play is being watched by 'A fellow, that has neither art, nor brain' (Induction, l. 177); the Scrivener in *Bartholomew Fair* addresses remarks to 'He that will swear *Jeronimo*, or *Andronicus* are the best plays ... Though it be an ignorance' (Induction, ll. 79–82); the Prologue in *Volpone* explains that in the forthcoming play 'no eggs are broken ... Wherewith your rout are so delighted' (Prologue, ll. 20–2). Jonson disdained the amphitheatrical spectators, perhaps because they had paid as little as a penny to enter the theatre and were looking for a good time for their money (private theatre audiences, conversely, had paid at least sixpence for entrance and tended to be upwardly mobile financially, socially and intellectually).

Ambivalence about the public theatre audience also affected Jonson's attitude to the stage itself. There were entire features of round playhouses that Jonson avoided, feeling that they were used merely to give the rabble what it wanted – a depth to which he refused to sink. He did not, for instance, employ the trapdoors that went down to a belowstage area known as 'Hell'. He equally avoided the opposite extreme, the 'Heavens' – an internal roof over the stage, decorated with stars and other sky symbols that protected the actors from the rain and aided with the amplification of their voices. This may, of course, be because his plays do not involve devils or gods, who are explicitly associated with such sites of spectacular entrance. But there seems to be more to it than that, for Jonson shunned Hell and Heaven with great consciousness of the possibilities they offered, boasting in one prologue that he would eschew all Heaven-housed props:

> [No] creaking throne comes down, the boys to please,
> Nor nimble squib is seen, to make afeared
> The gentlewomen, nor rolled bullet heard
> To say it thunders.
> *(Every Man In His Humour,* folio, Prologue, ll. 16–19)

He also regularly refers to the Hell and Heaven areas of the stage verbally, consciously drawing attention to the parts of the stage he will not employ. Asper in the Induction to *Every Man Out of His Humour* wonders who can see 'hell gaping under us' without yearning to 'strip the ragged follies of the time' (Induction, ll. 7, 15), the 'us' on one level referring to everyone but on another referring to the actors themselves striding backwards and forwards over the hell-trap as they perform. Later he exclaims to Mitis sarcastically, 'You might as well have told me yond is heaven, / This, earth' (Induction, ll. 125–7), reminding the audience not just that the painted heavens are indeed above but that the 'earth' – both the world and, of course, the Globe – is below. Jonson's ability to hold the attention of the audience while avoiding the gimmicks relied upon by other playwrights is being purposely highlighted by such exchanges.

Other features of the stage received use – but only sparing use – from Jonson. The posts that rose upwards from the middle, for instance, supporting the 'Heavens', are only clearly employed in *Every Man In His Humour*. The revised version of that play supplies stage-directions instructing '*Master Stephen*' to be seen '*practising* [fighting], *to the post*', and Bobadil later too '*practises at a post*' (3.5.109; 4.7.11). The explanation for having these two mirroring moments is that Stephen has been learning manners and attitudes from Bobadil: here, as Stephen is seen first, it becomes clear that the unfortunate learning process is going both ways. But it is also telling that the two men are made to attack the substance of the theatre. Jonson is always ambivalent about the stage's fixed features. And, for the most part, he chooses to occupy the space inventively rather than practically, using stage-posts purely for their metatheatrical possibilities. So Carlo, observing the bearing of the prologue-speaker to *Every Man Out of His Humour*, concludes that 'he would ha' made a good column an he had been thought on, when the [play]house was a building' (Induction, ll. 297–9).

So what does Jonson bring to a stage whose features he questions? And why was it that Herrick and Cockain associated Jonson overwhelmingly with round theatres? One major talent that Jonson had was an incredibly subtle sense of the possibilities offered by the wide and deep amphitheatrical stage. Unlike private theatres that had small stages – made smaller still by the fact that audience members could hire stools and sit on them – round theatres had huge stages that 'thrust' out into the middle of the standing audience. Jonson relished the opportunity to fill the thrust stage with people, having Cordatus ask in *Every Man Out of His Humour*:

> is it not an object of more state to behold the scene full, and relieved with variety of speakers to the end, than to see a vast empty stage, and the actors come in one by one as if they were dropped down with a feather, into the eye of the audience? (2.2.321–4)

Believing that plays should conform to the unity of time and place, so that all action should occur in 'real' time and be set in a single location, Jonson filled his stage with groups of contrary people observing one another and commenting on what they see. As a result, the real spectators watch what is happening in the play and receive a staged judgement about it, which divides their focus and reminds them that neither the action nor the commentary is necessarily reliable. In *Every Man Out of His Humour*, Cordatus and Mitis are 'critics' who, like the actual audience, evaluate the action happening in front of them; yet they do not share opinions, so that the real audience has to learn to see past their commentary and to analyse for themselves. Moreover, the framing does not end there. Even characters within the action, Macilente and Carlo Buffone, offer commentary on the other players. So the audience is given, in this play, a multiple split focus to think through. The same technique is used in *Bartholomew Fair*, where the disguised Justice Overdo is able to make a (foolish) commentary on the antics of the fair happening around – but somewhat aside from – him; similarly, in *Sejanus,* Arruntius' dissidents comment politically on the action while it takes place, overheard by 'us' but not by the other characters. The device is pervasive. When Face is being Captain in *The Alchemist* and is teaching Kastril how to quarrel, Abel Drugger simply observes what is happening – but in doing even this he provides a levelling, evaluative presence: the audience sees a tableau in which the watcher is as important as the action being staged. Divided 'readings' on the action are thus regularly supplied simply by Jonson's making use of the generous proportions of the round theatre stage: the width and depth of the stage is occupied physically and intellectually, filled with contradictory material that 'teaches' the audience how to watch thoughtfully, cryptically and, ultimately, cynically.

The size of the stage also has an effect on Jonson's choice of setting. It allows him to situate his plays in recognizably large, crowd-filled sites – sites that also complicate the audience's 'reading' of what they are watching. His round theatre plays are often set in large London places known to be thronged with varieties of people – Paul's Walk in *Every Man Out of His Humour,* Bartholomew Fair in the play of that name, a house and lane in Blackfriars in *The Alchemist*. Again, this affects the way the audience receive the play they are watching. In some sense the spectators at the round theatres must feel that they themselves are being 'staged': first, because they and their habits are being held up fictionally in front of them; but next because they and their commentaries, like the commentaries of the watching characters, come to define and describe that fiction – the audience become critically aware 'because they are in a position to comment on the accuracy of the representation' and because they see 'The familiar rendered unfamiliar' in front of their eyes.[3]

There were a few other features of the playhouses that Jonson also allowed himself to use. He was ready to occupy the upper galleries overhanging the stage, for instance, provided that they could be part of the single space that his fiction demanded. So sometimes he expanded his crowd scenes upward into this space as when, in 2.1 of *Every Man Out of His Humour* the area 'above' represents the upper floor of Puntarvolo's house: this allows twelve actors to be placed on the stage at the same time, with only the audience conscious of every person. Similarly Celia must be situated here when she first sees the 'mountebank' in *Volpone,* for she throws her handkerchief *'down'* to him (2.2.187): there may also be a suggestion, in this instance, that the elevation is spiritual as well as physical – Celia will never willingly give in to Volpone's lust. Certainly Jonson was alert to the interpretative possibilities of the space, for in *Sejanus* (or, to give it its full title, *Sejanus His Fall*), a play about toppling from political height, Sejanus is situated 'above' to hear the lines 'How like a god, speaks Caesar' (1.379): from here he can only 'fall', a point thoughtfully argued by Frances Berry.[4]

A consciousness of the meanings an area of stage could convey also shaped Jonson's use of the space situated between the two doors of entrance. This covered area is, in *Volpone,* the place where Bonario is put so that 'concealed, [he can] hear all' (3.6.1); in *Sejanus,* it is the area where Rufus and Opsius 'place [them]selves, between the roof, and ceiling' to reveal themselves later (4.95). In other words, it is a space used for secrecy, lying and hiding. The result is that everything associated with this space comes to seem potentially duplicitous. It is from here that the bed is thrust out for Volpone's phoney 'deathbed' scene, for instance. And it is, of course, from here that Volpone's treasure is first revealed ('Open the shrine, that I may see my *saint*' [1.1.2]); retrospectively, that fact can come to seem meaningful too: Volpone, who glories 'more in the cunning purchase of my wealth / Than in the glad possession' will finally be duped by and of the wealth itself (1.1.31–2).

One other aspect of round theatres sometimes taken on by Jonson was their natures: their individual names and their individual situations. Whenever he knew which theatre his play was destined for (and he did not always: *The Alchemist* appears to have been written with a Blackfriars performance in mind, though actually the Globe became its first home) he used the fact as one of his framing devices. In the Induction to *Every Man Out of His Humour,* Asper 'notices' the circle of spectators surrounding the stage of the Globe Theatre:

> I not observed this thronged round till now.
> Gracious and kind spectators, you are welcome.
> (Induction, ll. 49–50)

In *Bartholomew Fair,* too, the Hope Theatre and its audience are similarly 'visible' in the Scrivener's induction. This time 'Articles of Agreement' are drawn up 'between the spectators or hearers, at the Hope on the Bankside, in the County of Surrey on the one party; And the author of *Barthol'mew Fair* in the said place and county on the other party: the one and thirtieth day of October, 1614' (Induction, ll. 49–52). The environment the theatre occupied also works its way into the text. The Hope was playhouse and bear-baiting house by turns – 'A Play house for stage Playes on Mundayes, Wedensdayes, Fridayes, and Saturdayes. And for the Baiting of the Beares On Tuesdayes and Thursdayes. the stage being made to take up and downe when they please' – and it was, because of the meat, the blood and the slaughter that regularly filled the place, a smelly theatre in which to perform.[5] That is, at first, frankly acknowledged: 'The play shall presently begin. And though the Fair be not kept in the same region … yet think that therein the author hath observed a special decorum, the place being as dirty as Smithfield, and as stinking every whit' says the Scrivener (Induction, ll. 116–20). But later Jonson enwraps this olfactory fact into the fiction of his play too: Ursula's 'hang your vapours, they are stale, and stink like you' (3.2.84) gets its brutal humour – and, as ever, forces the audience to re-evaluate – by displacing the smell from environment to person.

In all, Jonson's technique was to use excellently those features of the round theatres of which he approved, always with the goal of 'teaching' the audience to watch more thoughtfully. Sometimes this worked spectacularly – though it could only do so with an audience prepared to watch the play more than once to take its complexity in. 'The Pit / The first time saw, the next conceiv'd thy Wit' explains Mayne; 'His Comedies were above the Vulger', enlarges Fuller, 'and took not so well at the first stroke as at the rebound, when beheld the second time.'[6] For audience members who wanted something a little less taxing and more simply enjoyable, Jonson was never the writer of choice: Mayne commented of performances of *The Alchemist* that 'th'unlearned' frankly 'lost their money, and / Schollers sav'd onely, that could understand'.[7]

Jonson's amphitheatre plays always divided the spectators. The very people whom the playwright described as too ignorant for his dramas 'proved' that to be the case by avoiding or hissing his work. Famously, *Sejanus* was damned in its first performance at the Globe by the 'multitude' who:

> screwed their scurvy jawes and look't awry,
> Like hissing snakes adjudging it to die:
> When wits of gentry did applaud the same,
> With Silver shouts of high lowd sounding fame.[8]

But even Jonson's more popular amphitheatre plays continued to alienate some of the spectators. Against the claims that 'thy Foxe' (*Volpone*) and 'thy Alchymist' were as popular after their tenth performances as at their first, are stories of the reverse: people who 'hist / At thy unequal'd Play, the *Alchymist*'; and who thought 'all was ill' in productions of *Volpone*.[9] Even years later, when the plays were revived, actors might 'Behold their Benches bare', when they offered to speak 'great Johnsons verse'; and performances of *Volpone* and *The Alchemist* sometimes 'scarce defrai'd the Seacoale fire' – they hardly garnered enough revenue to pay for heating the space.[10] Jonson had total mastery of the breadth and depth and height of the amphitheatrical stage and the interpretative possibilities raised by using its dimensions – but he never really understood, or wanted to understand, all of its patrons.

NOTES

1. Aston Cockain, *Small Poems of Divers Sorts* (1658), p. 108.
2. Robert Herrick, 'Upon M. Ben Johnson. Epig.', in *Hesperides* (1648), p. 173.
3. Helen Ostovich, '"To Behold the Scene Full": Seeing and Judging in *Every Man Out of His Humour*', in Martin Butler (ed.), *Re-Presenting Ben Jonson: Text, History Performance* (Basingstoke: Macmillan, 1999), pp. 76–92; pp. 76, 90.
4. Frances Berry, 'Stage Perspective and Elevation in *Coriolanus* and *Sejanus*', in Ian Donaldson (ed.), *Jonson and Shakespeare* (London: Macmillan, 1983), pp. 163–78; pp. 168–9.
5. *Manuscript Additions to a Copy of John Stowe's The Annales of England* (1631), Folger Shakespeare Library MS, v.b.275.
6. Jasper Mayne, 'To the Memory of Ben. Johnson', in Brian Duppa (ed.), *Jonsonus Virbius* (London, 1638), p. 30; Thomas Fuller, *History* (1662), p. 3H4a.
7. Jasper Mayne, 'To the Memory of Ben. Johnson', in Brian Duppa (ed.), *Jonsonus Virbius* (London, 1638), p. 30.
8. William Fennor, *Fennors Descriptions* (1616), Sig. B2a.

9. Mayne, 'To the Memory of Ben. Johnson', p. 30; Robert Herrick, 'Upon M. Ben Johnson. Epig.', in *Hesperides* (1648), p. 173; Henry Parrot, *The Mous Trap* (1606), Sig. F1b.
10. Thomas Carew, prefatory verses to William Davenant, *The Just Italian* (1630), Sig. A4a; Leonard Digges, 'Upon Master WILLIAM Shakespeare, the Deceased Authour, and his POEMS', prefixed to *William Shakespeare, Poems* (1640), *4a.

CHAPTER 13

The Whitefriars Theatre and the children's companies

Lucy Munro

In late 1609 or early 1610, Jonson's *Epicene* was among the first plays performed at a small indoor playhouse in Whitefriars precinct by a company that on 4 January 1610 gained a royal patent as the Children of the Queen's Revels.[1] Both the playhouse and the company had a past. The playhouse had been used in 1607–8 by a company known as the Children of the King's Revels, while the Queen's Revels name had been used until 1608 by a troupe performing at another indoor theatre, the Blackfriars. The Queen's Revels company of 1609–10 certainly included some actors who had previously worked at Blackfriars, and it may have included some boys or young men who had performed at Whitefriars in 1607–8.

A prologue written for an early performance of *Epicene*, published in the 1616 folio edition of Jonson's *Works*, plays with an audience's prior knowledge of the district and possibly its previous occupants. 'The Poet' asks, the prologue says, developing a line of gastronomic imagery, asks that the audience sit:

> and when his cates are all in brought,
> Though there be none far-fet, there will dear-bought
> Be fit for ladies; some for lords, knights, squires,
> Some for your waiting wench and city-wires,
> Some for your men and daughters of Whitefriars.
>   (Prologue, ll. 20–4)

Although the prologue may gesture towards local residents in the audience, the last line is double-edged, since the popular reputation of the Whitefriars, despite its proximity to the fashionable Strand and what was beginning to become the West End, was as a hive of criminal activity and, in particular, the sex trade. In *The Bellman of London* (1608), Thomas Dekker claims that Whitefriars is famous as a meeting place for prostitutes, while Thomas Middleton in *The Black Book* (1604) makes a casual reference to 'The Dice running as false as the Drabbes in *White-Fryers*'.[2] Jonson himself uses the Whitefriars' seedy associations elsewhere: he includes in the *Epigrams* a portrait of the disreputable Lieutenant Shift, who is 'not meanest among squires, / That haunt Pikthatch, Marshlambeth and Whitefriars' (*Epigrams* 12, ll. 1–2), and in *Volpone* Lady Politic Would-Be excoriates Peregrine, thinking he is a disguised whore, by telling him that she is none of his 'Whitefriars nation' (4.2.51). The reference in the *Epicene* prologue to '*men* and daughters of Whitefriars' may refer to pimps or whoremasters, or, as Mary Bly argues, the 'men' may also have been selling themselves to paying customers.[3]

Explicit reference to the district was not a new manoeuvre for Whitefriars playwrights. Lording Barry's *Ram Alley*, which was probably first performed by the King's Revels company at Whitefriars in 1607–8, is named after a particularly notorious street in the precinct, in which much of the action takes place, and its dialogue is larded with references to other local streets. Fittingly, given this precedent, *Epicene* is the first of Jonson's plays – the collaborative Queen's Revels play *Eastward Ho!*, written with George Chapman and John Marston in 1605, excepted – to have a verisimilar London setting. However, in contrast with *Ram Alley*, and with his own later work, *The Alchemist*, in *Epicene* Jonson flirts with the locally specific but does not wholly pin down the action of his play. Morose's house, located as it is in a dingy alley too narrow to allow the passage of noisy and disruptive coaches, would not be out of place in the Whitefriars, and it would have been a characteristically perverse choice of habitat for the wealthy but radically antisocial Morose. But for the main part, locations in *Epicene* are defined by where they are not, or are not quite: the house rented by the socially self-conscious Sir Amorous La Foole may be in the modish Strand, but Clerimont's lodgings, where the play opens, are not, La Foole declaring that they would be 'almost as delicate' as his own 'if [they] were i' the Strand' (1.4.4, 6).

Although Jonson does not aim for the unity of theatrical and dramatic location found in *Ram Alley* and *The Alchemist*, he does take advantage of the Whitefriars in other ways, seemingly capitalizing on its unusual configuration. Scholars have differed on the precise location of the playhouse and therefore on its dimensions. Glynne Wickham and Jean McIntyre both place it in the refectory, which seems to have measured 85 feet by 35 feet.[4] However, Herbert Berry draws on Martin Slater's contract with the King's Revels company and locates the playhouse in the longer, narrower room labelled 'The Hale' in an early seventeenth-century survey of the district, which measured 90 feet by 17 feet.[5] The latter would have been a particularly odd, extreme space for performance, but either set of dimensions would have produced something rather different from the Blackfriars playhouse, which seems to have measured 46 feet from east to west and 66 feet from north to south.[6]

Truewit's description of the room in which he humiliates La Foole and Daw probably accords with the set-up of the Whitefriars stage:

> Do you observe this gallery? Or rather lobby, indeed? Here are a couple of studies, at each end one: here will I act such a tragicomedy between the Guelphs and the Ghibellines, Daw and La Foole. Which of 'em comes out first will I seize on. You two [Dauphine and Clerimont] shall be the chorus behind the arras, and whip out between the acts and speak. (4.5.23–7)

This comment and other sources suggest that the doors were placed on the inner corners of the stage, and the discovery space seems to have been proportionally larger than in other playhouses; the 'above' playing area may, however, have been atypically small and difficult to access quickly. Richard Dutton suggests that the fact that the discovery space is not used 'in any marked way' adds to the 'effect of confinement' in the play.[7] He also notes that the peculiar stage direction, 'Haughty, Centaur, Mavis, Mrs Otter, Epicene, Trusty, *having discovered part of the past scene above*' (4.6.0.1), which McIntyre views as a 'literary' addition to the playtext, makes sense if one recalls the probable small size and relative inaccessibility of the playhouse balcony. Instead of the six actors squeezing into the balcony, he argues, 'They must, rather, have appeared individually or in pairs, and mimed responses to what they saw below.'[8]

Specific information relating to the Queen's Revels company and their plays also provides an important context for *Epicene*. Although they were known as the 'Children of the Queen's Revels', the name is misleading, as some of the performers are known to have been in their late teens and early twenties. In the 1616 folio, Jonson lists eight of the 'principal comedians' who appeared in *Epicene*:

NAT. FIELD.	WILL. BARKSTED.
GIL. CARIE.	WILL. PEN.
HVG. ATTAWEL.	RIC. ALLEN.
JOH. SMITH.	JOH. BLANEY.[9]

Nathan Field, the first actor named, was twenty-two when *Epicene* was first performed; William Barksted was at least twenty and may have been a year or two older, while Hugh Attwell was at least seventeen. Another Queen's Revels actor, Emmanuel Reade, is not listed by Jonson but may have appeared in a smaller role; he was also seventeen. Giles Cary, who had recently played the boy in Jonson's *Key Keeper* entertainment of April 1609 (also known as the *Entertainment at Britain's Burse*), may have been one of the younger members of the company; Robert Cecil's accounts refer to him and fellow *Key Keeper* performer William Ostler (shortly to join the King's Men) as 'Ostler the player' and 'his boye'.[10]

The information we have, therefore, suggests that the actors working at the Whitefriars in 1609/10 were not the children aged between ten and fourteen that Jonson would have found when he first wrote for the children's companies in 1600–1. Instead, the leading actors were young adults, some of whom had nearly a decade of public performance behind them. They may have been extremely proficient. Robert Keysar referred to them in a 1610 lawsuit as a 'Companye of the moste exparte and skillful acto^{rs} wthin the Realme of England to the number of eighteane or Twentye persons all or moste of them trayned vp in that service, in the raigne of the late Queene Elizabeth for Ten yeares togeath^{r}'.[11] He may have been exaggerating the number of actors and their expertise, but he was not challenged by Richard Burbage and Henry Condell, whose responses have survived, and in 1611 Prince Otto von Hess-Cassel was to refer to them as 'The best company in London'.[12] Six out of the eight actors listed by Jonson had sustained careers with adult companies: Attwell with Prince Charles's Men; Barksted with Lady Elizabeth's Men and Prince Charles's Men; John Blaney with Queen Anna's Men and Queen Henrietta Maria's Men; Cary with Lady Elizabeth's Men; Field with Lady Elizabeth's Men and the King's Men; William Penn with Lady Elizabeth's Men and the King's Men.

We know a little about the casting of *Epicene*, thanks to an early reader who annotated his copy of the play with the information that Hugh Attwell played Sir Amorous La Foole and William Barksted played Morose.[13] A few tantalizing scraps of information have survived about each of these performers. Attwell appears to have been short or slight, since an elegy written for him by William Rowley on his death in 1621 describes him as a 'little man'.[14] A reference to Amorous La Foole as 'a precious manikin' (1.3.18), may therefore suggest that Jonson was tailoring at least some aspects of roles to the physicality and capabilities of his actors. Barksted's reputation as a comedian is attested by cameo appearances in three jest-books; in one, *The Book of Bulls,* he is described as 'The best Comedian that ever trod on *English* Stage'.[15]

Sadly, we do not know for certain the role played by Nathan Field, the company's leading actor. Dutton notes that Jonsonian roles later associated with Field, Voltore in *Volpone* and Face in *The Alchemist*, 'require verbal authority (in bogus causes), the energy to press an argument, the capacity to change tack plausibly at a moment's notice'; although he does not mention another of Field's known parts, the fiery title character in Chapman's *Bussy D'Ambois,* it would also fit this characterization.[16] Dutton suggests, and I agree, that the most likely role for Field in *Epicene* is Truewit. In addition to its internal characteristics, Truewit is by far the longest role in the play, with more than double the number of lines of the next largest (Clerimont and Morose), and evidence from other companies suggests that leading actors often took the largest role in a given play. The two other Queen's Revels plays that have been convincingly dated to 1609–10, Field's *A Woman Is a Weathercock* and Francis Beaumont and John Fletcher's *The Scornful Lady,* have similar casting patterns. Each has one role that outstrips those around it, and in each case the character is a verbose young man: Scudamore in *A Woman Is a Weathercock,* and Elder Loveless in *The Scornful Lady.*

We know little about the distribution of female roles. David Kathman's recent study of boy actors in adult companies suggests that they were generally aged between around thirteen and twenty-one.[17] The maximum age here is similar to that of the Queen's Revels company of 1609–10, but we do not know whether actors would have swapped between adult male and female roles, or whether a compressed version of the adult system would have developed, in which the younger boys played most if not all of the female roles. Dutton suggests that Giles Cary may have doubled Clerimont's Boy and Epicene, noting that 'such a doubling has a bearing on the "surprise" of Epicene's true nature, which is no surprise at all in the printed text.'[18] Possible support for this hypothesis may be found in a later play, Richard Brome's *The City Wit* (c. 1630), also performed by a children's company, in which an audience think that a boy actor is doubling the roles of an apprentice and a Doll-Common-esque trickster, only to find out that the apprentice is in fact masquerading as the mysterious woman. Brome draws heavily on *Epicene,* here as in other plays, so it is possible that he was inspired by the original casting of Jonson's play.

Epicene is both a response to earlier children's performance and a reshaping of its contours to the specific needs of the new company and its Whitefriars environment. The play's opening dialogue both recalls and reworks earlier children's company conventions, featuring an extended dialogue between Clerimont and his boy servant, a sardonic child who would not have been out of place in Jonson's Blackfriars plays, or even in John Lyly's comedies of the 1580s. The actor playing Clerimont is constructed as an adult in comparison, whatever his real age, but we quickly learn from Truewit that Clerimont is himself in some ways juvenile, or at least adolescent, in his habits: 'Why, here's the man that can melt away his time, and never feels it! What between his mistress abroad and his ingle at home, high fare, soft lodging, fine clothes, and his fiddle, he thinks the hours ha' no wings or the day no post-horse' (1.1.18–21).

The reference to Clerimont's 'ingle', or catamite, might have recalled to at least some members of the audience the strategies of the King's Revels company, which, as Mary Bly has argued, aimed to appeal specifically to a desiring male spectator. But the allusion to male homoeroticism is juxtaposed with explicit references not only to female audience members (in the prologue quoted above) but also to desiring female subjects within the play itself. The Boy complains that the collegiates 'play with me and throw me o' the bed', and that Lady Haughty 'kisses me with her oiled face, and puts a peruke o' my head, and asks me an' I will wear her gown, and I say no; and then she hits me a blow o' the ear and calls me innocent, and lets me go' (1.1.10–14). As the play's narrative progresses, it becomes clear that for all its obsession with policing the limits of socially acceptable female behaviour, *Epicene* is always liable to fall back into the criticism of questionable male behaviour, whether it comes from Morose, or from Amorous La Foole and John Daw.

Epicene also left a lasting mark on subsequent Queen's Revels plays, which include Beaumont and Fletcher's *The Scornful Lady*, Field's *A Woman Is a Weathercock* and *Amends for Ladies*, Chapman's *The Revenge of Bussy D'Ambois* (probably written to accompany a revival of an earlier Blackfriars play, *Bussy D'Ambois*), Robert Daborne's *A Christian Turned Turk* and *The Insatiate Countess* (revised by Barksted and Lewis Machin from a possibly unfinished play by John Marston). In addition to *Bussy D'Ambois* they also seem to have revived Middleton's *A Trick to Catch the Old One*, Chapman's *May Day* and *The Widow's Tears*, and Beaumont and Fletcher's *Cupid's Revenge* and *The Coxcomb*.[19] Close relationships can be tracked throughout this repertory. *Epicene* itself may be indebted to *May Day* in its use of the cross-dressing motif, while a specific debt to Jonson's play can be traced not only in *Amends for Ladies* – which uses cross-dressing to such an extent that the motif becomes hopelessly overdetermined – but also in *The Scornful Lady*, which not only reworks the 'silent woman' motif, but also juxtaposes her with alternative models of female garrulity and with a miserly older man in (fruitless) search for a wife.

The earliest performances of *Epicene* followed a prolonged closure of the theatres due to a virulent outbreak of plague in London. What was presented to paying audiences was therefore something novel: a company that called themselves children but who were probably the oldest and most proficient 'children' that the indoor theatres had seen. *Epicene* plays with this paradox: it draws on established traditions of children's company dramaturgy, but it also twists and inverts those traditions in ways that were to prove fruitful for dramatists working at Whitefriars and beyond.

NOTES

1. On the date of *Epicene* and its original performance contexts see Richard Dutton (ed.), *Epicene* (Manchester: Manchester University Press, 2003), pp. 1–5.
2. *The Blacke Booke* (London, 1604), sig. D4r.
3. Mary Bly, *Queer Virgins and Virgin Queans on the Early Modern Stage* (Oxford: Oxford University Press, 2000), pp. 140–2.
4. Glynne Wickham, *Early English Stages* (London: Routledge & Kegan Paul, 1963–72), vol. I, pp. 122–3; vol. II, pp. 2, 80; Jean McIntyre, 'Production Resources at the Whitefriars Playhouse, 1609–1612', *Early Modern Literary Studies*, 2 (3) (1996): 2.1–35, available online at http://purl.oclc.org/emls/02-3/maciwhit.html.
5. Herbert Berry, 'Playhouses, 1560–1660', in Glynne Wickham, Herbert Berry and William Ingram (eds.), *English Professional Theatre, 1530–1660* (Cambridge: Cambridge University Press, 2000), pp. 285–674.
6. Berry, 'Playhouses', pp. 501–2, 504–5.
7. Dutton, *Epicene*, p. 56.
8. Dutton, *Epicene*, p. 56.
9. Ben Jonson, *Workes* (London, 1616), sig. 3D4v.
10. Scott McMillin, 'Jonson's Early Entertainments: New Information from Hatfield House', *Renaissance Drama*, 1 (n.s.) (1968): 153–66; p. 159, transcribing Hatfield MSS, Bills 35/1.
11. C. W. Wallace, 'Shakespeare and his London Associates as Revealed in Recently Discovered Documents', *University Studies of the University of Nebraska*, 10 (1910): 261–360; p. 350, transcribing Keysar v. Burbage *et al.*, Court of Requests, February–June 1610, National Archives, REQ 4/1/1, no. 1.
12. E. K. Chambers, *The Elizabethan Stage*, 4 vols. (Oxford: Clarendon Press, 1923), vol. II, p. 369. Dutton suggests that the company 'could normally count on fourteen actors, at most fifteen', *Epicene*, p. 9.
13. See J. A. Riddell, 'Some Actors in Ben Jonson's Plays', *Shakespeare Studies*, 5 (1969): 285–98; pp. 295–6.
14. G. E. Bentley, *The Jacobean and Caroline Stage*, 7 vols. (Oxford: Clarendon Press, 1941–68), vol. II, pp. 352–3.
15. *The Book of Bulls, Baited with Two Centuries of Bold Jests, and Nimble Lies* (London, 1636), sigs. b5v–b6r. Barksted also appears in John Taylor's *Wit and*

Mirth (1629) and *Taylor's Feast* (1638). For further discussion of Barksted's career see Bly, *Queer Virgins and Virgin Queans,* pp. 122–5.
16. Jonson, *Epicene,* p. 8.
17. David Kathman, 'How Old Were Shakespeare's Boy Actors?', *Shakespeare Survey,* 58 (2005): 220–46.
18. Dutton, *Epicene,* p. 7.
19. For discussion of the dates and company attributions of these plays, see Lucy Munro, *Children of the Queen's Revels: A Jacobean Theatre Repertory* (Cambridge: Cambridge University Press, 2005), pp. 170–8.

CHAPTER 14

The Blackfriars Theatre and the indoor theatres

Janette Dillon

Jonson, unlike Shakespeare, never became a company man. He did not write solely or mainly for one company and therefore did not have a particular association with one playhouse. In the early years of his career he wrote for different companies and for both outdoor and indoor playhouses. That said, however, he wrote more plays for the Blackfriars Theatre than for any other, and his association with it was long and varied, stretching over more than thirty years. He also lived in the Blackfriars district of London for some of that time. He signed the letter he prefaced to *Volpone*, 'From my house in the Blackfriars this 11 of February, 1607'; and besides occupying a house of his own in the Blackfriars at this date, he also spent two periods of several years either side of this date living in the Blackfriars residence of Esmé Stuart, Seigneur d'Aubigny and Gentleman of the King's Bedchamber.[1]

The Blackfriars district was a fashionable and elite neighbourhood at the time Jonson was writing, and Esmé Stuart was one of many well-born residents living there in the early seventeenth century.[2] Though it was inside the city walls it had, until 1608, the status of a liberty (an area free of city jurisdiction) because of its former status as a Dominican friary. This was also the reason why it was a good place to build a theatre. From the beginning of commercial theatre-building in the 1560s, theatres had been constructed either outside the city of London or inside its liberties.[3] London, in turn, had actively tried to push theatrical performance out of the city and had more or less managed to put an end to performances in city inns from the mid 1590s.

The Blackfriars playhouse was a conversion within the Upper Frater of the former friary, carried out in 1596 by James Burbage for the Chamberlain's Men. This was the second Blackfriars playhouse; the first, built by Richard Farrant for the Children of the Chapel Royal in a different part of the friary, had closed in 1584. Rectangular in shape and measuring 66 feet by 46 feet, the second Blackfriars, with a capacity of 600–700,

Figure 14.1 Study of a seated actor by Rembrandt Harmenszoon van Rijn.

was bigger than the first, but smaller than the outdoor amphitheatres. As in the outdoor playhouses, the stage was backed by the tiring house, with a gallery, including a music room, above; and the audience surrounded it on three sides in galleried tiers. Because the theatre was indoor, however, it was artificially lit by candelabras in addition to the light coming in through the windows, and this created very different effects from performance in the open-air spaces and natural light of the amphitheatres.

But this is to look forward. In 1596, when Burbage wanted to start performances in the Blackfriars playhouse, the residents successfully opposed him, and the Privy Council 'forbadd the use of the said howse'.[4] The Chamberlain's Men were not to perform in it until after they took over the lease as the King's Men in 1608 and the plague epidemic ceased at the end of 1609. In the interim, Burbage's sons, James Burbage himself having died in February 1597, leased the Blackfriars from 1600 to 1608 to a new company of Chapel Children, who quickly became known as the Blackfriars Children. Their superior social status compared with the adult playing companies, together with the fact that they played only once a week, made them acceptable to the Blackfriars residents where the Chamberlain's Men were not.

It was this boy company that gave Ben Jonson his first opportunity to write for the Blackfriars Theatre: *Cynthia's Revels* was performed during their first season, in autumn 1600.[5] This season was to launch the new company straight into the so-called War of the Theatres, giving their repertory a satirical edge from the start that was to be their downfall. Jonson was right at the centre of this fashion for satire, and he quickly followed up *Cynthia's Revels* with *Poetaster* (1601), written in a mere fifteen weeks and including a mercilessly comic picture of Crispinus (John Marston) vomiting up his 'terrible windy words' (5.3.490). It was now, with *Satiromastix* (1601), written in response to *Poetaster,* that Thomas Dekker began the joke about Jonson's bricklaying days that was to haunt him for the rest of his career.[6]

This vogue for satire flourished partly because of the location of the Blackfriars playhouse in a district not only wealthy and fashion-conscious generally but also immediately adjacent to two of the Inns of Court, the Inner and Middle Temple (where Marston himself was in chambers at this time). Law students always formed part of the relatively elite Blackfriars audience, and Jonson had many personal connections with lawyers.[7] Within a few years, indeed, he was collaborating with Marston and George Chapman on the writing of *Eastward Ho!* for the Blackfriars Children in 1605. Satire was again the dominant mode of this play, but this time the satire was more dangerous. It went well beyond the frivolous lampooning of fellow-dramatists to poke fun at the King and his Scottish favourites, and all three dramatists were imprisoned as a result. It was probably the intervention of Jonson's patron, Esmé Stuart, that resulted in their pardon.[8]

Eastward Ho! also marked the beginning of Jonson's participation in another, less dangerous, theatrical fashion: that of setting his plays within the city of London and making that location central to the meaning and effect of the play. The play, following its action through some very particular London locations (Wapping, Eastcheap, Whitefriars, Billingsgate, Cuckold's Haven and many more), ends with an address to London itself:

> Now London, look about,
> And in this moral, see thy glass run out.
>
> (5.5.181–2)

That sense of physical immediacy and local specificity was to become very important to Jonson's Blackfriars plays, allowing him to make the audience feel very directly addressed by his fictions and tying in with his regular adherence to the classical unities of time and place. The confined space of the Blackfriars, moreover, offered the perfect forum and stimulus for Jonson's tightly constructed and claustrophobic plays. As Martin Butler puts it, 'his art was unlocked by the physical conditions for which he wrote.'[9]

Thus, in *The Alchemist* (1610), Lovewit's house and the street outside, where all the action takes place, are located in precisely the same spot as the Blackfriars Theatre, 'here, in the Friars' (1.1.17) and the action unfolds over almost exactly the same period of time as does the play itself.[10] The very word 'house' comes to have particular resonance in this play and others, punning as it does on playhouse and fictional house. A similar equation carries on through *The Staple of News* (1626), where the conceit of the play is that an office where news is brought together has been '[n]ewly erected / Here in the house' (1.2.31–2), and *The New Inn* (1629), where the new inn is still 'The old house' (Prologue, l. 2), and on into Jonson's last Blackfriars play, *The Magnetic Lady* (1632). Here, though no direct equation is made between Lady Loadstone's house and the playhouse, much of the play is effectively a play-within-a-play, and the word 'house' resonates almost obsessively through both its fiction and its frame.

By the time Jonson came to write *The Alchemist,* the King's Men had regained possession of the Blackfriars and had begun performing there in the winter seasons. The Blackfriars Children had had to disband as a company after taking their satire a step too far. Their offence elicited a vow from King James that 'They should never play more, but should first begg their bred and he wold have his vow performed.' It was, as Andrew Gurr notes, 'The most direct and personal response' to a play by King James on record.[11] The Blackfriars Boys nevertheless managed to re-form as a new company with the Children of the King's Revels the very next year under a new manager, Robert Keysar, and Jonson wrote his last 'children's' play for them: *Epicene*. (They were scarcely children any more by this date, however; Nathan Field was twenty-two or twenty-three when he performed in this play.) Performed in the winter season of 1609–10, *Epicene* was probably one of the plays that launched the opening season at the new Whitefriars playhouse, and it again managed to offend the authorities.[12] When the King's cousin, Arbella Stuart, took exception to a reference to the Prince of Moldavia (5.1.20), Jonson had to write a new prologue denying any personal edge to the allusion and chiding his audiences for 'wrest[ing]' what he wrote to 'make a libel which he made a play' (*Epicene*, Second Prologue, ll. 12–14).[13] The condemnation of 'application' on the part of audiences – that is, reading plays as commenting directly on topical matters and living individuals – was one of Jonson's favourite topoi; yet it has to be set against the number of occasions on which his plays gave offence. 'Application' cannot thrive without something to feed on.

At the very end of his life Jonson wrote one more play for an indoor theatre other than the Blackfriars: *A Tale of a Tub* was played by Queen Henrietta's Men at the Cockpit in 1633. From 1610 to 1632, however, he maintained an extended and almost exclusive relationship with the King's Men at the Blackfriars.[14] *The Devil is an Ass* was performed there in 1616, *The Staple of News* in 1626, *The New Inn* in 1629 and *The Magnetic Lady* in 1632. There are, of course, long gaps of up to ten years in this sequence, but those do not indicate that Jonson was writing other plays for other companies. Besides writing poetry, he continued to write masques and entertainments for the court during this period, as he had done more or less continuously since 1605. One of his least well-known entertainments, possibly written in 1620 for the christening of Charles Cavendish, second son of the Earl of Devonshire, was performed in the Blackfriars precinct.[15]

Jonson's periods of long silence for the public stage are partly explicable as the result of his deeply contested relationship with the theatre and its audiences. His plays conduct an ongoing critical and self-justifying dialogue with audiences, developing through increasingly self-referential structures. The self-referentiality of *The Alchemist* and the signature use of the term 'house' have already been discussed, but *The Devil is an Ass* took this metadrama to a new level of directness in its engagement with both contemporary theatre and theatre history. The Prologue alludes to an earlier and highly popular King's Men's play, *The Merry Devil of Edmonton;* and when Fitzdottrel wants to visit the theatre, the play he is going to see is called *The Devil* (1.4.44). When Engine hands Fitzdottrel the playbill he is almost certainly brandishing before the audience the very playbill printed for *The Devil is an Ass;* and in talking of actors, Engine makes reference to 'Dick Robinson' (2.8.64), an actor with the King's Men who was very probably taking the part of Wittipol in this production.[16] The playhouse Fitzdottrel plans to visit is of course the Blackfriars, and this allows Jonson a further opportunity to tease his audience:

> Today I go to the Blackfriars Playhouse,
> Sit i' the view, salute all my acquaintance,
> Rise up between the acts, let fall my cloak,
> Publish a handsome man, and a rich suit,
> As that's a special end why we go thither,
> All that pretend to stand for't o'the stage.
>
> (1.6.31–6)

The teasing is more than half-serious. Again and again in his plays Jonson expressed, with varying levels of vitriol, his recognition that many spectators came to Blackfriars to be seen more than to see. He may have been choosing the King's Men and the Blackfriars as the most fashionable and elite company and venue in London, but in doing so he was also forced to encounter the worst excesses of a fashionable audience.[17]

The play also plays much more wittily and humorously with the theatre history of devils on stage – not just with popular Elizabethan plays such as *The Merry Devil of Edmonton,* but with the much older morality tradition of plays that centred 'fifty years agone, and six' around the figure of the 'Vice ... In his long coat, shaking his wooden dagger' (1.1.84–5) and typically ended with the Devil carrying off the damned soul on his back. Instead, Jonson turns this tradition on its head and has the Vice carry off the boy-devil, Pug, on his back with the usual (and archaic) effects of noise and smoke, while commenting explicitly on the reversal:

> The Devil was wont to carry away the evil;
> But now the evil out-carries the Devil.
>
> (5.6.76–7)

The Staple of News and *The Magnetic Lady* both use a structure of Induction and 'Intermeans' punctuating the acts to comment on the play, a structure that allows Jonson to anticipate and mock negative or stupid responses and to offer his own correctives to them. The names of those who offer their opinions in these structural interstices offer a clear window into Jonson's intentions. In *The Staple of News* they are called Mirth, Tattle, Expectation and Censure, and their triviality is openly acknowledged as they come on looking for stools on the stage (another characteristic feature of the Blackfriars, but evidently, from the onstage discussion that ensues, not a form of seating usually taken up by women): 'we are persons of quality, I assure you, and women of fashion, and come to see and be seen' (Induction, ll. 7–8). As in *The Devil is an Ass* (to which *The Staple* makes explicit reference [First Intermean, ll. 32–3]), Jonson is still working out his irritation with an audience whose preferences remain stuck in the morality drama of the past. The gossips look for a Vice and dismiss those characters who come closest to that archaic mode because they don't fulfil all the old expectations:

Tattle.
But here is never a fiend to carry him away. Besides, he has never a wooden dagger! I'd not give a rush for a Vice that has not a wooden dagger to snap at everybody he meets.

Mirth.
That was the old way, gossip, when Iniquity came in like Hocus Pocus, in a juggler's jerkin, with false skirts like the Knave of Clubs! But now they are attired like men and women o' the time, the Vices, male and female! (Second Intermean, ll. 9–14)

Probee and Damplay in *The Magnetic Lady* conduct both sides of the dialogue about how to judge a play (Probee approves [from Latin *probare*], while Damplay damns). They represent Jonson's most extended attempt to justify his dramaturgical practice and to teach his audience how to judge his plays. As an exposition and analysis of the proper relations between plays and audiences, their implied critique is both general and also very particular to the Blackfriars. When Probee claims to the company 'Boy' who meets them on stage ('a pretty prompt boy for the poetic shop' [Induction, l. 4]) that he and Damplay are 'sent unto you ... from the people' (Induction, 19), the Boy questions him about precisely which people, and a mocking dialogue about the Blackfriars audience ensues:

Probee.
Not the faeces or grounds of your people, that sit in the oblique caves and wedges of your house, your sinful sixpenny mechanics –

Damplay.
But the better and braver sort of your people! Plush and velvet-outsides! That stick your house round like so many eminences –

Boy.
Of clothes, not understandings? They are at pawn. (Induction, 23–7)

The cheapest seats at the Blackfriars cost sixpence each, which already made them considerably more expensive than the amphitheatres; but even the richest members of the audience, Jonson jokes, do not have brains to match their clothes.[18]

Although Jonson had been attacking his audiences for failing to understand him from a very early date, the attack in *The Magnetic Lady* was the more bitter and extended because it followed on from the failure of *The New Inn* three years earlier.[19] The dedication to the reader that Jonson wrote to accompany the publication of *The New Inn* in 1631 shows how much he was still smarting from that encounter two years after the play's performance, as does his famous vow to 'leave the loathèd stage, / And the more loathsome age' in the famous 'Ode to Himself', written in the same year as that first performance.[20] His own vitriol provided his most oppositional audience with exactly the material they needed. Alexander Gill's verses on *The Magnetic Lady* pulled no punches, not hesitating to drag in the old bricklaying joke or even to mock Jonson's physical affliction (he was by now very disabled by a stroke). Ironically, Gill's attack was as closely tied to the specificity of the Blackfriars audience as was Jonson's own, and quoted his own words to point up to him the risk he took in inviting 'silks and plush and all the wits' to censure him, while hearing 'Themselves styled Gentle Ignorance'.[21] If the stage was to be loathed, it was, according to Gill, 'for thou hast made it such'.[22] Several of the Blackfriars audience wrote in Jonson's defence after *The New Inn,* but Jonson had mainly himself to blame for relentlessly goading those less admiring members of his audience to attack.

NOTES

1. On Jonson's relationship with Esmé Stuart, see further Ian Donaldson, 'Jonson's Duplicity: The Catholic Years', in Ian Donaldson, *Jonson's Magic Houses: Essays in Interpretation* (Oxford: Clarendon Press, 1997), pp. 47–65.
2. Those who signed the petition against the Blackfriars Theatre in 1596 (see below) included Lady Elizabeth Russell and Lord Hunsdon, Lord Chamberlain and patron of the Chamberlain's Men.
3. The Rose, built *c.* 1587 in the liberty of the Clink in Southwark, was the only playhouse built in the liberties before 1596.
4. Irwin Smith, *Shakespeare's Blackfriars Playhouse,* quoted in Andrew Gurr, 'London's Blackfriars Playhouse and the Chamberlain's Men', in Paul Menzer (ed.), *Inside Shakespeare: Essays on the Blackfriars Stage* (Selinsgrove, Pa.: Susquehanna University Press, 2006), pp. 17–30; p. 24.

5. *The Case Is Altered,* an earlier play, was performed by the Blackfriars Children but not written for them. Andrew Gurr notes that Jonson first sold it to Philip Henslowe; *The Shakespearian Playing Companies* (Oxford: Clarendon Press, 1996), p. 241.
6. Jonson had briefly followed his stepfather's trade as a bricklayer.
7. See, for example, David Riggs, *Ben Jonson: A Life* (Cambridge, Mass.: Harvard University Press, 1989), pp. 192–3. Henry Fitzjeffrey, who published his 'Notes from Blackfriars' in 1617, was a lawyer in Lincoln's Inn.
8. See Riggs, *Ben Jonson,* pp. 122–6.
9. Martin Butler, 'Jonson's London and its Theatres', in Richard Harp and Stanley Stewart (eds.), *The Cambridge Companion to Ben Jonson* (Cambridge: Cambridge University Press), pp. 15–29; p. 26.
10. See further R. L. Smallwood, '"Here, in the Friars": Immediacy and Theatricality in *The Alchemist*', *Review of English Studies,* 32 (ns) (1981): 142–60; and Ian Donaldson, 'Jonson's Magic Houses' and 'Clockwork Comedy: Time and *The Alchemist*', in *Jonson's Magic Houses: Essays in Interpretation* (Oxford: Oxford University Press, 1997), pp. 66–88, 89–105.
11. Gurr, *The Shakespearian Playing Companies,* p. 354. The play was almost certainly *Chapman's Conspiracy and Tragedy of Byron.*
12. On the Whitefriars Playhouse and Whitefriars Children, see further Richard Dutton's introduction to his edition of *Epicene* for the Revels series (Manchester: Manchester University Press, 2003), pp. 2–11, 52–8.
13. The full title of the second prologue to *Epicene* is 'Another / Occasioned by some person's impertinent exception'.
14. The exception was the performance of *Bartholomew Fair* by the Lady Elizabeth's Men at the opening of the new Hope Theatre (an outdoor playhouse) in 1614.
15. See James Knowles's edition of *The Cavendish Christening Entertainment* in The Cambridge Edition of the Works of Ben Jonson (Cambridge: Cambridge University Press, forthcoming) for a revised argument about the context for this text.
16. See Peter Happé's note to these lines in his edition (Manchester: Manchester University Press, 1994).
17. See further William A. Armstrong, 'The Audience of the Elizabethan Private Theatres', *Review of English Studies,* 10 (ns) (1959): 234–49. Henry Fitzjeffrey, in his 'Notes on Blackfriars' (1617) also made a point of detailing the expensive clothes of some of the gallants in the audience.
18. On prices at the Blackfriars, see further Armstrong, 'The Audience of the Elizabethan Private Theatres'.
19. For discussion of reasons for the play's failure at the Blackfriars see further Martin Butler, 'Late Jonson', in Gordon McMullan and Jonathan Hope (eds.), *The Politics of Tragicomedy: Shakespeare and After* (London: Routledge, 1992), pp. 166–88; and Andrew Stewart, 'Some Uses for Romance: Shakespeare's *Cymbeline* and Jonson's *The New Inn*', *Renaissance Forum,* 3 (1998), available online at www.hull.ac.uk/renforum/v3no1/stewart.htm.

20. 'Ode to Himself', in *Poems,* ed. Ian Donaldson (Oxford: Oxford University Press, 1975), p. 354.
21. Gill's verses and Jonson's reply are reprinted in *The Magnetic Lady,* ed. Peter Happé (Manchester: Manchester University Press, 2000), Appendix 1.
22. Happé, *The Magnetic Lady,* Appendix 1.

CHAPTER 15

Provinces, parishes and neighbourhoods

Steve Hindle

By the time Ben Jonson was at the peak of his writing career, it was almost a century since Henry VIII's principal secretary Thomas Cromwell had declared in the preamble to the 1533 Statute in Restraint of Appeals that 'this realm of England is an empire', a sovereign jurisdiction that denied the claims of rival sources of political or legal authority, be they internal (principally the 'over-mighty' subjects, who had pretension to rule their estates as if they were kings) or external (especially the papacy, with its powers to review cases tried in English ecclesiastical courts).[1] The claims of the Tudor and Stuart regimes may well have been 'imperial', especially in the context of the expansion during the century after 1533 of the royal writ to run directly not only through lowland England but also in the peripheries (including not only the Welsh marches and the northern borderlands but also Wales itself and ultimately even Ireland).[2] 'Empire' (with its connotations of untrammelled political authority, perhaps even absolutism) is nonetheless in many respects an inappropriate term to describe the Jacobean and Caroline state. After all, many contemporaries idealized their society not as an empire but as a participatory 'commonwealth' in which rulers and ruled were enmeshed in networks of mutual obligation and interdependence.[3] What held the English polity together was not the naked exercise of political power (though the Tudors and Stuarts were perfectly capable of sporting the iron fist rather than the velvet glove) but the negotiation of social authority, especially in the exchange of obedience and deference on the part of subjects for protection and paternalism on the part of their rulers.[4]

Of course there was a hierarchy in this political community (as in all communities), but the patterns of interpersonal relations that underpin Jonson's plays are best understood in social-structural and spatial terms by locating them within the concentric spheres of social and political authority of which the early modern state was composed.[5] It is helpful to think of the community of the realm as being constituted by a series of county communities extending through the provinces and, in turn, of each county as a network of parish communities, each of them made up of collections of households united by an ethos of mutuality and solidarity which is best understood as neighbourliness.[6] Although the mapping of provinces, parishes and neighbourhoods across England takes us away from the metropolitan locale that provided the context for much of Jonson's writing, it nonetheless helps us to understand the ways in which Jonson's contemporaries might have understood the vertical and horizontal social relationships depicted in many of his plays, not least the drama of the Caroline period.

PROVINCES

The royal presence was far from extensive in early Stuart England. Although the court was peripatetic and monarchs (some more frequently than others) occasionally journeyed on progress away from Whitehall, the heartland of Stuart influence was very much the metropolis and its immediate hinterland.[7] This was the lowland region, thickly settled with royal palaces, with which James I and (more especially) Charles I were personally most familiar and where Englishmen were most conscious of Stuart rule. Beyond the home counties, however, the crown's presence was most often symbolic, characteristically represented on the coinage and in the royal arms painted onto the whitewashed walls of parish churches and carved into the wainscoted fireplaces of gentry parlours. This was an environment in which the monarch exerted little personal influence and the problem of political communication (compounded by the tyranny of distance which dictated the speed of epistolatory exchange) was accordingly fundamental to the process of governing.[8] The governance of Stuart England therefore depended upon the principle of delegated authority, the crown using its significant reservoir of patronage to appoint officers who could be relied upon (almost invariably without remuneration and thus at their own expense) to maintain the peace and stability of the provinces.[9] This hierarchy of offices extended downwards from the Lords Lieutenant (noblemen who were responsible for the military governance of one or more counties); to assize judges (trained lawyers responsible for administering criminal justice by trying those suspected of felony in each county town twice a year); to justices of the peace (JPs, thirty or forty landed gentlemen who served in the King's Commission of the Peace in each county and who were responsible for the administration of social policy and the keeping of the King's peace).[10] The authority of these office-holders was informally upheld by those landed gentlemen who were expected, by the exercise of charity and hospitality on their estates (a series of practices celebrated in Jonson's 'To Penshurst'), to take care of their tenants.[11] The gentry as a class were accordingly idealized as paragons of virtue whose vigilance ensured the quiet of the market towns and of the countryside in deep England. To ask whether the gentry saw themselves as members of the community of the realm or of the 'county community' is to miss the point, since the structure of the Stuart polity ensured that they could be confident that there was no necessary opposition between these two identities.[12]

The provinces were therefore governed through lengthy chains of command, which, although they were lubricated by royal patronage, could sometimes be made to rattle only very faintly.[13] The twice-yearly presence in county towns of Assize Judges ensured that the rhetoric of royal addresses first delivered in the court of Star Chamber at Westminster was repeated in the hearing of the provincial elites, but the crown enjoyed only limited powers of coercion in securing compliance with its requests.[14] This system of 'self-government at the king's command' implied that the independently minded gentlemen who held local office might either conveniently ignore those royal requests to which they and their networks of clientage and association were unsympathetic or take personal initiatives in social regulation which were not explicitly sanctioned by the crown.[15] This was a world in which Justice Adam Overdo of Jonson's *Bartholomew Fair* could thrive, since the political system allowed very considerable discretion to those JPs, especially those activists who, in partnership with puritans like Zeal-of-the-Land Busy, sought to be busy controllers of the towns and parishes over which they exercised authority.[16]

PARISHES

As Overdo found to his cost, however, a conscientious magistrate seeking to suppress vice and disorder in the marketplace might well have to run a gauntlet of scorn and abuse, perhaps even of violence. Magistrates were very thinly scattered across counties, and a majority (perhaps as many as two-thirds) of all parishes lacked not only a resident magistrate but even a resident gentleman.[17] This power vacuum was filled at the local level by the middle sort of people – yeoman tenant farmers, craftsmen and tradesmen – who were appointed to local office, usually by some combination of gentry patronage and neighbourly initiative.[18] By the early seventeenth century, most of the 9,000-odd parishes across England had an office-holding cadre of two churchwardens (responsible for collecting rates towards maintenance of the church fabric and for presenting moral offences, ranging from failure to attend communion to fornication, to the ecclesiastical authorities); two overseers of the poor (responsible for assessing the burden of poverty and providing relief, funded from local taxation, in cash or kind for the indigent); two supervisors of the highways (responsible for funding and organizing supplies of labour and materials to maintain the infrastructure of roads and bridges); and two parish constables (responsible for the apprehension of malefactors, the policing of vagrants and beggars and the punishment of petty offenders).[19] The parish had therefore by the early seventeenth century come to assume an institutional identity: an organic unit of ecclesiastical association, in which parishioners had lived, worked and worshipped together, had been transformed into a political unit of obligation and control. But this creation of the 'civil parish' under the terms of Elizabethan legislation assumed that the chief inhabitants of each parish would be willing to serve their local communities without payment, and this entirely characteristic Stuart insistence on local government on the cheap ensured that the quality of office-holders was inconsistent. All these officers were, moreover, dependent on the willingness of their neighbours to complain to them about local abuses, and some of those complaints might be unfounded or even malicious. Toby Turf, constable of the Middlesex parish of Kentish Town in Jonson's *A Tale of a Tub,* is sufficiently conscientious to pursue and apprehend John Clay when the tilemaker is suspected of theft, despite the fact that the accusation made against him was trumped up by Clay's rival for the hand of Turf's daughter. This situation entirely captures the dilemmas of the constable's office, caught between public obligations of law enforcement on the one hand and the private interest of neighbours on the other.[20] Men like Constable Turf doubtless heard their fair share of cock-and-bull stories but their legal responsibility was to investigate them nonetheless. Parishes were most likely to remain stable and peaceful where there was cooperation between justices like Overdo and constables like Turf, but that cooperation could not always be assumed, and even where it was forthcoming, both county and parish officers were vulnerable to popular opposition. The concept of order enjoined by the officers of the Stuart state (rehearsed in the homilies read from the pulpits and the royal proclamations pinned to the doors of parish churches) was not invariably shared by their neighbours, and Jonson fully exploited the comedic potential of that divergence of opinion.[21]

NEIGHBOURHOODS

If the parish was, therefore, a 'little commonwealth', it was in turn made up of an association of smaller household commonwealths, in which fathers and husbands exercised their patriarchal duties of care, provision and discipline over their wives, children and servants.[22] The extent to which the members of these households might see themselves as neighbours to one another depended very largely on the pattern of settlement in each local community. In the countryside, settlements might be located somewhere on a spectrum between two extreme ideal-types: on the one hand, the small-scale, nucleated, face-to-face communities of lowland fielden England in which traditions of solidarity and mutuality were fostered both by geographical propinquity and by the presence of a resident landlord and clergyman; and, on the other, the larger, dispersed, back-to back communities of upland pastoral England where the spirit of independence might thrive beyond the shadow of the manor house or the rectory.[23] The quality of social relations, especially the extent to which the traditions of mutual obligation and charity might thrive, was also inflected by population size (neighbourliness was bound to be more resilient in smaller parishes) and especially by levels of in-migration (charity was said to begin, perhaps even to end, at home, and strangers might be regarded with suspicion, perhaps even hostility).[24] Population turnover was nonetheless a very significant structural characteristic of late sixteenth-century and early seventeenth-century local communities: Elizabethan and Stuart men and women did not invariably live out their lives in the parishes of their birth. The increasingly intensive economic pressures of price inflation and social polarization, principally driven by demographic growth, encouraged out-migration from lowland arable parishes, with most of those leaving these migrant-remitting communities heading for the migrant-accepting communities of the upland wood-pasture zones, the towns and, especially, the metropolis.[25] By the midseventeenth century, perhaps one in six of the population had some experience of living in the metropolis, though a significant proportion of them drifted back to the provinces.[26] Local communities therefore had shifting constituencies of inhabitants among whom the ideals of neighbourliness were fragmenting and its practices diminishing. This was especially true in the more anonymous communities of the towns and of London, especially in its suburbs, although the tendency of migrants to assimilate themselves to networks of kin who had migrated from the countryside before them ensured that sub-communities might form among the neighbours huddled together in the densely packed tenements on the streets of provincial towns and of the capital.[27]

Although, therefore, the traditions of mutual aid – especially the extension of credit in cash or kind, the practice of alms-giving to the known neighbourhood poor and the provision of post-mortem charity – were idealized in Jonson's England, they were increasingly undermined by a number of social pressures.[28] To population turnover and kin dispersal might also be added the role of Puritanism, which in its desire to reform the manners of the disorderly poor might result in campaigns to suppress those alcohol-fuelled *fora* of sociability (especially those alehouses and parish festivals such as wakes and church-ales with which Jonson's *A Tale of a Tub* was preoccupied) which had brought the local community together in an atmosphere of carnival and celebration.[29] It is very significant that the one parish festival to survive, and even to be encouraged in the aftermath of, the Reformation was the annual beating of the bounds, which perpetuated knowledge of parish boundaries among those sufficient male inhabitants and their children who were expected to perambulate each year.[30] A further pressure was created by the increasing determination of the gentry to spend less time on their estates and more in the city, where they could pursue their financial and legal interests in the law courts and participate in the fashionable cycle of social gatherings of the London season.[31] Absentee landlordism created its own cultural difficulties for those who sought to make their own way in the metropolis, and Jonson had a great deal of fun with provincial ingénues (such as Kastril and his sister Dame Pliant in *The Alchemist*) falling foul of city con-men, but it also had profound implications in the countryside, where traditional expectations of lordly paternalism and hospitality were ground under the wheels of gentry coaches bowling towards the capital.[32]

Whether or not local communities enjoyed the benefit of a resident landlord, they certainly did contain hierarchies of wealth and power that constrained the nature of local social relations. If there was a continuum of belonging to the local community, in which households of social equals were tied together through an ethos of charity and neighbourliness, there was also a hierarchy of belonging, in which the reciprocal expectations were less those of mutuality and affection than of deference and subordination.[33] This was true even in those numerous communities which were governed by chief inhabitants who lacked the natural authority implied by gentle status but who were nonetheless sufficiently confident in their self-image as men of discretion to insist that their social inferiors should know their place, in both geographical and social-structural terms.[34] Perhaps the most obvious expression of this hierarchy was the seating plan for the pews in the parish church – the better sort in the prominent pews closest to the pulpit; their poorer neighbours, tenants and servants, several rows behind, and the poor of the parish at the rear – in which the social and gendered parameters of belonging were inscribed.[35]

CONCLUSION: COMMUNITIES, MOBILITY AND BELONGING IN JONSON'S ENGLAND

Jonson's England was therefore a world in which the gentry were an increasingly homogenous social group, united by their experience of grammar school and university education, of participation in the national political culture of self-government at the King's command and of access to the fashionable world of metropolitan 'society'. To be sure, gentlemen were culturally amphibious, alternating their lifestyles (and doubtless their accents) between those thought most suitable for the country and for the city, but the ease with which they moved in different social worlds bespeaks their social confidence and political authority. Those of less elevated social status also participated in communities of different kinds (of work, of worship, of neighbourhood) but their freedom of manoeuvre was much more constrained both by law and by custom. The social order was at its most fluid in its middle ranks, where the fact that there were no patents for gentility created opportunities for social mobility.[36] After all, if gentility was in the eye of the beholder, and a gentleman was to be recognized not by his ancient lineage or his tenure of office but principally by his lifestyle, ample opportunities were created for a politics of disguise.[37] One of Jonson's finest achievements as an observer of social relations was to recognize the comedic potential of the threats and opportunities created by geographical and social mobility. England may have been a unitary sovereign state with a high degree of curial integration and political participation, but Jonson and his contemporaries were extremely sensitive to the minute gradations of status and honour in the local communities of which that polity was composed.

NOTES

1. G. R. Elton, *The Tudor Revolution in Government: Administrative Changes in the Reign of Henry VIII* (Cambridge: Cambridge University Press, 1953).
2. S. Hindle, 'County Government in England', in R. Tittler and N. L. Jones (eds.), *A Companion to Tudor Britain* (Oxford: Blackwell, 2004), pp. 98–115; S. G. Ellis, 'Defending English Ground: The Tudor Frontiers in History and Historiography', in S. G. Ellis and R. Esser (eds.), *Frontiers and the Writing of History, 1500–1850* (Hanover: Wehrhahn, 2006), pp. 73–93.
3. P. Collinson, '*De Republica Anglorum*: Or History with the Politics Put Back', in *Elizabethans* (London: Hambledon, 2003), pp. 1–30; M. Peltonen, *Classical Humanism and Republicanism in English Political Thought, 1570–1640* (Cambridge: Cambridge University Press, 1995); J. F. McDiarmaid (ed.), *The Monarchical Republic of Early Modern England: Essays in Response to Patrick Collinson* (Aldershot: Ashgate, 2007).

4. M. J. Braddick and J. Walter, 'Introduction: Grids of Power: Order, Hierarchy and Subordination in Early Modern Society', in M. J. Braddick and J. Walter (eds.), *Negotiating Power in Early Modern Society: Order, Hierarchy and Subordination in Britain and Ireland* (Cambridge: Cambridge University Press, 2001), pp. 1–42.
5. S. Hindle, *The State and Social Change in Early Modern England, c. 1550–1640* (Basingstoke: Palgrave Macmillan, 2000).
6. C. Holmes, 'The County Community in Stuart Historiography', *Journal of British Studies*, 19 (2) (1980): 54–73; Collinson, '*De Republica Anglorum*'; K. Wrightson, 'Mutualities and Obligations: Changing Social Relationships in Early Modern England', *Proceedings of the British Academy*, 139 (2006): 157–94.
7. J. E. Archer, E. Goldring and S. Knight (eds.), *The Progresses, Pageants, and Entertainments of Queen Elizabeth I* (Oxford: Oxford University Press, 2007); cf. J. Richards, '"His Nowe Majestie" and the English Monarchy: The Kingship of Charles I before 1640', *Past and Present*, 113 (1986): 70–96; P. Harrison and M. Brayshay, 'Post-horse Routes, Royal Progresses and Government Communications in the Reign of James I', *Journal of Transport History*, 18 (1997): 116–33.
8. M. Brayshay, P. Harrison and B. Chalkley, 'Knowledge, Nationhood and Governance: The Speed of the Royal Post in Early Modern England', *Journal of Historical Geography*, 24 (1998): 265–88.
9. P. Williams, 'Securing Compliance', in *The Tudor Regime* (Oxford: Oxford University Press, 1979), pp. 351–406.
10. A. Fletcher, 'Part I: The Context of Magistracy', in *Reform in the Provinces: The Government of Stuart England* (New Haven, Conn.: Yale University Press, 1986), pp. 3–83.
11. F. Heal and C. Holmes, 'Civility, Sociability and the Maintenance of Hegemony', in *The Gentry in England and Wales, 1500–1700* (Basingstoke: Macmillan, 1994), pp. 276–318. Cf. Jonson, 'To Penshurst'.
12. Holmes, 'County Community'.
13. P. Williams, 'Chains of Command', in *The Tudor Regime* (Oxford: Oxford University Press, 1979), pp. 407–20.
14. J. S. Cockburn, 'Assizes and Local Government', in *A History of English Assizes, 1558–1714* (Cambridge: Cambridge University Press, 1972), pp. 153–87; C. W. Brooks, 'Political Realities and Legal Discourse', *Law, Politics and Society in Early Modern England* (Cambridge: Cambridge University Press, 2009), pp. 51–92.
15. Hindle, 'County Government'.
16. P. Collinson, 'Magistracy and Ministry', *The Religion of Protestants: The Church in English Society, 1559–1625* (Oxford: Oxford University Press, 1979), Chapter 4; Jonson, *Bartholomew Fair*.
17. S. Hindle, 'The Governance of the Parish', in *The State and Social Change in Early Modern England, c. 1550–1640* (Basingstoke: Palgrave Macmillan, 2000), pp. 204–30.

18. S. Hindle, 'The Political Culture of the Middling Sort in English Rural Communities, c. 1550–1700', in T. Harris (ed.), *The Politics of the Excluded, c. 1500–1850* (Basingstoke: Palgrave Macmillan, 2001), pp. 125–52; and M. Goldie, 'The Unacknowledged Republic: Officeholding in Early Modern England', in T. Harris (ed.), *The Politics of the Excluded, c. 1500–1850* (Basingstoke: Palgrave Macmillan, 2001), pp. 153–94.
19. Hindle, 'The Governance of the Parish'.
20. J. R. Kent, 'Constables' Conduct: The Pressures of the Office', *The English Village Constable, 1580–1642: A Social and Administrative Study* (Oxford: Oxford University Press, 1986), pp. 222–81.
21. K. Wrightson, 'Two Concepts of Order: Justice, Constables and Jurymen in Seventeenth-Century England', in J. Brewer and J. Styles (eds.), *An Ungovernable People: The English and Their Law in the Seventeenth and Eighteenth Centuries* (London: Hutchinson, 1980), pp. 21–46.
22. Hindle, 'The Governance of the Parish'; S. D. Amussen, 'Political Households and Domestic Politics', in *An Ordered Society: Gender and Class in Early Modern England* (Oxford: Blackwell, 1988), pp. 34–66.
23. J. Thirsk, 'English Rural Communities: Structures, Regularities and Change in the Sixteenth and Seventeenth Centuries', in B. Short (ed.), *The English Rural Community: Image and Analysis* (Cambridge: Cambridge University Press, 1992), pp. 44–61.
24. S. Hindle, 'Exclusion Crises: Poverty, Migration and Parochial Responsibility in English Rural Communities, c. 1560–1660', *Rural History,* 7 (1996): 125–49; K. D. M. Snell, 'The Culture of Local Xenophobia', *Social History,* 28 (1) (2001): 1–30.
25. R. B. Outhwaite, 'Progress and Backwardness in English Agriculture, 1500–1650', *Economic History Review,* 2nd ser., 39 (1) (1986): 1–18.
26. E. A. Wrigley, 'A Simple Model of London's Importance', *People, Cities and Wealth: The Transformation of Traditional Society* (Oxford: Blackwell, 1987), pp. 133–56.
27. J. Boulton, 'Social Relations in the Urban Community', in *Neighbourhood and Society: A London Suburb in the Seventeenth Century* (Cambridge: Cambridge University Press, 1987), Chapter 9; P. Griffiths, 'Streets', in *Lost Londons: Change, Crime and Control in the Capital City, 1550–1660* (Cambridge: Cambridge University Press, 2008), pp. 98–134.
28. C. Muldrew, 'Part II: The Culture of Credit', in *The Economy of Obligation: The Culture of Credit and Social Relations in Early Modern England* (Basingstoke: Macmillan, 1998); S. Hindle, 'Shift', in *On the Parish? The Micro-Politics of Poor Relief in Rural England, c. 1550–1750* (Oxford: Oxford University Press, 2004), Chapter 1; Wrightson, 'Mutualities and Obligations'; K. Wrightson, 'The "Decline of Neighbourliness" Revisited', in N. L. Jones and D. Woolf (eds.), *Local Identities in Late Medieval and Early Modern England* (Basingstoke: Palgrave Macmillan, 2007), pp. 19–49.

29. W. Hunt, 'Part II: The Sword of God's Word', in *The Puritan Moment: The Coming of Revolution in an English County* (Cambridge, Mass.: Harvard University Press, 1983).
30. S. Hindle, 'Beating the Bounds of the Parish: Order, Memory, and Identity in the English Local Community, c. 1500–1700', in M. J. Halvorson and K. E. Spierling (eds.), *Defining Community in Early Modern Europe* (Ashgate: Aldershot, 2008), pp. 205–27.
31. F. Heal, 'The Crown, the Gentry and London: The Enforcement of Proclamation, 1596–1640', in C. Cross, D. Loades and J. J. Scarisbrick (eds.), *Law and Government Under the Tudors: Essays Presented to Sir Geoffrey Elton on His Retirement* (Cambridge: Cambridge University Press, 1988), pp. 211–27.
32. See e.g. Jonson, *The Alchemist*, 4-2-9.
33. K. Wrightson, 'The Politics of the Parish in Early Modern England', in P. Griffiths, A. Fox and S. Hindle (eds.), *The Experience of Authority in Early Modern England* (Basingstoke: Palgrave Macmillan, 1996), pp.10–46.
34. S. Hindle, 'Hierarchy and Community in the Elizabethan Parish: The Swallowfield Articles of 1596', *Historical Journal*, 42 (3) (1999): 835–51.
35. C. Marsh, 'Order and Place in England, 1580–1640: The View from the Pew', *Journal of British Studies*, 44 (2005): 3–26.
36. H. R. French, *The Middle Sort of People in Provincial England, 1600–1750* (Oxford: Oxford University Press, 2007).
37. F. Heal and C. Holmes, 'Introduction', in *The Gentry in England and Wales, 1500–1700* (Basingstoke: Macmillan, 1994), pp. 1–19.

CHAPTER 16

The court

Malcolm Smuts

At the beginning of the seventeenth century, the English royal household had no official position of court poet. Although Jonson became the leading author of masques and occasional verse for James VI and I and Queen Anna, we should not imagine him moving into an established niche. Instead, he drew upon a number of English and European precedents to define an essentially novel role for himself, as the preeminent literary spokesman for the King and court elite. His pretentions in this respect were always open to challenge and largely collapsed under Charles I. But for more than two decades Jonson exploited his association with the court to enhance his social standing, his literary reputation and the particular kinds of poetry he favoured. To understand how he did this we need to look first at the institutional arrangements and social conditions that Jonson encountered as he pursued court patronage, and second at the way he responded to the opportunities and challenges court employment offered.[1]

Theatrical entertainments and occasional verse had long been part of royal life, and kings since the Middle Ages had retained the services of poets and pageant-makers. But these writers had either been literary amateurs retained by the court in other capacities or men of fairly modest status, paid on an ad-hoc basis for services rendered, in much the way that the royal household paid artisans to manufacture luxury objects. Even the award of a pension, like the one of 100 marks Jonson received in 1616, did not alter this relationship, since the Crown also awarded pensions and designations like 'saddle maker to his Majesty' to individual tradesmen. From an institutional perspective, Jonson's position resembled that of any craftsman retained to contribute to the ceremonial apparatus surrounding the King. He had no formal supervisory powers over other poets or the teams of musicians, tailors, scene-painters and actors who collaborated to produce a masque. This authority belonged instead to the Master of the Revels, an official of the Chamber responsible for overseeing the logistics for court entertainments as well as for censoring plays on the public stage. Jonson received a second reversion to this office in 1619, meaning that he stood to receive it after the death of the present incumbent and his designated successor. Had he become Master of Revels Jonson might have consolidated his control over the whole production of court masques while also acquiring power over other playwrights, but he died before the reversion took effect.

This comparison of Jonson to a court tradesman is also somewhat misleading, however, since the development of a humanist court culture in the sixteenth century had given literature a prestige that artisanal activities completely lacked. Gentlemen and even noblemen wrote poems, while in Scotland King James himself published an anthology of verse and a discourse on Scottish poetry.[2] From about 1580 English courtiers had developed a special genre of love poems aimed at the Queen, while younger men hoping to enter court service wrote verse to advertise their talents.[3] At the same time, the expansion of the printing industry and the emergence of public theatres created opportunities for less privileged writers to live by their pens. The cumulative effect of these trends produced a court intensely interested in literary culture, confronting a greater variety of literary output and a much bigger pool of potential talent than had ever existed in the past.

But it was by no means clear, in the closing years of Elizabeth I's reign, where these changes were leading. Although interested in literature and drama, the Queen had not attempted to establish a uniform literary culture at her court or to replace the tournaments and masques inherited from her predecessor with more modern entertainments. In any case, her reign was drawing towards a close, and no one knew what changes a new dynasty might bring. The Queen's death in March 1603 presented ambitious poets with a fluid situation in which they might seek to capture the new court's attention. Like Samuel Daniel, Thomas Dekker and others, Jonson tried to position himself by writing a string of entertainments and panegyrics for the new royal family.[4] His aggressive attitude towards Dekker after they shared the work of writing pageants for the King's formal entry into London in March 1604 suggests how determined he felt to win this competition: refusing to collaborate on a printed text of the entry, he published his own pageants separately with notations in which he disparaged his rival's work.

Early in the new reign, Jonson improved his opportunities for winning court patronage considerably by moving into the household of Esmé Stuart, seigneur d'Aubigny, who was not only a gentleman of the Bedchamber, well positioned to help his friends and clients win royal patronage, but the King's cousin, the brother of the Duke of Lennox and the younger son and namesake of James's first great favourite, who had died in 1583.[5] The poet may also have benefited from his relationship with Lucy Countess of Bedford, who became a bedchamber servant and confidant of the Queen. In January 1605, *The Masque of Blackness* – Jonson's first commission from Queen Anna and first collaboration with Inigo Jones – seems to have established him as the favoured writer of court entertainments, a position he held until the late 1620s.

Many writers would have been content simply to receive the lion's share of royal patronage but Jonson evidently wanted more than this, since from the outset he used his writings for the court to advance claims for the dignity and moral value of his art that went beyond those of most other contemporary writers. To appreciate these claims we need to recognize that in the early seventeenth century the concept of literature had a broader meaning than it does today, embracing the totality of literary and intellectual culture and, more especially, knowledge of the Greek and Roman classics. Throughout much of Europe court culture had been progressively classicized during the sixteenth century, as medieval forms, like royal entries, were treated as Roman triumphs and embellished with triumphal arches and pageants steeped in classical mythology. This trend also led to a new genre of lavishly illustrated pageant books that implicitly instructed readers about the proper way to view such events, by concentrating on the learned underpinnings fashioned by humanist scholar-poets, rather than outward spectacle. Although aware of this trend, the English court did not follow it: the closest we come to a Continental-style Elizabethan pageant book is an illustrated volume commemorating the Earl of Leicester's progress through the Netherlands in 1585, produced by Dutch printers and engravers. The self-conscious revival of medieval forms characteristic of much late Elizabethan court culture and the underdeveloped state of English engraving inhibited the kind of synthesis of classicist erudition, modern visual culture and printed texts that had developed on the Continent.

But the classical tradition nevertheless enjoyed enormous prestige in England. Jonson had grown up in an artisan's household in a small alley very near the court before studying at the prestigious Westminster grammar school, under the pioneering scholar of Roman Britain, William Camden. Camden enjoyed some court patronage, while one of Jonson's friends at Westminster, the antiquarian Robert Bruce Cotton, also began to establish contacts with the court early in James's reign. It was while studying Latin under Camden that Jonson first came into contact, if not with court society in the proper sense, at least with an intellectual milieu that had meaningful court connections. He must have learned to appreciate, at an early age, that classical erudition might open doors by allowing him to establish bonds with people who outranked him considerably in social terms.

The entertainments that he and Jones devised for the early Jacobean court involved a considerable effort to update older Tudor formulas. The English masque had originated in the reign of Henry VIII, as an eruption of disguised male figures into a court dance, intended to frighten and disconcert the ladies present. The form had subsequently evolved, acquiring poetic scripts and dramatic elements, but remained less sophisticated than the French *ballets de cours* and Italian entertainments of the period. From the beginning, masques had overtones of disorder, further reinforced when they were incorporated into the court's Christmas revels, traditionally a celebration of chaos and misrule. The form developed by Jonson and Jones allowed disorderly elements to flourish in burlesque anti-masques, before containing them through an invocation of the presence of the main royal spectator, after which the anti-masquers disappeared and the main masque, celebrating the court's virtue, appeared. The Jacobean masque thus allowed plentiful opportunities for broad humour while ultimately celebrating the King's power to transform chaos into order and the beneficent characteristics of his reign. Jones introduced perspective stage scenery and mechanical devices allowing for spectacular scenic effects. The genre also served as a platform for the latest innovations in music and court dance. It provided plenty of spectacle and entertainment in the most basic sense, at the same time that it decorously praised the King and court and brought English entertainments somewhat closer to the European mainstream.[6]

We should see this achievement as the result of a true collaboration between men of similar background – Jones had also begun life as a London artisan – who shared a fascination with classical and humanist culture, an ambition to better themselves through association with the court and a determination to use Roman and modern European models to update native English forms.[7] Despite the famous quarrel that finally destroyed their partnership, Jones and Jonson were engaged in very similar projects and probably initially saw each other as kindred spirits. But it is also notable that even before *The Masque of Blackness* Jonson began to insist, in printed editions of his court entertainments, on the distinction between his erudite literary contribution and superficial outward spectacle.

After describing the first of his two pageants for the 1604 entry, Jonson commented that his 'device' had expressed 'The very site, fabric, strength, policy, dignity and affections of the city', as 'The sharp and learned' would understand; 'and for the multitude, no doubt but their grounded judgements gazed, said it was fine and were satisfied'.[8] In this text and the printed editions of masques he further emphasized the point by equipping his verse with marginal notes, similar to those found in humanist editions of classical texts, explaining the sources of his imagery and commenting on fine points of classical scholarship. This strategy of self-presentation offers an aggressive parallel to the festival books of the Continent, except that Jonson's printed texts differed from their European counterparts in lacking illustrations. Whereas in a typical Continental festival book 'devices' are presented through both verbal and visual media, making poetry, art and architecture complementary, in Jonson's texts artistic imagery needs to be conveyed through words, implying that it originated in a poet's mind and that the mental image, rather than its actualization in paint and carpentry, is what matters. We do not know whether Jonson wished from the outset to demote the significance of visual representations. But the absence of illustrations in all early printed editions of Stuart masques certainly helped in giving priority to texts over scenery, dance and costume, serving Jonson's desire to promote his own art over that of Jones and other collaborators.[9]

Jonson's use of classical and humanist culture in fashioning a new court literature ultimately extended beyond matters of self-presentation, however. Some of the classical forms most fashionable around the turn of the century – especially Tacitean history and Roman satire – lent themselves to acrid criticism of courts much more readily than to panegyric. This did not stop them becoming popular in court circles, in part because bitter factional conflicts and dissatisfaction with the rule of an ageing Queen had produced deep currents of disenchantment among some members of the ruling group, especially the associates of Robert Devereux, Earl of Essex.[10] Jonson always displayed ambivalence towards the court: if he praised it in his masques he also wrote bitter satires of individual courtiers, and his tragedy *Sejanus* (1603–4) ranks among the most disillusioned portrayals of a degenerate court society produced by any writer of the period. Twice – over *Sejanus* and *Eastward Ho!* (1605) – his work for the stage landed him in prison for insulting the King or for alleged sedition.

More clearly than any other writer of his generation Jonson recognized that Latin literature provided two nearly antithetical models of an imperial court and imperial rule, both applicable to seventeenth-century

England. One was the image of Augustus conveyed by several odes, panegyrics and passages of Virgil's *Aeneid:* a reforming Emperor who brought peace to a society torn by civil war, attempted to restore the moral values of old Roman society and distributed enlightened patronage that produced a flowering of literary and artistic brilliance. The other was the picture developed by historians like Tacitus and satirists like Juvenal: a society corroded by luxury, decadence and sycophancy, presided over by weak and vicious emperors surrounded by even more vicious spies, informers and flatterers. Jonson had responded to this negative image partly from the perspective of an English Catholic.[11] Many Catholics regarded themselves as victims of an Elizabethan tyranny that worked by convicting people of treason on flimsy evidence, collected and embroidered by government spies and their managers, and the dark histories of Tacitus reminded them of their predicament. Even before *Sejanus* Jonson alluded to such practices in the figure of Lupus in *Poetaster* (1601), a venal informer who enflames Augustus's wrath against Ovid and tries unsuccessfully to ruin Virgil through a tendentious interpretation of a drawing found in the poet's study. Tyranny, as Jonson here portrays it, derives less from the personal vice of a ruler than the manipulative talent of lesser men who succeed in exploiting the ruler's fears and jealousies. On one level this vision drew upon Jonson's fascination with irrational obsessions, gulls and confidence tricksters, displayed in comedies such as *Epicene* (staged 1609; printed 1616) and *Volpone* (staged 1605; printed 1607). But it also reflected the ways in which a Catholic minority applied histories of Roman tyranny to its own experience.

By drawing upon both positive and negative Roman models and holding them in tension with each other, Jonson fashioned a poetry in which panegyric and satire alternate and draw strength from each other, as opposing mirrors revealing both the corruption threatening to degrade Jacobean society and the moral virtues that provide a possible antidote. This is especially striking in the early 'Panegyre on the Happie Entrance of James, our Soveraigne, to his First High Session of Parliament' (1604), in which praise for the King's virtuous acts in purging vice and maintaining peace alternates with dark descriptions of vice and a scathing denunciation of the crimes of Henry VIII in perverting the law to serve his lust and rapacity. But the technique is equally apparent in some relatively late work, such as 'The Epistle Answering to One that Asked to be Sealed of the Tribe of Ben' (*c.* 1620; printed 1641), and in the alternation between poems of praise and satiric volleys encountered by a reader of Jonson's collected verse.

This corpus of work does not especially lend itself to interpretations of the period as one dominated by ideological struggle between absolutist and republican values, because Jonson does not approach politics as a choice between alternative institutional systems. He is fundamentally republican in the sense that he sees governance as ideally an exercise of human virtue in the service of the public good, and fundamentally royalist in so far as he tacitly accepts the idea that the best government is that of a wise and virtuous prince. But he typically sees politics more from an ethical than a constitutional perspective. He shows no confidence in the ability of good institutions to rescue a corrupt society: in the world of *Sejanus,* the ruler, his court, the Senate and the Roman populace seem equally depraved, making it difficult to imagine any kind of constitutional change that might cure Rome's debasement.[12] But Jonson's alternation of satire and panegyric tends to convey a sense that in Jacobean society the forces of corruption and virtue are sufficiently balanced that individual effort and choice will make a real difference. If the King and other members of the ruling group resist the flattery, venality and paranoia that surrounds them a reasonably free and peaceful society may result; if they succumb to these snares things will rapidly get worse. The calling of the court poet is to remind the elite of its responsibilities and the consequences of forgetting them.

It is pointless to criticize Jonson for failing to adopt a different attitude more in keeping with contemporary political values. But it can be illuminating to examine how the kind of poetry he developed represented an active choice over other possible alternatives. It was probably inevitable that Jacobean court literature would depart from the chivalric and Petrarchan models of the previous reign, but Jonson may have accentuated the shift away from the heroic and warlike themes that had flourished under Elizabeth and continued to attract favour in the court of Prince Henry. Although not always averse to war, Jonson seems to have felt little attraction for the militant chivalry of the Accession Day jousts and Spenserian epic, perhaps because he associated it with forms of Protestant bellicosity he disliked. Jonson's emphasis on Augustan themes corresponded to one facet of the image James VI and I had already defined for himself in works such as *Basilikon Doron* (1599). But the poet gave much less emphasis to James's concept of himself as a modern Solomon. Eschatological themes, which continued to figure in court sermons, are conspicuously absent from his work, and although Jonson occasionally quoted the Bible he made little effort to give his poetry a Protestant colouration, even after his return to the Church of England around 1610. Some critics have been too ready to read Jonson as a proponent of Jacobean ideology, as if such a thing already existed fully formed in 1603, needing only to be adopted and translated into rhyme and meter. This unduly minimizes both the variety of options available to a poet working for the court and his own agency in choosing among them.

NOTES

1. Previous treatments of Jonson's role as a court poet include David Riggs, *Ben Jonson: A Life* (Cambridge, Mass.: Harvard University Press, 1989), Chapter 6; Julie Sanders, 'Jonson, King and Court', in Patrick Cheney, Andrew Hadfield and Garrett A. Sullivan Jr. (eds.), *Early Modern English Poetry: A Critical Companion* (Oxford: Oxford University Press, 2007), pp. 253–63; and Leah Marcus, 'Jonson and the Court', in Richard Harp and Stanley Stewart (eds.), *The Cambridge Companion to Ben Jonson* (Cambridge: Cambridge University Press, 2000), pp. 30–42.
2. James VI, *Ane Schort Treatise conteining some Reulis and Cautelis to be observit and eschewit in Scottis Poesie* (Edinburgh, 1584); *The Essayes of a Prentise, in the Divine Art of Poesie* (Edinburgh, 1584); *His Majesties Poeticall Exercises at Vacant Houres* (Edinburgh, 1591).
3. Steven May, *Elizabethan Courtier Poets* (Columbia, Miss.: Pegasus Press, 1991). The aspiring courtier poets of the 1590s included John Donne, as well as others with whom Jonson exchanged verse, such as Sir Thomas Roe and Sir Henry Wotton.
4. These are briefly listed in *The Oxford Dictionary of National Biography* article by Ian Donaldson: an entertainment for Queen Anna and Prince Henry at Althorp in the summer of 1603; a number of epigrams celebrating the King's policies and his poetry; three pageants during James's formal entry into London in March of 1604; the 'Panegyre' on James's opening of his first Parliament and another entertainment of the King at Highgate the following May. There may have been additional entertainments or speeches that have since vanished.
5. Riggs, *Ben Jonson*, p. 115, who misses, however, the full significance of d'Aubigny's connections at court. We know little about d'Aubigny's relationship with Jonson but the Scottish courtier would have been just the sort of patron the poet needed to establish a direct connection to the King and royal family. The pivotal importance of Scottish Bedchamber servants in the distribution of James I's patronage is documented by Neil Cuddy, 'The Revival of the Entourage: The Bedchamber of James I, 1603–1625', in David Starkey, D. A. L. Morgan, John Murphy, Pam Wright, Neil Cuddy and Kevin Sharpe (eds.), *The English Court from the Wars of the Roses to the Civil War* (London: Longmans, 1987), pp. 173–225. D'Aubigny was among the leading recipients of James's bounty, garnering over £18,000. As Riggs and Marcus both suggest, Jonson's relationship with the Countess of Bedford, a Lady of the Bedchamber to Queen Anna, must also have helped in winning her patronage (Marcus, 'Jonson and the Court', 34; Riggs, *Ben Jonson*, p. 118).

6. For two recent discussions of the evolution of the masque form, with citations to specialized studies, see Suzanne Westfall, 'Performances in the Great Households', in Arthur Kinney (ed.), *A Companion to Renaissance Drama* (Oxford: Oxford University Press, 2002), pp. 266–80, esp. pp. 272–80; and R. Malcolm Smuts, 'Progresses and Court Entertainments', in Arthur Kinney (ed.), *A Companion to Renaissance Drama* (Oxford: Oxford University Press, 2002), pp. 281–93, esp. pp. 282–5. The classic study of Jonson's reworking of the form is Stephen Orgel, *The Jonsonian Masque* (Cambridge, Mass.: Harvard University Press, 1965). John C. Meagher, *Method and Meaning in Jonson's Masques* (Notre Dame, Ind.: University of Notre Dame Press, 1966) usefully complements this by giving more attention than Orgel to scenery, music, lighting and dance. For more recent work see the essays collected in David Bevington and Peter Holbrook (eds.), *The Politics of the Stuart Court Masque* (Cambridge: Cambridge University Press, 1998). The most recent comprehensive study is Martin Butler, *The Stuart Court Masque and Political Culture* (Cambridge University Press, 2009).
7. The scholarly and bookish nature of Jones's approach to architecture, which invites comparison to Jonson's close readings of classical poetry, is effectively brought out in Christy Anderson, *Inigo Jones and the Classical Tradition* (Cambridge: Cambridge University Press, 2007).
8. Malcolm Smuts (ed.), 'The Kinges Entertainment through the Citie of London', in Gary Taylor and John Lavagnino (eds.), *Thomas Middleton: The Collected Works* (Oxford: Oxford University Press 2007), pp. 219–79; pp. 240–1.
9. The difference between masque performances and masque texts is usefully discussed in Jerzy Limon, *The Masque of Stuart Culture* (Newark, Del.: University of Delaware Press and London: Associated University Presses, 1990), Part 1. For the roles of music and dance, see Barbara Ravelhofer, *The Early Stuart Masque: Dance, Costume and Music* (Oxford: Oxford University Press, 2006).
10. The way in which sympathy for Essex may have influenced Jonson's early satiric treatment of the court is ably discussed by Tom Cain, '"Satyres, That Girde and Fart at the Time": *Poetaster* and the Essex Rebellion', in Julie Sanders with Kate Chedgzoy and Susan Wiseman (eds.), *Refashioning Ben Jonson: Gender, Politics and the Jonsonian Canon* (Basingstoke: Macmillan, 1998), pp. 48–70.
11. For an elaboration of this point, see Peter Lake, 'From *Leicester His Commonwealth* to *Sejanus His Fall*: Ben Jonson and the Politics of Roman (Catholic) Virtue', in Ethan Shagan (ed.), *Catholics and the Protestant Nation: Religious Politics and Identity in Early Modern England* (Manchester: Manchester University Press, 2005), pp. 128–61.
12. Cf. Robert Evans, '*Sejanus*: Ethics and Politics in the Early Reign of James', in Julie Sanders with Kate Chedgzoy and Susan Wiseman (eds.), *Refashioning Ben Jonson: Gender, Politics and the Jonsonian Canon* (Basingstoke: Macmillan, 1998), pp. 71–92; esp. pp. 84–5.

CHAPTER 17

Masques, courtly and provincial

Karen Britland

In John Marston's play *The Insatiate Countess,* two young women discuss their husbands' participation in a masque for a noble marriage. Clearly perturbed by her spouse's ancestry – his rival, Rogero, calls him the son of a mountebank – Abigal remarks that she is 'glad there's Noble-men i'the Masque / With our Husbands[,] to ouer-rule them', continuing:

I saw a show once at the marriage of a *Magnificero's* daughter, presented by Time: which Time was an olde bald thing; a seruant, 'twas the best man; hee was a Dyer, and came in likenesse of the Raine-bow in all manner of colours, to shew his Art, but the Raine-bow smelt of vrine, so wee were all afraid the property was chang'd, and look'd for a shower. (1613, sig. C1r)

Abigal's comments reveal a set of social anxieties and economic relationships that foreground the masque form as a point of intersection between various elements of a community. In Abigal's tale, a masque to celebrate a high-status marriage is co-opted by its low-status performers to display their skills and goods. Any metaphysical pretensions contained in the masque are undermined by its participants' bodies: 'Time' and 'Justice' are not transcendent personifications, but are held down to earth, and up to ridicule, by the materiality of their actors' occupations. In other words, Abigal's humorous condescension foregrounds the physical realities of the dyer and his art and makes it clear that both he, and his cloth, smell of the urine that is an essential ingredient of his trade. By contrast, noble masquing, she implies, is more endowed with decorum and taste. This masquing moment at once brings to the fore the economic underpinnings of masque (buttressed by the efforts of cloth-workers, embroiderers, seamstresses, vizard-makers and the like) at the same time as Abigal is shown to believe that masques performed by noblemen somehow manage to transcend the labour that gives rise to their costumes and effects. For Abigal, then, masquing by noblemen is a noble enterprise that will socially elevate her husband, but when citizens copy it, it becomes a debased and comic form.

What this passage opens up is the many-faceted face of masquing, which comprised not only the large and elaborate royal masques performed in the Banqueting House at Whitehall but also smaller, more intimate noble shows such as running masques, country dances and country-house entertainments, as well as grander pageants sponsored and performed by the London guilds and civic authorities. Early masque criticism, focusing on the royal entertainments, saw courtly performances as expressions of the will of the monarch that shadowed his political and iconographical agenda.[1] More recent writings, again focusing on royal masques, tend to read them as negotiations between various courtly factions.[2] Only very recently, in essays such as James Knowles's brilliant investigation into the miners' protests that formed the backdrop to *Love's Welcome at Bolsover* (the Earl of Newcastle's 1634 entertainment for Charles I) have specific economic and class realities behind masquing begun to be investigated.[3] Here I want to consider masques, both courtly and provincial, as phenomena that necessarily involved cross-class collaboration, plotting their development during the Stuart period, at the same time as investigating Ben Jonson's contribution to the genre.

Stuart court masques grew out of and were informed by several types of entertainment, not least the elaborate festivals sponsored by the Médicis in Florence and the entertainments performed at the universities of Oxford and Cambridge, the Inns of Court and the grammar schools. Most significantly, during the early years of James I's reign, they were influenced by summer progress entertainments provided for Queen Elizabeth. These entertainments helped to promulgate Elizabeth's personal iconography, drawing, for example, on Edmund Spenser's figurations of her as the Fairy Queen: the Elvetham entertainment of 1591 saw the Fairy Queen dancing with her attendant ladies, while, as Knowles notes, a 1578 entertainment at Hengrave Hall (home of the Kytson family) saw the Fairy Queen present Elizabeth with a gift.[4] By the end of Elizabeth's reign, performances were being conceived that prefigured the structure of the Jacobean masque: as Peter Davidson and Jane Stevenson have noted, a 1592 wedding entertainment staged for her daughter by Elizabeth, Lady Russell, involved elaborate costumes, a rudimentary plot about eight muses seeking a lost sister and dances performed by young noblewomen.[5] Not only does this establish a precedent for the kind of masquing favoured by Queen Anna of Denmark, it also emphasizes the significance of entertainments sponsored by non-royal families in the development of the masque genre.

With the possible exception of critical work on John Milton's 1634 *Masque at Ludlow*, the connections between courtly, provincial and civic entertainments have been insufficiently researched. That said, new work is emerging that explores the connections between royal and noble masquing and between the city and the provinces.[6] Most interestingly, Matthew Steggle has shown that an eclogue performed as part of the City of London's 1606 celebrations for the visit of King Christian VI of Denmark was reproduced in John Marston's 1607 *Entertainment at Ashby* for Alice, Dowager Countess of Derby, and concludes that, although Marston is usually remembered as a 'snarling satirist', his last known works 'constitute a link both to the country-based patronage network of the Huntington family, and also to that most public and community-conscious of forms, the City of London civil entertainment'.[7] Royal and noble masques, I suggest, need to be considered both within the context of civic and provincial shows, as well as alongside the economic and social circumstances of those who helped to fashion them.

Ben Jonson's first Jacobean entertainment was presented to Queen Anna and Prince Henry in 1603 at Althorp, Sir Robert Spencer's house in Northamptonshire, as they made their way from Scotland to London to join England's new king. They were received with an Elizabethan-like show in a manner that, like Samuel Daniel's 1604 *Vision of the Twelve Goddesses* (the first Jacobean royal masque), emphasized continuity with the previous reign. However, where Daniel's entertainment would align Anna with martial virginity, this production, as Knowles notes, revised the former queen's Diana imagery into that of Anna Oriens, whose princely son 'is the greatest felicitie of Kingdoms' (sig. A4r). Knowles also astutely notes that James recognized the importance of his wife's journey to London 'in "anchoring" his regime', commenting that, by the time Anna reached the Midlands, her entourage had been allowed to swell to over 200 people.[8]

Jonson's text reflects this superfluity of people when it recognizes that Spencer's house was overwhelmed by 'The throng of the Countrey' (sig. B2v). While some of this throng were undoubtedly lords and ladies hoping to attach themselves to Anna's court, it is also likely that some were locals. Not enough work has yet been done on the social composition of masque audiences, and even less has been undertaken on the kind of people who would expect to witness a provincial or progress entertainment. What is certain, however, is that the Althorp entertainment took place in a difficult local moment and provides an example of the strategies of social inclusion and exclusion that would underpin the festive ideology of the Jacobean reign. In the late 1590s and early 1600s, the rural, working people in the county of Northamptonshire were in distress because of rising grain prices and the trouble caused by ambitious, enclosing landlords. Indeed, in the 1604 Parliament, they would, through their spokesman, Sir Edward

Montagu, present a grievance about the 'depopulation and daily excessive conversion of tillage into pasture' in their county.[9] At Haselbech, 10 miles from Althorp, Sir Thomas Tresham had turned nearly 1,000 acres of arable land into grazing for sheep, causing about sixty people to lose their livelihoods, reducing the area upon which grain could be grown and thus exacerbating the problem with rising prices.[10] Jonson, who, Knowles suggests, was likely to have been at Althorp for the entertainment, cannot have failed to be aware of these social problems, which, I argue, manifest themselves obliquely in his text.

Jonson's 'Morris of the Clowns' (disingenuously presented as something that was 'sodainly thought on') was introduced by a speech by 'Nobody', clad in a complicated 'pair of breeches which were made to come up to his neck, with his arms out at his pockets, and a cap drowning his face' (sig. B2v) in a manner that participated in a tradition of festive grotesque that finds humour in the distorted bodies of working men and women.[11] As such, he might be considered to participate in the politics of festive mirth, investigated by Leah Marcus as the Stuart regime's policy for creating social cohesion.[12] Nobody is respectful to his noble audience and excuses the rusticity of his fellows' performances as a result of their lack of ambition and honest desire to please. However, in the context of local discontents over land management, the introductory speech itself is fascinating for the insistent prevalence of images of property. 'There's none of these doth hope to come by / Wealth, to build another Holmby' (1616 folio *Works*, p. 877) says Nobody, referring, as Knowles suggests, to the nearby Holdenby House and the supposed rise to prominence of Sir Christopher Hatton, its owner, through dancing. Knowles argues that the speech 'presents a critique of Elizabeth by suggesting that the new Jacobean court will involve more "solid learnings" than the ability to dance'.[13] This seems plausible, and I would add that it also makes a promise that no huge estates will be the reward for Spencer's entertainment. 'Property' becomes more a metaphysical attribute than a physical one as Nobody maintains:

> I not deny where graces meet
> In a man, that quality
> Is a graceful property.
> (1616 folio *Works*, p. 877)

Combined with the exhortation, 'Come on, clowns, forsake your dumps' (1616 folio *Works*, p. 877) it seems to me that Nobody's speech, like Jonson's poem, 'To Penshurst', promises a nostalgic return to rural community in the face of obvious hardship and aristocratic selfishness.

This impression is strengthened if one considers the literary precedents for the figure of Nobody. Jonson's character and its costume seems to be directly inspired by the stage Nobody from the commercial London play, *Nobody and Somebody*.[14] Nobody begins the play as a countryside benefactor who is slandered by the devices of Somebody. The play concludes, however, with Somebody revealed as a swindler at the same time as Nobody's pockets are found to contain 'liedge bonds forfeit[ed] by poore men, / Which he releast out of the vsurers hands', and 'Leases likewise forfeited, / By him repurchast' (sig. I2r). The play's social criticism is biting, emphasizing a lack of charity and community feeling which sees Nobody/nobody helping the poor and dispossessed. Jonson's entertainment contains resonances of this, at the same time as it gestures towards a hopefulness about the new regime in a manner that is reinforced by its closing encomium to Prince Henry. Presented, significantly, by a group of younger sons (a financially vulnerable section of society), this encomium constructs Henry as a warrior prince who will lead the nation's youth 'ouer the strict Ocean' where their swords 'Shall speake [their] action better then [their] words' (sig. B4r). Just as in Jonson's later masques for Henry, the prince is figured here as a nascent national hero whose actions will unite the country and solve social ills by rewarding virtue and eliminating envy and flattery.

What is most revealing about the Althorp entertainment, though, is that – as the retrospectively printed text indicates – it was irreparably marred by the 'Multitudinous presse' of people who had come to see the Queen. Whatever message the fictional Nobody and his fellows had to offer was disrupted by a crowd of the very people these characters claimed to represent. Rather than being deferentially circumscribed by the proprieties of the entertainment, the local gentry and countryfolk came to pay their own respects and, perhaps, to make their own voices heard. In doing so, they upset the carefully choreographed visit that had absorbed so much of their labour before the royal arrival, substituting in its place a more unformed and potentially dangerous sort of spectacle. Four years later, Haselbech would become one of the sparking points of the Midland Riots when social discontent boiled over into violent protest. Jonson's printed text holds these energies in suspension, painting a sympathetic portrait of rural values that nevertheless pokes fun at the rustic, labouring body and that clearly resonates with the author's irritation that his spectacles were marred by the audience's lack of attention. Rendering the working body a figure of innocent mirth, it cannot contain the dangerous potential of a crowd that threatens social disorder.

If the entertainment at Althorp participated in a tradition of Elizabethan country-house entertainments, then Jonson's next two public productions saw him working alongside the civic authorities when he was employed to contribute to the pageants that celebrated James I's 1604 entry into London and was then paid by the Haberdasher's Company to compose their contribution to the 1604 Lord Mayor's show. It was not until 1605, after Daniel had written the inaugural court masque of the Stuart reign, that Jonson got his first royal commission, perhaps, as Helen Ostovich suggests in this volume, because of the intervention of Lucy, Countess of Bedford. His *Masque of Blackness* infamously caused a stir because Anna and her ladies appeared as blackamoors and gave rise to Dudley Carleton's oft-cited comment that their costumes were 'too light and curtisan-like'.[15] The *Masque f Blackness* was also the first occasion upon which the Queen danced on a raised stage with moveable scenery designed by the court surveyor and architect, Inigo Jones. This spectacular presentation was succeeded by a companion masque, *The Masque of Beauty* (1608), which renovated and washed clean the improprieties of the former and which, although it was again expensively staged, was structured in a way similar to Continental entertainments, with a rudimentary plot fleshed out by elaborate costumes, dances and songs plus a stage populated by abstract virtues and mythological figures. With the 1609 *Masque of Queens,* however, there came an apparent innovation, and one that Jonson carefully, but somewhat ambivalently, attributed to the will of his patron.

In the preface to the printed text of the masque, he notes:

And because her majesty (best knowing that a principal part of life, in these spectacles lay in their variety) had commanded me to think on some dance or show that might praecede hers and have the place of a foil or false masque, I was careful to decline, not only from others', but mine own steps in that kind, since that last year I had an antimasque of boys [in the masque at my L(ord) Hadding(ton's) wedding.]: and therefore now devized that twelve women, in the habit of hags [...] should fill that part. (ll. 8–17)[16]

At once insisting that he elaborated on the anti-masque form because of a royal command, Jonson nevertheless manages to intimate that the queen's desires were sparked by his own practices in the entertainment for Lord Haddington's wedding. What also happens here is an attempt to separate off the disruptive elements of the masque which then appear to be superceded and reformed by the presence of the virtuous queen and her companions.

The development of the anti-masque introduced a bi-partite structure into the court masque that operated along class lines. Professional actors and court servants took on histrionic personae in the anti-masque, while expensively clad courtiers danced silently as incarnations of their essential selves in the main masque. In other words, the comic debasement of the bodies of working people became encoded in the masque form itself, with the humorous or disruptive anti-masque preceding the serious, reformative, moral message of the main masque. Indeed, Laurie Ellinghausen notes that, although labouring characters appeared in masques by other writers, Jonson 'aligns the working orders specifically with *theatrical* labor and machinery' in a manner that 'erects barriers between Jonson and [his collaborator Inigo] Jones's respective kinds of creation'.[17] Just as Marston's depiction of masquing in *The Insatiate Countess* saw labourers' performances contaminated by the physicality of their trades, so Jonson aligns the architect Jones's craft with the physical nature of the anti-masque, reconfiguring poetry and intellectual aspiration as the entertainment's more lasting and transcendent soul.

Jonson's creative practices gave the masque the innovative double form that established it as a specifically English phenomenon. However, in the Caroline period, the lure of a histrionic role became too great, and some courtiers, notably the Duke of Buckingham, began to appear in the anti-masques. At the same time, Jonson's star at court was waning, in part because of his continuing feud with Jones who, he asserted, desired to be 'The music-master, fabler, too; / He is, or would be, main Dominius Do- / All in the work!'[18] Jonson's last masque commissions, while written and performed for Charles I, were commanded not by the monarch but by William Cavendish, Earl of Newcastle, and were performed on Newcastle's estates at Welbeck and Bolsover. In many ways, his masque career had come full circle, concluding, as it had begun, with a country-house entertainment. Moreover, the social discords that had been prevalent during the production of *Althorp* in 1603 were equally present in 1634.

The Bolsover entertainment which, like *Althorp*, adapted the form of the Elizabethan progress entertainment, took place in a countryside to which the trained bands had been summoned. As Knowles explains, about 300 miners had mounted a petition against Sir Robert Heath (who was attempting to gain mining rights in the area) and were trying to present it to Charles I. In contradistinction to this riotous mass, Knowles suggests that the artisans created by Jonson in *Bolsover* belong 'to a more innocent version of labour', located 'within Caroline conceptions of order', their work 'regulated by proper holidays celebrated with "statute-tunes and dances"'.[19] Here, as in *Althorp*, we are presented with a safe version of labourers whose 'craftsmanship sits well with Caroline cultural programmes'.[20] Nevertheless, without the more problematic labour of the discontented miners, or *Althorp*'s agricultural workers, or the women who sewed cloth and weeded Sir Robert Spencer's garden, the masques and entertainments of the Stuart period could not have taken place. Abigal and her companions in *The Insatiate Countess* might sneer at dyers and servants, constructing an idea of noble taste built on the denigration of their activities, yet the economic and social forces underlying such entertainments are fascinating, revealing ideological cracks and tensions that, themselves, contributed to the development of the Jonsonian masque form.

NOTES

1. See, for example, Stephen Orgel and Roy Strong, *Inigo Jones: The Theater of the Stuart Court*, 2 vols. (Berkeley, Calif.: University of California Press, 1973) and Graham Parry, *The Golden Age Restor'd* (Manchester: Manchester University Press, 1981).
2. See Kevin Sharpe, *Criticism and Compliment* (Cambridge: Cambridge University Press, 1987) and Martin Butler, 'Courtly Negotiations', in David Bevington and Peter Holbrook (eds.), *The Politics of the Stuart Court Masque* (Cambridge: Cambridge University Press, 1998), pp. 20–40.
3. James Knowles, 'Jonson and the Miners' Strike', unpublished paper presented at Keele University's Early Modern History Seminar, 2005.
4. James Knowles, 'Headnote' to *The Entertainment at Althorp*, in The Cambridge Edition of the Works of Ben Jonson (Cambridge: Cambridge University Press, forthcoming).
5. Peter Davidson and Jane Stevenson, 'Elizabeth I's Reception at Bisham', in Jayne Elisabeth Archer, Elizabeth Goldring and Sarah Knight (eds.), *The Progresses, Pageants, and Entertainments of Queen Elizabeth I* (Oxford: Oxford University Press, 2007), pp. 207–26; p. 222.
6. See, for example, Lauren Shohet, *Reading Masques: The English Masque and Public Culture in the Seventeenth Century* (Oxford: Oxford University Press, forthcoming).
7. Matthew Steggle, 'John Marston's *Entertainment at Ashby* and the 1606 Fleet Conduit Eclogue', *Medieval and Renaissance Drama in England*, 19 (2006): 249–55.
8. Knowles, 'Headnote'.
9. HMC, *MSS of Lord Montagu of Beaulieu*, p. 42.
10. Felicity Heal and Clive Holmes, *The Gentry in England and Wales, 1500–1700* (Stanford, Calif.: Stanford University Press, 1994), p. 109.
11. The references to the Althorp entertainment are to the edition that appeared in Jonson's 1616 folio *Works*, p. 877. Spellings have been modernized.
12. Leah Marcus, *The Politics of Mirth* (Chicago, Ill.: University of Chicago Press, 1986).
13. Knowles, 'Headnote'.

14. For plausible dating of this play to 1602, see Roger Bourke, 'Falstaff, Nobody, and Will Kemp's "Giant Hose"', *Notes and Queries*, 55 (2) (June) (2008): 183–5.
15. State Papers, 14/12/6.
16. All masque citations refer to line numbering in Stephen Orgel (ed.), *Ben Jonson: The Complete Masques* (New Haven, Conn.: Yale University Press, 1969).
17. Laurie Ellinghausen, *Labor and Writing in Early Modern England, 1567–1667* (Ashgate: Aldershot, 2008), pp. 68–9.
18. 'An Expostulation with Inigo Jones', ll. 63–5.
19. Knowles, 'Jonson and the Miners' Strike'.
20. Knowles, 'Jonson and the Miners' Strike'.

CHAPTER 18

Music

David Lindley

In the course of his career as a writer Jonson was involved with music and musicians at many points: in the theatre; at court in his provision of scripts for masques; and as a poet whose lyrics were set at the time by composers such as Alfonso Ferrabosco and William Lawes and have subsequently attracted many others, including the anonymous musician who provided probably the most famous setting of any Jonson lyric, 'Drink to Me Only', in the eighteenth century.

Undoubtedly, however, the most significant involvement in terms of musical history was his work as the principal provider of masque libretti for some twenty-five years from 1605. These entertainments called upon the full range of the resources of the royal musical establishment, 'The largest and most proficient group of professional musicians in England' at the time.[1] Some idea of the scale and scope of that musical resource is indicated in the first stage direction of Thomas Campion's *Lord Hay's Masque* (1607):

right before [the screen] was made a partition for the dancing place, on the right hand whereof were consorted ten musicians with bass and mean lutes, a bandora, a double sackbut, and an harpsichord, with two treble violins. On the other side, somewhat nearer the screen, were placed nine violins and three lutes; and, to answer both the consorts (as it were in a triangle) six cornetts and six Chapel voices were seated almost right against them, in a place raised higher in respect of the piercing sound of those instruments.[2]

Throughout his masque Campion informs us of the physical arrangement of musicians in the performance space, gives details of instrumentation, specifies the movement of singers and their accompanists and suggests something of the style of music being employed. This account is frequently cited, not least because there is simply no other printed Jacobean masque that even comes close to providing such a clear picture of the musical arrangements which formed so significant a part of the evening's entertainment and, like the costume, scenery and dance, contributed to the genre's declaration of courtly magnificence.

By contrast, Jonson offers much less detail. We do get occasional information about instrumental resources in the earlier masques: the 'rare and full music of twelve lutes' which accompanied the dancers in *Hymenaei*,[3] or the ensembles of cornetts and violins that performed successive dances in *The Masque of Queens*,[4] for example, together with the often strange percussive instruments that accompanied the entrance of anti-masque figures from the witches in *Queens* onwards. But in the later masques even these sparse indications disappear. This is partly consequent on the fact that Jonson largely abandoned the considerable effort involved in the retrospective revision of his performance scripts in order to incorporate details of staging and performance. But it also indicates that in the process by which masques were put together Jonson may not necessarily have even been aware of how the music and songs his scripts called for would actually be realized in the performance. Once the initial 'invention' of the device, its central story, was decided, and a libretto constructed, responsibility for each aspect of the masque would probably have been parcelled out, to the scene designer (usually Inigo Jones), the composer(s) and choreographer(s), and it is by no means clear how much continued conversation there then was between these various parties. Indeed, one of Jonson's criticisms of Inigo Jones, in his 'Expostulation', that he planted 'the music where no ear can reach' ('An Expostulation with Inigo Jones', l. 53), suggests that cooperation was not necessarily close at all.

A strong sense of Jonson's own priorities emerges in his description of the main masque in *The Haddington Masque*.

Here the musicians, attired in yellow, with wreaths of marjoram and veils like Hymen's priests, sung the first staff of the following epithalamion; which, because it was sung in pieces between the dances, showed to be so many several songs, but was made to be read an entire poem. After the song they came forth, descending in an oblique motion from the zodiac, and danced their first dance. Then, music interposed (but varied with voices, only keeping the same chorus) they danced their second dance. So after, their third and fourth dances, which were all full of elegancy and curious device. The two latter were made by Master Thomas Giles, the two first by Master Jerome Herne, who, in the persons of the two Cyclops, beat a time to them with their hammers. The tunes were Master Alfonso Ferrabosco's. The device and act of the scene, Master Inigo Jones his, with addition of the trophies. For the invention of the whole and the verses, Assertor qui dicat esse meos, Imponet plagiario pudorem.[5]

For all that he tells us that the beating of hammers functioned as a seventeenth-century drum kit for dancing, Jonson's priority is clearly the preservation of the integrity of his literary imitation of a classical epithalamium. The hammers, indeed, are specified because they are appropriate instruments for the servants of Vulcan, and it is usually when there is a specific iconological interest that Jonson does offer more detail than usual. In *The Irish Masque,* for example, there is an obvious political symbolism at work in choosing bagpipes for the anti-masque dance and the music of two harps for the main masque. (Though Jonson was also seizing on the practical opportunity offered by the fact that Cormac MacDermott was, in 1605, the first harper to be employed at the English court since 1555.[6]) What, however, comes through overwhelmingly in the surviving texts of these early masques is Jonson's obsessive protection and celebration of his own intellectual-property rights, with scant attention to that which he did not control.

Jonson can, however, be generous in acknowledging the contributions of others, as he is in the quarto of *Hymenaei*:

> *The design and act of all which, together with the device of their habits, belongs properly to the merit and reputation of Master Inigo Jones; whom I take modest occasion in this fit place to remember, lest his own worth might accuse me of an ignorant neglect from my silence.*
>
> *And here, that no man's deservings complain of injustice – though I should have done it timelier, I acknowledge – I do for honour's sake, and the pledge of our friendship, name Master Alfonso Ferrabosco, a man planted by himself in that divine sphere, and mastering all the spirits of music; to whose judicial care, and as absolute performance, were committed all those difficulties both of song and otherwise; wherein, what his merit made to the soul of our invention would ask to be expressed in tunes no less ravishing than his . . .*
>
> *The dances were both made and taught by Master Thomas Giles; and cannot be more approved than they did themselves. Nor do I want the will, but the skill to commend such subtleties; of which the sphere wherein they were acted is best able to judge.*[7]

This is a very revealing passage. Not only does Jonson confess his ignorance of the technicalities of dance but in the very different tones of the commendation of Jones and Ferrabosco one might see both the early signs of the tension that was later to erupt in open warfare between poet and designer and also the way in which, for Jonson, music contributes directly to the 'soul' of his work, whereas design is specifically allocated to its merely external 'body'. In his theory, then, Jonson sets a high premium on music, even if he does not choose to descend to specifics about the practicalities of its performance.

Ferrabosco provided several songs for earlier Jonson masques and then disappears until a brief return in 1622. The reason for his absence is not known. To modern ears Ferrabosco's songs are much less appealing than, for example, the music of his older contemporary, John Dowland.

He published only one book of airs, in 1609 (to which Jonson contributed a rather conventional laudatory poem), and much of his work is lost. Whether directly influenced by Italian practice or not, many of his songs project the words in a style that is called 'declamatory'. The result is often music of a rather angular character, but one which both suited the need to make the words heard by the audience, and also was likely to appeal to Jonson himself. The theories promulgated contemporaneously in the writings of Monteverdi and other Italian theorists and followed in Ferrabosco's practice, that the words should be mistress of the harmony, would have accorded absolutely with Jonson's own sense of priorities.

This was music that looked towards the future, and later in his career Jonson may have contributed to the further movement of the masque towards a kind of operatic performance. According to the 1640 folio, in *The Vision of Delight* Delight '(*Spake in song*, stylo recitativo)'[8] and in *Lovers Made Men* 'The *whole masque was sung after the Italian manner* (stylo recitativo) *by Master Nicholas Lanier.*'[9] Both these entertainments date from 1617. The second of them was also published in quarto in that year, but in this earlier version there is no mention of recitative. This absence, which might suggest that the references to recitative are later additions, has led to controversy about the nature of the music for these masques,[10] but whatever precisely is meant, it is clear that in the masque – and perhaps partly because of the demands it made for clarity of diction and verbal projection – musical experiment went alongside the development of scenic techniques as an essential part of the genre's assertion of stylistic sophistication.

Within the structure of the masque, the assertion of practical as well as symbolic harmony in the main masque is often explicitly in contrast to the strangeness of the music that might accompany the anti-masque. Yet the masque itself often finds it necessary to police the potentially dangerous association of dance and music with licence and lechery. In *Pleasure Reconciled to Virtue,* for example, the masquers are sent to take out the ladies to dance, but are reminded that 'what is noble should be sweet, / But not dissolved in wantonness'.[11]

It is music's troubling doubleness, as both an image of the divine and also the siren song of debauchery that playwrights in the period negotiated, and in almost all of Jonson's theatrical uses of music and song he chooses to render problematic any straightforward response to the harmony one hears. His most extended use of song is found in the two plays written for the Children of the Chapel at Blackfriars, *Cynthia's Revels* and *Poetaster.* The children's companies had musical resources that the adult companies at this stage lacked,[12] and because of their relatively infrequent performances they had time to rehearse new music and therefore to commission it from composers in a way that the adult companies with their crowded repertoires almost certainly could not. The children seem to have provided concerts before the play as part of the entertainment – if the oft-quoted testimony of Frederic Gershow who attended such a performance in 1602 is representative of their normal practice.[13] They certainly included, as a matter of routine, music between the acts to allow for the trimming of candles in the indoor arena (though Jonson, unlike his contemporary Marston, does not refer to it).

In 4.3 of *Cynthia's Revels* the vanity that is the play's target is satirised in a scene where both Hedon and Amorphus sing songs of affected exaggeration. Part of the satire is carried by the fact that they accompany themselves on the lyra viol, which was just then coming into fashion; more is suggested by the way in which Amorphus comments on his own efforts:

AMORPHUS: How like you it, sir?
HEDON: Very well, in troth.
AMORPHUS: But 'very well'? Oh, you are a mere mammothrept in judgement then! Why, do you not observe how excellently the ditty is affected in every place? That I do not marry a word of short quantity to a long note, nor an ascending syllable to a descending tone? Besides, upon the word 'best' there, you see how I do enter with an odd minim and drive it through the breve, which no intelligent musician I know but will affirm to be very rare, extraordinary and pleasing. (4.3.231–9)

This parodies the conventional advice given to would-be composers – and suggests that Jonson had read Thomas Morley's *Plaine and Easie Introduction to Practical Music,* published some three years earlier in 1597. Jonson, characteristically, knows and delights in the specialized language of the composer, and uses it to satirize pretension. The surviving manuscript setting of his song, almost certainly used in the first performance, bears out the leaden affectedness of the matching of word and note of which Amorphus boasts.[14] These two characters, presumably, perform in a fashion which invites laughter, but even Echo's exquisite lyric, 'Slow, slow, fresh fount' (1.2.65) from earlier in the play – which seems designed to invite the composer to musical illustration and must be performed with skill – is, in its dramatic situation, represented as excessive indulgence of feeling. In the last act, however, music – from the song to Cynthia, 'Queen and huntress', to the final epilogue song – reasserts the power of truth and harmony. This deployment of music's positive associations was not, however, to be the common tendency in the plays that followed.

In *Poetaster,* the songs contribute principally to the satirizing of Crispinus – a figure for the playwright Marston who was, in point of fact, both adept in his use of music in his plays and comparatively careful in prescribing its instrumentation. Like *Cynthia's Revels,* the play concludes with an epilogue song, but, as Mary Chan observes, in this play the songs 'have a simple and purely parodic function as satires on folly and immorality'.[15] In Jonson's later work songs feature much less frequently. In *Epicene* Clerimont's praise of artlessness in the song he has taught his page, 'Still to be neat' (1.1.71) is a finely turned lyric, and appropriate enough to the play's themes of disguise and deceit, but scarcely feels essential to the action of the play, seeming something of an intercalated set-piece.

The best-known song episode in Jonson's work is that in *Volpone* (3.2), where Volpone sings twice as part of his attempt to persuade Celia to surrender to his amatory advances. These lyrics, too, are elegantly written, adaptations of Catullus's most famous lyric, *Vivamus, mea Lesbia,* and thematically it is possible to see the songs as continuing the self-flattering sexual fantasy that Volpone presents to Celia in the speech which precedes them. At the simplest level, then, there is a collision between the learned sophistication of the song and the base motivation of its singer. This is a disjunction Jonson exploited again in Wittipol's serenade in *The Devil is an Ass,* where the erotic fantasy his singing represents is interrupted by the appearance of the husband of the object of his attention, Fitzdottrel, who threatens him with death. An elegant manuscript setting of 'Have you seen but a white lily grow', probably by Robert Johnson, survives and might well have been used at the play's first performance.[16] In the dramatic situation it is important that the song is sung well so that the audience might respond to the attractiveness of the music of the song but not thereby identify with the aspirations of the singer. This is precisely the effect of the Shakespearian serenades in *The Two Gentlemen of Verona* and *Cymbeline* and indeed seems characteristic of most serenades in Renaissance drama, where singing rarely leads to success.

A Ferrabosco setting of Volpone's 'Come my Celia' was published in his 1609 *Ayres.* Though it is often assumed that this would have been used in performance, it is by no means certain. It is written in Ferrabosco's declamatory and extended style and if Volpone himself sings it, then its very length would be awkward at the least to accommodate on stage. Peter Walls argues that the setting justifies 'Volpone's claims to virtuosity as an entertainer' but also suggests that it is possible that the song is to be sung offstage by another actor while 'Burbage enacted some "graceful gesture" and "footing"'.[17] There is a further problem with the Ferrabosco setting in that it is generally believed that the King's Men at this stage of their evolution did not employ composers to provide special settings of individual songs.[18]

The real difficulties with this scene, however, are, it seems to me, theatrical. Where the traditional serenade imposes a physical separation between singer and addressee (who might, indeed, not even appear to hear it) the proximity of the two characters here has, at least in productions I have seen, led to an awkward kind of semi-operatic stasis. In the end Jonson seems really to be thinking about the imitation of Catullus as much as the effect or effectiveness of this *as a song* in its dramatic situation. Mary Chan argues that 'The song, in itself a superb example of the "eloquence" of music-for-words, and intended as a heightening of Volpone's persuasion, in fact deflates that persuasion; it is a mockery of itself, and Volpone's performance of it merely mimics himself.'[19] But this seems to me untrue to the way in which we actually experience songs in a theatrical setting. It is possible to write songs whose music, like their words, satirizes a musical style – as in Hedon's song; and it is possible to perform songs badly for comic effect. But Ferrabosco's setting is not parodic, and once one takes it in any way seriously, then the effect of the music cannot simply be overridden and overwritten by the 'comic' situation. Indeed, to render Volpone's assault on Celia as merely comic would surely be to mistake the tone of the scene as a whole. This, then, is an extreme example of the way in which musical effect and dramatic situation may be put deliberately at odds.

The other songs in *Volpone* have a simpler function. The first is sung as part of Mosca's entertainment of Volpone in 1.1, and the two songs in 2.1 are both intended to drum up trade for Volpone-as-mountebank. The musical invitation to buy offered by street-sellers was both a reality in early modern streets and the source for sophisticated compositions based on them. Shakespeare represents the genre in Autolycus's songs 'Lawn as White as Driven Snow' and 'Will You Buy Any Tape' in *The Winter's Tale*, Act 4.

Perhaps Jonson's most successful musical creation is Nightingale in *Bartholomew Fair*. He is a familiar figure – a professional seller of ballads, who would advertise his wares by singing to a gathered crowd. His stock would be varied; his songs, printed on a single sheet, and hence known as 'broadsides', might include lyrics on news, real or imagined, narratives of love and seduction, reports of criminals going to execution and the like. The list Nightingale offers in 2.4, including a ballad called 'The Windmill

Blown Down by the Witch's Fart', only minimally exaggerates the kinds of material that contemporary hack writers were prepared to turn into verse. These ballads might be printed with a woodcut illustration; Mrs Overdo asks Cokes whether the example he looks at has a 'fine picture' (3.5.38), and he in turn reports that he had many sheets pasted up 'over the nursery-chimney' (3.5.39). This no-doubt-common practice underlines the fact that ballads were the most widely distributed of literary kinds and must, for many, have been their principal 'literary' experience. Few ballads were actually printed with music; in general they were simply described as 'To the tune of' a popular air. Importantly, then, when Nightingale actually sings, it is to the tune of 'Paggington's Pound', one of the most widely used melodies in the whole ballad literature. The audience in the theatre, just as much as the onstage audience, would certainly have known, and therefore have been able to identify with, the music, and be drawn, as it were, into the circle that surrounds Nightingale. (In a good deal of the drama of the period written for the adult companies it is, indeed, likely that most, if not all of the songs would have been versions of popular material, or at the very least sung to existing well-known tunes.) In the event, of course, Nightingale sings in order to create the opportunity for his accomplice, Edgworth, to pick the pocket of the foolish Cokes, ironically committing the crime while Nightingale is actually singing a warning song about the dangers of cutpurses. This representation of ballad-singing as a cover for criminal activity is entirely conventional (Autolycus, in Shakespeare's *The Winter's Tale,* plays the same kind of trick), and here the comedic effect is clear; we may ourselves feel something of the attractiveness the music has for Cokes, and since Nightingale is singing an already well-known popular tune an audience is likely to identify cheerfully with the singer rather than his victim.

It seems, perhaps, characteristic that one of Jonson's most successful dramatic deployments of song is in the context of deception and suspicion. There is little evidence in Jonson's work as a whole of any real inwardness with music. He uses it in his masques as an image for the harmony of the well-ordered state, and he certainly can write lyrics well adapted for musical setting, but in the bulk of his poetry musical imagery is notably thin on the ground. He told Drummond that he wrote all his verses 'first in prose, for so his master Camden had learned him' (*Informations* 15, 293), and this perhaps suggests that the rhythms of music were not central to his poetic inspiration, as the comparative paucity of detail about music in the stage directions of both masques and plays indicates that it was not for him a high priority.

NOTES

1. Peter Walls, *Music in the English Courtly Masque, 1604–40* (Oxford: Oxford University Press, 1996), p. 148.
2. David Lindley (ed.), *Court Masques* (Oxford: Oxford University Press, 1995), pp. 100–7.
3. Ben Jonson, *The Complete Masques*, ed. Stephen Orgel (New Haven, Conn.: Yale University Press, 1969), l. 245.
4. Jonson, *The Complete Masques*, l. 492.
5. Jonson, *The Complete Masques*, ll. 290–303.
6. Peter Holman, 'The Harp in Stuart England: New Light on William Lawes's Harp Consorts', *Early Music*, 15 (1987): 188–203.
7. These comments were excised, along with all mention of the occasion of the masque, in the 1616 folio. They are printed in Jonson, *The Complete Masques*, p. 475, n. 616.
8. Jonson, *The Complete Masques*, l. 4.
9. Jonson, *The Complete Masques*, ll. 16–18.
10. The topic is fully explored by Walls, *Music in the English Courtly Masque*, pp. 86–103.
11. Jonson, *The Complete Masques*, ll. 282–3.
12. See Lucy Munro, *Children of the Queen's Revels: A Jacobean Theatre Repertory* (Cambridge: Cambridge University Press, 2005).
13. Quoted, for example, in Andrew Gurr, *The Shakespeare Company, 1594–1642* (Cambridge: Cambridge University Press, 2004), p. 80. More generally on the music of the children's companies, see Linda Austern, *Music in English Children's Drama of the Later Renaissance* (Philadelphia, Pa.: Gordon and Breach, 1992).
14. Printed in Mary Chan, *Music in the Theatre of Ben Jonson* (Oxford: Clarendon Press, 1980), pp. 59–60.
15. Chan, *Music in the Theatre of Ben Jonson*, p. 69
16. Chan, *Music in the Theatre of Ben Jonson*, pp. 106–8.
17. Peter Walls, 'Come my Celia', in John Creaser (ed.), *Volpone* (London: Hodder & Stoughton, 1978), pp. 289–90.
18. I argue this in my *Shakespeare and Music* (London: Cengage Learning, 2005), and it's a position Ross Duffin adopts in his *Shakespeare Songbook* (New York: Norton, 2004). It is a position open to challenge, and Jonson had worked closely enough with Ferrabosco on masques to suggest that this song might be an exception to the general rule.
19. Chan, *Music in the Theatre of Ben Jonson*, p. 98.

CHAPTER 19

Dance

Barbara Ravelhofer

In *The Devil is an Ass,* Satan fantasizes about an 'almain leap into a custard' (1.1.97) as one of the minor, mildly entertaining vices. Dancing, like food, proved irresistible for Jonson's poetic imagination and coloured his works to both comic and serious effect. As dance played an important role in the social life of early modern England and Europe as a whole, his attitude seems natural. The art was taken very seriously and sparked off lively debates between zealous practitioners in court and city, apologists for whom dancing was pleasurable, wholesome and gracefully ennobling, and detractors who considered it a waste of time and regarded even a harmless, small almain leap as the first step towards damnation (as the indefatigable Puritan polemicist William Prynne memorably put it, 'as many paces as a man maketh in Dauncing, so many paces doth he make to Hell').[1] Jonson was familiar with literature on the topic; for instance, he owned a copy of Balthasar de Beaujoyeulx's famous *Ballet comique de la Royne* (1581) which is now held by the New York Public Library. As a Londoner, he encountered a range of different dance genres both English and imported from abroad; as a dramatist, he knew the stage jigs that concluded a theatre performance, and as a court writer devising masques and entertainments he regularly worked with musicians and dancers over a period of some thirty years.

In early modern England, ambitious individuals were not only expected to speak well but also to move well. Those who showed too much talent, though, were viewed with suspicion, such as Jonson's witty Sempronia in *Catiline* (1611), who is not only able to 'compose in verse, and make quick jests' but also dances 'better than an honest woman need' (2.1.46–51). The Duke of Buckingham, one of the finest dancers of his time, saved the situation in Jonson's masque *Pleasure Reconciled to Virtue* (1618) by charming the bored king with improvised capers – athletic 'caprioles', nimble foot movements performed during a high jump. Playing a shifty Gypsy in Jonson's countryside entertainment *The Gypsies Metamorphosed* (1621), he introduced an innovation of French *ballet de cour* which allowed aristocrats to take risqué character roles. Buckingham specialized in another such role, that of a fencing master, for which he was singled out by certain contemporaries as too histrionic for a courtier and privy counsellor.[2] Buckingham employed a French ballet professional, Montagut, who later became instructor of Charles I and a member of Henrietta Maria's household. Montagut performed in court masques and was quite likely involved in productions that Jonson prepared for Buckingham and the Caroline court.[3]

A keyword in Jonson's oeuvre and ethics was 'measure' – which, in his days, covered, according to the *Oxford English Dictionary*, a range of meanings: capacity, quantity, or limit; moderation, restraint; prudence; due proportion, symmetry, balance; a duration of time, and, in the later seventeenth century, a full line in print. Furthermore, 'measure' was a musical note; it signified rhythm in poetry and music; and, importantly, 'measure' was synonymous with 'dance'. On occasion, the word was also applied to a group of traditional social dances of Elizabethan origin. When applying the word, Jonson plays with most of these meanings, and we must be particularly attentive to its musical, rhythmical, dance-like resonance. *Timber; or, Discoveries* connects 'measure' with classical harmony: 'A poet is ... a maker, ... expressing the life of man in fit measure, numbers, and harmony, according to Aristotle' (1665–7). One feels that Jonson welcomed unaffected, restrained elegance in courtly dancing. Excess is an issue in *Cynthia's Revels*. 'Did I not dance movingly last night?' asks Lady Philautia, to which her guardian Moria responds, 'Movingly! Out of measure' except that her charge 'wanted the swim i' the turn'. Mercury (disguised as a page) comments, 'A happy commendation, to dance out of measure'. Philautia angrily retorts, 'both the swim and the trip are properly mine. Everybody will affirm it that has any judgement in dancing' (Quarto, 2.4.38–44). In performance, this dialogue was probably accompanied by the appropriate movements; the characters must have imitated modish French slides and turns and opened and closed their arms before their chests as in a swimming fashion. The conversation takes place on two levels – one is about dancing, the other about moral standards. Lady Philautia ('Self-love') fishes too eagerly for compliments, an opportunity for others to tease her. Mercury recognizes Moria's double-edged praise: Philautia dances rarely but immoderately in some way. Philautia's own sharp remark reveals an involuntary ambiguity – the 'trip' may not simply be an innocent step but refer to a lady's misconduct. In a few moments, we learn much about Lady Philautia and the atmosphere at Cynthia's court. Here, as in other examples of Jonson's drama, a dance episode works like a play within the play; it makes character relations transparent in an economic snapshot.

In Renaissance England, dancing was heavily encoded. Certain popular genres had a particular reputation or were associated with a particular geography, as, for instance, the saraband, supposedly lewd, agitated and (as a Protestant audience might not have been surprised to hear) of Spanish origin. Dance activated the audience's collective memory and prompted certain reactions. In English drama of the period, costumes, settings, props and speeches were supplemented by a kinetic theatrical vocabulary, that of dance. This served several dramatic purposes, such as highlighting a character's profile, adding local colour or making a moral statement about a figure or scene.

Jonson frequently mentions Spanish pavins, brawls, corantos, almains, measures and the like in his plays with specific intent. In *The Staple of News*, Pennyboy Senior watches with alarm the performance of a 'bawdy saraband' which transforms the dancers into mindless revellers ('All things ... Move but their brain') (4.2.137–41). *Cynthia's Revels* begins by sternly reminding the audience that a court should be like a fountain of manners or a polished looking-glass for the common man's admiring emulation. Hence, well-proportioned bodies and elegant movement are major themes, which invites, as we have seen, many dance-related jokes. The play is populated by a narcissistic cast who are less accomplished than they believe, and not even the gods escape censure. Mercury snipes at Cupid's small size, calling him a 'dancing braggart in decimo-sexto' (1.1.37). The traveller Amorphus's efforts in balletic self-improvement are continually frustrated: having pestered everybody with his dancing lessons and galliard tricks, the common verdict is that he now walks like a rope dancer (2.3.87). The spindly gallant Anaides, it appears, 'puts off the calves of his legs with his stockings every night' (4.1.55–6). This alludes to a common, much-derided practice of the period: men, especially dancers, stuffed their stockings with bombast (a kind of cotton) so as to suggest muscles where the thin leg was found wanting – thus Jonson confronts us with, as it were, the equivalent of the wonder-bra for the early modern male. Amidst general jocularity, the play registers discomfort as courtiers mercilessly scrutinize each other, relishing the certain discovery of flaws; individuals struggle to live up to the ideals imposed upon them. The microcosmos of Cynthia's court reflects the rigorous standards of contemporary dance and conduct literature. Here, readers were, for instance, told not to spread their legs apart as if wanting to urinate; nor should they pull tight gloves off with their teeth. Some books spent many pages simply on the topic of sitting down properly. Avid learners might be confronted with up to several hundred rules for steps. Dancing schools and academies of comportment were urgently recommended. Amusingly cruel, *Cynthia's Revels* proceeds with the purging of flaws in manner and physique until Cynthia declares her court reformed ('A virtuous court, a world to virtue draws', 5.5.261). While appreciating Jonson's satirical didacticism one feels slightly sorry for some protagonists' treatment on the thorny path towards perfection.

In *Epicene*, where silence plays an eminent role, it follows that body language should be observed with particular attention. Indeed, the sign language invented by Morose becomes emblematic of the quiet world he so desires. Fearful of noise, Morose employs a mute servant who communicates with his master by making legs and gestures, and he proposes to Epicene, whom he believes to be a lady capable of answering with 'silent gestures' (2.5.32). However, in the course of the play, a Jonsonian *volta* turns the meaning of movement to its opposite extreme. Hitherto the signifier of peace, movement is now represented by dancing and begins to indicate riot. As the wedding celebrations hit Morose he finds that the creature he espoused is not the quiet domestic angel he had hoped for ('The spitting, the coughing, the laughter, the neezing [sic], the farting, dancing, noise of the music, and her masculine and loud commanding ... makes him think he has married a Fury' [4.1.5–7]). At the end of romantic comedies, communal dancing traditionally emphasizes harmony and cohesion: it seals the auspicious union of happy lovers amongst friends and family. In a telling departure from this pattern, and quite in keeping with a more cynical kind of city comedy, the clamorous revels of *Epicene* – aural as well as kinetic torture – release the audience with a final outlook on the horrors of a community of people who could not care less for each other.

For Jonson, the most intense contact with dance came, of course, when he began to devise masques and countryside entertainments. For many critics, Jonson had some reason to nurse a grudge against those 'Mighty shows', as he called them in 'An Expostulation with Inigo Jones' (l. 39): if eyewitness accounts of performance nights may be trusted, audiences usually gazed at dancers, prominent guests and costumes, while paying little attention to the speeches. Also, audibility was not always good, to the point that protagonists occasionally approached the audience to shout into dignitaries' ears what might otherwise not be heard. The famous preface to *Hymenaei*, an early masque, therefore distinguishes between the 'body' and the 'soul' of a masque, the former being its physical performance and the latter being the Jonsonian creation that lived on after the occasion as a lasting printed or written text.

In the late entertainment *Love's Welcome at Bolsover* (1634) Jonson scoffs at domineering dancing masters whose pupils are unable to keep time unaided. 'Iniquo Vitruvius' (a thinly disguised swipe at Inigo Jones) directs a dance of 'mechanics', among them masons, carpenters and a plumber, who beat the time with their tools. Mock rhetoric parodies the exuberance of masque libretti at court: 'Well done ... my true mathematical boys! It is carried in number, weight, and measure, as if the airs were all harmony and the figures a well-timed proportion!' (ll. 55, 56, 58–9).[4] Iniquo's effusive praise fails to convince, and the calculated 'as if' removes any residual doubts as to the hulking misery of the performance. For Jonson, it was not minutely planned spectacular effect but finer, spontaneous charms that made an entertainment come alive and infused the dancing body with a soul.

Himself a frolicsome choreographer of the pen, Jonson occasionally put accents on words to suggest dance rhythm. The structure of a Jonsonian masque usually fell into two parts – the anti-masque representing the forces of chaos and disorder, where grotesque dancers (often actors or professional ballet artists) indulged in gesticulation, pantomime, complicated acrobatic jumps and turns and other demanding theatrical movements. Anti-masque dances, however, should not be misunderstood as improvised low-key foolery; every single movement must have been carefully cued, as the complicated surviving anti-masque scores with their pointed changes of rhythm and speed suggest, and the performance certainly required professional prowess.[5] After the grotesque part followed the courtly 'masque proper' where an ensemble of courtly dancers performed formal, specially devised theatre choreographies that they had rehearsed for several weeks. These dances often represented geometrical figures or letters, as was also common in French *ballet de cour* and Italian *intermedi* of the period. Then the so-called revels followed, where the masquers took out members of the audience for more dancing. This would have been commonly known popular repertoire of the period, therefore accessible to many spectators. Dancing thus became a communicative tool that enabled kinetic bonding in masques, with everybody temporarily sharing the illusion of moving in a perfect courtly world.

The Jonsonian masque relied on a lively, anarchically diverse cast: stock figures of European ballet such as furies (with their staple props of daggers, torches, snakes or bones), of which Jonson must have thought when characterizing Morose's wife, but also fairies, Roman 'pantomimi', dancing

Figure 19.1 Inigo Jones, final design for Prince Henry as Oberon.

'bears' and even bottles. The cast of memorable dancers included Anna of Denmark as a 'daughter of Niger' in Jonson's first court masque in 1605; Anna appeared in black make-up and a provocatively short gown, which showed her ankles – a sight from which certain members of the audience had to recover. To great acclaim, Prince Henry danced as the fairy Oberon, possibly making use of those stuffed stockings decried in *Cynthia's Revels*, as Inigo Jones's design for this role shows him with unrealistically muscular legs (see Figure 19.1).

The quest for perfection via dance is not only apparent in the regular choreographies of the masque proper but also in Jonson's poetry. A striking combination of choreographic patterning and poetic structure occurs in Jonson's Pindaric ode 'To the Immortal Memory and Friendship of That Noble Pair, Sir Lucius Cary and Sir Henry Morison' (1629).[6] The ode praises the short yet accomplished life of Henry Morison, who died aged twenty-one, and consoles his friend Cary. As the poem points out, it is not long life but one's actions that count. Emulating the dynamics of a dancing Greek chorus, Jonson's composition employs the triadic structure of the Pindaric ode (strophe, antistrophe and epode), with an ouverture (Jonson's 'Turn') answered by a 'Counter-turn' and a concluding 'Stand'. In three movements, Jonson traces three exemplary lives: a conspicuously short life (the newly born infant which, at the destruction of Saguntum, prefers to return to its mother's womb and die); another man's long life wasted with trifling matters; and finally Morison's seemingly premature death. The charged word 'measure' occurs again to describe the fullness of Morison's short life:

> All offices were done
> By him so ample, full, and round,
> In weight, in measure, number, sound,
> As, though his age imperfect might appear,
> His life was of humanity the sphere.
> (*The Underwood* 70, ll. 48–52)

In early modern usage, a 'turn' meant 'turning about a centre' or 'changing direction', but it could also be a valorous deed or task, as appropriate to Morison's well-rounded example. Poetically, a 'turn' could refer to nimble diction (as in 'this gallants tongue has a good turne' in *Poetaster*, 3.1.36–7).[7] The 'stand' may be a state of perplexity or arrested bodily motion. In the context of the ode, it is a pause, inviting the reader (or listener) to halt and reflect; it is a moment of observation, as in Shakespeare's *Romeo and Juliet*, when Romeo, entranced by Juliet's dance, says, 'The measure done, I'll watch her place of stand' (1.4.163).[8] It is a well-known phenomenon in drama that monosyllabic lines spoken aloud slow down a declamation. Intriguingly, such lines occur most often in Jonson's 'Stand' stanzas, making the speaker or reader almost stop.

The dual image of circle and centre was, as Thomas Greene has pointed out, an organizing principle in Jonson's work, signifying equilibrium and perfection.[9] In a fandango of circular movements, Jonson, Cary and Morison revolve around each other. Morison, who has leapt to Heaven, is now a star of higher spheres yet not out of reach:

> *The Counter-Turn*
> Call, noble Lucius, then, for wine,
> And let thy looks with gladness shine:
> Accept this garland, plant it on thy head,
> And think, nay, know thy Morison's not dead.
> He leaped the present age,

Possessed with holy rage,
To see that bright eternal day,
Of which we priests, and poets say
Such truths as we expect for happy men,
And there he lives with memory, and *Ben*
The Stand
Jonson, who sung this of him, ere he went
Himself to rest ...

(*The Underwood* 70, ll. 75–86)

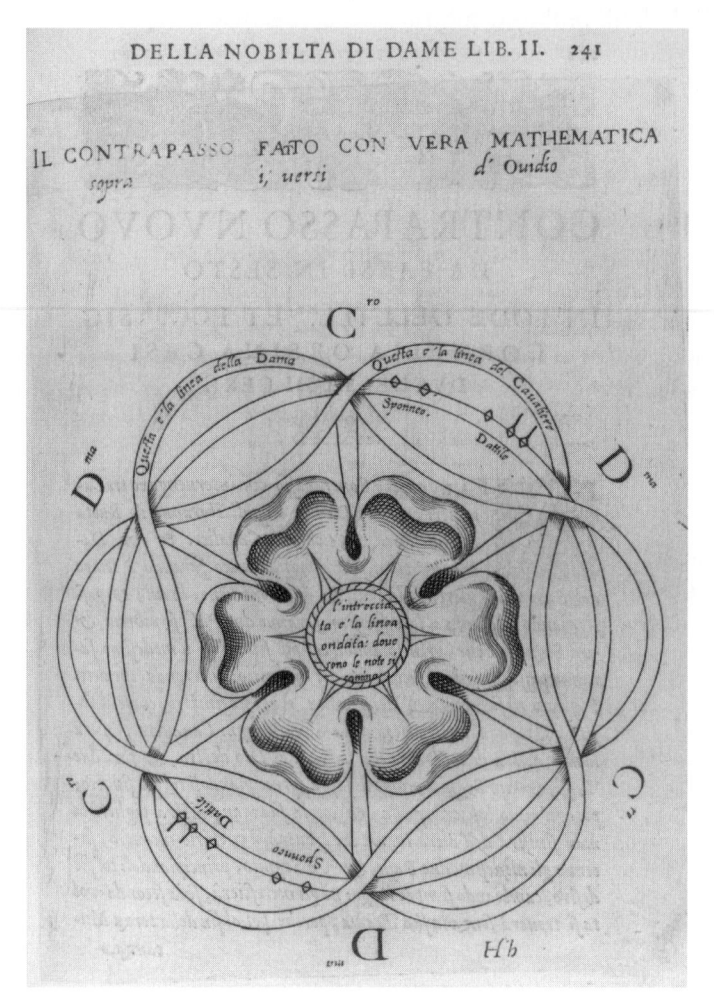

Figure 19.2 Fabritio Caroso's circular choreography from *Nobiltà di dame* (1600).

In a striking enjambment, Jonson's lyrical performance bridges the gap between the living and the dead. The informal 'Ben' of the 'Counter-turn' – priest and poet, offering song and wine to Lucius and yet joining Morison's eternal dance of the spheres – is at the same time the earthbound, distant Jonson, who imagines himself in the past, dead, in the 'Stand'. His song will be the condition upon which the 'memory' of three true friends will be preserved.

Two stanzas artfully counterpoint past, present and future, with Jonson, whose name has been self-consciously inserted into the ode as the necessary link, leading the complex turns. Jonson's 'Counter-turn' makes one think of an Italian choreographer, Fabritio Caroso. Caroso composed a *Contrapasso,* a circular choreography inspired by verse meter, to express perfection (Figure 19.2). Jonson may not have known Caroso's work but both were driven by the same desire, each from their particular professional point of view. The choreographer seeks immortal fame by drawing dance towards the condition of poetry. The poet, whose motto, ironically, was the broken compass ('deest quod duceret orbem') arranged his verse in a circular choreography to defy death. Having come full circle in the survey of Jonson's works, we find no Morose but a poet who appreciated the supple lightness of dancing and, in darker hours, turned to dance to celebrate life.

NOTES

1. William Prynne, *Histrio-Mastix* (London, E.A. and W.I. for Michael Sparke, 1633), p. 229.
2. His role as fencing master, which required balletic agility, was considered 'too histrionical'. Letter, December 1626, in Stephen Orgel and Roy Strong (eds.), *Inigo Jones: The Theatre of the Stuart Court,* 2 vols. (London: Sotheby Parke Bernet, 1973), vol. 1, p. 389.
3. On Montagut and Buckingham, see Barthélemy de Montagut, *Louange de la danse,* edited by B. Ravelhofer (Cambridge: RTM, 2000) and James Knowles, 'The "Running Masque" Recovered? A Masque for the Marquess of Buckingham (c. 1619–20)', *English Manuscript Studies,* 8 (2000): 79–135.
4. The edition of *Love's Welcome at Bolsover* cited is that in David Lindley (ed.), *Court Masques* (Oxford: Oxford University Press, 1995).
5. Standard works on masque dance and music include Jean Knowlton, 'Some Dances of the Stuart Masque Identified and Analyzed', 2 vols., Ph.D. thesis (Bloomington, Ind., 1966); Andrew Sabol (ed.), *Four Hundred Songs and Dances from the Stuart Masque* (Hanover, NJ: University Press of New England, 1982); and Peter Walls, *Music in the English Courtly Masque, 1604–1640* (Oxford: Clarendon Press, 1996).

6. The following discussion is inspired by Susanne Woods, 'Ben Jonson's Cary-Morison Ode: Some Observations on Structure and Form', *Studies in English Literature, 1500–1900*, 18 (1) (1978): 57–74.
7. The edition of *Poetaster* cited is that edited by Tom Cain for the Revels Plays series (Manchester: Manchester University Press, 1995).
8. The edition of *Romeo and Juliet* cited is that edited by Jill. L. Levenson (Oxford: Oxford University Press, 2000).
9. Thomas M. Greene, 'Ben Jonson and the Centered Self', *Studies in English Literature, 1500–1900*, 10 (2) (1970): 325–48.

CHAPTER 20

Manuscript culture and reading practices

James Knowles

[T]hough it hath proved a work of some difficulty to me to retrieve the particular authorities ... to those things which I writ out of fullness and memory of my former readings, yet, now I have overcome it.[1]

Jonson has often been typed as 'The poet of printed books', his career understood in relation to publication, with the 1616 folio as pivotal point in his trajectory.[2] Jonson's attention to the processes and visual effects of textual production – the deliberate recreation of the apparatus of a classical edition – are designed to assert his control and create 'textual legitimation' for himself and his texts.[3] The chronological ordering and the careful exclusion of unfitting texts, a process of 'self-documentation in a canon', echoes the academic treatment of classical texts and authors, and the reinvention of the classical text as English classic construes the claim that 'Jonson as a writer is a classic'.[4] Even the plethora of dedications that seem to draw the folio back into the world of patronage rather than nascent consumerism paradoxically renders Jonson as the only fixed point of the galaxy of dedicatees and patrons. Thus, the author's 'sovereign power' is asserted.[5] Indeed, the 1616 folio has been identified as the instant at which a new kind of authorial ownership alongside a new idea of the author and authority emerge. The combination of this generation of a name and identity that is both created in, valorized by and valorizing of the work – Jonson – with its typical typographic precision, has been described as a demonstration of 'bibliographic ego', where commercial and intellectual ownership meet. It has been argued that this ego emerges at a key point in the restructuring, even invention, of the literary marketplace, as patronage gives way to printing house and courts are superseded by commerce.[6]

From 'B.ION: HIS PART' proclaimed on the title page of the *Royal Entertainment* (1604) through to the standardized closing tag of 'The Author B.I'. in the entertainment and masque texts printed in 1616, Jonson's repeated claims of ownership make him not only the begetter of his texts, differentiated from the player's poet, but also marks their summation as his name usurps the place of colophon or royal imprimatur: 'Written by BEN: IONSON.'; or, more abbreviated and assertively, '*And thus it ended. / BEN. IONSON.*'.[7] Yet many of these apparently 'print' features (classical lettering styles, standardized spelling that makes variation meaningful, the erased printer's colophon and 'cum privilegio') are echoed in the sequence of manuscripts that shadow the masque quartos of the period 1604–9.[8] Thus the *Panegyre*, *Blackness* and *Queens* all survive in the Royal Manuscripts, while printed texts of *Blackness* and *Queens* have manuscript paratexts, and the Salisbury entertainments, especially *The Entertainment at Theobalds* (1607), as we shall see below, also circulate through manuscript publication that announces poetic authority: 'Hos ego versiculos feci / Ben: Ionson'.[9] Similarly, the complex marginalia of the early masques are often conceived of in manuscript, and it has even been argued that the typography of some early quartos was designed to give a 'manuscript-like' immediacy of access to the author.[10] This method of lending printed text the authority or individuation of manuscript through a range of supplementary inscriptions endows the particular copies with additional resonance and authority, instantiating 'credit' in a transmission medium that was still often associated with the cheap and the commercial. These instances drawn from Jonson's earlier career and from print *and* manuscript suggest how Jonson's imprintedness is just as often inscriptedness, and the continued use of manuscript throughout his canon to authorize print suggests that Jonson's use of both manuscript and print was highly strategic. This ability to move *between* publication systems and the continued use of manuscript to render printed texts credit-worthy, suggests that we need to reconsider the conceptualization of, or at least the assumption of the printed manifestation of, authority in Jonson's texts.

The interplay between print and manuscript is evident in *The Masque of Queens* and its paratextual materials (manuscript plus epistle, quarto, quarto copy plus manuscript dedication, folio) and Jonson's 'minute' that renders account of his recollection of the 'particular authorities', the textual fragments that through the 'memory' of the poet reconstitute the 'memory of my former readings' and their 'fullness' (abundance, completeness). Here 'Writ out' expresses not only this creative synthesis but also the laborious double *action* of both copying and creating that shaped the final product as if the very 'work of some difficulty' provides the authority of the text. The echo of Jonson's 'antiquity and solid learnings' in *Hymenaei* (l. 14) is deepened as the poet combines reading in print (and presumably manuscript), with the act of creation in script, which is recreated in the act of manuscript copying to lend authority to the performance and to its print publication. The *interaction* of the 'second labour of annotation' and the 'first of invention' through the figure – and literally the pen – of the poet yokes poet and authority and provides that sense of inherent authority that has been traced to print.[11] Significantly, the manuscript 'minute' (moment in time, opportunity, but also formal notation) carefully distinguishes between publication and the intimacy which it claims, as the term itself suggests not the formal public document but the rough copy in 'small writing' offered as a private gesture. Jonson's use of italic scripts in this manuscript has been noted for its evocation of classical and humanist forms, just as its often miniscule size embodies the project's intense effortfulness, but another suggestion may lie in the strategic use not just of manuscript in combination with print but in the differentiation within manuscripts to give specific (and highly strategic) social significance to the choice of letter form.[12]

The intensity of the complexly bookish culture of Jonson's *Masque of Queens* – intimate, learned and centred upon the book as material object beyond any print/script binary – requires us to reconsider the image of Jonson as the poet of print. Interestingly, recent approaches to the history of the book also require a modification of the conceptualization of print itself that has underpinned such accounts, not perhaps in its outline but in exactly how it operates. Printing, it has often been suggested, produced a new reliability in books, encouraging standardization of key features, fixity, preservation through dissemination. Print, in this interpretation, provides books – in a way not present in manuscript – with a completeness and finishedness that closes the text from readerly interference, either in the inaccuracy of transmission or in the deliberate process of appropriation and reappropriation that manuscript-copying encouraged. It has been suggested that this very process of standardization allowed writers such as Jonson to make meaning precisely because they can vary from an established norm, as in his own typographical reshaping of his name, or in his 'particular' allusions to other texts. Indeed, it is even suggested that the combination of accuracy and correctness further the idea of 'propriety', that is ownership, and helps to produce the Jonsonian author.

More recent studies, however, have questioned the simple linkage of technology to culture, highlighting how authority does not inhere in print technology per se but had to be constructed into book culture. Books had to be endowed with the properties of accuracy and fixity, and these had to be given cultural meaning. Adrian Johns in *The Nature of the Book*

(1998) has argued that even in scientific circles where the book might be seen as the absolute instrument of new discoveries based on accuracy of reproduction, fixity and so on, print had to be shaped and given the property of credit.[13] In the case of Tycho Brahe, often seen as one of the first to use print to propagate his ideas, Johns suggests that his printing press was almost entirely divorced from the book trade's structures so that the printed texts are 'barely published at all, but were to be distributed as gifts to patrons', and that the most prestigious were 'hybrids', often hand-coloured and individualized for specific recipients. If this interpretation of Brahe's publishing can be applied more widely, it raises some difficult issues about how communities of readers – and the idea of a community of readers (such as the republic of letters) – might have emerged but also requires a more careful consideration of how such communities and ideas, and even the overarching ideal of 'credit' in the book, were constructed.

Although Jonson's situation differs in key ways as his work is more clearly engaged with commercial structures of printing houses, stationers and the theatrical market, the Brahe example suggests how printed texts did not simply supplant manuscripts and how different patterns of commerce and patronage overlapped and interconnected.[14] No examples of individualized printed volumes linked to Jonson have survived, but many books that record patronage and friendship do. In one copy of *Cynthia's Revels* (1601) inscribed to Lucy, Countess of Bedford, Jonson sends his 'little book' complete with gilt-stamped binding neatly requesting reward while seeming only to ask the 'kiss' of her 'white hand' in accepting the gift.[15] Such association copies embody a delicately balanced relationship between patron and poet, where manuscription becomes a way of asserting the equality and significance of the poet, a strategy that parallels the creation of independence and creditability often attributed to print.[16]

Again, more recent studies have argued that 'publication' covers three differentiated actions: performance, scribal publication and print publication.[17] Jonson clearly recognized the significance of each of these forms, and even as late as *News from the New World Discovered in the Moon* (1620), the news on offer from the Chronicler, Factor and Printer includes manuscript material alongside gossip (a kind of performance), and printed newsbooks, and part of the joke against these incompetent newsmongers is not only that they recycle old news but that for all their claims of novelty, the main medium of news-transmission is the oldest: manuscript. Print is seen, largely, as a lower-class medium – represented by the Chronicler (of City news), and the Printer who recycles old wonder pamphlets, such as that about the Sussex serpent. Of course, such recycled news undermines the claims of print to authority and fixity, as the Printer cheerfully admits he peddles 'lies' for the 'common people' (*News from the New World Discovered in the Moon*, l. 48).

Although *News from the New World Discovered in the Moon* concerns a particular kind of print publication, it articulates the anxieties of print which also pressed poets towards manuscription. Indeed, our interpretation of the poet of print should be modified by an awareness of the interplay between different dissemination systems, by attention to Jonson's considered use of those different systems and media at various points in his career, and by recognition of the instances of print and the 'profession of publication', especially in the early quartos, as polemical and persuasive rather than simply inherently authoritative. These 'strategic' uses of print are most apparent in the crucial and still underestimated 1604 volume of entertainments that sought differentiation between the 'momentary and local' associations of 'pageantry' and the new aesthetic that Jonson was in the process of creating. Joseph Loewenstein, one of the few critics sensitive to the shifts in Jonson's evolving sense of textuality and its potential deployments, traces both a much more combative and polemical attitude towards rivals alongside a much more 'deferential' attitude to performance and spectators in the early masques which are obscured by the folio fetish.[18]

To develop these contentions, especially the fluidity of Jonson's engagements with different modes of publication and the complex developments in Jonsonian ideas of textuality, the rest of this chapter considers how Jonson used the resources of manuscript in a range of ways but crucially as a supplement to publication. The examples of Jonsonian manuscript publication suggest not only that we should modify our description of him as the poet of the printed book but that we should consider more carefully how the Jonsonian ideal textuality developed and that if we shift away from the folio fetish that has obscured much of Jonson's earlier and later careers, we can trace a jointly conceived deployment of a range of different self and textual presentations using the full range of media available.

'READ BY ALL': JONSON AND THE CIRCULATING TEXT

Jonson's extensive and complex involvement with manuscripts has only ever been partially discussed. Surveying the multiple manuscripts extant and particularly the number of holograph copies of Jonson's poems sent or given to patrons, friends and associates, such as the Drummond leaves containing 'My Picture Left in Scotland', Peter Beal characterizes Jonson as the first poet to give autographs.[19] In addition to these specific poetic and personalized gifts we should add the numerous fragments and drafts of Jonson's works that can be associated with his patrons; the reciprocal verse epistles; the multiple copies of Jonson's texts, such as the 'Cock Lorel' ballad begged by Chamberlain and others and then copied many times, adapted, extended, cast and recast; and the poetic texts written in defence of his work that inspired extensive dialogues that crossed between manuscript and print in the latter part of his career.

One of the earliest –and also the best-documented – instances, the circulation of *An Entertainment at Theobalds* (1607) suggests that Jonson was alert to the possibilities of scribal publication. Staged by Robert Cecil, 1st Earl of Salisbury, to mark the transfer of Theobalds, his father's massive palace in Hertfordshire, ostensibly to Queen Anna but in fact to James I, Jonson's text skilfully glossed the property exchange in which Cecil not only alienated a key part of his patrimony but also made considerable profit as some contemporaries suggested. The 'blessed change' that is 'no less glad than strange' is celebrated in a debate between the Genius of the house, Mercury, who explains the logic of the exchange and provides divine sanction, and the Three Fates who support the need for obedience in the face of what is cast as a providential 'good event' (outcome). In the printed text in the 1616 folio, Jonson provided elaborate descriptions of the scenery and action, closing the text with a two-stanza song to celebrate how 'gentle winds breed happy springs / And duty thrives by breath of kings', even though earlier sections of the text had been addressed to Bel-Anna the 'fair queen'.

Although the contemporary documents suggest the two-stanza version was that performed in 1607, two other manuscript copies of this entertainment offer a very different text, culminating in a four-stanza version of the song that recalls the 'foundress' of Theobalds, Elizabeth I, who the house had been built to entertain:

> SOLOIST: But thank that queen
>   Whose bounty it hath been
>   Such liking first to take,
>   And of our cell her palace make.
> CHORUS: So prosper still those happy walls
>   That are not raised by other falls.
> SOLOIST: Joy then fair place,
>   Joy in thy present grace,
>   Joy in thine innocence,

>   Joy in thy founder's good expense;
> CHORUS: So this great day shall still to thee
>   In reverence kept holy be.
>   (ll. 125–36)

Both of the copies that present these stanzas can – albeit tentatively – be tracked back to Jonson: one comes from the hand of Sir Henry Goodyere, a well-known literary intermediary, and the collection of Sir Edward Conway, a collector of Jonson texts; the other derives from the papers of Dudley, Lord North, and the antiquary Peter Le Neve, but is also likely to have originated with Jonson. Certainly, by 1616, two versions of the entertainment circulated: one a James-centred event that appeared in print, and which with minor revisions and some additions probably reflects what was staged in May 1607, and the other an Anna-centred event, which posited an almost matrilineal origin and descent for the house, as the keys of the 'cell' become 'palace' for 'Eliza, now a star', are handed on to the 'present grace' of the new queen.

Although it is tempting to interpret the versions either as stages towards a final text or as instances of the Jonsonian self-fashioning that translated his early career into a seamless progress towards royal service, the simultaneous circulation of print and manuscript versions of different redactions of the same event suggest a more complex, less linear pattern, in which Jonson deploys strategically the different opportunities offered by transmission systems and media. The printed, published and public text proclaims loyalty to the monarch and situates Jonson as the king's poet. Yet the alternative, but equally authorized, version speaks to other audiences as both manuscript copies are linked to those close to Prince Henry, perhaps insinuating a different duty to the next king while also aligning the poet with the Queen's view of the princely role. The two versions also imply that there is not a single 'authorized' Jonson available through print but a more flexible figure, able to offer differently authoritative texts as circumstance – and the different medium – requires. This is a poet able and willing to use the open matrix of the manuscript – the unfinished qualities that print is supposed to expunge – to speak to different audiences.

It is here that the local pressures on Jonson's production, what Martin Butler calls 'the micropolitics of interest and obligation, competition and local advantage' meet with the larger arguments about Jonson's typographical self-production as a manifestation of new forms of authorship and new interactions with the developing print market.[20] The creation of the poet as author and the generation of a sense of authority is not simply an effect of print but part of a dual process in which both print and manuscript can be deployed. Clearly the size and range of dissemination differs between manuscript and print (though the extent of circulation of even a single text in manuscript should not be underestimated), but the effects are an interconnected creation of authority. The printed folio text of the Theobalds entertainment manifests Jonson as the authoritative royal poet, and through the scale and material richness (and cost) and typographical elaboration of the printed volume with its columnar printing, massed headings and entries, and elaborate marginalia creates a visible public and authoritative persona. The manuscript text also creates its own authority rooted in the ties of obligation and interest and in the claim to exclusivity, which mark a different kind of authority. But both kinds of authority are required to create the full, plenipotentiary sense of Jonson's overarching poetic authority.

Jonson's career is shaped not only by the trajectory towards printed volumes but by a consistent double use of print and scribal circulation. Although Jonson's plays seem to have been disseminated through print, the most extensive evidence for scribal publication of dramatic work is provided by *The Gypsies Metamorphosed* (1621), which existed in at least five, differently complete manuscript copies, a tally that rivals the most widely circulated dramatic text of the period, Middleton's *A Game at Chess* (1624; five extant manuscript copies). One of the surviving manuscripts, the Newcastle Manuscript, can be linked to the household of William Cavendish, Earl of Newcastle, while the second, the Bridgwater Manuscript, appears in the library of the 1st Countess of Bridgwater in 1627 but is clearly a professional scribal copy. Both the Earl and Countess had widespread literary associations and acquired some playbooks and dramatic manuscripts in the 1620s, possibly through Ralph Crane, the King's Men's scrivener, although Jonson himself has no particular known connection with the Egerton family. The Bridgwater copy, as well as providing a careful collation of the different versions of the text contains material missing in both the two duodecimo issues and second folio print versions. Interestingly, like another no-longer-extant manuscript, the Huygens copy, the Bridgwater manuscript is described as a 'quarto' in the 1627 catalogue, raising the possibility that they were similar kinds of copy that circulated contemporaneously with the masque staging. John Chamberlain's desire to acquire the Cock Lorel ballad suggests that the demand for scribal publication was generated by its popularity, and although, as I have remarked elsewhere, this extensive circulation takes on a life of its own, which bears no necessary resemblance to or connection with the original masque occasion, some of the extant part copies do originate in contemporary textual circulations.[21] Although it is impossible to ascertain if these represent instances of authorial scribal publication, given the auspices and controversial nature of the text it must be likely.

Many of Jonson's texts in the 1620s circulate in these multiple authorities, and important poems such as 'An Execration Upon Vulcan' survive in manuscript texts that suggest distinct and different versions of the poem originating with the author were in circulation. Although Jonson fails to match the massive scribal publication of lyric poems by writers such as Donne, the multiple copies/versions should alert us to the ongoing use of manuscript by Jonson. Indeed, rather than regarding the lack of printed texts as a sign of failure and diminishing power, we might need to consider how Jonson used the different publications available to him at different points in his career, especially in the 1620s, where the pressures on Jonson's political position, the kind of compromises he attempted in the mid-decade masques and which publicly collapsed in *Neptune's Triumph* (1624), required the use of different methods of self-presentation and dissemination.

Jonson's own writing about the process of transmission, amid its sideswipes at failing printers, pilfering plagiaries and those unable to point his pauses and lines, reflects not only on the mechanics of circulation but also on its politics. Jonson recounts how he has offered Sir Kenelm Digby verses which 'he doth love' and so:

> will look
> Upon them (next to Spenser's noble book)
> And praise them, too. Oh, what a fame 'twill be!
> What reputation to my lines and me,
> When he shall read them at the Treasurer's board!
> The knowing Weston and that learnèd lord
> Allows them! Then what copies shall be had,
> What transcripts begged! How cried up, and how glad
> Wilt thou be, muse, when this shall them befall!
> Being sent to one, they shall be read by all.[22]

As a member of an important Catholic coterie (Jonson's text also mentions Richard Weston, Earl of Portland), Digby's philosophical interpretation published in 1624 contrasted with the militantly Protestant Spenserian poets of the late 1620s.[23] Although it is hard to trace Jonson's sympathies with the various Catholic coteries that he engaged with in this period, the contrast with Spenser may combine politics and publication. Jonson differentiates his poetic 'lines' from 'The noble book', that is the printed text and contrasts his writing with the Protestant 'print-fixated writer' for whom print publication was an indispensible part of his self-announced national and international epic significance.[24] Jonson, against the print audience and its claims of authority and reach, claims his own authority through the reach of manuscript. Crucially, manuscript circulation is not simply an elite prerogative for the learned lord but creates a different kind of mass audience. Indeed, the poem's final clauses, with their shift into the pithier, aphoristic and chiastic sentence, punch out the countering proposition that even this form of publication can lead to being 'read by all', a phrasing that implies reach far beyond elite circulation. It is a classic demonstration of Jonson's strategic use of manuscript brought to us through print. It reminds us – powerfully – that if we are to celebrate Jonson as the creator of a 'bibliographic ego' then that ego depended not only on printing the mind but also involved theatrical and scribal publications that themselves write out the 'fullness and memory of ... former readings'.

NOTES

1. British Library Royal MS 18.A.xlv, as transcribed in D. Lindley (ed.), *Court Masques* (Oxford: Oxford University Press, 1995), p. 226. All quotations from masques in this chapter unless otherwise indicated are from Ben Jonson, *The Complete Masques,* ed. Stephen Orgel (New Haven, Conn.: Yale University Press, 1969).
2. Richard C. Newton, 'Jonson and the (Re-)Invention of the Book', in C. Summers and Ted-Larry Pebworth (eds), *Classic and Cavalier: Essays on Jonson and the Sons of Ben* (Pittsburgh, Pa.: University of Pittsburgh Press, 1982), pp. 31–55; p. 36.
3. Timothy Murray, 'From Foul Sheets to Legitimate Model: Antitheater, Text, Ben Jonson', *New Literary History,* 14 (1983): 641–64; p. 657.
4. Newton, 'Jonson and the (Re-)Invention of the Book', p. 37.
5. Martin Butler, 'Jonson's Folio and the Politics of Patronage', *Criticism,* 35 (1993): 377–90; p. 379.
6. Joseph Loewenstein, 'The Script in the Marketplace', *Representations,* 12 (1985): 101–14; p. 101.
7. *The Masque of Queens* (1609), title page; and *The Entertainment at Highgate* (1604) in *Works* (1616), p. 885. In 1604 the *Panegyre* was called 'B.I. HIS PANEGYRE'.
8. William H. Sherman, 'The Beginning of "The End": Terminal Paratext and the Birth of Print Culture', unpublished lecture. I am grateful to Professor Sherman for sharing his research with me.
9. Copies of the *Panegyre* and *Blackness* are in MS Royal 17.B.xxxi.
10. John Jowett, 'Jonson's Authorization of Type in *Sejanus* and Other Early Quartos', *Studies in Bibliography,* 44 (1991): 254–65; p. 257.

Manuscript culture and reading practices 191

11. Autograph dedication to Queen Anna in quarto copy of *The Masque of Queens* (1609), British Library C28.g.5.
12. Harold Love, *The Culture and Commerce of Texts: Scribal Publication in Seventeenth-Century England* (Amherst, Mass.: University of Massachusetts Press, 1998), p. 109, suggests some of the cultural meanings of italic.
13. Adrian Johns, *The Nature of the Book: Print and Knowledge in the Making* (Chicago, Ill.: University of Chicago Press, 1998).
14. The individualization of printed texts took many forms, such as the insertion of printed dedicatory pages, while more prestigious volumes, such as Drayton's *Polyolbion,* survive in hand-coloured, high-status copies. The copy of STC6498.2, Dekker's *The Double PP: A Papist in Arms, bearing ten several shields* (1606), in the Pforzheimer Collection contains an inserted dedication to Sir Henry Cocks (*The Carl H. Pforzheimer Library Catalogue: English Literature, 1475–1700,* 3 vols. (New York, 1940), vol. I, pp. 264–5); the hand-coloured copy of Drayton's *Polyolbion* (1612) that once belonged to Princess Elizabeth (of Bohemia) is in the Bodleian Library, Oxford.
15. *The Fountain of Self Love; or, Cynthia's Revels* (1601), Clark Library, Los Angeles, PR2609.A1 1601*, MS epistle.
16. Loewenstein argues that one of Jonson's distinctive contributions to the development of the social structures of literature lies in the construction of a literary coterie beyond the aristocratic household: see 'The Script in the Marketplace', p. 101.
17. Love, *The Culture and Commerce of Texts,* pp. 35–6.
18. Joseph Loewenstein, 'Printing and "The Multitudinous Presse": The Contentious Texts of Jonson's Masques', in Jennifer Brady and W.H. Herendeen (eds.), *Ben Jonson's 1616 Folio* (Newark, Del.: University of Delaware Press, 1991), pp. 168–91.
19. Peter Beal, *Index of English Literary Manuscripts,* Vol. I, *1450–1625* (London: Mansell, 1980), p. 234.
20. Butler, 'Jonson's Folio and the Politics of Patronage', p. 379; but see also p. 386.
21. James Knowles, '"Songs of Baser Alloy": Jonson's *Gypsies Metamorphosed* and the Circulation of Manuscript Libels', *Huntington Library Quarterly,* 69 (2006): 153–76.
22. 'An Epigram to My Muse, the Lady Digby, on Her Husband, Sir Kenelm Digby', *The Underwood* 78, ll. 23–32.
23. David Norbrook, *Poetry and Politics in the English Renaissance,* 2nd edn (Oxford: Oxford University Press, 2002), p. 206. Spenser's *The Faerie Queene* had been reissued in 1628. Digby lauded Spenser as 'thoroughly versed in the mathematical sciences, in philosophy, and divinity': see *Observations on the 22 Stanza of the 9th Canto of the 2nd Book of Spencer's 'Faery Queen'* (1643), sig. A4v.
24. Love, *The Culture and Commerce of Texts,* p. 145.

CHAPTER 21

Print culture and reading practices
Alan B. Farmer

Ben Jonson was one of the most innovative dramatists in early modern England, an author whose creativity in the theatre was matched by his inventiveness in the book trade. Of the thirty-one books published during his lifetime, the majority (nineteen) were editions of professional plays, that is, plays performed by one of London's professional playing companies. The rest included ten books of court masques, one of royal entertainments and a collection of plays, masques, entertainments and poems. Soon after his death there followed a translation of Horace's *Art of Poetry* (1640) and a second edition of his collected works (1640–1), expanded to three volumes and containing several never-before-published plays and masques, an English grammar and a series of short prose observations.[1] Although these publications established Jonson's reputation as one of the most formidable authors in Renaissance England, his books did not sell particularly well. The plays of Shakespeare, Thomas Heywood, Francis Beaumont and John Fletcher, Thomas Dekker, Thomas Middleton and James Shirley were all published in more editions than Jonson's were, and only two of his plays were definite hits with readers: *Every Man Out of His Humour* (1600) and *Eastward Ho!* (1605) (which he co-wrote with George Chapman and John Marston). Despite this paucity of best-sellers, Jonson's playbooks arguably did more than those of any other playwright to change the material form and to elevate the literary status of printed plays from the professional stage. His playbooks would end up being some of the most influential publications in all of early modern English literature.

Discussions of Jonson and print culture often centre on his 1616 folio, a book that brought together his diverse literary writings under the title of *The Workes of Beniamin Jonson* (henceforth *Works*). Printed in two issues – one on luxury, large-paper stock and the other on regular paper stock – *The Works* was a lavish publication, and at 257 sheets and more than 1,000 pages, the longest English book ever to include plays: nine from the professional stage, eighteen court masques and entertainments, as well as 148 poems. The title *Works* was intentionally evocative, meant to suggest the *opera* of classical authors like Virgil, Cicero and Ovid. Jonson took meticulous care to ensure that his book was exquisitely produced, proofreading and correcting typographical and textual errors as it was being printed.[2] With a similar concern for shaping his authorial persona, he omitted his earliest collaborative plays and extensively revised the early comedies he did include. Perhaps most important, he arranged the book's disparate texts to create a compelling narrative of literary and social advancement: Jonson's *Works* begins in the competitive world of the London commercial theatre, moves to a series of poems to noble patrons and ultimately arrives in triumph with masques and royal entertainments at the court of James I.[3]

Although the 1616 folio was undoubtedly a monumental edition, it was less original than has often been maintained. The frequently quoted quip in *Wits Recreations* (1640) mocking Jonson for calling his plays works – 'Pray tell me *Ben*, where doth the mystery lurke, / What others call a play you call a worke' (sig. G3v) – misrepresents the history of printed drama before 1616, for Jonson's plays were not the first to be sold as 'works'. Several closet dramas (plays written primarily for reading and not for performance) were called works on their title page or by their author.[4] *An Interlude of Minds* (1574) was advertised as 'A worke in Ryme', while *1 and 2 Promos and Cassandra* (1578) was marketed as '*The worke of* George Whetstones Gent'.[5] Using language clearly directed at Jonson but writing three years before 1616, John Stephens emphasized in the dedicatory epistle of *Cynthia's Revenge; or, Maenander's Ecstasy* (1613) that his play was a 'worke' regardless of whether readers 'praise or dispraise' it:

> The worke (no doubt) is in it selfe a worke, though naked, yet neuer to bee amended, with beautifull and faire acceptance[;] praise and dispraise after Impression bee alike, they do neither adde, nor can detract from things simply considered, so inherent is the name of *Worke* to each composure; but I can truely say, your im-partiall acceptance will make it a good worke to mee.[6]

Stephens's dedication was surely inspired by Jonson, who had referred to both *Volpone* (1607) and *Catiline* (1611) as 'works' when they were published, as did a commendatory poem in each playbook.[7] But Stephens was so convinced his own play was a 'worke' that he vowed he would not 'descant (like some sage fabulist) vpon reall difference betwixt Readers, and vnderstanding Readers' or 'prescribe a formall limitation who should, with my consent, sur-vey this Poem'.[8] Stephens was gesturing here to the addresses 'To the Reader in ordinarie' and 'To the Reader extraordinary' in *Catiline*, in which Jonson claimed that 'neither praise, nor dispraise from' the ordinary reader 'can affect mee' (sig. A3r), a boast Stephens plainly doubted.[9]

Furthermore, as Jeffrey Knapp has recently stressed, Jonson was not the first English (or British) dramatist to publish his collected 'Works'.[10] George Gascoigne's 1587 collection included four plays and went by the title of either *The Whole Works* or *The Pleasantest Works*. Samuel Daniel's *The Works* (1601), also a folio, contained the closet drama *Cleopatra*, and the two-play collection, *1 and 2 A Satire of the Three Estates*, was reissued in 1604 as *The Workes of the Famous and Worthy Knight, Sir David Lindsaie*. Nor was Jonson's 1616 folio the first collected 'Works' to contain a professional play. Two editions of Samuel Daniel's *Certain Small Works* (1607; 1611) included *Philotas*, which had been performed by the Queen's Revels Children, but even Daniel's was not the first professional play to be sold as a 'work'. Robert Wilson's *The Three Ladies of London* was advertised as 'a worke right worthie to be marked' on the title pages of both its 1584 and 1592 editions.

The evidence from these other playbooks is not meant to minimize the impressive authorial self-fashioning and labour that went into Jonson's folio, but they should cause us to hesitate before too easily crediting the idea that Jonson was breaking new ground in calling his poems and plays, professional or otherwise, 'works'. Jonson's *Works* appeared after both Gascoigne's and Daniel's, and, while other dramatic collections followed Jonson's, it did not have the transformative impact on play publication that scholars have sometimes claimed. Only a few folio play collections were printed after Jonson's – posthumous editions of Shakespeare (1623; 1632) and of Beaumont and Fletcher (1647) – which is perhaps unsurprising given the expense of producing such massive tomes. In contrast, the play quartos of Jonson's published in the first decade of the seventeenth century clearly changed printed drama and dramatic authorship in early modern England. In many ways, the 1616 folio was the culmination of innovations Jonson had introduced in his earliest playbooks.

Beginning with the first edition of *Every Man Out of His Humour* in 1600, Jonson radically altered how professional plays were sold to readers. Originally performed in 1599, *Every Man Out of His Humour* was not the earliest play Jonson ever wrote, nor do many modern critics consider it his finest comedy. It would prove to be a stunning success in the book trade, however, with three editions published in 1600 (no other professional play had ever been printed in that many editions in a single year).[11] *Every Man Out of His Humour* was a revolutionary playbook, starting with how it was advertised to readers on its title page: '*The Comicall Satyre of* EVERY MAN OVT OF HIS HVMOR. *AS IT WAS FIRST COMPOSED* by the AUTHOR B. I. *Containing more than hath been Publickely Spoken or Acted*. With the seuerall Character of euery Person' (see Figure 21.1, depicting the title page to the third edition of 1600, which contains the same innovative features

Print culture and reading practices

> *The comicall Satyre of*
> # EVERY MAN
> ## OVT OF HIS
> ### HVMOR.
>
> As it was first composed by the Author B. I.
>
> *Containing more then hath been publikely spoken or acted.*
>
> With the seuerall Character of euery person.
>
> *Non aliena meo pressi pede | * si propius stes*
> *Te capient magis | * & decies repetita placebunt.*
>
> LONDON,
> Printed for Nicholas Linge.
> 1600.

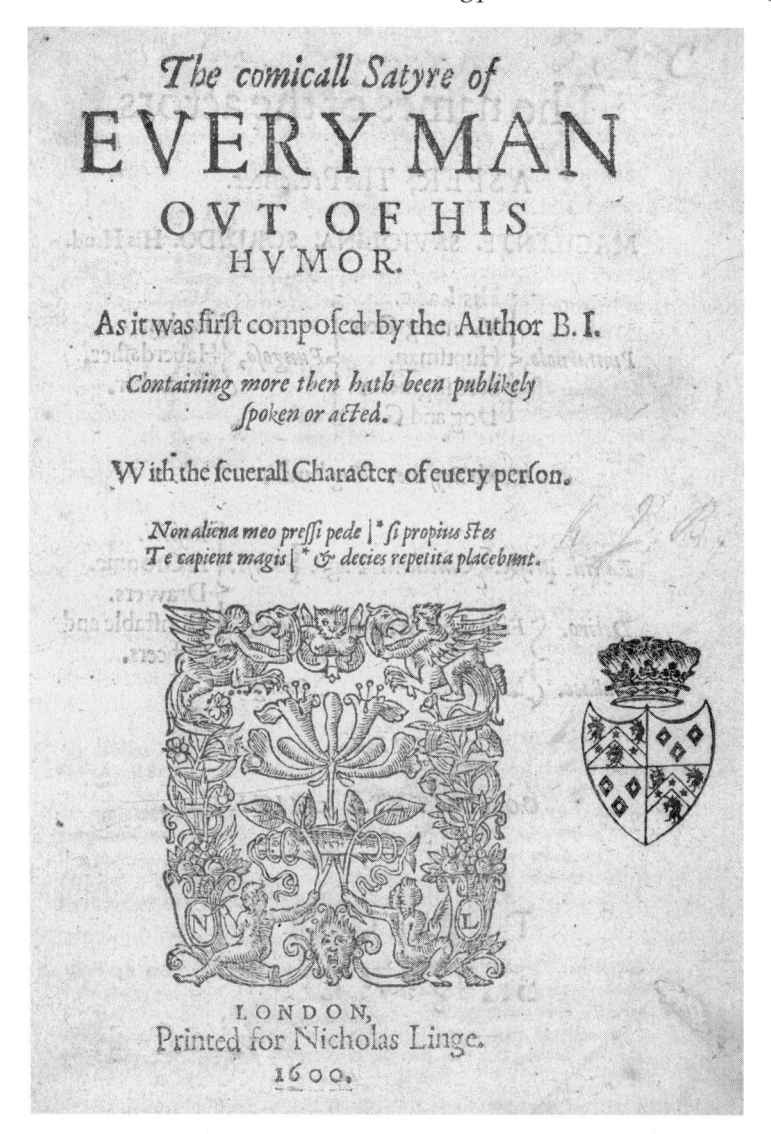

Figure 21.1 Title page to the third edition of *The comicall satyre of Euery Man Out of His Humor.*

as the first). Displayed in bookshops as well as hung on posts and walls in London, title pages were the primary means of advertising books in early modern England, and the one for *Every Man Out of His Humour* was unlike any before it. To begin, the title page prioritizes the text authored by Jonson over that performed by the Lord Chamberlain's Men, who go unmentioned. Claiming the play was printed 'AS IT WAS FIRST COMPOSED' reversed the usual marketing strategy of selling plays as they were performed on stage.[12] Almost two-thirds of professional play title pages published from 1590 to 1600 repeated some version of the refrain 'As it was played' or 'As it was sundry times acted' or 'As it hath been publicly acted', a phrase Jonson co-opted for his written text. In addition, one reason the playbook contained 'more than hath been Publickely Spoken or Acted' is that Jonson printed two endings to the play. When it was initially performed, the last scene involved a character representing Queen Elizabeth, which, according to Jonson, 'many seem'd not to rellish' (sig. R3r). He therefore wrote a new ending but also published the original one with a five-part defence of it. No other play had ever been printed with multiple endings.

Before Jonson, moreover, only one dramatist had ever been called an 'Author' on a title page: Seneca, who was lauded as 'the most graue and prudent author' in Jasper Heywood's translation of *Troas* (1559; 1559; [1562?]). By aligning himself with a canonical Latin author, Jonson was signalling the classical tradition in which he wanted his play to be read, an impression furthered by the Latin motto he adapted from Horace's *Ars poetica* for use on his title page: '*Non aliena meo pressi pede* | ** si propius stes / Te capient magis* | ** & decies repetita placebunt*'. ('I did not follow in the footsteps of others | if you examine it up close, / it will strike you the more | and will continue to please after ten repeated viewings').[13] Jonson was obviously well aware of the originality of his first publication.

This originality was furthered by the unusual decision to advertise the characters he created for the play. Whereas a few earlier professional plays had been printed with a simple list of characters, either on the title page or on the first couple of pages inside the book, Jonson provided both a list of 'The Names of the Actors' (i.e. characters) and an elaborate description of each one. The main character Asper, for example, is described as '*an ingenious and free spirit, eager and constant in reproofe, without feare controuling the worlds abuses*' (sig. A3r). These extended character descriptions were intended to aid readers of the play, not spectators, and Jonson would include them again in several later playbooks.

The ground-breaking bibliographic features Jonson introduced in *Every Man Out of His Humour* were a harbinger of other innovations he would make in subsequent play quartos. *Cynthia's Revels* (1601) was the first professional play to be dedicated to a patron, and other dedications followed in *Volpone*, *Catiline* and *The Alchemist* (1612).[14] *Cynthia's Revels*, *Poetaster* (1602) and *Sejanus* (1605) contain short addresses to readers, as did *Every Man Out of His Humour*. *Sejanus, Volpone* and *Catiline* were three of the first four professional plays to be preceded by commendatory verses praising the play and its author; the fourth, John Fletcher's *The Faithful Shepherdess,* was issued with a commendatory poem written by Jonson. Lastly, *Sejanus* was the first professional playbook, or one of the first, to contain an 'Argument' summarizing the play and situating it in a larger historical context.[15] In the 1580s and 1590s, almost no professional plays were printed with paratextual material, but in the wake of Jonson's quartos, more and more began to include them. Such material could summarize the action of the play, help readers to understand and keep track of characters, explain or defend controversial aspects of the play and its performance history, and answer or anticipate criticisms from readers. More broadly, the inclusion of paratextual material caused professional plays to resemble closet and classical dramas, publications that Jonson used as models for both the content of his plays and their appearance in print.

Jonson's strong sense of authorial identity remained conspicuous in his play quartos too. Every edition of Jonson's professional plays advertises his name or initials on its title page – occasionally calling him an 'Author' – and almost every one contains a Latin motto.[16] The address to readers of *Sejanus* reveals a remarkable fact about the authorship of the play, which 'is not the same with that which was acted on the publike Stage' (¶2v). The play had been co-written with another unnamed dramatist, but before it was printed, Jonson replaced all of the other author's contributions with passages of his own. Jonson's authorial presence also emerges in the play's copious marginal notes, in which he defends his play against its critics and aggressively demonstrates his classical knowledge. In making *Sejanus* look like a classical play, Jonson used for the first time the technique of continuous printing, in which a verse line split between two speakers is printed on a single line to preserve the full metrical unit. Continuous printing privileges the integrity of the poetic line over the separation of dramatic speeches and hence the literary over the theatrical. Like paratextual material, it was used most often in university plays and translations of Latin authors, making it ideally suited to the literary ambition of Jonson, who would employ it afterward in the quartos of *Volpone, Catiline* and *The Alchemist,* and in his 1616 folio.[17]

In part because the printed texts of *Every Man Out of His Humour* and *Sejanus* differ from the versions performed on stage, scholars have sometimes argued that Jonson worked to establish his authorial identity by distancing his plays from the commercial theatre. And while Jonson did routinely disparage the professional stage, he nevertheless took unprecedented steps to advertise the theatrical origins of his plays. He was the first to name a commercial theatre on a title page, initially on *Cynthia's Revels* in 1601, and then on *Poetaster* in 1602, both with the statement, 'As it hath beene sundry times priuately acted in the Black-Friers'. These attributions were the earliest to associate indoor playhouses with 'private' performances. Indoor playhouses were actually as public as outdoor amphitheatres like the Globe, but they were often thought to cater to audiences of a higher social rank because, among other reasons, they charged higher admission prices and had smaller seating capacities. Building on the example of Jonson, later playbooks regularly named playhouses on their title pages and were instrumental in securing the reputation of indoor theatres as 'private houses'.[18] Furthermore, although it does not name any theatres, the 1616 *Works* does print the names of the principal actors who performed in Jonson's plays. This was the first time actor lists were supplied for professional plays, though Jonson had done the same in several earlier editions of his masques, beginning with *Hymenaei* (1606), the first printed masque to feature the names of the performers. As these examples show, Jonson's periodic antitheatrical statements did not prevent him from introducing both theatres and actors into his printed plays. Many others would soon follow his lead.

If we look at the playbooks of the 1630s, in the decade before the closing of the theatres, we can better appreciate Jonson's influence on the publication of drama. Whereas almost no professional plays in the 1590s contained any paratexts – a few had a list of characters (5 per cent of editions) or an address to readers (8 per cent of editions) – those in the 1630s were filled with a range of paratextual material: 64 per cent contain a list of characters; 38 per cent a dedication; 22 per cent an address to readers; 16 per cent commendatory verses; 5 per cent a list of actors (concentrated in the years 1629–33); and 4 per cent an argument (almost always in historical plays). The marketing of authors and theatres and the use of Latin mottoes on title pages likewise increased significantly: author attributions rose from 34 per cent in the 1590s to 74 per cent in the 1630s; theatre attributions from 0 per cent to 56 per cent; and Latin mottoes from 3 per cent to 26 per cent. The advertising of theatres and authors also shows Jonson's influence: almost half (46 per cent) of the indoor theatres named on title pages in the 1630s were called a 'Private House', and in the final years before the closing of the theatres, from 1636 to 1642, a quarter (25 per cent) of professional playwrights named on play title pages were labelled an 'Author'. As these trends suggest, the material appearance of playbooks changed greatly between the 1590s and the 1630s in ways that can be traced back directly to Jonson's earliest quartos.

Most of these paratextual materials – character lists, addresses to readers, dedications, commendatory verses, even Latin mottoes – were aimed at readers of a play and intended to shape their judgement of it. When Jonson began using these features in the 1600s, there was no way to know that they would eventually become standard methods of selling professional plays as 'literary drama'. Nor was this the only way that the advertising of professional plays could have developed. The playbooks of Shakespeare, for example, greatly outnumbered and outsold those of Jonson, and they contained almost no paratextual material and never called Shakespeare an 'author'. But the changes introduced by Jonson ended up being more influential so that by the time the theatres closed in 1642, most playbooks included elements that originated in his first publications. The 1616 folio certainly contributed to this transformation, but it was Jonson's quartos that initiated it and, in the end, seem to have had the greater impact, turning plays originally performed in the commercial theatre into texts written by authors and intended for readers.

NOTES

1. All the statistics in this essay are derived from W. W. Greg, *A Bibliography of English Printed Drama to the Restoration*, 4 vols. (London: Bibliographical Society, 1939–59), and A. W. Pollard and G. R. Redgrave (eds.), *A Short-Title Catalogue of Books Printed in England, Scotland, & Ireland and of English Books Printed Abroad, 1475–1640*, 2nd edn, rev. W. A. Jackson, F. S. Ferguson and Katharine F. Pantzer, 3 vols. (London: Bibliographical Society, 1976–91).
2. See, for example, David Gants, 'The Printing, Proofing and Press-Correction of Ben Jonson's Folio *Workes*', in Martin Butler (ed.), *Re-Presenting Ben Jonson: Text, History, Performance* (Basingstoke: Macmillan, 1999), pp. 39–58.
3. Martin Butler, 'Jonson's Folio and the Politics of Patronage', *Criticism*, 35 (1993): 377–90.
4. For an incisive discussion of the genre of 'closet drama', see Marta Straznicky, *Privacy, Playreading, and Women's Closet Drama, 1550–1700* (Cambridge: Cambridge University Press, 2004), pp. 1–6.
5. It is unclear whether Whetstone's plays were unacted or performed in a commercial theatre.
6. John Stephens, *Cynthia's Revenge; or, Maenander's Ecstasy* (1613), dedicatory epistle, sig. A2r.
7. Ben Jonson, *Volpone*, ¶2v, ¶3v, A1v; Ben Jonson, *Catiline*, sigs. A3r, A4r.
8. Stephens, *Cynthia's Revenge*, sig. A2v.
9. Stephens, *Cynthia's Revenge*, sig. A3r.
10. Jeffrey Knapp, 'What Is a Co-Author?', *Representations*, 89 (2005): 1–29, esp. pp. 19–20.

11. For the date of the third edition of *Every Man Out of His Humour,* see Ben Jonson, *Every Man Out of His Humour,* edited by Helen Ostovich, The Revels Plays (Manchester: Manchester University Press, 2001), p. 4.
12. John Jowett, 'Jonson's Authorization of Type in *Sejanus* and Other Early Quartos', *Studies in Bibliography,* 44 (1991): 254–65, esp. pp. 256–7.
13. *Every Man Out of His Humour* (Revels Plays), p. 98.
14. Jonson wrote two dedications for *Cynthia's Revels,* one to William Camden and the other to Lucy, Countess of Bedford; each dedication appears separately in single extant copies of the play. Prior to *Cynthia's Revels,* Thomas Dekker dedicated *The Shoemaker's Holiday* (1600) to shoemakers ('all good Fellowes, Professors of the Gentle Craft'), and Whetstone dedicated *1 and 2 Promos and Cassandra* (1578) to William Fleetwood.
15. In 1605, two other professional plays were published with 'Arguments', John Marston's *The Dutch Courtesan* and Samuel Daniel's *Philotas.*
16. For the connection between dramatic authorship and Latin mottoes, see Alan B. Farmer and Zachary Lesser, 'Vile Arts: The Marketing of English Printed Drama, 1512–1660', *Research Opportunities in Renaissance Drama,* 39 (2000): 77–165, esp. pp. 97–103.
17. Zachary Lesser, *Renaissance Drama and the Politics of Publication: Readings in the English Book Trade* (Cambridge: Cambridge University Press, 2004), pp. 66–70. *The Case Is Altered* also contains continuous printing, even though Jonson may not have been involved in its publication.
18. Farmer and Lesser, 'Vile Arts', pp. 82–95.

CHAPTER 22

Visual culture

John Peacock

Jonson's shifting attitude towards the visual culture of his time can be gauged from two different areas of his work: the plays and the masques. The rationale of this attitude is stated in two succeeding sections of *Discoveries,* on 'Poetry and picture' and 'Picture'. Like his contemporaries, Jonson understood 'picture' to mean visual representation or even imaging in general:

Poetry and picture are arts of a like nature, and both are busy about imitation. It was excellently said of Plutarch, poetry was a speaking picture, and picture a mute poesy. For they both invent, feign, and devise many things, and accommodate all they invent to the use and service of nature. Yet of the two, the pen is more noble than the pencil [i.e. painter's brush]; for that can speak to the understanding, the other, but to the sense. (1074–9)

Whosoever loves not picture is injurious to truth, and all the wisdom of poetry. Picture is the invention of heaven: the most ancient and most akin to nature. It is itself a silent work, and always of one and the same habit; yet it doth so enter and penetrate the inmost affection – being done by an excellent artificer – as sometimes it o'ercomes the power of speech and oratory. (1083–7)

From Plutarch, quoting a famous dictum of Simonides, Jonson takes up the idea of poetry and picture related by complementary kinship and rivalry; and in praising picture he stresses their cultural interdependence. Yet his introductory remarks assert the superiority of poetry, which can 'speak to the understanding', not merely the 'sense'; and the very characterizing of representation as a kind of speech, a deployment of language, makes his point before he completes it. This belief, while it may have intensified as his long collaboration with Inigo Jones turned sour, underlies all his work.

Several comedies comment on the place of 'picture' in education. Castiglione had suggested that a knowledge of painting should form part of the liberal education of courtiers, women as well as men. Jonson satirises this idea in *Volpone*, by having Lady Would-Be suggest she has followed the recommendations of *The Courtier:*

> I have, a little, studied physic; but now
> I'm all for music; save i'the forenoons
> An hour or two for painting. I would have
> A lady, indeed, to have all, letters and arts,
> Be able to discourse, to write, to paint.
>
> (3.4.67–71; cf. 4.2.35)

In the earlier *Cynthia's Revels* Cupid says sarcastically of Philautia: 'She has a good superficial judgment in painting, and would seem to have so in poetry. A most complete lady' (2.4.32–4). The last phrase anticipates *The Compleat Gentleman* (1622) of Henry Peacham, who urges the practice of drawing and painting as part of a gentry education. Jonson's scepticism, previously directed against supposedly pretentious ladies, emerges thereafter in *The New Inn,* where Lovel praises the traditional system of placing an elite youth as a page in a noble household to be trained in 'letters, arms' and good conduct, learning especially 'to speak / His language purer' (1.3.44, 48–9). There is no mention of the visual arts, which Sir Thomas Elyot had already allowed in the education of his 'governor' a century before.[1] Rather, the aesthetic dimension of Lovel's programme would be for young men '"To make their English sweet upon their tongue", / As reverend Chaucer says' (1.3.68–9). Invoking the arch-poet of an idealized past, Jonson imagines a world inhabited by his noble patrons where 'picture' offers no rivalry to the prestige of his own medium.

A more explicit claim for the primacy of his own art is made in the long section of *Discoveries*, 'On Poetry', where Jonson equates the power of the orator with that of the poet, especially the poet who writes comic drama:

> because in moving the minds of men and stirring of affections – in which oratory shows and especially approves her eminence – he chiefly excels. What figure of a body was Lysippus ever able to form with his graver, or Apelles to paint with his pencil, as the comedy of life expresseth so many and various affections of the mind? (1797–81)

While the poet expresses the mind, his rivals figure the body. As the supreme masters of their age, Lysippus and Apelles enjoyed exclusive rights to sculpt and paint the image of Alexander the Great; so Jonson is claiming for the comic poet a kind of sovereignty in representation surpassing that of the greatest visual artists, but exercised on a more demotic and inclusive level. The imperious populism of his own comedies resonates with this claim.

Ironically, the spirit of 'the comedy of life' came to be eloquently captured in visual form by Inigo Jones. A sheet of sketches for characters in the anti-masques of *Britannia Triumphans* (1637) (Figure 22.1) suggests that, despite their eventual falling out, the designer had learned a great deal from his competitive colleague about comic portrayal.

Figure 22.1 Inigo Jones, A sheet of sketches for characters in
the anti-masques of *Britannia Triumphans* (1637).

In the Dedication to his *Epigrams,* many of which are addressed to patrons, courtiers and friends, Jonson described those poems as 'The pictures I have made of them' (15). The picturing of individuals in the comedies becomes, understandably, a more turbulent affair, as characters comment on each others' appearance and behaviour with exorbitant figurative ingenuity. *Bartholomew Fair* intensifies this process by moving into the urban panorama of London, so that the energy with which the characters picture each other interacts with the vividly sketched locations around which they move. Wasp complains of his master, the naive squire Cokes: 'yesterday i'the afternoon we walked London, to show the gentlewoman he shall marry ... Why, we could not meet that heathen thing all day, but stayed him: he would name you all the signs over, as he went, aloud, and where he spied a parrot or a monkey, there he was pitched' (1.4.81–7). The feeling of the city as an itinerary of exhibits that induce disarmed fascination drives not only Cokes but the entire posse of leading characters, who come alive in terms of their enthrallment with the 'sights' of London, condensed into the microcosm of the Fair. Jonson invites the same fascination from his audience, as his Induction itemizes some of the attractions to come: 'A wise justice of peace meditant ... A civil cutpurse searchant. A sweet singer of new ballads allurant, and as fresh an hypocrite as ever was broached, rampant' (Induction, ll. 93–5). The mock-heraldic jargon gives a preview of Overdo, Busy and the rest in stills or freeze frames, prior to the drama about to be launched as a succession of moving pictures.

An ironic motto for the animated scenes that follow is supplied by Zeal-of-the-Land Busy, and repeated by his disciple Dame Purecraft: 'the vanity of the eye' (1.6.62; 3.2.57). It invokes Psalms 119:37: 'Turn away mine eyes from beholding vanity.' This text had troubled the painter Nicholas Hilliard who, by complaining that 'we are all generally commanded to turn away our eyes from beauty of human shape, lest it inflame the mind',[2] had seen it as a focus of anxiety for practitioners of 'picture'. Jonson the poet, in his most ambitious project to depict 'the comedy of life', seems less troubled by the Psalmist's petition, and deals with the anxieties it generates by displacing them onto the ridiculous figure of Busy the puritan. As the 'hypocrite ... rampant' promised in the Induction, he declaims against 'toys ... hobby-horses, puppet-plays' and all the paraphernalia of the Fair as idols (Prologue, ll. 4–5), but only after gourmandizing on Ursula's roast pig. Knockem observes, 'He eats with his eyes, as well as his teeth', indicting him for the idolatry he denounces (3.6.40). A comic creation who far outgrows the heraldic stereotype that introduced him, he registers with fervour the conflicting allure and distastefulness of the Fair's ultimately specious fascinations. Jonson, in a prologue addressed to King James for a performance at court, offered the play as a sportive satire on Puritan dislike of carnival commerce, with all its appeal to 'the vanity of the eye' (1.6.62, 3.2.57). In the end this seems to misrepresent a comedy which is much more ambivalent about Busy's watchword and about its own portrayal of Jacobean London as an early modern society of the spectacle.

A major locale of spectacle, as Jonson was only too restively aware, was the playhouse itself. Again and again he rebukes his audiences for their tendency to regard plays as 'shows', instead of attentively following the dialogue and the dramatic action. In the mock contract with the playgoers drawn up in the Induction to *Bartholomew Fair* the Scrivener first categorizes them impartially as 'spectators or hearers' but goes on to indicate that the latter are more welcome for their 'grounded judgments and understandings' (Induction, ll. 56–7). In the prologues and epilogues that he wrote for performances at court, Jonson could be ruder about the mere 'spectators' back in the public theatre, 'The vulgar sort / Of nut-crackers, that only come for sight' (*The Staple of News*, Prologue, ll. 7–8) and look to address 'men that have more of ears / Than eyes to judge us' (*The New Inn*, Epilogue, ll. 6–7). A more diplomatic tone is exemplified by the theatre prologue to *The Staple of News*, which conveys the playwright's hopes to the audience:

> For your own sakes, not his, he bade me say,
> Would you were come to hear, not see a play.
> Though we his actors must provide for those
> Who are our guests, here, in the way of shows,
> The maker hath not so; he'd have you wise
> Much rather by your ears than by your eyes.
>
> (Prologue, ll. 1–6)

This preference for the ear rather than the eye as an organ of understanding is in line with the contrast between the dramatist who expresses the mind and the visual artist who figures the body, and with the fundamental priority given to poetry over picture.

The rivalry of ear and eye works as a dramatic opposition in the tragedy of *Catiline*. In his address to the people on being elected consul, Cicero stresses that he is a 'new man', possessing none of the ancestral memorials and images that identify a member of the governing class:

> I have no urns, no dusty monuments,
> No broken images of ancestors
> Wanting an ear or nose.
>
> (3.1.14–16)

With a clever stroke of anachronism, Jonson has him anticipate the broadside which opens Juvenal's critique of nobility in Satire VIII, with scorn for the crumbling busts and other impedimenta that signify patrician lineage.[3] Cicero has risen through his talent for oratory, and his subsequent attack on the renegade aristocrat Catiline is launched with speeches in the Senate. Catiline fights back by branding him an enemy of the senatorial order, an upstart rabble-rouser, 'A boasting, insolent tongue-man' (4.2.99–102). Cicero's riposte is delayed but effective. In a later episode he confronts the patrician Lentulus with a treasonous letter, sealed with the image of the latter's patriotic grandfather, and poses the question:

> Was not his picture,
> Though mute, of power to call thee from a fact
> So foul –
>
> (5.3.88–90)

The answer and its implications are obvious. The aristocrat, whose pre-eminence is signified by the potency of dumb images, is overcome by the articulate energy of the man of words. In the context of Jonson's claims for his own art, *Catiline* is as much a cultural parable as a political tragedy.

In warning of the insufficiencies of visual representation, Jonson's drama reserves its heaviest scepticism for the art of painting. The reason lies in the ambiguity of the term 'painting' itself, which can refer either to the work of the 'picture-maker', who in England at this time would most likely be producing portraits, or to the use of cosmetics. Both the portraitist and the make-up artist could be seen as painters of faces, as could the women (and men) who made themselves up with substances supplied by professional cosmeticians or 'painters'. Like many of his contemporaries, sustained by a tradition reaching back to pagan antiquity and the Church Fathers, Jonson was obsessed with female cosmetics as images of falsehood. Drummond reports that he often recited an epigram by Donne:

> Thy flattering portrait, Phryne, is like thee
> Only in this, that ye both painted be.
>
> (*Informations* 18, 510–11)

To this way of thinking, the creative feigning of reality which is involved in 'picture' can be compromised by the capacity of 'painting' to falsify human features, either with cosmetics or by the artist's idealization.

The duplicity of 'painting' is signalled at the start of *Every Man Out of His Humour*, when Asper declares his compulsion to castigate wickedness:

> ... my language
> Was never ground into such oily colours
> To flatter vice and daub iniquity.
>
> (Induction, ll. 11–13)

It is not clear whether the 'oily colours' are those of the portraitist or the cosmetician, nor does it need to be: it is the 'colours' themselves which are perilous substances, prone to unctuous misrepresentation. Asper's counterpart in *Cynthia's Revels,* the more composedly censorious Crites, allows the necessary distinction to emerge. Describing to Mercury the ladies of the court, he sums them up as 'all disdaining but their painter and apothecary,' 'twixt whom and them is this reciproque commerce: their beauties maintain their painters, and their painters their beauties'; Mercury responds 'Sir, you have played the painter yourself, and limned them to the life' (Folio 5.4.41–5). In this exchange the identities of cosmetician and portraitist are discriminated, and the latter aligned with realistic representation; but the joke only works because the same word covers both roles, as if they were potentially interchangeable.

To conceive of pictorial art in terms of its material medium was a habit that English culture in Jonson's time had not entirely outgrown. He himself reveals disparate attitudes in different areas of his work. In *Discoveries,* the long section 'On Picture', based on Pliny and Quintilian, respectfully summarizes the progress of pictorial art in antiquity, with the proviso that the capacity for representation was learnt by painters from poets: 'Picture took her feigning from poetry' (1102). In the plays, 'picture' usually figures as 'painting' and the issue of its kinship to cosmetics is left wide open. Crites in *Cynthia's Revels* plays on this association to compliment Cynthia. He plans a masque in which a succession of allegorical females symbolize her virtues, expressing 'Their several qualities ... in several colours' and each carrying an *impresa* shield with a visual 'device' and a motto. The final figure is Apheleia or Simplicity, dressed in white, 'without colour, without counterfeit ... Her device is no device', that is, her shield is blank, with the motto 'omnis abest fucus' (5.2.39–43). As 'fucus' literally means cosmetic paint or wash, the meaning is: 'devoid of all dissimulation', referring to Cynthia's purity. The description plays on terms like 'colour', 'counterfeit' and 'device', which evoke the element of pictorial symbolism crucial to court entertainments while at the same time suggesting potentially negative connotations. The notion of the pictorial is collapsed into that of the cosmetic, to produce the conceit that Cynthia's purity is beyond representation, unsusceptible of being 'painted'.

In Jonson's texts for the court masques, 'picture' is allowed its proper esteem, and not characterized in material terms. This adjustment can be gauged from *The Masques of Blackness and Beauty,* his two initial pieces for Queen Anna in 1605 and 1608. In each case Jonson describes the scenic machine in which the masquers appear. For *The Masque of Blackness,* this was a 'great concave shell' (46) floating towards the shore of:

> a vast sea ... from the termination, or horizon of which ... was drawn, by the lines of Prospective, the whole work shooting downwards from the eye; which decorum made it the more conspicuous, and caught the eye afar off with a wandering beauty. (65–70)[4]

Jonson is concerned to explain that the scene achieves visual and aesthetic coherence through the use of linear perspective, and also to show that he appreciates this fundamental aspect of modern pictorial science, which would be unfamiliar to many spectators. For *The Masque of Beauty,* the corresponding scene was a floating island, with an elaborate tier of seating 'called the throne of beauty', which revolved in one direction while its stepped base revolved contrariwise. Jonson praises the engineering of this scene, while criticizing its visual effect: 'The painters, I must needs say ... lent small colour to any, to attribute much of the spirit of these things to their pencils. But that must not be imputed a crime either to the invention or design' (228–31). The culprits he picks on are the scene painters, who failed to do justice to the overall conception of the inventor (Jonson himself) who devised the scene, and the designer (Inigo Jones) who realized it in detailed drawings. These distinctions show that Jonson is familiar with the modern Italian theorist Lodovico Dolce, who divided *pittura* into three parts: invention, design and colour.[5] Like his previous praise, his partial criticism here implies an understanding of 'picture' in advance of many contemporaries.

How deep this understanding went is open to question: certainly not as deep as the Vitruvian architectural aesthetic which Anthony Johnson has detected in the structure of the early masques. Nonetheless, Richard Peterson, in his study of Jonson's encomiastic poetry, has shown how he could deploy metaphors of sculpture, about which he probably knew very little, to powerful effect.[6] What matters for Jonson the masque writer is his determination to figure not just as one specialist in a team of collaborators but as the 'inventor', the artist responsible for the informing fiction of the whole work and therefore capable of understanding the various arts of which it was compounded. This magisterial knowledge could be expressed in a published masque in descriptive passages, or the poetic text itself, or interpolated compliments to performers and collaborators. He was especially concerned to demonstrate his grasp of the 'arts of design', the visual disciplines of painting, sculpture and architecture which made up Inigo Jones's special province as scenographer and producer.

Jonson's quarrel with Jones has been analysed in a classic essay by D. J. Gordon.[7] The sticking point for Jonson was that the fiction invented and articulated by the poet was the 'soul' of the work, while the material representation on stage was only the 'body'. This being allowed, he was prepared, at least in the early years, to lavish attentive approval on the visual dimension of the masques; hence his tribute to the main scene of *The Masque of Blackness,* which 'caught the eye afar off with a wandering beauty' (ll. 69–70), although he then concludes, 'So much for the bodily part' (l. 71). Elsewhere he gives freer rein to evocative descriptions of spectacle. *Hymenaei* (1606), his first published masque text, begins with a manifesto about the distinction between 'soul' and 'body' (ll. 1–9), but also offers an affective response to the occasion:

> Such was the exquisite performance, as ... that alone ... was of power to surprise with delight, and steal away the spectators from themselves. Nor was there wanting whatsoever might give to the furniture, or complement, either in riches, or strangeness of the habits, delicacy of dances, magnificence of the scene, or divine rapture of music. Only the envy was that it lasted not still, or, now it is past, cannot by imagination, much less description, be recovered to a part of that spirit it had in the gliding by. (ll. 522–32)[8]

This is itself an 'exquisite performance' by Jonson, which aims to evoke in its readers the same feeling ascribed to the spectators of the masque, to 'steal' them 'away ... from themselves'. Part of its effect is an imaginative generosity towards the poet's fellow artists, especially Jones, responsible for both 'the habits' and 'the scene'. But as a literary tour de force it also appropriates their achievements: it textualizes the spectacle and annexes it to the poet's domain.

Within these limits Jonson is more than willing to celebrate the visual appeal of the masque, not only in reportage but also in his verse. *Pleasure Reconciled to Virtue* (1618) places the masquers under the guidance of Daedalus, the 'artificer' (Jonson's stand-in), and their three formal dances are envisaged as following the patterns of three successive labyrinths, dedicated to Pleasure, Beauty and Love. As they trace the first labyrinth, Daedalus sings:

> ... let your dances be entwined,
> Yet not perplex men unto gaze;
> But measured, and so numerous too,
> As men may read each act you do.
> (ll. 219–22)

The pattern must be meaningful, but not so intricate as to cause mere amazement: the spectator should be able to 'read' it intelligibly – a typical

Jonsonian position. However, Daedalus moves beyond it in his second song:

> And now put all the aptness on
> Of figure, that proportion
> Or colour can disclose;
> That if those silent arts were lost,
> Design and picture, they might boast
> From you a newer ground.
>
> (ll. 234–9)

Using pictorial terms such as 'figure', 'proportion' and 'colour', this compliments not only the masquers and the choreographer but also Inigo Jones, 'Design, and Picture' being his province. Even their designation as 'silent arts' is ennobled by association with the quiet aloofness of the dancing courtiers. Jonson forgoes his usual entrenched superiority to empathize with the 'mute poesy' of his co-worker and rival, as if masques were 'pictures with light and motion'.[9]

That last phrase was of course used by Jones triumphantly after their partnership had been dissolved and Jonson ousted from the masque productions. In 1631, the year of the rupture, two masques were published with credits to both partners as 'Inventors'. It seems that Jonson had been forced to give ground, although he ensured that his own name had precedence. He also introduced the King's masque, *Love's Triumph through Callipolis*, with a preface headed 'To make the Spectators Understanders' (l. 1),[10] as if he feared that the courtiers had become no better than his theatre audiences who had to be constantly reminded to listen to the words instead of revelling in the 'show'. After the break-up he could express this fear openly and pin the responsibility on his rival, in the 'Expostulation with Inigo Jones':

> O shows! Shows! Mighty shows!
> The eloquence of masques! What need of prose
> Or verse, or sense to express immortal you?
>
> (ll. 39–41)

The gracious even-handedness which he could extend to the visual appeal of the masque in years past, when he felt confident of his own primacy, has turned into outrage at the apparently irresistible claims of spectacle. Turning his own doctrine on its head, he exclaims, 'Painting and carpentry are the soul of masque!' (l. 50). 'Painting' here does not mean 'picture', but cosmetic daubing and dissembling. Excluded and aggrieved, Jonson regresses to the bitter tone of Asper, whose 'language / Was never ground into ... oily colours' (Induction, l. 11),[11] and revives the suspicious anxieties that his plays entertain towards 'painting' and other snares in the domain of the visual.

NOTES

1. Sir Thomas Elyot, *The Boke Named The Governour* (London and New York: Everyman's Library, 1907), pp. 28–32.
2. Arthur F. Kinney and Linda Bradley Salamon (eds.), *Nicholas Hilliard's Art of Limning* (Boston, Mass.: Northeastern University Press, 1983), p. 23.
3. G. G. Ramsay (ed. and trans.), *Juvenal and Persius* (Cambridge Mass.: Harvard University Press, 1961), 159, Satire VIII, ll. 1–5.
4. The editions of *The Masque of Blackness* and *The Masque of Beauty* cited throughout are from Ben Jonson, *The Complete Masques,* edited by Stephen Orgel (New Haven, Conn.: Yale University Press, 1969).
5. Mark N. Roskill, *Dolce's Aretino and Venetian Art Theory of the Cinquecento* (Toronto: University of Toronto Press, 2000), pp. 116–17.
6. See Anthony Johnson, *Ben Jonson's Poetry and Architecture* (Oxford: Clarendon Press, 1994) and Richard Peterson, *Imitation and Praise in the Poems of Ben Jonson* (New Haven, Conn.: Yale University Press, 1981).
7. D. J. Gordon, 'Poet and Architect: The Intellectual Setting of the Quarrel Between Ben Jonson and Inigo Jones,' in Stephen Orgel (ed.), *The Renaissance Imagination* (Berkeley, Calif.: University of California Press, 1975), pp. 77–101.
8. The edition of *Hymenaei* cited throughout is that from Ben Jonson, *The Complete Masques,* edited by Stephen Orgel (New Haven, Conn.: Yale University Press, 1969).
9. Aurelian Townshend, *Tempe Restored,* ll. 49–50, in Stephen Orgel and Roy Strong, *Inigo Jones: The Theatre of the Stuart Court,* 2 vols. (Berkeley, Calif.: University of California Press, 1973), vol. II, p. 480.
10. The edition of *Love's Triumph through Callipolis* cited throughout is from Ben Jonson, *The Complete Masques,* edited by Stephen Orgel (New Haven, Conn.: Yale University Press, 1969).
11. The quartos of *Every Man Out of His Humour* which preceded the folio text read 'soul' for 'language'.

CHAPTER 23

The body

Ben Morgan

Ben Jonson does not like the fact of being in a body. When bodies intrude on his texts, it is usually in the context of their capacity to be degraded, to be ridiculed or to carry contagious disease. Crispinus, one of the bad poets of his self-referential *Poetaster*, eventually vomits up his pretentious Latinate speech – a moment paralleled in the onstage vomiting at the end of *Bartholomew Fair*. In the final scene in Newgate in *The Devil is an Ass*, the junior devil and general mischief-maker, Pug, is led out on the back of the Vice, Iniquity, where usually the Devil would have carried off the Vice – a witty exploitation of the conventions of role and physicality which reminds us that not even a devil can measure up to the reality of human corruption. And in *The New Inn*, the socially presumptuous tailor's wife, Pinnacia Stuff, is stripped of her clothes as a punishment for wearing finery commissioned by her social superiors during sex with her husband. Throughout his drama, Jonson uses players' bodies in a state of indignity or disgrace to spice up the bitterest elements of his comedy.

But the body is not only a vehicle for Jonson: it is also a subject. The body's constant potential for baseness, disease and obscenity is also part of his passionately asserted, neo-classicist aesthetic credo. At crucial moments, especially in his poetry, the body's baseness becomes identified with everything he despises in literary production itself: that it might merely cater to the appetites of its audience, and that its sheer physical presence in the world makes it part of the – for Jonson – filthy transactions of advertising and crowd-pleasing in the nascent literary and theatrical marketplace. As he puts it in the preface to *Sejanus*:

[L]est in some nice nostril the quotations might savour affected, I do let you know ... I ... have only done it to show my integrity in the story, and save myself in those common torturers that bring all wit to the rack; whose noses are ever like swine spoiling and rooting up the muses' gardens, and their whole bodies, like moles, as blindly working under earth to cast any – the least – hills upon virtue. (ll. 18–23)

Bad and ignorant criticism is commonly characterized by bodily indignity in Jonson's writing. By catering for an audience – by being in their physical presence – the text becomes indistinguishable, in a sense, from their desires for it. It becomes a consumable commodity. Here, 'wit', in the hands of what elsewhere Jonson calls 'my merely English censurer', is given its own figurative body, stretched on the rack of critics' misunderstanding. And, in an economy visible throughout Jonson's work, if bad critics force wit, tortuously, into the flesh, it is because their own cultural taste fails to transcend the purely physical: in the garden of the Muses, they are the moles. Their 'spoiling', 'rooting', 'blind' criticism belongs to a body without spiritual or aesthetic vision. As we will see, it is not an exaggeration to say that, for Jonson, the misunderstood text assumes a body of its own, a body which actually *tastes* of its audience's debased appetites. Here, the Muse's naturally rather abstract and symbolic garden has been given a disturbing real presence – soil, moles – in the text.

It is in his distrust of theatrical audiences, of course, that the deep ambiguities of Jonson's position become ambivalent. He is one of the most skilled theatrical choreographers of his period, fully aware that without players, and the physical space in which their bodies play, his theatre would be robbed of its own currency. As author of *The Alchemist* and *Volpone,* he is brilliant, for example, at the highly physical idiom of farce. So when he writes against the 'sluggish gaping auditor' of the playhouse, he also writes against the conditions of his very medium: theatrical performance, and the real, physical space where that happens.

Tracing this problem, the two halves of this chapter work in some ways as mirrors of each other. The first concentrates on his poetry, and its language for publication and performance, while the second looks at a representation of the poet onstage: taking performance, and seeing how it speaks about poetry. What he writes about in his poems, then, Jonson attempts to perform in *Poetaster:* but, as I will suggest, the victory of (aesthetically chaste, disembodied) neo-classical taste over the merely physical taste of the ignorant is visibly compromised, in *Poetaster,* by the very conditions of theatrical performance, and the kind of pleasure that performance offers. Embodied performance *is* the theatre's disease, which neo-classical genre, represented at the end of the play by the administering of a literal purgative, can never hope to cure.

EXPOSURE: THE POETRY

Jonson is known now, and was known in his lifetime, for the brilliance and ferocity of his satire. But in his Epigram, 'To My Book', the poet hopes his poetry will rise above the 'gall' of mere satire towards something higher-minded and – as we will see – less *embodied*:

> It will be looked for, book, when some but see
> Thy title, 'Epigrams', and named of me,
> Thou shouldst be bold, licentious, full of gall,
> Wormwood, and sulphur; sharp, and toothed withal ...
> And by thy wiser temper let men know
> Thou are not covetous ...
>   ... with lewd, profane and beastly phrase,
> To catch the world's loose laughter or vain gaze.
>   (*Epigrams* 2, ll. 1–12)

On one literal level, the argument here is a simple one: Jonson wants his satire to have a moral purpose, its potential to improve the sensibilities of its audience uncompromised by the ambition to entertain them. But behind this straightforward textual politics lies something murkier: a distrust of the economy between author and audience which appears as an instability within the language's own economy between literality and metaphors. '[F]ull of gall', 'toothed', 'lewd' and 'beastly': the text condemned here almost *has* a body, and it is a sick and degraded one. It also provokes an obscene response: 'loose laughter' and 'vain gaze'. The imagery makes the poet–audience relationship into a corrupting quasi-sexual transaction.

The transaction, crucially, is reflected at the level of the language as well as in the argument. The words Jonson uses could refer to a text, to its reader, or to the range of feelings it represents and provokes: any of these could be toothed, tempered, profane, beastly. The text's crime, in this light, is to transgress all these boundaries. Its body is leaky: the aesthetic contingent on this body also breaks and miscegenates the different categories of text, reader and reader-response. It is literally impossible to say which of the three Jonson is referring to here. In fact, it is the exchange between categories – the way text becomes body, and body becomes text – to which he seems to be objecting:

> It is the same logic which informs this epigram:
> Playwright me reads, and still my verses damns:
> He says I want the tongue of epigrams;
> I have no salt. No bawdry he doth mean.
> For witty, in his language, is obscene.

> Playwright, I loathe to have thy manners known
> In my chaste book: profess them in thine own.
> ('To Playwright', *Epigrams* 49, ll. 1–6)

'[N]o salt', 'no bawdry', 'obscene' and 'chaste': the bodily politics here is also a textual politics. In fact, the text is bad in so far as it *is* sexual: that is to say, both *discussing* and *provoking* sexual response. The ambiguity of the adjective 'chaste' – is the book filled with chastity, or chaste itself? – makes his argument: the kind of epigram Jonson rejects not only speaks of promiscuity, but is promiscuous, facilitating an embodied transaction between reader and text which he fears and resents.

As the epigram 'To My Bookseller' makes clear, the economic reality that inspires and reinforces Jonson's imagery is distinctively early modern. In this poem, Jonson, in writerly persona, asks his bookseller not to do anything so vulgar as advertise his book:

> But crave
> For the luck's sake it thus much favour have;
> To lie upon thy stall till it be sought;
> Not offered as it made suit to be bought;
> Nor have my title-leaf on posts or walls,
> Or in cleft sticks, advanced to make calls
> For termers, or some clerk-like serving-man,
> Who scarce can spell th'hard names; whose knight less can.
> (*Epigrams* 3, ll. 3–10)

Most obviously, it is illiteracy to which Jonson objects here. But more subtly, he is – once again – raising a total objection to the physical fact of the published and circulated text itself. The objects of his ire are as much 'title-leaves', 'posts', 'walls' and 'cleft sticks' as they are bad readers like the 'clerk-like serving man' and his knight. As far as the text is a physical object, with a literal, and figurative, body of its own, it betrays the neo-classical high culture to which Jonson aspires to contribute. Like the textual body of the previous epigram, this physical presence breaks up the text's aesthetic unity, dispersing the meaning of the text across different visible, and tangible, locales.

The epigram entitled 'On Poet-Ape' expresses the problem at, perhaps, its fullest. The epigram is about plagiarism – the man who 'takes up all, makes each man's wit his own' – which it swiftly makes a problem of bodily continence and consumption:

> Tut, such crimes
> The sluggish gaping auditor devours;
> He marks not whose 'twas first: and after-times
> May judge it to be his, as well as ours.

> Fool, as if half-eyes will not know a fleece
> From locks of wool, or shreds from the whole piece?
> (Epigrams 56, ll. 9–14).

If the synecdoche of posts, walls and sticks split the text of 'To My Bookseller', it is thievery which splits this one, tearing it into 'locks of wool' and 'shreds'. But again it is the undiscriminating audience member whom Jonson really condemns: the fact, by implication, of audience–poet transaction itself. This figure literally interposes its own degraded ('sluggish, gaping') body onto the text. The text is inappropriately digested both by its plagiarist and its recipient: neither respect the author's grip on it ('May judge it to be his, as well as ours'). Jonson is objecting to a consumerist attitude towards literature, one which values it only for the pleasure and profit it can afford those involved with its entry into public life. The 'tremulous and private body' of the text itself is degraded by this objectification.

Jonson is ambivalent, then, about audience per se, and the figure through which he chooses to express this ambivalence is, repeatedly, embodiment. This figure of embodiment, in turn, stands for the appetites which literary entertainment gratifies and which reciprocally carnalize and contaminate the text. If we want to know why Jonson chooses this figure, we need look no further than 'On Poet-Ape', with its figure of the auditor. After all, where is an 'auditor', sluggish and gaping or otherwise, likely to be found, except in the theatre? In my second section, I will suggest that, if the text risks sickness by being published, the theatre is where, for Jonson, it inevitably catches cold. My example comes from Jonson's longer, and more complex, theatrical treatment of the 'Poet-Ape', or false artist: *Poetaster*.

DISEASE: *POETASTER*

If we have so far discussed the difference between Jonson's highly educated, even elitist, aesthetic and the very conditions of publishing and performance in Elizabethan and Jacobean London, then it is this *mise en scène* that informs *Poetaster*. Part of the famous 'war of the theatres', in which Jonson and his rivals John Marston and Thomas Dekker bitterly satirized each other in their plays, *Poetaster* dramatizes Jonson's own predicament as the innocent subject of ignorant criticism. Jonson's figure of the poet, the young Horace, is, it turns out, both perfect classical author *and* cultural medic: the play ends with his administering a series of purgatives to one of his critics which makes the unhappy man cough up his ill-chosen words.

We will return to that scene in a moment. But to investigate the textual politics at work here, and the way they inevitably encode a view of culture, and theatre, as *embodied*, it is worth beginning at the beginning of the play. In fact, *Poetaster*'s discourse of infectious disease, and its intimate connection to theatrical performance, begins with the play's prologue. Its speaker, Envy, embodies everything that Jonson thinks is wrong with contemporary ways of reading, especially ways of reading Jonson himself. Envy is a kind of self-made Medusa, whose venom is ready to transmit itself to its victim:

> Here will be subject for my snakes and me.
> Cling to my neck, and wrists, my loving worms,
> And cast you round in soft and amorous folds,
> Till I do bid uncurl: then break your knots,
> Shoot out yourselves at length, as your forced stings
> Would hide themselves within his maliced sides
> To whom I shall apply you.
> (Induction, ll. 5–11)[1]

What emerges clearly here is that if Envy is being condemned, it is partly because the figure is *physical*. Its envy of real artistry is part of what keeps it trapped in a sensual transaction with its audience which is both debasing and debased. So the language revels in the figure's serpentine form, mimicking it with its slither of fricatives and sibilants; and the logic of that language echoes another property of consumerist writing which Jonson has identified, its tendency to break the text's integrity, transgressing boundaries, ontological and literal. Envy's 'worms' are instructed to 'uncurl', '[s]hoot out', move from imaginary beings into real ones. And Envy's practice, unjust criticism, is also figured as a repulsively bodily phenomenon:

> Here, take my snakes among you, come and eat,
> And while the squeezed juice flows in your black jaws,
> Help me to damn the Author. Spit it forth
> Upon his lines, and show your rusty teeth
> At every word or accent: or else choose
> Out of my longest vipers, to stick down
> In your deep throats, and let the heads come forth
> At your rank mouths; that he may see you armed
> With triple malice, to hiss, sting and tear
> His work and him ...
> (Induction, ll. 44–53)

What distinguishes Envy and its followers is what is in their *mouths*: 'squeezed juice', 'rusty teeth', vipers. Images of perverse or sexualized orality are Jonson's familiar figures for bad reading. Rather than understanding, these figures are eating, grinning, spitting. Envy is the fulfilment of the fears about the embodied relations of a text's public life which Jonson expresses in his poetry, and it enacts the way a text and the appetites it provokes might become indistinguishable from each other.

But something is importantly different. Envy is *on stage*. And if the figure possesses a wholly physical mode of cognition, it is exactly the right mode in which to recognize the physical conditions of theatrical performance:

> Stay! The shine
> Of this assembly here offends my sight;
> I'll darken that first, and out-face their grace.
> Wonder not if I stare: these fifteen weeks
> (So long as since the plot was but an embrion)
> Have I with burning lights mixed vigilant thoughts
> In expectation of this hated play ...
> (Induction, ll. 11–17)

'[T]his assembly here' is, of course, the audience Envy is addressing. With its hissing snakes, and assertion of the power of its 'stare' over that of the audience, Envy is so present on stage that the figure seems to stand for stage presence per se. It recognizes, like any player, that its role is to 'out-face' the audience, commanding their attention and manipulating their sense of reality. Even the figure's language for its interiority is bound up with the exigencies of stage production: its 'vigilant thoughts' are somehow interspersed, perhaps illuminated by, the internalized 'burning lights' of stage lighting. In other words, if Envy stands for an unhealthy, consumerist attitude towards text, it also brilliantly represents the performative essence of theatre. The critical attitude Jonson condemns, and the literal currency in which he, as playwright, trades, are in structural tension with each other. Theatre is sick, just like Envy is.

It further becomes apparent that Envy is in tension with the generic situation of neo-classical drama itself: Rome, the play's setting. On seeing what must be the board announcing the play's scene, he starts back:

> 'Rome?' 'Rome?' and 'Rome?' Crack eye-strings, and your balls
> Drop into earth! Let me be ever blind!
> I am prevented; all my hopes are crossed,
> Checked and abated; fie, a freezing sweat
> Flows forth at all my pores, my entrails burn!
> What should I do? 'Rome'! 'Rome'! O my vexed soul,
> How might I force this to the present state?
> (Induction, ll. 28–34)

Confronted with its own generic setting, the purely performative Envy is appalled. In this moment, we see the crowd-pleasing, purely sensual and transactional essence of performance ekphrastically confronting its own generic context. It knows that Rome is an idea, as well as a real place:

> O my vexed soul,
> How might I force this to the present state?

Envy wants to assert *presence,* the embodied moment, over the absent presence which is genre. But for Envy, a mere body, 'Rome' has the blinding, almost neo-Platonic clarity of a moral Form. And Envy's reaction is, consequently, the reaction of a tormented physical being:

> Crack eye-strings, ... a freezing sweat
> Flows forth at all my pores, my entrails burn!

In short, Envy is everything that Jonson the dramatist seeks to contain *about his own drama* – its own inherent theatricality, which means its status as an act of exchange between performer and audience, in which classical genre can never 'out-face' its performative context. And it speaks of this phenomenon in the language of sickness, perversion, poison and disease. Perhaps nowhere in Jonson's canon is the tension between the diseased body of performance and the *mise en scène* of neoclassical drama, clearer.

It is in the light of this tension between genre and performance that we can profitably assess the play's conclusion, in which the ideal author (Horace) is figured as *curing* bad taste in the pseuds and critics who surround him. At the end of the play, Horace is in the presence of Virgil and Caesar, who embody the perfect arbitration of classical taste. About to treat his enemy Crispinus' envy and ignorance, Horace explains:

> Ay. Please it, great Caesar, I have pills about me,
> Mixed with the whitest kind of hellebore,
> Would give him a light vomit that should purge
> His brain and stomach of these tumorous heats ...
>
> (5.3.385–8)

When Crispinus finally takes the pills, what he vomits forth are words:

CRISPINUS: O – retrogade – reciprocal – incubus.
...
O – glibbery – lubrical – defunct – O –
...
Chilblained – O – O – clumsy –
HORACE: That clumsy stuck terribly.

(5.3.460, 465, 479–80)

This conclusion is full of the ambivalence I have been tracing throughout this chapter. It simultaneously disowns the unenlightened, unreflective transaction between audience and text and, by provoking the most embodied of pleasures, laughter, risks enacting it. If Envy, after all, stood for that element in performance which is always purely physicalized, and always trying to provoke pleasure, then a similar quality seems to attach to verbal utterance itself in this scene. We *feel* Crispinus's words all the more intensely for their being vomited up, rather than spoken; the stage becomes a place where language itself is given a body, its audible texture central to its meaning. The very effect Jonson has been writing against in the texts I have mentioned – the replacement of a word (or text's) moral meaning with its physical, sensual form – is exactly the effect he generates here, in the name of a satirical closure. At the very moment the embodiment of Jonson's poetic ideals ministers to his critic's ignorance, the visible, embodied element of the drama – the fact that what an audience sees is one man holding another man's head while he vomits – generates a second meaning, and mode of appreciation, which precisely traps those ideals in the flesh.

When I call Jonson's a problem of taste, then, I precisely mean that his is a theatre that operates on the borderline between entertainment and instruction, unsure whether it is playing *to* and *with* physical presence (the player's and the audience's) or *against* them. It is also operating on the borderline between physical fact and metaphor – the problem with the player's body is it straddles the divide, blurring the very metaphysical truths Jonson would like it to express. In arguing that genre, for Jonson, operates on, and tries to medicate, performance, then, I do not suggest that this is 'simply' a metaphor. No such boundary is sustainable in a meta-literary discourse which is exactly about the transgression of such boundaries. If Jonson's work has a moral, then, it is simply that the playtext can never cure the play of its real disease: the always-embodied, always-transactional theatre and the literary marketplace that theatre exemplifies.

NOTES

1. The edition of *Poetaster* used throughout is that edited by Tom Cain for the Revels Play series (Manchester: Manchester University Press, 1995).

CHAPTER 24

Law, crime and punishment

Lorna Hutson

Ben Jonson's dramatic career is throughout characterized by an unusually focused attention to the relation between law, especially criminal law, and theatre. We can see his fascination with the connection between courtroom and theatre – and the relationship between deceived spectators and judges of evidence – in all of his plays, from the earliest, pre-canonical works, to the fragments we have of late drafts. For example, the final scene of Jonson's romantic comedy, *The Case is Altered* (first performed early in 1597), opens with a couple of servants-turned-gentlemen who are ready to bring a legal action for slander on their Lord for calling them 'hinds' (which means 'household servants'). Almost immediately, however, their 'pageant' is exposed, and the legal state of case is 'altered' by successive evidential revelations that include proof of their having stolen the gold that seemed to make them gentlemen. At the latter end of Jonson's writing life, the unfinished fragment of a tragedy, *Mortimer: His Fall* (published 1641), introduces after its third act a '*Chorus* of Country-Justices' who tell 'how they were deluded, and made believe the old King lived, by the show of him in Corfe Castle … with the description of the feigned lights, and masques there, that deceived 'em, all which came from the Court' (spelling modernized). In these plays, written thirty years apart, there's a strikingly consistent sense of affinity between the legal witness and the theatrical 'pageant' or 'show' that deceives spectators.

All the plays written in the thirty-odd years between are marked by a similar awareness. All of them likewise feature a surprising number of officers of the law. There are the justices of the peace (JPs): Justice Clement in the revised text of *Every Man In His Humour* (first performed 1598, revised 1616), Justice Overdo in *Bartholomew Fair* (1614), Justice Eitherside in *The Devil is an Ass* (1616) and Justice Preamble in *A Tale of a Tub* (performed 1633). Two plays feature justices' clerks – Roger Formall in *Every Man In His Humour* and Miles Metaphor in *A Tale of a Tub* – who, in different ways, facilitate legal deception. Below JPs come constables, inferior officers with restricted powers to apprehend suspects prior to examination. In the revised text of *Every Man In His Humour*, the waterbearer's wife, Tib, asks a stranger at her door, 'you are no constable, I hope?', and he immediately suspects her: 'Oh, fear you the constable?' (4.10.5–6). Constables figure similarly as officers of arrest in the last act of *The Alchemist*, when the duped clients of Subtle, Face and Doll attempt to bring the force of law to bear on the trio of swindlers (5.3.22–4; 5.5.1–89). In the Venice of *Volpone*, the *avocatori* play the role of English justices, hearing the evidence in the rape and adultery case against Volpone (4.5; 4.6). When Volpone thinks the game is up (for he is guilty of attempted rape), he vividly imagines not only that he hears the *saffi*, or Venetian constables at the door to arrest him, but that he feels the hot branding iron 'Hissing already, at my forehead' (3.8.18).

Jonson's tragedies, *Sejanus* and *Catiline* offer chilling scenes of the abuse of law's name in political trials. In *Sejanus*, Caius Silius is accused and condemned for being 'a traitor to the state' (3.190) by an orator, Afer, who acts both as accuser and judge. When Silius protests, and the Emperor Tiberius justifies the practice ('It hath been usual', 3.201), Silius denounces the terrifying regime in which 'this boast of a law, and law, is but a form ... to take that life by a pretext of justice / Which you pursue with malice' (3.244–7). In the comedy *Epicene*, a barber and a sea captain disguise themselves as a parson and a canon lawyer (a lawyer learned in the law of the Church) and debate the nice points of law that might allow the despairing bridegroom, Morose, to declare his marriage null and void. As Morose is driven, in desperation, to declare himself impotent 'by reason of frigidity', the assembled wedding guests tease and torment him further by observing that he'll need to prove it by being 'searched' by a jury of physicians – or even by the women there present (5.4.37–49). In the much later *A Tale of a Tub*, surreal comedy ensues when the rather dimwitted bridegroom-to-be, John Clay, suddenly comes under suspicion of armed robbery, although in fact the alleged crime is nothing but a hoax perpetrated by Justice Preamble, who is after Clay's bride. Poor Clay is so flustered that he speaks and behaves as guiltily as can be, declaring, with ludicrous truth, that he would be *hanged* if ever he had done such a thing (2.2.148–9).

The England in which Jonson set most of his plays – 'cause we would make known / No country's mirth is better than our own' (*The Alchemist*, Prologue, l. 6) – was characterized by a criminal-justice system unique in Europe. Throughout Continental Europe, nations were refining and developing criminal codes that relied on professional prosecutors examining the accused and witnesses in secret and assigning agreed arithmetical values to the emergent proofs.[1] In England, however, there were no professional prosecutors, and there was no agreed tariff of proof that said, for example, that two credible witnesses equalled conviction. In England, lay people judged the evidence, and a verdict could be reached without any witnesses at all. Local lay officers, known as Justices of the Peace, were appointed by commission and were empowered since a statute of 1360–1 to 'arrest all they may find by indictment or suspicion'.[2] Statutes passed in 1554 and 1555 required them to take written examinations of the 'fact', or alleged deed, and all its attendant circumstances, from witnesses and from the accused, before imprisoning or granting bail.[3] In addition to JPs and constables, the English criminal-justice system relied on the participation of the jury – an assembly of twelve supposedly local people, who were required to hear the case for and against the accused in open court and to give their verdict as to whether or not he or she was guilty or not guilty of committing the 'fact'.[4] Initially, when first established after the abolition of ordeal in 1215, the jury was expected to give its verdict according to local knowledge. By the sixteenth century, however, juries were increasingly being expected to be strangers to the case and to evaluate the evidence presented in court by witnesses.[5] Interestingly, though the causes of these changes are not known, the increased emphasis on jurors as evaluators of evidence coincided with the changes that required JPs to make more detailed and circumstantial evidential inquiries.[6] In the England in which Jonson was writing his plays, the language and habits of thought associated with evaluating evidence were not esoteric skills known only to professional prosecutors and judges but were broadly diffused in popular culture.[7]

Jonson jokes about the popular diffusion of these very skills of evidence evaluation in *A Tale of a Tub* when Toby Turf, High Constable of Kentish Town, asks Basket Hilts to describe the thieves whom he alleges recently robbed and bound himself and his captain. '[W]e that are officers', says Turf, 'Must 'quire the special marks, and all the tokens / Of the despected parties' (2.2.115–17). Turf's 'despected' is a garbling of the technical term, 'suspected', but his other technical term – 'tokens' – was a common synonym for 'evidence'. Sir Thomas Smith's *De republica anglorum*, written c. 1565, describes witnesses in criminal trials as those 'who were at the apprehension of the prisoner, or who can give any ... tokens which we call in our language evidence against the malefactor'.[8]

But if Jonson mocked Turf's wobbly grasp of these procedures (for constables were *not* actually empowered to inquire into the evidence), he was powerfully aware, as a dramatist, of the affinities between the judicial evaluation of evidence and the skills of make-believe in the theatre. The English word 'evidence' derives from the Latin *evidentia,* a rhetorical term meaning 'vividness' or 'clarity'. *Evidentia* was, according to Jonson's favourite author, Quintilian, what a clever lawyer could give to a narrative of the facts, whether true or false, by making all the circumstances seem coherent and plausible.[9] Interestingly, in the Continental neo-classical drama written in imitation of the ancients, the Aristotelian rule of unity of place, combined with the convention of fixed-locale staging, meant that many events could not be staged but were conveyed by narratives. (This actually happens in English Shakespearian drama, too; Hamlet's unstaged sea-voyage, narrated to Horatio, is one example.) Jonson was obviously interested in working within modified neo-classical rules.[10] Part of his interest was in the scope such dramaturgy affords for exploiting the rhetorical *'evidentia'*, the circumstantial realism of narratives of unstaged events, to produce a kind of surrogate theatrical spectacle – an illusion of seeing what is not actually there. We believe not what we see but the circumstances we piece together to understand the narrative. George Chapman went so far as to praise Jonson's tragedy, *Sejanus,* for transforming hearsay into visual illusion, by 'Performing such a lively Evidence / in thy Narrations, that thy Hearers still / Thou turnst to thy Spectators'.[11]

The affinity between the rhetorical 'evidence' (the vivid clarity that narratives acquire by circumstantial elaboration) and the legal evidence considered in criminal trial is key to Jonson's innovation as a dramatist. From his earliest plays, Jonson has his witty, clever figures act like lawyer/dramaturges, manipulating narratives so that other characters draw false inferences that persuade them that they have actually *seen* what does not exist. They become spectators of an illusion generated by their own desire to believe. In *Every Man In His Humour* (1616 folio version), the wits, Wellbred and Edward Knowell, manage to play so effectively on the suspicions of their kinsfolk, especially Wellbred's brother-in-law, Kitely, that by Act 4, both the Knowell and Kitely households have converged on the dwelling of Cob the waterbearer, convinced that it is a brothel to which their loved ones resort. Kitely takes matters into his own hands: 'I'll ha' you every one before a justice', he says (4.10.58), and the scene removes, for the last act, to Justice Clement's house, where an examination takes place. Justice Clement soon uncovers the root cause of the brothel hoax – it was a story put about by Wellbred, to enable Edward Knowell to elope secretly with Kitely's sister, Bridget. Rather amazingly, the JP sees no impropriety in this plot, even when he learns that it involved the faking of his own judicial authority by Knowell's servant, Brainworm, disguised as his clerk

(5.3.91–3). Indeed, the JP reserves his scorn not for those who exploit a general respect for legal authority but rather for those who too easily and unquestioningly obey the law.

At the same time as *Every Man In His Humour* was playing at the Curtain in September 1598 Jonson himself was indicted for manslaughter at the Old Bailey. The Middlesex grand jury found that Jonson 'feloniously and wilfully slew and killed' the actor, Gabriel Spencer, with a rapier in the fields at Shoreditch.[12] By pleading guilty, Jonson did not go before a trial jury (a procedure known as 'putting oneself on one's country'), but he was able to take advantage of the legal procedure known as 'benefit of clergy', which required reading a Latin verse from the Bible to escape hanging. This suggests Jonson's awareness of the rhetorical manipulability of evidence – he was not prepared to risk trusting the jury to find from the evidence that he had, as he later told William Drummond, slain Spencer in self-defence.

Jonson's great comedies continued to exploit an intense awareness of the relations between evidence manipulation and theatrical illusion. For *Volpone*, Jonson studied the details of the Venetian criminal-justice system in Lewis Lewkenor's translation of Gaspare Contarini's *The Government and Commonwealth of Venice* (1599). In 3.2 of *Volpone*, Mosca tells the young heir, Bonario, that he'll bring him where he'll be 'a witness of the deed' of his father's disinheriting him (3.2.63–5). What Bonario actually witnesses, however, is Volpone's attempt to rape Celia. Bonario and Celia, innocent victim and honest eyewitness, immediately go to the police, and when the judges or *avocatori* come in to the courtroom in the trial scene in 4.5, they are ready to think Volpone guilty. Mosca, however, not only primes the advocate Voltore to plead the opposite case – accusing Celia of whoredom – he actually recruits a complete outsider as unwitting corroborative witness. Earlier, in 3.5, Mosca had rid Volpone of the annoying Lady Would-Be by exciting her suspicion that her husband was seeing a courtesan on the Rialto. In 4.6, in a brilliant *tour de force*, Lady Would-Be comes on to identify Celia in court as the prostitute with whom her husband apparently consorted in a gondola (4.6.1–4; see 3.5.19–20). The case is altered: the advocates believe not the true eyewitnesses but the extraordinarily coherent illusion fabricated by Mosca's cunning circumstance and Lady Would-Be's snobbery and jealousy.

Jonson's early and middle comedies thus seem to celebrate the affinities between theatrical illusion and the manipulation of justice. In *The Alchemist*, the swindling Face persuades the neighbours (who swear that they've seen strange goings-on in his master's house) that what they thought they saw was all deception of their eyesight – 'all *deceptio visus*' (5.3.62). Face concludes the play by putting himself on trial by the jury of the audience ('I put myself / On you, that are my country' [5.5.162–3]), but whether for a moral or aesthetic crime is unclear.

Jonson's later comedies, however, engage more critically with law in its political aspect. Early Stuart England saw the sharpening of an ancient constitutional tradition that defined the monarch's power as existing to protect the public good. In its seventeenth-century version, this constitutionalism set the common law against the monarch, insisting it was not the King but the judiciary who had authority to define the public interest.[13] Jonson's *Bartholomew Fair* (1614) has fun with this idea, and with its main proponent, Lord Chief Justice Edward Coke. Justice Adam Overdo, who presides over the Fair's special court, 'professes himself the loyal servant of James I, but he consistently places the law before the king and assumes that he is its only true arbiter'.[14]

The Devil is an Ass (1616) represents a different departure again: here Jonson criticizes the King's and the law's preoccupation with punishing witchcraft, while being unable to discern the real work of the Devil in the perversions and cruelties wrought by greed. The play is set in a contemporary London in which conjurers and magic are prohibited by the King's proclamation of 1615 (1.7.16–17), but in which the financial sleights of projectors, far from being outlawed, form the basis of crown patronage and wealth. Merecraft the projector professes to be able to coin money out of 'cobwebs' (2.1.7), and all this 'without the devil / By direct means; it shall be good in law' (2.1.18–19). Called upon to examine Fitzdotterel's demonic possession (alleged to be the result of his wife's plot to get his estate), Justice Eitherside concludes that 'The proofs are pregnant' (5.8.77). But Jonson here mocks his own earlier evidential dramaturgy: in this scene, unlike its much earlier precursor in *Every Man In His Humour,* what turns out to be true is not what is most circumstantially probable but what seems to defy all probability. In *The Devil is an Ass,* the legally likely plot of poisoning for money with which Fitzdotterel charges his wife is actually false, but what *is* true beggars belief: the Devil has indeed come to London and has proved, by comparison with diabolic Londoners, to be an ass.

Finally, in *A Tale of a Tub,* the focus is on the impact of the tightening crown surveillance of the countryside and localities through the increased accountability of voluntary officers of justice. The participatory nature of judicial administration meant that officers were ideally both answerable to the political centre and responsive to local needs. Through the reigns of James I and Charles I, however, this balance shifted, and local judicial administration came increasingly to be used by the Crown as a tool of its own policies.[15] In *A Tale of a Tub,* the High Constable Turf is at first proud of representing the Crown: 'Does any wight parzent Her Majesty's person, / This Hundred, 'bove the high constable?', he asks (1.4.53–4). By Act 4, however, machinations on the part of the local JP, Justice Preamble, disillusion him. Preamble tricks Turf into believing that a robbery has taken place in the hundred, and that he, Turf, is accused 'Of being careless in the hue and cry' (that is, not performing his judicial office in ensuring capture of the thief [4.1.14]). In representing Turf's increasing bitterness at the impossible political accountability of his humble office, Jonson in this late play adumbrates with beautiful precision the tensions that would lead to the collapse of Charles I's personal rule, and the advent of civil war.[16] He does so, as ever, by exploiting affinities between courtroom and theatre.

NOTES

1. John Langbein, *Prosecuting Crime in the Renaissance* (Cambridge, Mass.: Harvard University Press, 1974), pp. 129–250.
2. *34 Edward III,* c.1 (1360–1).
3. *1 & 2 Philip & Mary* c.13 (1554–5); *2 & 3 Philip and Mary* c.10 (1555).
4. Barbara J. Shapiro, *A Culture of Fact: England, 1550–1720* (Ithaca, NY: Cornell University Press), pp. 8–33.
5. Edward Powell, 'Jury Trial at Gaol Delivery in the Late Middle Ages: The Midland Circuit, 1400–1429', in J. S. Cockburn and Thomas A. Green (eds.), *Twelve Good Men and True: The Criminal Jury in England, 1200–1800* (Princeton, NJ: Princeton University Press, 1988), pp. 78–116.
6. Langbein, *Prosecuting Crime in the Renaissance,* pp. 118–25.
7. See Shapiro, *A Culture of Fact,* p. 32.
8. Sir Thomas Smith, *De republica anglorum,* edited by Mary Dewar (Cambridge: Cambridge University Press, 1982), p. 114.
9. Quintilian, *The Orator's Education,* in 5 vols., ed. and trans. Donald A. Russell (Cambridge, Mass.: Harvard University Press, 2001), vol. II, pp. 250–1, Book 4.2.64–5.
10. See Peter Womack, 'The Comical Scene: Civility on the Renaissance Stage', *Representations,* 101 (2008): 32–56.
11. George Chapman, '*In Seianum Ben Ionsoni*', in Ben Jonson, *Sejanus: His Fall* (London: 1605) sig. ¶ 4v.
12. J. C. Jeaffreson, 'Editor's Preface', *Middlesex County Records,* vol. 1: *1550–1603* (1886), pp. xvii–lx. Available online at www.british-history.ac.uk/report. aspx?compid=65918 (accessed 7 October 2008).
13. See Alan Cromartie, 'The Constitutionalist Revolution: The Transformation of Political Culture in Early Stuart England', *Past and Present,* 163 (1999): 76–120.

14. Leah S. Marcus, *The Politics of Mirth: Jonson, Herrick, Milton, Marvell and the Defense of Old Holiday Pastimes* (Chicago, Ill.: Chicago University Press, 1986), p. 54.
15. Steve Hindle, *The State and Social Change in Early Modern England, c. 1550–1640* (Basingstoke: Palgrave Macmillan, 2000), pp. 3–13.
16. See Catherine Rockwood, 'Topicality and Dissent in Ben Jonson's *A Tale of a Tub*', *Ben Jonson Journal,* 10 (2003): 77–100.

CHAPTER 25

Religion

Julie Maxwell

In the middle of the sixteenth century, during a period of little over twenty years, England officially changed its religion three times. The ferocious religious disputes were not confined to Catholics and Protestants – or, if we are to avoid premature labels, conservatives and reformers. For decades after the break from Rome, Protestants disagreed fiercely among themselves as to what sort of church the Church of England ought to be. Here there were conservatives and reformers too. Ultimately, a few years after Ben Jonson's death, civil war resulted. Some of his finest writing had been inspired by this long religious turmoil.

Traditional medieval Catholicism was ousted by Henry VIII for reasons of personal and financial expediency, rather than theology, and he was not concerned to create a coherent replacement church. That was left to his children. His first heir, the young Edward VI, was under the tutelage of Thomas Cranmer and precociously Protestant. Had he lived longer, England would have been reformed comprehensively. Conversely, when Edward's Catholic half-sister Mary I acceded to the throne, her sole interest was a full-scale restoration of England to the old faith and in order to perpetuate her work she desired the wholehearted conversion of her half-sister and successor, Elizabeth I. But Elizabeth was unlike her siblings in matters of religious policy. She had been brought up a Protestant and only conformed nominally to Catholicism during Mary's reign to save her life. Inconsistency would characterize the church she headed. The thoroughgoing reformation that so many desired would never be undertaken.

Elizabeth's experiences under Mary crucially determined her policies as queen, and they matter here because they explain the sort of religious culture in which Jonson lived and against which some of his most memorable characters fulminated. What Elizabeth wanted was not logical consistency in her church but outward conformity to the church from her subjects. It was therefore compulsory to attend church, but this was not, of course, necessarily equivalent to believing what was said there. Elizabeth reportedly declared she had no wish to make windows into men's souls: the token performance of religious conformity she had once offered herself was acceptable. She was not inclined to probe further, as she had been repeatedly probed by Mary and her councillors. Adherence to the Act of Uniformity in religion could be an act. Unlike private religious belief, whose exact nature was not easily discoverable, nor measurable in political significance, public conformity could be taken as a demonstration of loyalty to the Crown. But it might not mean much else. Some people were, in fact, Church of Englanders in name only – distant ancestors of the modern Brits who write 'C of E' unblinkingly on their hospital forms.

A comical writer and satirist like Jonson, professionally fascinated by all kinds of performance, could not fail to notice such behaviour. In many writers we find references, of varying significance, to contemporary religious habits. But Jonson's detailed attention to his times is central to how his writing works. The early *Every Man Out of His Humour* (1599), for instance, dispenses with a conventional plot as far as possible in order to offer, instead, a satiric portrait of contemporary Elizabethan manners, including religious conformity. A lady's maid is asked if her master is religious. She replies: 'Religious? I know not what you call religious, but he goes to church, I am sure' (2.2.55–6). His piety is about as extensive as his travels, which have taken him once (or perhaps it was twice) to the faraway shore of France. Elizabethan religion is merely a civic duty for him, a matter of correct observance, one of the many he performs unfailingly because he is Mr Punctilious. (His strange name, Puntarvolo, means *punctilious*.) He is an Elizabethan Mr Men character, not so much two-dimensional (as Jonson's creations are sometimes accused of being) as deliberately one-dimensional. And he is the first example of Jonson taking an aspect of contemporary religious behaviour to its *reductio ad absurdum*.

Conformity did not necessarily mean religious indifference, of course. Many conformed gladly because they found genuine spiritual solace in the Church of England. There were also objectors to the national church, Protestant as well as Catholic, who nonetheless continued to conform outwardly, in order to avoid fines and other trouble. The Jonson who wrote *Every Man Out of His Humour* was one of them. Although a churchgoer, he had recently converted to Catholicism. The circumstances were dramatic and leave their mark on the play. Jonson, imprisoned for a fortnight pending trial for the manslaughter of an actor on 22 September 1598, was visited by a priest. He came close to being hung but escaped with his life via a legal loophole – benefit of clergy. Originally intended only for the clergy, who proved their status (in times of widespread illiteracy) by the ability to read a verse of the Latin Bible, by the fifteenth century the privilege had been extended to lay persons. It meant that first-time offenders could avoid the death penalty for manslaughter and other crimes. *Every Man Out of His Humour* features the religious awakening of a miserly farmer, Sordido, who also nearly hangs himself (it is a failed suicide attempt.) The scene is a comical reworking of Jonson's own distinctly unfunny experience. The rustics who cut Sordido down opine that it is 'chance-medley', or accidental manslaughter. Ludicrously inappropriate to the intentionality of suicide, chance-medley was rather a crime, like Jonson's, to which the legal loophole of benefit of clergy applied. *Every Man Out of His Humour* is also presented by a preachy, slightly deranged scholar-playwright whom contemporaries correctly recognized as a self-portrait. But they missed or ignored Jonson's self-irony: his comic ability to treat even his most intense personal experiences (in this case religious ones) with amused, intelligent detachment, in order to transmute them into art.

How Jonson's conversion affected his life practically – what exactly his conformity comprised – we can deduce from ecclesiastical records. Until the end of Elizabeth's reign, Jonson continued to take communion in the Church of England. (The accession of James I emboldened him, like many of Catholic persuasion, to stop.) Jonson's children were also baptized in the Church of England. Jonson was, in other words, what Protestants called a *church papist* and Catholics called a *schismatic* – a Catholic by conviction who nonetheless conformed, wholly or partly, to the state religion.

Being a church papist was not, as we might assume, necessarily clandestine, a way of cloaking one's true religious position. An impression has arisen, however, that Jonson was indeed secretive about his beliefs. In an influential study, Ian Donaldson proposes that Jonson's behaviour as a Catholic is best characterized by the term 'duplicity'.[1] But if Jonson was duplicitous, then how is it that he was widely known to be a Catholic? Theatrical rivals like Marston and Dekker quipped publicly about Jonson's popery in their plays. His church papistry was remarked in *The Whipping of the Satyre* (1601): Jonson (alias the Humourist) had been false to his baptismal vows in the Church of England and was inflamed with 'neuterisme'.[2] The term was sometimes applied rebukingly to church papists by those who thought that conformist churchgoing inevitably signalled spiritual apathy. However, others argued that a Catholic could use his presence in church actively to object to Protestantism.

Jonson's own behaviour in church between 1603 and 1606 can be documented. He is reported to have attended church but abstained from communion – in fact, he absented himself during that part of the service.

At court, James I's Catholic queen consort, Anna of Denmark, likewise abstained. Some Catholics believed that this was demonstration enough of one's inner faith: so far from being duplicitous, it drew attention to one's desire to be loyal to the Crown without compromising oneself spiritually. It also saved lives and fortunes – resources that would be needed in the event of England's restoration to Catholicism. This was the argument of Thomas Wright, a priest Jonson knew and who is sometimes thought to have converted him. Their acquaintance early in James's reign is proved by a dedicatory poem Jonson wrote. Wright advocated church papistry following harsh new anti-Catholic laws that targeted rich Catholic families after the failure of the Gunpowder Plot.

Wright's opinions were a revival of Thomas Bell's, which had been circulating in manuscript since the 1590s and encouraged the church papist to walk into his local parish church and declare out loud that he attended only for reasons of political loyalty.[3] Anyone who had the courage to make such a public statement (or *protestation of civil obedience,* as it was known) was manifestly not duplicitous either. Certainly Jonson was conscious that his behaviour in church could be a public statement when, abandoning his Catholicism and returning to the Church of England around 1610, he made a spectacular *resumption* of communion: 'after he was reconciled with the Church and left of to be a recusant at his first communion jn token of true Reconciliation, he drank out all the full cup of wyne.'[4]

Jonson made plain some of his theological views in his poetry – and discovering them helps to explain why he found the Church of England a more congenial place in 1610 than he did in 1598. Traditionally, critics tell us that 'Jonson's religion rarely appears in his writing, and its inner history is a sealed book to us.'[5] 'This is not to deny the strength and reality of Ben Jonson's religious convictions. It is merely to say that they did not penetrate that layer of his mind where his best poetry was made.'[6] However, Jonson frequently mentions one controversial theological idea: the role of human merit in the scheme of salvation: 'Our merit leads us to our meeds' in his epigram 'Of Life, and Death' (*Epigrams* 80, l.2). Jonson's characteristic emphasis on ethical self-determination is compatible with the Catholic belief (confirmed at the Council of Trent) that God makes the good works of humans meritorious. But it is wholly at odds with the mainstream Calvinist theology of the Elizabethan church. By 1610, however, anti-Calvinist thinkers had gained increasing prominence in the Church of England, particularly in the Jacobean court circles Jonson moved in. Jonson had repeated the term *merit* insistently in four plays following his conversion to Catholicism (*Every Man Out of His Humour, Cynthia Revels, Poetaster* and *Sejanus*). There, it is a latently theological metaphor applied primarily to his worth as a writer. It is unfortunate that Jonson harped on his merits, his misunderstood genius, in turgid passages – but eventually he would write plays of world-class distinction and from time to time, scattered through his oeuvre, it was theology that inspired him to great creative heights.

Take the nature of grace. Calvinists preached that God's grace was irresistible, in no way dependent on human response, whereas Catholics (and other anti-Calvinists) maintained that humans could (or even must) cooperate with divine grace when it was offered. This idea is expressed with lovely poignancy in the Echo scene of *Cynthia's Revels*. The classical nymph has spent 3,000 years able to do nothing but echo. She is offered the chance to regain her body and powers of speech and to ascend to heaven. But like recalcitrant 'worldlings', she 'prophan'st the grace' now available to her (1.2.93–4). Echo's refusal of grace is affecting. It isn't that she is wicked. She is just still too wounded by grief for Narcissus:

> Oh, I could still,
> Like melting snow upon some craggy hill,
> Drop, drop, drop, drop,
> Since nature's pride is now a withered daffodil.
>
> (1.2.72–5)

She is yearning to echo again, to lose herself in the repeated drop of dripping, not to grasp hands with God's sudden grace.

Equally anguished, equally wonderful, is Jonson's poem 'To Heaven'. It is in the speaker's psychological difficulty that the interest of the religious lyric lies, and Jonson characteristically feels misunderstood. People think his piety is merely an act, 'sad for show' (l. 6). But God can tell whether Jonson 'dare pretend / To aught but grace, or aim at other end' (ll. 7–8). Jonson *is* pretending, then: not faking, but *aiming* for Heaven, aspiring like the pretender to a throne, whose claim may be legitimate. The poem asks God to vouch for Jonson's sincerity, but its own strength vouches for that. Writing in a candid, earnest, supplicatory voice, Jonson manages to use religious formulae without sounding formulaic. 'As thou art all, so be thou all to me' (l. 9). This is the formula, he is saying, let it apply in my case. Please be 'My faith, my hope, my love: and in this state / My judge, my witness, and my advocate' (ll. 11–12). Jonson describes this state unflinchingly:

> I know my state, both full of shame and scorn,
> Conceived in sin and unto labour born,
> Standing with fear, and must with horror fall,
> And destined unto judgement after all.
>
> (ll. 17–20)

The last two words are brilliantly chosen. 'After all' means 'after all the events of my life are over' and also 'despite my hope that it might be otherwise'. Jonson has nursed a secret, desperate, hopeless hope that somehow judgement won't happen.

Very differently from this moving religious poetry, Jonson's finest writing about religion often coincides with his funniest. His treatment of religion's more bizarre extremes in *The Alchemist* (1610) and *Bartholomew Fair* (1614) is justly celebrated. Although Jonson's comedy can be understood by anyone who has ever been human, it is useful to look back to Elizabethan religious policy once again. We have seen how, intellectually and emotionally, there was a wide gulf between Jonson's Catholicism and the Calvinism preached by the typical Church of England vicar – although the sometimes ambiguous wording of the English liturgy itself could accommodate contradictory doctrinal positions. Institutionally, however, the Church of England had much in common with its pre-Reformation counterpart. The Elizabethan Church retained traditional clerical vestments, episcopal structure, unleavened wafers at Eucharist, tithing, canon law – partly to appease members of the old faith at home and Catholic governments abroad. One could believe that not too much had changed.

Unfortunately, that was exactly what the Church of England's detractors soon began to say. English clergymen who had been in exile for their faith under Mary were particularly distressed when a comprehensive reformation failed to materialize and bitter when they found themselves persecuted by the new Protestant prelacy for failing to conform to what they regarded as the unacceptable compromises of the Elizabethan church. This problem did not go away with time. On the contrary, in each subsequent generation, with the accession of James I and then of Charles I to the English throne, there were puritan clergy pushing for reformation of the national church or voicing their reasons for separating themselves from it.

It is in the nature of radicalism that there is always a step further to go, a finer scruple to propose – and it is this human propensity that Jonson's best comedies capture; every time a puritan objector sounds progressively shriller and competitively sillier. In *The Alchemist* Ananias is holier than his fellow extremist Tribulation Wholesome. In *Bartholomew Fair,* Zeal-of-the-Land-Busy hysterically perceives popish evil in gingerbread and the proximity of Goldilocks to the whore of Babylon in a scene that is itself hysterically funny. Busy's ultimate showdown with the puppets in the fifth act is the climax of the frenzy and of the comedy. The comic engine mimics the religious acceleration to extremity. Once again, there are, even within this tiny puritan community, conformists as well as zealots. John Littlewit and his wife Win-the-Fight, who has been brought up a strict puritan, make an appearance of conforming to Busy's spiritual leadership in order to get what they want: a day out in that treacherous mire of sin, the world of Bartholomew Fair.

Fiction is never stranger than truth when it comes to the behaviour of religious maniacs. Yet Jonson, like his literary heir Charles Dickens, has been criticized for inventing types so flat that their lungs could never have filled with air. Dickens replied, 'I have never touched a character precisely from the life, but some counterpart of that character has incredulously asked me: "Now really, did I ever really, see one like it?" '[7] Busy had real-life originals too: William Wheatley, preacher of Banbury, claimed to find his fellow believers too scrupulous, too inclined to imagine sins where there were none, but was clearly delighted to pontificate at length on their crises of conscience. It made his opinion important – as Busy's is when called upon to decide the circumstances in which a pure Christian can eat pig at a fair. The much-misunderstood Jonson mocks puritans as exemplary misinterpreters.

Jonson also derived his religious figures of fun from life in his late plays: Parson Palate of St Bartholomew-Exchange in *The Magnetic Lady* (1632) and Chanon Hugh, the vicar of Pancras in *A Tale of a Tub* (1633), glance at the real Caroline incumbents of those livings.[8] Now it was not only flagrant nonconformists Jonson was ridiculing, but, in a traditional vein of literary anti-clericalism, the corruptions of the establishment. And, in a new twist, the apparent conservatives had become reformers, vigorously promoting the controversial ecclesiastical policies of Archbishop Laud. Elizabeth had required conformity to some traditional externals of English worship, inclined rather to let things lie than to alter them yet again. But the Laudian pursuit of the beauty of holiness was actively disruptive and appallingly popish to puritans. Communion tables, for example, suddenly became altars – richly furnished, railed off, relocated to the east end and turned against the wall. This style was once a minority liturgical option at the Jacobean court (dubbed *avant-garde conformity* by historians), in private chapels, cathedrals and collegiate churches. Critics have found a programme for Caroline religious policy in the sometimes hymnal, high church-like spectacle of the Jonsonian masque.[9] But the masque also belonged at court or great private estates – whereas, in the 1630s, Laudian policies were instituted nationwide and adherence to them was demanded. Hence the phrase, avant-garde *conformity*. And hence the outrage. Bitter divisions were created, not least in the London parish where Jonson had set *The Magnetic Lady* in 1632. And it was rebellion, not conformity, still less uniformity in religion, that resulted.

NOTES

1. Ian Donaldson, *Jonson's Magic Houses: Essays in Interpretation* (Oxford: Clarendon Press, 1997), pp. 47–65.
2. Extract reprinted in C. H. Herford, Percy Simpson, and Evelyn M. Simpson (eds.), *Ben Jonson*, 11 vols. (Oxford: Clarendon Press, 1925–52), vol. XI, p. 363.
3. Alexandra Walsham, *Church Papists: Catholicism, Conformity and Confessional Polemic in Early Modern England* (Woodbridge: Boydell Press, 1999), pp. 56–9.
4. Herford *et al.*, *Ben Jonson*, vol. I, p. 141.
5. Herford *et al.*, *Ben Jonson*, vol. II, p. 391.
6. Marchette Chute, *Ben Jonson of Westminster* (London: Robert Hale, 1954), p. 328.
7. Charles Dickens, *Martin Chuzzlewit* (1843–4, repr. London: Penguin, 1994), p. 41.
8. See my 'Ben Jonson Among The Vicars: Cliché, Ecclesiastical Politics and the Invention of Parish Comedy', *The Ben Jonson Journal*, 9 (2003): 37–68.
9. David Norbrook, *Poetry and Politics in the English Renaissance*, 2nd edn (Oxford: Oxford University Press, 2002), pp. 14, 234–5.

CHAPTER 26

Politics

Andrew Hadfield

Jonson wrote a number of poems about friendship, a concept that was central to his intellectual and political vision. The epigram, 'Inviting a Friend to Supper', is a deceptively simple work that appears, on first reading, to be a straightforward celebration of men dining together:

> Tonight, grave sir, both my poor house and I
> Do equally desire your company;
> Not that we think us worthy such a guest,
> But that your worth will dignify our feast,
> With those that come, whose grace may make that seem
> Something, which else could hope for no esteem
> 					(*Epigrams* 101, ll. 1–6).

Jonson is following one of his favourite authors, Martial, and, as in Martial's poem of invitation (Book 5, no. 78), Jonson then lists the food they will be able to share even as he laments the limitations of his table – olives, capers and salad, then mutton, hen in lemon and wine sauce, as well as a variety of game birds. The joke, one Jonson makes elsewhere, is at his own expense, a comment on his gargantuan appetites. But it is also a celebration of the pleasures of equality and unrestrained discussion between equals. During the meal Jonson's servant will 'read a piece of Virgil, Tacitus, / Livy, or of some better book' (ll. 21–2) and the guests will be able discuss what they hear without fear: 'we'll speak our minds amidst our meat' (l. 23). The poem concludes with words that make it clear that the meal is as much about the need to exercise the political ideal of friendship as it is a celebration of eating and drinking:

> And we shall have no Poley or Parrot by,
> Nor shall our cups make any guilty men:
> But, at our parting, we will be as when
> We innocently met. No simple word
> That shall be uttered at our mirthful board

>   Shall make us sad next morning, or affright
>   The liberty that we'll enjoy tonight
>
>   (ll. 36–42)

These last lines are a sharp reminder that not all words are construed as innocent. (Jonson was imprisoned in 1597 after the staging of the now lost play, *The Isle of Dogs,* which he wrote with Thomas Nashe.) (Robert) Poley and (William) Parrot were notorious informers, Poley having helped ensnare and kill Jonson's fellow playwright, Christopher Marlowe, significantly enough, after supper.[1] In contrast, within the closed circle of their table talk the host and guests can say exactly what they want, knowing that no careless statements will have any consequences the next day. They will remain innocent and at liberty, whatever they discuss. Drink will be used as a stimulus to friendly conversation and not as a means of distorting words in order to incriminate and ensnare those whose opinions may be at odds with official doctrine.

The poem invites the reader, looking in on the pleasures enjoyed by the guests, to imagine what they might debate. The reading from Virgil, Tacitus or Livy, designed to set the tone for subsequent conversation, encourages us to speculate that Jonson wants his guests to participate in a discussion based on the history and politics of the Roman republic and its transformation into an empire after the rise of the Julio-Claudians. Livy's *History of Rome* charts the transformation of Rome from the corrupt monarchy of the Tarquins to the rise of the republic after Brutus's coup placed the people in control; Virgil's *Aeneid* is a reflection on the costs as well as the advantages of empire, written to advise the first Roman emperor, Augustus; and Tacitus's *Histories* and *Annals,* among the most widely read books in early Jacobean England, are a detached and critical analysis of the early Roman emperors, encouraging the need for balanced and informed political judgement of recent events.[2] The selection of books, again innocent enough as they were all easily available and read, indicates that table talk would revolve around politics and the ways in which ancient histories could be applied to the present.

One Roman author is conspicuously missing from the list, perhaps present although not named, if his work is intended as the 'better book'. Cicero's speeches and treatises were probably the most important classical element that made up sixteenth-century English culture.[3] One of Cicero's most widely read works was *De amicitia* (*Of Friendship*), written a year before his death in 44 BCE.[4] Throughout his life, Cicero was the great champion of the republic and its values of public debate and collective responsibility, a means of fostering a society of equals who would govern themselves. As this political ideal began to become ever more fragile and threatened, especially during the bloody civil wars that destroyed the fabric of Roman society after the assassination of Julius Caesar in 43 BCE, Cicero turned to the theme of friendship as the best means of preserving republican values in trying times. For Cicero, friendship was what separated men from beasts. True friendship was republican in that it would only work properly between equals, just as the republic itself required the participation of men who saw themselves at the same social level. Friends would encourage each other to behave virtuously – indeed, it would not work unless each friend was virtuous – and to think through complex and troubling problems in search of valuable solutions. Bad men could not be true friends. Cicero's reflections further implied that monarchs could never really enjoy proper friendship as they could have few equals, and none within the society they ruled.

Jonson's poem, therefore, demands to be read as a defence of a besieged ideal of republican values in a society that was intent on taking away the liberties of its subjects. We cannot be sure when 'Inviting a Friend to Supper' was written – the reference to Poley suggests an early date as Marlowe died in 1593. However, it was not published until 1616, as part of the volume of *Epigrams* in the folio of Jonson's *Works*. By this point James was well known for styling himself as the new Augustus through a series of verbal and visual comparisons, a *rex pacificus* ruling over a second Roman empire.[5] Jonson casts himself and his circle – the 'tribe of Ben' – as a repository of virtue within a nation that has badly lost its way and has succumbed to the vices of bad government: loss of liberty, servility, fear and lack of proper debate.

The relationship between political vice and virtue is further explored in two poems at the start of the second of Jonson's volumes of verse, 'The Forest', 'To Penshurst' and its companion piece, 'To Sir Robert Wroth'. 'To Penshurst', a celebration of the estate of the Sidney family who were generous patrons to Jonson, contains another description of the freedoms of proper dining.[6] As in 'Inviting a Friend to Supper', Jonson's account of the meal contains more than a hint of self-criticism, as well as a pointed reflection on what is really going on at and around the table:

> And I not fain to sit (as some, this day,
> At great men's tables) and yet dine away.
> Here no man tells my cups; nor, standing by,
> A waiter, doth my gluttony envy;
> But gives me what I call, and lets me eat
>
> (ll. 65–9)

Liberty is a fine ideal, but in the real world it is often misused by those who do not have a sense of rational control or balance required to make proper use of freedom, such as Jonson himself. Furthermore, the pointed contrast between the egalitarian table of the Sidneys and the hierarchical dining arrangements found at the houses of other great families sounds as if it is a compliment of their superior values and the republican character of their estate. However, one should also bear in mind that the courteous treatment that the poet receives may well be because the Sidneys are less favoured by the King and his allies than other eminent people and so feel the particular need to treat him well. Certainly the opening lines are as much a backhanded comment on the shabby nature of the Penshurst estate as they are praise of its lack of ostentation:

> Thou art not, Penshurst, built to envious show,
> Of touch or marble; nor canst boast a row
> Of polished pillars, or a roof of gold.
> Thou hast no lantern whereof tales are told,
> Or stair, or courts; but stand'st an ancient pile,
> And these grudged at, art reverenced the while […]
>
> (ll. 1–6)

Robert Sidney, Lord Lisle, earl of Leicester (1563–1626), as Jonson well knew, suffered from monetary difficulties throughout his life, partly because of his extravagant generosity, and the poem may well have been written during a particular financial crisis.[7] The lines perhaps allude to the poetry of Robert's brother, Sir Philip, killed in 1586, whose sonnet sequence, *Astrophil and Stella,* makes frequent references to the expensive stones, marble and touchstone (touch), most notably in Sonnet 9 ('Queen Virtue's Court'). Jonson appears to be reminding his readers that the Sidneys are rich in literary wealth but lacking real capital. They can write about marble and touchstone but cannot afford to buy it.

The economy of the estate is represented in terms of a fantasy, akin to that of the land of Cokaygne, the legendary place in which work was impossible and roast pigs ran around with carving knives sticking in them yelling 'Eat me! Eat me!'[8] Jonson describes the fish that live in the lakes and streams around the estate:

> Fat, agèd carps, that run into thy net,
> And pikes, now weary their own kind to eat,
> As loath the second draught or cast to stay,
> Officiously, at first, themselves betray;
> Bright eels, that emulate them, and leap on land
> Before the fisher, or into his hand […]
>
> (ll. 33–8)

The effect of this passage – and others like it – is to disguise the work that takes place to make the estate function. The example of the fish running into the net is so absurd and contrary to the reality of estate management that the lines actually draw attention to what they ostensibly hide and deny. We are made painfully aware of how carefully the rivers and fields at Penshurst need to be cultivated and maintained, and that nothing ever comes for free, or without work, even if that labour is not immediately visible. Jonson extends this insight to every aspect of the Sidneys' domains:

> And though thy walls be of the country stone,
> They're reared with no man's ruin, no man's groan;
> There's none that dwell about them wish them down,
> But all come in, the farmer and the clown,
> And no-one empty-handed, to salute
> Thy lord and lady, though they have no suit.
> Some bring a capon, some a rural cake,
> Some nuts, some apples; some that think they make
> The better cheeses, bring 'em; or else send
> By their ripe daughters, whom they would commend
> This way to husbands[.]
>
> (ll. 45–55)

Nothing in this passage is what it seems to be. We are reminded that everything comes at a cost and that everything is for sale. The estate at Penshurst looks old but is actually very recent. It was made to look older than it was to make the Sidneys appear as if they were one of the ancient families of England, when they were really much more arriviste.[9] The estate had, in fact, been relatively recently enclosed and walls erected through the hard labour of many who had undoubtedly had to make way for the new owners. As Raymond Williams put it, 'this magical extraction of the curse of labour is in fact achieved by a simple extraction of the existence of labourers.'[10] The rural folk may come to the feast professing that they have no particular motive in bringing produce for the lord and lady of the manor, but they are painfully aware that their livelihood depends on them. The lines move seamlessly from the production of fine cheese to the display of 'ripe daughters', a detail that only appears innocent if we are unaware of the significance of marriage in early modern England.[11] Most wealth existed in the form of land rather than money, which meant that families would try and arrange suitable matches in order to preserve and increase the wealth that they possessed. Marriage was probably the most important choice that people made in their lives. Yet, as Jonson observes, selecting marriage partners was, in many ways, not really that different from displaying and choosing goods in a market.

'To Penshurst' is not a hostile attack on the Sidneys and should not be read as such. Rather, it is a poem that shows that Jonson was acutely aware of the ways in which early modern English society functioned and how at odds ideal and reality usually were. The republican ideal of friendship, a political standard as well as a means of living everyday life, was fragile and almost impossible to maintain. It had to confront a rigidly hierarchical society that placed people in relationships of dependency, whatever the illusions to the contrary. Even the most generously treated workers on a well-run estate were aware of the power that their superiors had over them. And what might seem like debate between equals was often nothing of the sort but a skewed conversation between a hired hand and a master. Jonson's poem shows his own understanding of how dependent he was on his superiors for their bounty.

> In turn, of course, the Sidneys, have to serve their master:
> There's nothing I can wish, for which I stay.
> That found King James, when, hunting late this way
> With his brave son, the Prince, they saw thy fires
> Shine bright on every hearth, as the desires
> Of thy Penates had been set on flame
> To entertain them; or the country came,
> With all their zeal, to warm their welcome here[.]
>
> (ll. 75–81)

James's passion for hunting was legendary, as was his abuse of his richer subjects' hospitality, as he toured the country looking for parks and forests in which to indulge his desire. Wealthy families lived in fear of his visits which would invariably eat them out of house and home and leave the country without proper leadership while he remained away from London.[12] Yet, just as the people who lived on the Penshurst estate had to give their lord tributes in order to remain in favour, so did the Sidneys have to accommodate the desires of the monarch who had the power to distribute the property they owned and in which they lived.

If 'To Penshurst' shows Jonson reflecting on the role of the poet and the constraints under which he had to work, 'To Sir Robert Wroth' represents the poet in action, asserting his right and power to distribute proper advice to those who most need it. Sir Robert Wroth (c. 1576–1614) was married to Robert Sidney's daughter, Lady Mary (1587?–1651/3), a noted poet and author of *Urania* (published 1621). Evidence suggests that the marriage was not happy, and, when Wroth died, he left his wife with enormous debts of £23,000. Jonson himself commented that she was 'unworthily married on a jealous husband' (*Informations*, ll. 275–6).

Jonson's poem, as does its companion piece, draws attention to what it pretends to conceal or deny:

> How blest art thou canst love the country, Wroth,
> Whether by choice, or fate, or both;
> And, though so near the city and the court,
> Art ta'en with neither's vice nor sport;
> That at great times art no ambitious guest
> Of sheriff's dinner, or mayor's feast.
> Nor com'st to view the better cloth of state,
> The richer hangings, or crown-plate;
> Nor throng'st (when masquing is) to have a sight
> Of the short bravery of the night;
> To view the jewels, stuffs, the pains, the wit
> There wasted, some not paid for yet!
>
> (ll. 1–12)

Jonson is not praising Wroth for his abstinence, modesty and frugality, but pointing out a self-sufficient ideal, like the ideal of friendship in 'To Penshurst', that the profligate aristocrat should at least try to uphold. Wroth, as readers of the poem would have known, was guilty of the vices denied here and wanted to spend more time at court than at home, as well as buying costly objects that he could not afford. The poet, in pointing out Wroth's faults, is exercising his power to correct vice, a role that places him on the same level as his social and economic superior, rather like a republican friend. In doing so, Jonson casts himself as both a Ciceronian and a Tacitean, able to comment on the prevalence of vice but also capable of holding up a mirror which showed things as they really were and as they should be.[13]

NOTES

1. See Charles Nicholl, *The Reckoning: The Murder of Christopher Marlowe* (London: Picador, 1993).
2. Alan T. Bradford, 'Stuart Absolutism and the "Utility" of Tacitus', *Huntington Library Quarterly*, 46 (1983): 127–55.
3. Howard Jones, *Master Tully: Cicero in Tudor England* (Nieuwkoop: Bibliotheca Humanistica & Reformatorica, Vol. LVII, 1981); Jennifer Richards, *Rhetoric and Courtliness in Early Modern Literature* (Cambridge: Cambridge University Press, 2003).
4. Cicero, *Fowre Severall Treatises of M. Tullius Cicero: Conteyninge His Most Learned and Eloquent Discourses of Frendshippe, Oldage, Paradoxes: and Scipio His Dreame*, trans. Thomas Newton (London, 1577).
5. Anthony Miller, *Roman Triumphs and Early Modern English Culture* (Basingstoke: Palgrave, 2001), pp. 107–27.

6. David Riggs, *Ben Jonson: A Life* (Cambridge, Mass.: Harvard University Press, 1989), pp. 184–6.
7. Millicent V. Hay, *The Life of Robert Sidney, Earl of Leicester (1563–1626)* (Washington: Folger Shakespeare Library, 1984), pp. 51–7, passim; J. C. A. Rathmell, 'Jonson, Lord Lisle, and Penshurst', *English Literary Renaissance*, 1 (1971): 250–60.
8. A. L. Morton, *The English Utopia* (London: Lawrence & Wishart, 1978, first published in 1952), pp. 15–45.
9. Don E. Wayne, *Penshurst: The Semiotics of Place and the Poetics of History* (Madison, Wisc.: University of Wisconsin Press, 1984).
10. Raymond Williams, *The Country and the City* (London: Paladin, 1975), p. 45.
11. For discussion, see David Cressy, *Birth, Marriage and Death: Ritual, Religion, and the Life-Cycle in Tudor and Stuart England* (Oxford: Oxford University Press, 1997), Chapters 12–16.
12. Alan Stewart, *The Cradle King: A Life of James VI and I* (London: Chatto & Windus, 2003), pp. 167–85.
13. Blair Worden, 'Ben Jonson Among the Historians', in Kevin Sharpe and Peter Lake (eds.), *Culture and Politics in Early Stuart England* (Basingstoke: Macmillan, 1994), pp. 67–89.

CHAPTER 27

Rank

Clare McManus

> Kings being publike persons, ... are as it were set ... upon a publike stage, in the sight of all the people.[1]

Early modern theatre is inherently concerned with rank and the playful shifting of its terms. James VI and I's expression of monarchy as a theatrical act has often been a starting point for critical attention to the connection between rank, or social standing, and theatrical production in early modern England. This connection, of course, permeates early modern society beyond its royal figurehead and is a particular feature of its theatre. David Scott Kastan has alerted us to the class cross-dressing of the actor who, as the anti-theatricalist Stephen Gosson put it, took 'upon him the title of a prince with counterfeit port, and train', and Natasha Korda's work has outlined the circulation of aristocratic garments through the city theatres.[2] In both cases, early modern theatre is revealed as a forum for the players' physical inhabitation of alternative ranks through costume. The stages of the city theatres themselves, and especially plays like Middleton and Dekker's *The Roaring Girl*, are deeply concerned with both the theatricality of costume and the sheer value of textiles.[3] Moll Frith, Middleton and Dekker's flashy, bravura protagonist, is problematic partly because of the conspicuous consumption and social aspiration involved in the transvestism, which is in fact only one of the disruptive energies embodied in the roaring girl. In her case, and in a great deal of Jonsonian theatre, ostentatious displays of wealth in costume were clear social markers of aspiration, of 'acting up'. Many of Jonson's plays, *Epicene, The Alchemist* and *The Devil is an Ass* among them, mock the aspirant, socially mobile figure of the newly rich, satirizing their fashions and behaviours and implicitly supporting those aristocratic or conservative characters who wish to put them back 'in their place'.

The court masque was the most socially stratified of the theatrical forms for which Jonson wrote. Those masques that were danced at court, in the palaces of Whitehall or Hampton Court, attracted a great deal of attention. Masques were social occasions at which attendance implied courtly status, and the crowds were great, the jostling for position extreme, and great efforts made to police attendance and behaviour. Jonson himself, along with Sir John Roe, was ejected from a masque performance during the Christmas festivities at Hampton Court in January 1604 by Lord Chamberlain Suffolk.[4] Although seeming to reinforce discipline and to suggest parity between noble and non-noble audience members, this expulsion is far from constituting evidence of a fully contained elite theatrical experience. Jacobean letter-writers such as Sir Dudley Carleton depict masques not as polite, decorous events but in terms of riot:

> The confusion in getting in was so great, that some Ladies lie by it and complaine of the fury of the white stafes. In the passages through the galleries they were shutt vp in seueral heapes betwixt dores, and there stayed till all was ended. and in the cuming owt, a banquet wch was prepared for the k: in the great chamber was ouerturned table and all before it was skarce touched.[5]

In this light, Jonson's expulsion from the Great Hall of Hampton Court suggests the anxiety caused by the mingling of royalty, aristocrats and court servants and points to an effort to control their interactions.

Much remains to be uncovered about the composition of masque audiences and the interactions between performers and spectators, but Jonson's masques have also to engage with the interactions between distinct groups of performers themselves. The masque, certainly in its early incarnation as a primarily female performance genre under the patronage of Anna of Denmark, is a hybrid form which relied upon a mixed economy of performers. Professional dance masters trained aristocrats; musicians and singers provided the accompaniment for the silent courtiers' dances; players acted anti-masque parts and provided commentary for the entrance of the noble masquers. Indeed, both Inigo Jones as masque designer and Ben Jonson as librettist were court servants working for their royal patron. Jonson's *The Masque of Queens* (1609) partly credits the full emergence of the bipartite structure of anti-masque and main masque to Anna who 'had commanded [him] to think on some dance or show that might precede hers and have the place of a foil or false masque' (10–12),[6] and this division allowed nobility and professional players to rehearse and, to a certain extent, to perform separately from one another.[7] The division between performers is based not on gender but on rank.

This reliance upon social status is crucial to the history of women's engagement with early modern theatre. Dividing its performers only by rank, the masque genre required silence from its noble performers (whether male or female) to separate them from those paid court servants who spoke, sang or played instruments. Temporarily (in this theatrical form at least), the equal standing of aristocratic women and men facilitated women's theatricality and their performance on the masquing stage.[8] These theatrical women also participated in a transnational performance genre, part of a discourse of pan-European aristocratic theatricality: the Stuart court masque was a performance of European courtliness and a synthesis of the domestic and the foreign. Anna of Denmark herself, the daughter of the Danish court made Queen of Scotland and England by marriage, is doubly foreign for the English court. When the disgruntled courtier John Harington criticizes the Stuart court, he does so by writing an epistolary masque of 'The Coming of the Queen of Sheba' (figuring James as Solomon and Anna as the foreign queen) and imaginatively inscribes female performers into an early version of the anti-masque to censure the court that fostered and sustained women's performance.[9] Harington's attack depends on the mingling of performers usually separated by degree, on the suggestion of a dangerous association of noblewomen and city players which Jonson's later masques sought to avoid. It also depends on an imaginative connection between theatricalized femininity and the foreign woman, and this connection between femininity, theatre and rank is instructive for Jonson's depiction of rank in his public and private theatre plays.

Jonson's Jacobean plays satirize the theatricality involved in the creation of aristocratic, or would-be aristocratic, identities by such male and female characters as Sir Amorous La Foole of *Epicene* or Epicure Mammon of *The Alchemist* and such female characters as the Collegiates of *Epicene* or the Ladies Tailbush and Eitherside of *The Devil is an Ass*. Indeed, Jonson's experience of the noble female masquer intersects with his treatment of rank. In Lady Politic Would-Be, as Peter Parolin explains in his illuminating study of Jonson's theatrical woman in *Volpone,* Jonson offers a depiction of the English woman abroad. In Venice, Lady Would-Be's 'acting efforts can have free rein' since the cosmopolitan city is 'an urban performance space in which people are free to abandon fixed identity categories and remake themselves'.[10] This displacement allows Jonson to satirize a 'crude traveller' (4.1.7), 'so portable a thing' (4.1.88), whose geographical wanderings beyond England and beyond the control of her husband mirror her movement through the stratified categories of rank. Lady Would-Be is a version of those Scotsmen of *Eastward Ho!* whom Jonson depicts as 'dispersed over the face of the whole earth' (3.3.31). First and foremost a satire against the union of England and Scotland, the image of the Scots flooding over the world nonetheless models the fears of a mobility that also destabilizes the hierarchies of rank. In much the same way, Jonson's satire of the foppish La Foole in *Epicene* is part and parcel of that play's preoccupation with the policing of borders. In a play that describes itself as 'dear-bought' but not 'far-fet' (Prologue, l. 21) and whose central character, Morose, locks himself away in a room with 'double walls and treble ceilings', his 'windows close shut and caulked' (1.1.146–7), the foppish La Foole's frenchified name and fashions, and his description of himself as 'descended lineally of the French la Fooles' (1.4.31–2), mocks him as much for his efforts to move beyond England as for his move beyond his expected social standing.[11] Social aspiration is targeted throughout the play, and the bite of Jonson's satire is clear when La Foole takes the role of a waiter, 'sewing [carrying] the meat' across the stage (3.7.13 s.d.). Richard Dutton describes the social aspirant of *Epicene* as an animal 'to be baited', and this scene has La Foole enter bearing an emblem of his own end, foreshadowing his attack and consumption by the gallants.[12]

In Lady Would-Be, though, the danger that Jonson figures as inherent in social and geographical mobility is complemented by the threat of her theatricality and the slipperiness of theatre itself. Lady Would-Be's theatricality is a criticism of her social mobility. As Parolin argues, 3.4.1–38 finds the Englishwoman 'assembl[ing] and check[ing] her costume, cosmetics, and props, much as an actress would before mounting the stage'.[13] Believing Peregrine to be a courtesan in male disguise, Lady Would-Be confronts him with the accusation that he is 'A female devil in a male outside' (4.2.56), and the playfully self-reflexive gesture towards the cross-dressed boy actor completes the satire of the woman who is 'out of her place'.[14]

Perhaps unsurprisingly for a society that connects the aspirant woman, the theatrical woman and the woman abroad with a dangerous promiscuity, *Volpone* figures this dangerous bending of the structures of rank through the Venetian courtesan. The besieged Celia, virtuous Venetian wife of Corvino and the uncontained, garrulous and gullible English Lady Would-Be are sharply opposed yet parallel characters, linked by a shared theatricality and a connection to the courtesan. Celia's appearance at her upstairs window to watch and participate in Volpone's pretended mountebank show is a case in point (see Figure 27.1). Read through Jane Tylus's argument about Italian female spectacle and liminal theatrical space in her important article 'Women at the Windows', Celia's actions are revealed as crossing not only the boundary between private, interior

Figure 27.1 Quack addressing a crowd by Rembrandt Harmenszoon van Rijn (compare with the Scoto of Mantua scene in *Volpone*).

and public, exterior space but also that between spectator and actress.[15] Appearing at the upper window, Celia embraces a theatricality inherent to that other famous woman at a window – the Venetian courtesan.[16] In his account of his time in Venice, the English traveller Thomas Coryate paid special notice to the appearance of courtesans at theatres: 'their noble & famous Cortezans came to this Comedy, but so disguised, that a man cannot perceive them ... They were so graced that they sate on high alone by themselves in the best roome of all the Play-house.'[17] Sitting on high, on display yet hidden, the courtesan is a paradox of ostentatious display and withholding. Epitomising the foreign woman for English audiences, theirs is also an aspirational performance of femininity. Ann Rosalind Jones outlines the connections between *cortigiana* (the Italian feminine of 'courtier') and 'courtesan', and this connection recalls Dudley Carleton's accusation that the black make-up of *The Masque of Blackness* rendered Anna and her women 'Curtizan-like'.[18] The Venetian courtesans' performance of femininity, as they sat above in a gallery reserved only for them, is a visualization of their high social standing and so of the potential for theatricality and sexuality to facilitate social mobility. The opprobrium that faced them from some quarters was due not only to their sexual activities but also to their crime of social aspiration. Celia at the window, then, is both a confined woman seeking escape and a figure for the socially mobile, theatrical courtesan. Simultaneously, she also echoes Lady Would-Be and the elite English female theatricality which Jonson condemns in these satirical shadows of aristocratic female performers.

Jonson's 1616 play, *The Devil is an Ass,* brings *Volpone* back to London, 'Englishing' the Italianate theatrical representations of rank, theatricality and gender dramatized in Jonson's Venice. The plot centres around the gulling of squire Fitzdottrel and the potential seduction of his neglected young wife, Frances, by the gallant Wittipol who is recently returned home 'from travel' (1.4.10). Set firmly in the London of 1616 (the date of its first performance at the Blackfriars), Jonson's satire mirrors the lived experience of his audience. Wittipol bribes the jealous old husband, Fitzdottrel, to allow a meeting with Frances by offering him a rich cloak which 'cost fifty pound' (1.6.28), and Fitzdottrel reprimands her reticence with a fantasy of rehearsing his membership of a gallant, masculine playhouse society:

> Today, I go to the Blackfriars Playhouse,
> Sit i'the view, salute all my acquaintance,
> Rise up between the acts, let fall my cloak,
> Publish a handsome man, and a rich suit –
> As that's a special end why we go thither,
> All that pretend to stand for 't o' the stage
>
> (1.6.31–6)

Fitzdottrel is the counterpart of Sir Epicure Mammon who longs to 'purchase Devonshire and Cornwall / And make them perfect Indies!' (2.1.35–6) and whose association of wealth with status opens him to exploitation by the consummate theatrical tricksters, Face and Subtle, whose pretence to transform base metal into gold symbolizes their mark's desire to climb the social hierarchy. In 1616, even the Devil is in on the game, since Pug, 'The less devil', first appears to Fitzdottrel in the guise of 'a gentleman, / A younger brother; but in some disgrace' (1.3.2–3). Even more tellingly, in a jibe at King James's mass creation of knights that ties Fitzdottrel to the ridiculous Sir Petronel Flash of *Eastward Ho!*, the projector Merecraft plays on his target's weakness with a scheme to drain the fens intended not only to enrich him but also to ennoble him by, appropriately, making him the Duke 'of Drowned-land' (5.8.158).

Though the Ladies Tailbush and Eitherside of *The Devil is an Ass* are the successors of the Collegiates of *Epicene* and though Jonson's satire again connects female social mobility and theatricality, this time masculine theatricality is again under scrutiny. *The Devil is an Ass* extends the *commedia dell'arte* trope of the woman at the window in ways that indicate the difference that nation makes to the intersections of rank, theatre and gender. Set not in the open space of the Italian piazza but in crowded London streets where buildings jostle against each other, Jonson's 'Englished' conceit is doubled by having Frances and Wittipol speak and touch 'at two windows, as out of two contiguous buildings' (2.6.36 s.d.). Here the country squire's wife, whose husband squanders the riches she brought to a marriage depicted as morally and socially beneath her (4.6.18–23), is made visually equivalent to the city gallant. The cheek-by-jowl built environment of London gives Wittipol access to a woman whose husband thinks her safely locked away. Furthermore, when Fitzdottrel interrupts his wife's potential seduction and tells her, 'I could now find i' my very heart to make / Another lady Duchess and depose you' (2.7.41–2), the connection between the hierarchical structure of marriage and rank suddenly comes into plain view.

Rather than 'deposing' Frances, though, Fitzdottrel decides to fashion her into a fit wife for the Duke of Drowned-land, once more leaving her open to Wittipol's rewriting of well-known theatregrams. Wittipol follows his appropriation of the *commedia* seduction by playfully inverting the usual transvestite plot (the endangered young woman disguises herself as a young man) and cross-dresses as 'The Spaniard' (2.8.28), an English widow who, in a parody of an aristocratic education, knows 'from the duke's daughter to the doxy, / What is their due just, and no more' (2.8.38–9). Wearing the 'cioppinos' (3.4.13), or distinctive platform shoes of the Venetian courtesan, Wittipol protects Frances from the theatrical techniques of cosmetics, costume and fashion with which Tailbush and Eitherside will train her to become a city lady. Thus Jonson has a male character (perhaps originally played by Dick Robinson, the King's Men's former expert in transvestite parts) perform specifically in order to restrain a female theatricality that is characterized as whorish, connected to the crimes of the courtesan and which – most tellingly – symbolizes the greater crime of social mobility.

NOTES

1. James VI and I, *Basilikon Doron*, in *James I, The Workes* (1616), ed. by Marvin Spevack (New York: Georg Olms Verlag, 1971), pp. 137–89; p. 141.
2. David Scott Kastan, 'Is There a Class in this (Shakespearean) Text?', *Renaissance Drama* 25 (1993): 101–21; Stephen Gosson, *Playes Confuted in Fiue Actions* (London, 1582), sig. E5r; Natasha Korda, 'Women's Theatrical Properties', in Jonathan Gil Harris and Natasha Korda (eds.), *Staged Properties in Early Modern English Drama* (Cambridge: Cambridge University Press, 2002), pp. 202–29; p. 216.
3. This topic is fully explored in Ann Rosalind Jones and Peter Stallybrass, *Renaissance Clothing and the Materials of Memory* (Cambridge: Cambridge University Press, 2000).
4. David Riggs, *Ben Jonson: A Life* (Cambridge, Mass.: Harvard University Press, 1989), p. 106.
5. Sir Dudley Carleton to Sir Ralph Winwood, 1605, in C. H. Herford, Percy Simpson and Evelyn Simpson (eds.), *Ben Jonson*, 11 vols. (Oxford: Clarendon Press, 1925–52), vol. x, p. 449.
6. The edition of *The Masque of Queens* cited is from Ben Jonson, *The Complete Masques*, ed. Stephen Orgel (New Haven, Conn.: Yale University Press, 1969).
7. Anne Daye, 'The Jacobean Antimasque within the Masque Context: A Dance Perspective', unpublished Ph.D. thesis, Roehampton University 2008, pp. 300–2.
8. This argument can be found in full in Clare McManus, *Women on the Renaissance Stage: Anna of Denmark and Female Masquing in the Stuart Court (1590–1619)* (Manchester: Manchester University Press, 2002), pp. 1–17.
9. John Harington, letter to 'Mr. Secretary Barlow', in John Nichols (ed.), *The Progresses, Processions and Magnificent Festivities of King James the First* (London: J. B. Nichols, 1828), 4 vols., vol. 11, pp. 72–4; p. 72. For the full argument, see Clare McManus, 'When Is a Woman not a Woman? Or, Jacobean Fantasies of Female Performance (1606–1611)', *Modern Philology*, 105 (2008): 437–74.
10. Peter Parolin, '"A Strange Fury Entered My House": Italian Actresses and Female Performance in *Volpone*', *Renaissance Drama*, 29 (1998): 107–35; pp. 109–10.
11. Clare McManus, '*Epicene* in Edinburgh (1672): City Comedy beyond the London Stage', in Robert Henke and Eric Nicholson (eds.), *Transnational Exchange in Early Modern Theater* (Burlington, Vt.: Ashgate Press, 2008), pp. 181–96; pp. 185–6.
12. Richard Dutton (ed.), *Epicene; or, The Silent Woman* (Manchester: Manchester University Press, Revels Plays, 2003), p. 71.
13. Parolin, 'A Strange Fury', p. 123. For analysis of theatrical and social cosmetic discourses, see Farah Karim-Cooper, *Cosmetics in Shakespearean and Renaissance Drama* (Edinburgh: Edinburgh University Press, 2006).

14. Parolin, 'A Strange Fury', 125.
15. Jane Tylus, 'Women at the Windows: Commedia dell'arte and Theatrical Practice in Early Modern Italy', *Theatre Journal*, 49 (1997): 323–42; Parolin, 'A Strange Fury', pp. 111–15.
16. Tylus, 'Women at the Windows', p. 336.
17. Thomas Coryate, *Coryat's Crudities,* 2 vols. (Glasgow: James MacLehose and Sons, 1905), vol. 1, p. 386.
18. Parolin, 'A Strange Fury', p. 112, citing Ann Rosalind Jones, 'City Women and Their Audiences: Louise Labé and Veronica Franco', in Margaret Ferguson, Maureen Quilligan and Nancy Vickers (eds.), *Rewriting the Renaissance: The Discourses of Sexual Difference in Early Modern Europe* (Chicago, Ill.: University of Chicago Press, 1986), pp. 289–316; p. 304. Carleton to Winwood, p. 448.

CHAPTER 28

Households

Kate Chedgzoy

Households are important places in Jonson's poetry and plays. He made a unique contribution to the literature of the household with 'To Penshurst', a work which helped to inaugurate the country-house poem as a distinctive early modern genre concerned with the politics of the domestic. More than merely a place, the poem shows, the early modern household was also a dynamic social formation, shaped by complex relationships among people of varying ages, genders and social status, connected both by kinship and by relations of authority and dependency. And, as such, it carried considerable social and ideological weight as a microcosm of the functioning of early modern society more broadly. It is this combination of social dynamism with metaphorical importance that makes the household such a significant dramatic location in Jonson's plays. The urban household (whether in London or in an Italian city) is a key location in comedies written throughout Jonson's career, from *Every Man In His Humour*, by way of *Volpone*, *Epicene* and *The Alchemist*, to *The New Inn*. Jonson structures the comic action of these plays by drawing together a motley group of characters at a particular household where they believe their materialistic desires and social aspirations will be gratified. Despite the larger location signalled by its title, even *Bartholomew Fair* begins in Littlewit's house: like those other comedies, its point of departure is an urban, non-aristocratic household whose stability and status will be called into question by the comic action of the play.

The significance of domestic locations in Jonson's works is thus shaped by and reflects their wider importance in early modern culture, both as actual places and in representation and ideology. Early modern English writers frequently invoked the analogy – influential in ancient Greece, and revived in Renaissance political thought – between the domestic and civic spheres (*oikos* and *polis*) which enabled the household to serve as a tool for thinking about the relationship between the individual and larger social structures. Not merely a microcosm of the state, in this model the household was the foundation of virtuous, disciplined civic behaviour in a hierarchical society. It was, according to the rules for domestic life prescribed by William Perkins, 'the Schoole, wherein are taught and learned the principles of authoritie and subjection'.[1] This chapter explores how studying Jonsonian households, represented in verse and drama, can enhance our understanding both of his works and of the politics of domesticity in early modern culture. An awareness of historical specificity and change both in household structure and in ways of thinking about the domestic as part of a larger social world can enrich our responses to Jonson's stagings of the domestic realm. At the same time, studying Jonson's dramatic and poetic representations of the household can complicate and challenge our perceptions of the history of domestic life.

The material and ideological importance of the early modern household mean both that it is of great significance for scholars across a range of disciplines who want to make sense of the early modern world, and that it has left behind a wide range of sources for them to use. How might these sources of evidence, and the methods that scholars employ to analyse them, help us think about Jonsonian households and their inhabitants? Prescriptive writings delineating the form an orderly, well-run household should take have been analysed by cultural historians and literary scholars who have revealed the gap that often opened up between ideological precept and domestic practice. *Epicene*, Jonson's satire on gendered expectations about domestic behaviour, both exaggerates and subverts the rulings that people such as William Perkins laid down. Relentlessly and noisily questioning Morose about the state of his health, for example (*Epicene* 4.4.25–50), the new bride Epicene parodies the good housewife's care for the well-being of the inhabitants of her household that was not only exhorted in treatises on domestic management, but was also valued by early modern women as a practical skill.[2]

Public records of birth, marriage, death and economic activity allow social historians using quantitative methods to highlight the wide range of economic, educational and sociable activities that took place in and around the typical early modern urban household and the importance of intergenerational and cross-status dynamics among its diverse inhabitants.[3] Such evidence can help us to appreciate how Jonson's plays map the physical and social space of the household and the complex and often fraught personal interactions that took place within and around it. Master–servant relations, for instance, were a very important part of early modern household life. In *The Alchemist*, Lovewit's house is exploited, during his absence in the country, as a site for profitable charlatanry by his housekeeper Face and the latter's seedy cohorts Subtle and Doll Common. Hissing at Face and Subtle to hush their quarrelling – 'Will you have / The neighbours hear you?' (1.1.7–8) – Doll provides dramatic evidence to complement the work of social historians such as Laura Gowing who have shown that the close quarters provided by urban households could often result in unlooked-for intimacy and community surveillance between households.[4] The social and material aspects of the household as building and community intersect at such moments, and we can further enrich our response to them by learning from archaeologists and social historians to use evidence from material culture to make sense of the geographies of early modern households. Such work provides a context in which we can analyse the dramatic significance on Jonsonian stages of household features and material objects, such as the windows that facilitate illicit conversations across the boundaries of two households in *The Devil is an Ass* (2.6), or the 'couch' where Volpone repeatedly holds court (*Volpone*, 1.2.85).

As Doll's awareness of the neighbours' proximity in *The Alchemist* suggests, households were not discrete entities but coexisted in varied urban landscapes. To understand the full significance of the domestic in Jonson's theatrical worlds, we must therefore attend not only to the internal geographies of households but also to the relations and differences between them. The opening scenes of *Every Man In His Humour*, for example, stage striking contrasts between different households. The play begins in front of the citizen Knowell's house with a focus on masculine familial relations. These father–son and cousinly encounters are shaped by expectations concerning the transmission of property between male kin, a process which was crucial to the social functioning of the early modern patriarchal household. Then the scene moves to the humbler house of Cob the water-bearer, whose lodger Captain Bobadil can be found drunkenly sleeping wrapped in his cloak on a bench. Bobadil's preference for 'lodg[ing] in such a base obscure place' reveals him to be a transient, socially dislocated man who has dropped out of the mode of masculinity proper to his class – namely, the version associated with fatherhood and its attendant reponsibilities for dependents and property already modelled by Knowell (Folio 1.4.28–9, 32–4). The juxtaposition of these two contrasting households within the wider urban landscape typical of Jonsonian comedy depicts a range of different household economies and kinds of alliance between men.

But these alliances – and thus the fate of the household – are dependent in important ways on women. And this is a source of much anxiety and comedy in Jonson's domestic dramas. Two key strands in the comic plot of *Every Man In His Humour* are concerned with Knowell Jr.'s courtship of Bridget – a young woman whose fortunes and social status do not correspond to his own – and Kitely's worries about his wife's fidelity. Jonson's men seek to use the exchange of women to enhance and consolidate the wealth and standing of their households; but the fact that those women are not merely objects of domestic property, but have their own dramatic agency, complicates and often thwarts these ambitions.

Though the citizen's urban household is the most prominent domestic location in Jonson's plays, his principal attempt to conceptualize the household and find a representational language for a particular ideology of it can be found in 'To Penshurst', a poem which, as Ian Donaldson says, is centrally concerned with 'the kind of life that the *house,* in its fullest sense – a dynasty, a household, an edifice and an estate – is capable of fostering and sustaining'.[5] Drawing on classical literary precedents, Jonson celebrates the Kent seat of his patron Robert Sidney as an idealized site of natural abundance, harmonious (if strictly hierarchical) social order and magnanimous aristocratic hospitality. Country-house poems used the household as an image of the good society – one characterized by stable, enduring harmony between the natural and the social, and among the various hierarchically ordered components of society. In an account which has had a germinal role for later discussion of the poem, Raymond Williams argued that by presenting Penshurst thus, Jonson undertook a deliberate act of ideological misrepresentation designed to make a particular, highly unequal way of ordering society seem natural and inevitable.[6] For example, 'To Penshurst' situates the house in an agricultural landscape which Jonson portrays as spontaneously offering its bounty to the householder to whom it all naturally belongs:

> Each bank doth yield thee conies; and the tops
> Fertile of wood, Ashore and Sydney's copse,
> To crown thy open table, doth provide
> The purpled pheasant, with the speckled side[.]
>
> (ll. 25–8)

In doing so, the poem occludes both the labour of those who work the land and fundamental questions about how all this comes to be in the ownership of one household. Indeed, Jonson specifically excludes the possibility that exploitation was involved in the building of the house:

> And though thy walls be of the country stone,
> They're reared with no man's ruin, no man's groan.
> There's none that dwell about them wish them down,
> But all come in, the farmer and the clown[.]
>
> (ll. 45–8)

Depicting the dynamic between master and servant as one in which the latter gladly embraces his subordination, Jonson presents a view of this crucial household relationship which contrasts sharply with Face's lack of any such loyalty to Lovewit in *The Alchemist,* and with the ambivalence and conflict that characterizes the relationship between Mosca and his master in the closing scenes of *Volpone* (and which, in performance, often makes itself felt earlier in the play).[7] Taking plays and poems together offers a more complex and uneven portrait of life within the early modern household than Williams's account of the poem allows, one which explores and plays with ideologies of domesticity rather than simply propounding them.

In 'To Penshurst', Jonson mystifies relations not only of class and wealth but also of gender. Women feature in the poem as symbols of a way of imagining society and as accessories to men, not as persons in their own right. Revealing how place, property, family and power are all interconnected, the poem makes plain that men depend on women's reproductive labour to secure all these things:

> Thy lady's noble, fruitful, chaste withal.
> His children thy great lord may call his own:
> A fortune, in this age, but rarely known.
>
> (ll. 90–2)

For the aristocratic wives whose fertility secures the transmission of property between generations, as for the farmer's 'ripe daughters' who emblematize the fertility of nature, the world of Penshurst is one in which a woman's greatest aspiration should be to receive '[t]he just reward of her high huswifery' (l. 85). In contrast, Jonson's plays show little interest in the domestic comforts that should be furnished by a skilled housewife: indeed, wives are conspicuously absent from the principal households in plays such as *The Case is Altered, Volpone* and *The Alchemist,* and these male-run households are bleak and squalid places.

Where female domestic roles *are* staged, what is foregrounded is the urgency of the male householder's desire for control over the women who dwell under his domestic authority. Where Shakespeare's plays often test the limits of this authority and explore the householder's anxieties about it, by staging plots in which daughters disobey their fathers, Jonson's men are – as Ann Christensen has noted – rendered more anxious by disorderly wives.[8] *Every Man In His Humour* dramatizes Kitely's paranoia about the security of his household and the chastity of his wife in terms that reveal that he sees them as coterminous (Folio 3.3.6–39). Just as the desperate measures born from Morose's obsessive urge to control female speech are frustrated by the fake bride of *Epicene*, so it is Kitely's very over-insistence on securing the boundaries of his marriage and home that makes him vulnerable to the thing he fears.

Since the gendered ideology of the early modern household required that women's bodies metonymically represent the domestic sphere and its vulnerabilities, they all too easily become a site of contest over the meanings of the domestic between men of varying status and power. This is most vividly illustrated by the contest between Volpone and Signior Corvino over the latter's beautiful young wife Celia. Mosca describes her and her position in Corvino's household to his master thus:

> She's kept as warily as is your gold:
> Never does come abroad, never takes air,
> But at a window.
> (1.5.118–20)

As much as the exotically valuable orient pearl Corvino presented to Volpone via Mosca earlier in the same scene, Celia is a precious possession; but, unlike the pearl, she initially derives her value from being kept off the market – closed away within the marital household from the possibility of either use or exchange. Corvino is furious when she exposes herself to public view at a window, a transgression which he views as tantamount to adultery:

> Why, if you'll mount, you may; yes, truly, you may –
> And so you may be seen, down to th'foot.
> (2.5.19–20)

The integrity – and putative violation – of the woman's body and the patriarchal household are here conflated, in a powerful metonymy with implications for the politics of the sexual and the domestic.

A disorderly, compromised site of conflict, the urban household of plays such as *Volpone* contrasts strongly with the idealized rural aristocratic household of 'To Penshurst'. This dichotomy appears to confirm the argument put forward in a now-classic essay by Thomas M. Greene, who contended that Jonson's poems and masques depict domesticity as an important value, whereas the plays dramatize its disruption in a variety of dissolute households.[9] But a different dynamic comes into view if we contrast both the rancid Venetian households of *Volpone* and the ideologically saturated glories of Penshurst with the ramshackle but ultimately regenerative household of Jonson's late comedy, *The New Inn*. For the particular form that domesticity takes in the latter suggests that a more positive, expansive spin can be put on Greene's analysis of Jonson's theatrical households. The tavern which gives this play its title is one of Jonson's most intriguing domestic locations, not least because here he moves out of the city to set the household where his dramatic action unfolds in a market town a few miles beyond London. While Anne Barton sees the Inn as 'a heightened and extraordinary environment' in which transformations and second chances are made possible in a vein of romantic comedy, Michael Hattaway takes a less positive view of the volatile, metamorphic qualities of the household that dwells under the sign of the Light Heart in Barnet, seeing it as 'the anti-type of Penshurst . . . a figure for the social mobility, fashion following and rootlessness of the times'.[10] Is Hattaway right to contend that *The New Inn* is a nostalgic lament for the disintegration of the conservative vision of the household epitomised by Penshurst? Or does the play rather stage a more expansive, fluid and inclusive version of the household as a space where the virtues of hospitality and reciprocity can be practised by a cast of people drawn from a wider and more diverse social world than Penshurst can imagine?

Such questions are fundamental to the politics of the household throughout Jonson's dramatic canon, because they centre on the conflict between precept and practice – between the ideology of domesticity and the reality of the multifarious forms that households could take. And this conflict is a vital source of dramatic tension in the genre of city comedy, the mode in which many of Jonson's households are staged. As we have seen, prescriptive texts such as William Perkins' *Christian Oeconomie* write about how households ought to be when everything is going right. But domestic dramas make their theatrical material from an exposé of things going wrong. Depending on genre, this may involve frustrated courtships, adultery, mix-ups about children and inheritance, theft or murder.[11] Rather than promoting a certain ideology of the domestic, such dramas must engage with its cultural power but may also complicate, subvert and play about with it. Drama – particularly perhaps Jonsonian drama – is by nature a multivocal and volatile form, better suited to laying out sites of potential conflict than to prescribing idealized conduct. Mario DiGangi's delineation of the tension between 'the early modern householder's deepest aspirations – a reputation for civility, generosity, and effective domestic government – and deepest fears – the public exposure of private disorder, the proliferation of illicit sexual practices, the treachery of unruly subordinates' is a precise analysis of Jonson's domestic dramas.[12] Playing out the tensions between these aspirations and fears in modes that veer between comic and tragic, Jonson dramatizes the strains of characters who aspire to put these precepts into practice.

In *Epicene,* for instance, Morose's attempt to make his house a haven of peace in a distressingly noisy and turbulent world is an extreme manifestation of the common injunction that a virtuous wife should be silent. In dramatizing the tricking of Morose, conned into marrying a boy disguised as a woman who acts out the stereotype of the noisy, volubly disobedient wife, Jonson shows how easily such aspirations could be subverted or disordered. The joke is on Morose – but also on women, eliminated from the marriage plot in which they would normally play a key role, present in relation to it only as the butt of a sustained misogynist joke about female speech and behaviour. This is complicated, however, by the juxtaposition of the 'silent woman' plot with the staging of the Collegiate Ladies as a kind of anti-household that subverts dominant ideologies of domesticity and gender. Though for Nicholas McDowell the unwomanly freedom the Ladies enjoy in the public, commercial realm of the city reveals by contrast the high value Jonson's culture placed on domesticity and chastity, the dramatic spectacle of female characters enjoying a certain theatrical freedom beyond the confines of the household can have subversive, creative effects.[13]

Jonson's plays do not stage simple contrasts between ideal and disorderly households, but reveal the ways in which domesticity might often take up a contradictory, unstable position in early modern discourses on the management of self and society. Jonsonian households are porous, diverse, populous places, which reunite gatherings of people that are not merely different from, but counterposed to, the normative ideal of the patriarchal household, reminding contemporary readers and audiences that the early modern household was often an expansive, inclusive and eclectic place.

NOTES

1. William Perkins, *Christian Oeconomie; or, A Short Survey of the Right Manner of Erecting and Ordering a Family* (1609), in Wendy Wall, *Staging Domesticity: Household Work and English Identity in Early Modern Drama* (Cambridge: Cambridge University Press, 2002), pp. 1–2.
2. For the quasi-medical responsibilities of the good housewife, see Linda Pollock, *With Faith and Physic: The Life of a Tudor Gentlewoman, Lady Grace Mildmay, 1552–1620* (New York: St Martin's, 1995).
3. See, for example, J. P. Boulton, 'London 1540–1700', in Peter Clark (ed.), *The Cambridge Urban History of Britain*, Vol. II, *1540–1840* (Cambridge: Cambridge University Press, 2000), pp. 315–46.

4. Laura Gowing, *Domestic Dangers: Women, Words, and Sex in Early Modern London* (Oxford: Oxford University Press, 1996).
5. Ian Donaldson, *Jonson's Magic Houses: Essays in Interpretation* (Oxford: Oxford University Press, 1997), p. 69.
6. Raymond Williams, *The Country and the City* (Oxford: Oxford University Press, 1975), pp. 7–32.
7. Simon Russell Beale's performances of both roles at the National Theatre are illustrative: Mosca in 1995 in a production directed by Matthew Warchus, Face in 2006 (director Nicholas Hytner).
8. Ann C. Christensen, 'Reconsidering Ben Jonson and the "Centered Self"', *South Central Review,* 13 (1) (1996): 1–16; p. 6.
9. Thomas M. Greene, 'Ben Jonson and the Centred Self', *Studies in English Literature, 1500–1900,* 10 (1970): 325–48.
10. Anne Barton, *Ben Jonson, Dramatist* (Cambridge: Cambridge University Press, 1984), p. 259; Michael Hattaway (ed.), *Ben Jonson's The New Inn,* The Revels Plays (Manchester: Manchester University Press, 2001), Introduction, p. 22.
11. Frances E. Dolan, *Dangerous Familiars: Representations of Domestic Crime in England, 1550–1700* (Ithaca, NY: Cornell University Press, 1994).
12. Mario DiGangi, *The Homoerotics of Early Modern Drama* (Cambridge: Cambridge University Press, 1997), p. 93.
13. Nicholas McDowell, 'Interpreting Communities: Private Acts and Public Culture in Early Modern England', *Criticism,* 46 (2) (2004): 281–98. On the complexities of *Epicene*'s sexual politics in performance, see the Introduction to Ben Jonson, *Epicene; or, The Silent Woman,* edited by Richard Dutton, The Revels Plays (Manchester: Manchester University Press, 2003), pp. 85–9.

CHAPTER 29

Foreign travel and exploration

Rebecca Ann Bach

Throughout his dramatic and poetic works, Ben Jonson shows his acute consciousness of his country's foreign trade and his compatriots' interests in foreign travel and exploration. That consciousness appears in his works both as theme and in passing. Jonson lards his plays and poems with foreign money and goods, foreign travellers, braggart soldiers boasting of foreign exploits, bumbling Irishmen and references to the Virginia colony and Pocahontas. Although critics disagree over whether Jonson's masque Irishmen lampoon the Irish or criticize English policy towards Ireland, most critics who have looked at Jonson's representations of trade, travel and exploration see the poet as attempting to shore up English power against the threats posed by what is foreign.[1]

I have argued in earlier work that in his plays Jonson seeks to domesticate colonial savagery; especially in later work such as *The New Inn,* Jonson imagines exotic otherness brought home and made English.[2] Likewise, Karen Newman suggests that in '*Epicene,* the talking woman represents the city *and* what in large part motivated the growth of the city – mercantilism and colonial expansion'.[3] The play, thus, promotes masculine authority in relation to feminized foreign commodity culture. Reading Jonson's commendatory poems, Barbara Fuchs suggests that Jonson transforms British colonial belatedness into 'an exceptional national achievement', and Jonathan Gil Harris sees Jonson's treatments of foreign drugs and diseases in *Volpone* as envisaging an English national economy that 'although dependent for its welfare on transactions with other such [national economies] engages the 'foreign' in often aggressively self-protective and even xenophobic fashion'.[4] In these readings, Jonson becomes a poet of nascent empire, but always a supremely English poet, suspicious of foreign trade and travel, while at the same time eager to rewrite colonial 'achievement' by Spain as England's own.

These accounts capture a significant trend in the poetry and drama. Jonson evidently hated aspects of English foreign trade, particularly the influx of tobacco that in his lifetime became a fixture of the London scene. He also never reserves his scorn for English men and women strutting in foreign fashions. That scorn appears again and again in plays and is perfectly captured in his epigram 'On English Monsieur':

> Would you believe, when you this monsieur see,
> That his whole body should speak French, not he?
> That so much scarf of France, and hat, and feather,
> And shoe, and tie, and garter, should come hither,
> And land on one whose face durst never be
> Toward the sea further than half-way tree?
> That he, untravelled, should be French so much,
> As Frenchmen in his company would seem Dutch!
> Or had his father, when he did him get,
> The French disease, with which he labours yet?
> Or hung some monsieur's picture on the wall,
> By which his dam conceived him, clothes and all?
> Or is it some French statue? No: 't doth move,
> And stoop, and cringe. Oh then it needs must prove
> The new French tailor's motion, monthly made,
> Daily to turn in Paul's, and help the trade.
>
> (*Epigrams* 88, ll. 1–16)

This piece of poetry exhibits the anxiety about the foreign that critics such as Harris and Newman have located in Jonson's plays. In the epigram we see an instance of what Harris finds in *Volpone,* a link between foreign affect and bodily pathology. The poem floats the fantasy that this man's devotion to French attire might stem from his father's having sired him while suffering from venereal disease, 'The French disease'. His French attire thus becomes a disease symptom 'with which he labours yet'. The epigram also points to the dynamic Newman perceives as motivating *Epicene:* the poem's other origin fantasy for the English *monsieur* blames his French devotions on his animalistic mother, who in response to his father's early modern pin-up of a Frenchman, 'conceived' this man fully clothed as French.

Jonson's epigram ends by blaming the English *monsieur* directly on foreign trade. The speaker attacks the man as a walking advertisement for a French tailor, thereby linking trade to a ludicrous and 'cringing' spectacle. Although he is located in London at St Paul's, the French tailor appears in this epigram as a foreign contaminant. The trade he hopes to stimulate seems to have the potential to turn real Englishmen into imitations of the tailor's 'motion', ridiculous fake Frenchmen. Thus, the epigram can be read as demonstrating Jonson's potential for xenophobic protectionism.

However, the epigram also reveals a contrary feature of Jonson's engagement with foreign trade and travel. The poem criticizes its target, the English *monsieur*, for wearing and loving French apparel, but the epigram is equally critical of its target's ignorance about France. The English *monsieur*'s dress is more French than a Frenchman's, but he does not speak French, and he has not travelled.

His French aspirations go only as far as foreign fashion, a realm that, like tobacco-smoking, Jonson seems to have held in general contempt from the beginning to the end of his career. That contempt is directed at both male and female devotees of fashion. In *Every Man Out of His Humour*, Asper, who according to David Riggs 'symbolizes the creative pole of Jonson's imagination',⁵ calls it 'more than ridiculous':

> ... that a rook in wearing a pied feather,
> The cable hatband or the three-piled ruff,
> A yard of shoe-tie, or the Switzer's knot
> On his French garters, should affect a humour.
> (Induction, ll. 108–11)

In the same play, Jonson ridicules the idiot courtier Fastidious Brisk who is introduced in the outline of the play's characters as 'one that wears clothes well, and in fashion' and who later in the play tells a story involving his ruffled boots made of Spanish leather (l. 28). Later in Jonson's career, *Volpone*'s Lady Politic is ludicrous not only because of her incessant chatter and ridiculous jealous fantasies but also because of her devotion to foreign fashion. She worries that she will be laughed at by the foreigners around her:

> Besides, you seeing what a curious nation
> Th'Italians are, what will they say of me?
> 'The English Lady cannot dress herself'.
> Here's a fine imputation to our country!
> (3.4.32–5)

Lady Politic's pathetic confusion of English pride with fashion-consciousness is Jonson's satirical target here. Like the English *monsieur*, Lady Politic knows nothing about Italy and Italians but aspires to be a foreign fashion-plate. In its display of the English *monsieur*'s affected fashion and also of his lack of actual engagement with France, Jonson's epigram suggests that he may be as critical of English people who pretend to knowledge of foreign lands and languages as he is xenophobic. It is this less remarked angle of Jonson's engagement with foreign travel that the remainder of this short chapter will explore.

As Asper's comment above suggests, *Every Man Out of His Humour* makes hay with foolish characters who misunderstand the significance of foreign travel or who pretend to knowledge of foreign lands and mores. In that play, Deliro attempts to defend the poorly clothed Macilente (Asper in disguise) to Fastidious Brisk as 'a man worthy of regard':

FASTIDIOUS: Why? What has he in him of such virtue to be regarded? Ha?
DELIRO: Marry, he is a scholar, sir.
FASTIDIOUS: Nothing else?
DELIRO: And he is well travelled.
FASTIDIOUS: He should get him clothes. I would cherish those good parts
    of travel in him, and prefer him to some nobleman of good place.
                                                        (2.3.267–72)

Deliro's account of Macilente echoes Jonson's own in his outline of the character of the persons: 'A man well-parted, a sufficient scholar, and travelled' (l. 6). That Jonson links scholarship with travel indicates his own regard for travel as the mark of a significant man. Fastidious's intense foolishness manifests in his disregard for what Jonson seems to see as the true 'good parts of travel', knowledge of the world, and his attachment to what Jonson despises, 'clothes'.

Every Man Out of His Humour also displays for ridicule the 'vain-glorious knight' Puntarvolo, an early version of Lady Politic's ludicrous travelling husband, Sir Politic Would-Be. In *Every Man Out of His Humour*, Puntarvolo plays a game with his waiting-gentlewoman in which he pretends to be a stranger asking her about her master and she responds to his cues with compliments about himself. In answer to Puntarvolo's cues, the waiting-gentlewoman lauds her master's generosity, his courtesy, his constancy in love, his beautiful wife and his facility with foreign languages:

PUNTARVOLO: Is he learned?
GENTLEWOMAN: Oh, ay, sir, he can speak the French and Italian.
PUNTARVOLO: Then, he is travelled?
GENTLEWOMAN: Ay, forsooth, he hath been beyond-sea once or twice.
                                                        (2.2.49–52)

Carlo Buffone comments to the men watching this silliness, 'As far as Paris, to fetch over a fashion and come back again' (2.2.53). Just as Puntarvolo's 'noble' virtues are a figment of his imagination, so his identity as a learned traveller exists only in his brain; to other men, he looks like a traveller for fashion, the kind of foreign traveller Jonson despises.

Foolish men in Jonson's middle comedies are also distinguished by their ignorance of foreign languages and customs. Jack Daw in *Epicene* identifies the title of a Roman law book as the name of a 'civil lawyer, a Spaniard' (2.3.72). Likewise, Kastril, the stupid fighting boy in *The Alchemist*, cannot tell the difference between languages. In that play, Face takes full advantage of this ignorance when they are conversing about Surly wooing Kastril's sister:

FACE: Is't not a gallant language that they speak?
KASTRIL: An admirable language! Is't not French?
FACE: No, Spanish, sir.
KASTRIL: It goes like law-French,
  And that, they say, is the courtliest language.
                                                    (4.4.59–62)

Just as Jack Daw mistakes an ancient noun for a Spanish name, Kastril hears Norman French in contemporary Spanish. He cannot tell the difference between a law court and courtliness, and he cannot distinguish between or understand foreign languages. In contrast, Jonson gives Surly, his pretend Spaniard, accurate Spanish to speak. In these plays, Jonson seems not averse to foreign languages or to foreign travel, but he repeatedly demonstrates his aversion towards men whose ears are deaf to languages. Kastril is also a target because of his ignorance of foreign customs. After Face and Subtle convince Kastril that Spain produces the best horses, beards, clothes, dances and weapons, Subtle pushes him to encourage his sister's sexual advances to Surly:

> 'Ods will, she must go to him, man, and kiss him!
> It is the Spanish fashion for the women
> To make first court.
>   (4.4.66–8)

Surly relies on Kastril's ignorance about Spain to motivate his quasi-prostitution of his sister, and Jonson may well be relying on his audience's knowledge that Spanish women were protected by their male relatives to make Kastril's falling for this piece of misinformation even funnier.

Jonson's plays are especially critical of men and women who learn nothing from their foreign encounters. While Kastril has apparently never ventured anywhere, the self-proclaimed world traveller Sir Politic famously misunderstands everything he has seen during his travels: he thinks that mountebanks are learned scholars and plans to cater to Italian tastes with red herrings. The Venetians in *Volpone,* far from welcoming Sir Politic's schemes, cannot wait to applaud his exit from their country. In the fifth act of the play, Peregrine enters with three unnamed merchants whom he has enlisted for his revenge on the travelling knight. Their conversation reveals their distaste:

SECOND MERCHANT: If you could ship him away, 'twere excellent.
THIRD MERCHANT: To Zant or to Aleppo?
PEREGRINE: Yes, and have's
  Adventures put i' th' Book of Voyages,
  And his gulled story registered for truth!

(5.4.3–6)

We can hear Jonson speaking through Peregrine and the merchants here. He registers both his contempt for Sir Politic's ignorant pretence and his own ability to discriminate between the truth of foreign travel and the stories recorded in travel narrative collections and taken 'for truth'. Unlike the Politics, as Robert M. Adams says, 'Jonson takes great pains to make his Venetian details specific and accurate'.[6] Thus, Jonson repeatedly demonstrates his own comfort with the Continent and Continental languages at the same time that he ridicules the ignorant.

Jonson also enjoys lampooning braggart soldiers boasting of their world travels. In *Every Man In His Humour,* Brainworm/Musco disguises himself as a maimed soldier and tells the audience that he now must 'create an intolerable sort of lies, or else [his] profession loses his grace' (Quarto 2.1.3–4).[7] His inflated tales of service in 'Bohemia, Hungaria, Dalmatia [and] Poland' and of his life 'at America in the galleys' convince the gulled country boy Stephano to part with his money for a fake Spanish rapier even when his friend Edward Knowell Lorenzo Jr tries to persuade him otherwise (Quarto 2.1.47–8, 51).[8] *Every Man In His Humour* also features a real braggart soldier, Bobadil[la], whom Jonson uses to simultaneously ridicule braggart soldiers and to criticize tobacco-traders. Bobadil[la] boasts of his encounter with 'divine' tobacco: 'I have been in the Indies, where this herb grows, where neither myself, nor a dozen gentlemen more, of my knowledge, have received the taste of any other nutriment in the world for the space of one-and-twenty weeks, but tobacco only' (Quarto, 3.2.56–9). We can hear Jonson's wry commentary in Edward Knowell/Lorenzo's response: 'this speech would have done rare in pothecary's mouth' (Quarto, 3.2.70–1). In Bobadil[la]'s and Brainworm/Musco's relations to the men around them, we see Jonson's divided discourse in relation to foreign trade and travel. The foreign import, tobacco, is corrupting in itself, but not for every Englishman; the foreign traveller or soldier is corrupt only if he lies about his travels. However, the braggart soldier can only gull the unknowing. In Edward Knowell/Lorenzo's reaction to Bobadil[la]'s lies and in Brainworm/Musco's encounter with Stephano and Edward Knowell/Lorenzo, we see the intelligent (English)man who can discern truth precisely because he knows more about the world than the gulls around him.

Jonson also indulges himself in ridicule of the braggart soldier in the epigram 'To Captain Hungry', which asks the 'captain' not to 'abuse' the speaker's ears with stories of world travel. He invites Captain Hungry to tell his stories to other men, 'gross Dutch[men]', who will listen to his 'grosser tales', stories of his 'services and embassies / In Ireland, Holland, Sweden (pompous lies), / In Hungary and Poland, Turkey too' (*Epigrams*, 107, ll. 5, 11–13).

Although Jonson identifies the captain's auditors as Dutch and stereotypically maligns them as 'gross', he calls the Englishman's lies 'grosser', hardly elevating what is English. As Jonson says in the Prologue to *The Alchemist*:

> Our Scene is London, 'cause we would make known,
> No country's mirth is better than our own.
> No clime breeds better matter for your whore,
> Bawd, squire, imposter, many persons more.
> (Prologue, ll. 5–8)

Jonson's backhanded national pride is on full display here and in the epigram. The braggart soldier may fool foreigners but he is, sadly, one of Jonson's compatriots. In the braggart soldier, Jonson could see a distorted mirror of his own exploits in the early 1590s when he served as an English soldier in the Netherlands. Unlike his characters, Jonson appears to have come back from the Continent not wanting to engage his countrymen with ridiculous stories; rather, in some cases, at least, his plays and poems commend a scholar's attitude towards foreign lands and languages.

Jonson's masques and late plays anticipate England's empire, displaying colonial desires; but what these masques and plays also reveal is Jonson's close engagement with England's foreign relations and affairs. Jonson travelled to Europe for the second time as Wat Raleigh's tutor in 1612, and, after his return to England, he socialized with men such as Samuel Purchas and John Selden, men at the centre of English discourse on the foreign world. Of course, this discourse hardly reflected the reality of the world outside of England, but Jonson seems to have tried to understand the world around him to the best of his ability. In *The Devil is an Ass* (1616), Jonson reprises his cony-catching fakery involving Spanish customs from *The Alchemist*. In an effort to get close to Frances Fitzdottrel, Wittipol dresses as an 'English widow, who hath lately travelled' and who 'is called the Spaniard, 'cause she came / Latest from thence, and keeps the Spanish habit' (2.8.27–9). Wittipol has actually travelled, and he uses his knowledge of Spain to fool the play's gullible noblewomen and his special target, Frances's husband Fabian Fitzdottrel. Riggs calls Wittipol 'a man who resembles the author himself'.[9] Jonson gives Wittipol detailed knowledge about Spanish women's lives, their servants and slaves and even their shoes. If Bobadil[la] is the distorted mirror image of Jonson the soldier, Wittipol seems like a relatively accurate reflection of Jonson the traveller, a man who may have relied on John Smith's tall tales about Virginia but who prided himself on accuracy in relation to Spain and the Continent. Jonson's scorn for the would-be traveller predicts his own more complex and scholarly relation to the foreign world.

NOTES

1. See Andrew Murphy, *But the Irish Sea Betwixt Us: Ireland, Colonialism, and Renaissance Literature* (Louisville, Ky.: University of Kentucky Press, 1999); David Lindley, 'Embarrassing Ben: The Masques for Frances Howard,' *English Literary Renaissance*, 16 (1986); Lesley Mickel, *Ben Jonson's Antimasques: A History of Growth and Decline* (Aldershot: Ashgate, 1999).
2. Rebecca Ann Bach, *Colonial Transformations: The Cultural Production of the New Atlantic World, 1580–1640* (New York: Palgrave, 2000).
3. Karen Newman, 'City Talk: Women and Commodification in Jonson's *Epicoene*', *English Literary History*, 56 (1989): 509.
4. Barbara Fuchs, 'Jonson's Commendatory Poetry and the Translation of Empire', *Modern Philology*, 99 (2002): 347; Jonathan Gil Harris, '"I Am Sailing to My Port, Uh! Uh! Uh! Uh!": The Pathologies of Transmigration in *Volpone*', *Literature and Medicine*, 20 (2001): 109.
5. David Riggs, *Ben Jonson: A Life* (Cambridge, Mass.: Harvard University Press, 1989), p. 60.
6. Ben Jonson, *Plays and Masques*, edited by Robert M. Adams (New York: Norton, 1979), p. 28, n. 1.
7. The textual situation here is complicated. This is the quarto reading, and in the quarto, this character is called Musco. I will be quoting from the quarto but giving both quarto and Folio character names.
8. Jonson revises this in the Folio to 'a gentle-man slave in the galleys' (2.4.54–5).
9. Riggs, *Ben Jonson*, p. 242.

CHAPTER 30

Domestic travel and social mobility
Julie Sanders

In his poem 'Masques', the contemporary poet Geoffrey Hill imagines the arrival of London nobility at a court masque collaboratively staged and designed by the tetchy but brilliant artistic partnership of Ben Jonson and Inigo Jones.[1] He describes with brilliant precision the round-bellied shapes of the coaches, pregnant, as it were, with their charges. What Hill captures in this poem is a moment in early modern society when the arrival of widespread coach travel began to impact not only on the habits but also the social relations, and even the built environment, of the world in which Ben Jonson and his contemporaries moved. Jonson lived through the period in which coach travel was not only introduced to England but became mainstream. By the 1630s, coaches and carriages were omnipresent in the streets of London to the extent that there were protests against them and a stream of parodic and polemic literature in response to them.

According to the waterman-poet John Taylor in his 1623 prose pamphlet *The World Runnes on Wheeles; or, Oddes betwixt Carts and Coaches*, the first coach had been brought to London in 1564. In the early days, usage of these expensive items was limited to the most wealthy of noble families and, even then, coaches were regularly shared between estates. Yet, by the 1620s and 1630s when Taylor was writing, they had become so commonplace that not only were royal proclamations issued that attempted to control their usage (in 1629 and 1635), but the hiring of them became open to those of all social ranks and levels, much to Taylor's evident concern:

> when euery *Gill Turntripe*, Mrs *Fumkins*, Madam *Polecat*, and my Lady *Trash*, *Froth* the Tapster, *Bill* the Taylor, *Lauender* the Broker, *Whiff* the Tobacco seller, with their companion Trugs, must be Coach'd to *S. Albanes, Burntwood, Hockley-in-the Hole, Croydon, Windsor, Uxbridge*, and many other places, like wilde Haggards prancing vp and downe.[2]

Taylor was, of course, a waterman, someone who made his primary living from the fares obtained for ferrying Londoners and visitors to the city alike in his wherry-boat up and down the Thames to key locations such as the playhouses on Bankside and the noble houses on the Strand (which all had waterside access and frontages at this time). That his text is dedicated to fellow watermen, whose trade is threatened by the rise of coach travel, offers rapid explanation for the hyperbolic and deliberately excessive claims of the pamphlet. It blames coaches for all manner of ills in contemporary society from a dearth of natural resources (on account of all the timber felled to build them and maintain their wheels) to widespread obesity and ill-health due to the reliance on coaches to carry people from place to place. Nevertheless, it is a text that gives us a direct glimpse into what were massive social transformations taking place in the early seventeenth century, of which coach travel might at least be regarded as a symptom if not the sole cause.

The places catalogued in Taylor's complaint above are tellingly all located to the north of the city of London and register a shift of perspective away from the river Thames to the ever-expanding suburbs of the city. A similar map is provided by Henry Peacham's witty 1636 pamphlet, written this time in the form of a small play, where he actually has a coach and a sedan-chair debate who is superior, only to be bested by a passing brewer's cart (see Figure 30.1). In the guise of describing all that he does not do, the sedan chair makes a list of the lower rank members of society and the dubious social locations served by the coach, which is remarkably similar to that described in Taylor's earlier pamphlet:

we carrey no Lackquies or Footboyes, when we are emptie, nor have we to do with *Dol Turn-up*, and *Peg Bum-it,* your silken wenches of *Hackney,* to carry them to the *Red Bull,* and other Play-houses, to get trading, or Citizens wives to St Albanes, South-mimmes, Barnet, Hatfield, Waltham, Ilford, Croidon, Brainford, and other places ...[3]

The implicit association of the coaches with theatregoing is clear in several contemporary references. There are records of complaints from those living in the vicinity of theatres such as the Blackfriars about the noise and pollution, as well as overcrowding in the streets themselves, caused by the gathering of coaches outside the playhouses on performance nights.[4] Jonson alludes to these complaints when he creates the scene of the discontented neighbours in *The Alchemist*. They berate Lovewit for the strange gatherings that have been taking place at his house while he has been absent during the plague weeks (5.1). This is, also, the social and cultural geography of Jonson's 1629 Blackfriars Theatre play *The New Inn*. This drama is set entirely in an innhouse in Barnet, in a northern suburb of London, on the post-road to St Albans in Hertfordshire, yet another of Taylor's identified locales in his diatribe against the new leisure activities of London's service classes.

Figure 30.1 Woodcut frontispiece to Henry Peacham's *Coach and Sedan, pleasantly disputing for Place and Precedence*, 1636.

Jonson's play makes huge comic capital of the very same social phenomenon described by Taylor. A central strand of *The New Inn*'s complicated plotlines is a dress, commissioned from a tailor called Nick Stuff. It is intended for the purposes of some licensed play-acting on the part of the

Lady Frampul's chambermaid, Prudence, during their joint sojourn at the Barnet inn. Near the start of the play, however, the dress has failed to materialize. It will eventually appear on stage, although not worn by its rightful owner. In the fourth act it attires the tailor's wife, Pinnacia. She is using it for the purposes of a little play-acting of her own, in which she imagines herself a countess and casts her husband in the role of her subjugated footman, made to run alongside the coach that she has hired in order to visit 'The Light Heart':

> It is a foolish trick, madam, he has;
> For though he be your tailor, he is my beast.
> [...]
> When he makes any fine garment will fit me,
> Or any rich thing that he thinks of price,
> Then I must put it on and be his countess
> Before he carry it home unto the owners.
> A coach is hired and four horse; he runs
> In his velvet jacket thus to Romford, Croydon,
> Hounslow, or Barnet, the next bawdy road;
> And takes me out, carries me up, and throws me
> Upon a bed –
>
> (4.3.63–74)

An earlier scene in the same act has prepared audiences for Pinnacia's rather wholehearted approach to her performance of a countess. Barnaby the coachman has arrived bedraggled and browbeaten at the inn, in need of a stiff drink (or two). He explains to the Light Heart employees, such as Jug the tapster, how his hat had blown off en route at Highgate (also in the north of the city) but how his mistress 'Would not endure me 'light to take it up, / But made me drive bare-headed i' the rain' (4.1.16–17). The reason for this prohibition is quickly understood by the inn-workers who comprehend the social semiotics which state that the coachmen who worked for noble families went bare-headed. Jonson's sympathy here for the fate of the workers who are subject to the whims of those who are their paymasters is typical, and we see another knowing version of this in the extended scene between those inn-workers who are employed not behind the bar or in the kitchens of the Light Heart but in its stables.

As social historian Joan Thirsk has made clear, horses had always been a significant part of medieval and early modern culture, required as they were even when the river was a main source of transportation since they were the easiest means of embarking and disembarking goods and commodities, but they became increasingly significant in the era of widespread coach-travel.[5] The costs though of stabling these horses, in addition to paying for the staff to maintain them, and their uniforms or livery, was considerable, and these costs necessarily increased when owners were on the move, staying at inns and taverns like the Light Heart on the common roads and highways. A horse required 141 pounds of hay per day along with 7 pounds of straw, a peck of oats (a peck was a specific measurement, equivalent to a quarter of a bushel) and half a peck of peas.[6] On top of that there would be stabling costs.[7] In a brilliant, if sometimes overlooked, scene, Jonson brings all of these realities on to the stage of *The New Inn* when he depicts Peck, the appropriately named ostler, whose role it was to take care of guests' horses in these ways, reflecting on a complex series of scams he has been operating in order to deprive those same guests of their money. In a scene replete with the kind of professional and subculture jargon which Jonson loved and displayed to such effect in plays such as *The Alchemist* and *Bartholomew Fair*, we hear from Pierce the drawer in some detail of Peck's previous schemes:

PIERCE: When,
   You know, the guest put in his hand to feel
   And smell to the oats, that grated all his fingers
   Upo' the wood –
   [...]
                  You were then there
   Upo' your knees, I do remember it,
   To ha' the fact concealed. I could tell more:
   Soaping of saddles, cutting of horse tails,
   And cropping – pranks of ale and hostelry –

(3.1.117–25)

Peacham's playlet-pamphlet makes reference to similar, obviously well-known hustles and scams in the observations of the knowing and experienced brewer's cart. He stresses that Coach should take care of the horses he relies upon to pull him:

See your man give to his horses their due allowance in Hay and Oates, and that he beguiles them not ... Your man also shall leave that old knavish tricke of tying a horse haire very straight about the ... feete (which present will make him halt) then to tell your Master hee is lame, and will not serve his turne.[8]

A similar detailed evocation of the world of the animals and servants who sustained and made possible the world of early modern social display, as well as the practical movement and mobility represented by the coach, is present in Jonson's earlier collaborative dramatic production, *Eastward Ho!* (co-written with George Chapman and John Marston in 1605). In that play, the ambitious goldsmith's daughter Gertrude is married off to the apparently wealthy knight Sir Petronel Flash and immediately envisages the performance of her new status in the form of travelling in her personal coach: 'As I am a lady, I think I am with child already, I long for a coach so' (3.2.34–5). The sense of theatre involved is enhanced by the provision of an onstage audience in the form of the easily impressed Mistresses Fond and Gazer: 'here's a most fine place to stand in' (3.2.14), but we also catch glimpses of Hamlet the footman, who dashes onto and off the stage in an attempt to serve his demanding mistress, and Potkin, a former tavern-worker, who is soon to be metamorphosed into the blue livery of a noblewoman's servant (a shorthand signifier to the audience of Gertrude's willingness to spend of the highest to make a statement of her new status to the world).

The obvious alternative to horse travel, either on horseback or by pulled coach, was walking, and, while in many ways the development of coach travel was understandably seen as a huge advance on the difficult and limited pedestrian opportunities available on poorly made-up roads and surfaces, offering as it did protection from the elements, it is intriguing that in some ways the massive urban expansion that had been witnessed in London during Jonson's lifetime also saw the beginnings of a particular mode of fashionable walking, especially in the city and particularly in certain areas of the city with which Jonson had strong associations. The Strand, Fleet Street and the areas surrounding the Inns of Court more generally became the site of this quotidian practice. This was rapidly reflected in the literature of the age, including not only Jonson's city comedies – *Epicene* in 1609 centres on this aspirational district with its shopping malls and sites of conspicuous consumption but also the ambitious eye that those residing in Strand townhouses and lodgings like Clerimont at the start of this play had to the court – but also the poetry of significant contemporaries such as Donne. His *Satires* reflect the fact that these London streets, but also the ways in which one moved through and traversed them, literally and socially, were a 'crucial part of the topography of the new metropolis'.[9] This was, of course, also the world that various disciples of Jonsonian theatre in the 1630s, such as Richard Brome and James Shirley, would depict as the heart of the social and cultural geography of their own town-based comedies.

John Taylor's pamphlet drew attention to the desirability of walking for health reasons, but *The World Runnes on Wheeles* is, as we have seen, pervaded by concerns that widespread coach travel has blurred clear distinctions that previously existed in terms of different social ranks' access to alternative forms of travel and transportation. In an associated move, it has often been seen as a surprising decision that Jonson conduct his high-profile journey to Scotland in 1618–19 (he was invited to court afterwards to describe his experiences) not by coach or horse but resolutely on foot.[10] If the prospect of a heavyweight man no longer in the prime of youth making the epic journey north from London and back again as a pedestrian seems out of kilter with his considerable social status by this stage in his career, it is helpful to think of this walk as a form of performance art. Jonson certainly envisaged publishing work relating to his experiences – his 1623 poem 'An Execration Upon Vulcan' in which he notes in a long list of lost works and possessions lost in a library fire:

> ... among
> The rest, my journey into Scotland sung,
> With all the adventures.
> (*The Underwood* 43, ll. 93–5)

In this way, it might be helpful to think of this walk less as leisure activity or even domestic travel than as conscious performance art akin to more contemporary narrative accounts of walking journeys by writers such as Robert Macfarlane and Iain Sinclair.

For biographers and scholars of Jonson alike, the fact that the intended poetic work on the journey was never completed (or at least is not extant) remains a frustration, the impact of the experience can still be registered in Jonson's canon in a number of ways. Looking at his plays, masques and entertainments authored after 1618, we can see new kinds of attention being paid to the 'North' as a subject matter, not least in works such as the unfinished *The Sad Shepherd*. The patronage of North Midlands aristocrat William Cavendish must also be viewed as influential on this aspect of his writing, but, nevertheless, the detailed attention to be found in the available fragments of this playtext to matters such as regional weather cycles and landscape features, including the seasonal flooding of the Lincolnshire wolds, give us a hint of what the intended 'fisher play' set around Loch Lomond – which he seemingly intended to write following the Scottish trip – might have featured (*Informations* 18, 519). Exchanges with one of his Scottish hosts, William Drummond of Hawthornden, in which he asked for research materials relating to this intended pastoral play, indicate that Jonson too was becoming interested in the kind of place-specific works more readily associated with Michael Drayton in this period. Of course, there were important precedents for Jonson's Scottish walk. Just a year before, King James VI and I had made his own 'salmon-lyke' progress to his home nation, a journey that had ensured the large-scale improvement of roads and bridges on the route that can only have facilitated Jonson's trip.[11] And, even earlier, William Camden's impressive and extensive peregrinations during his teaching vacations from the Westminster School, where he taught the young Ben and which formed the research for *Britannia* provided obvious inspiration. Jonson was imitated as well as imitating others. John Taylor undertook his own highly publicized journey to Scotland, seeking to carry no money and to rely on hospitality en route. An account of this was published under the title *The Pennyles Pilgrimage* in 1618, though it should be added that Taylor's typically lively account suppresses the crucial detail that he was accompanied by a horse carrying his belongings for much of the journey.

Taylor has long been an important point of access for social historians to the practical world of domestic travel and mobility in this period, be it in the form of these more spectacular and artistically directed forms of travel (Taylor also published accounts of staged journeys by boat and horse) or their everyday patterns of practice. He was a waterman and had a deep understanding of riverine culture as a result, but his published writings also bring to life for us the world of the early modern roads and highways. In 1637 he published *The Carriers Cosmographie*, a fascinating compendium of which inns in London held and dispatched post to which areas of the country. The Black Bull in Smithfield, for example, was the recipient of post coming to and from Bingham in Nottinghamshire, with carriers resident on Fridays.[12] In this example, Taylor provides us with yet another intriguing form of social cartography, mapping for us the postal routes and networks of early modern England in the moment just prior to the formation of a national postal system and linking us back in turn to the world of Jonson's *The New Inn* where the Light Heart is clearly located on one of the main postal networks in and out of north London. This is why Jug, the tapster, is described within the play as a 'thoroughfare of news' (see Persons of the Play, 49); like the inn-house itself he has become a recipient of gossip and information. The ever-expanding road network in England, Scotland and Wales, however, did bring along with an emergent sense of national identity and connectedness concomitant fears and anxieties about the homeless and the unemployed who frequently travelled on it, sometimes begging, sometimes indulging in more criminal activities. The old certainties of parish structures were placed under pressure by these developments in the built environment.

Jonson, like Taylor, was alert to all the social consequences of the increased mobility, literal and social, of the early modern period, be it by road or river. *Eastward Ho!* maps this out in comic fashion by two heavily prescribed journeys eastwards in that play. Gertrude's high hopes for her socially ambitious marriage are soon thwarted by her husband's intention merely to secure and to spend her wealth, and Sir Petronel's own ambitious plans for a voyage to the newly founded colony of Virginia in New England is, in the end, reduced to a very localized and highly domestic journey down the Thames to the Isle of Dogs. Jonson was someone whose own biography had seen him traverse spaces and sites as diverse as the Bricklayers Hall to the glamour and glitter of Whitehall Palace. Yet John Aubrey's retrospective comment that he 'was wont to weare a coat like a coach-man's coate, with slitts under the arme-pitte'[13] would imply that he never forgot the downstairs world of service and practical transport that drove events such as extravagant and expensive court masques for the King and Queen. The world of Peck the ostler, Jug the tapster and Potkin the drawer, is one that Jonson knew and remembered throughout his dramatic career. This vivid social memory ensured that his drama never became static in terms of the spaces, actual and imaginative, that it created and mobilized.

NOTES

1. The poem appears as part of his collection *A Treatise of Civil Power* (London: Penguin, 2007).
2. John Taylor, *The World Runnes on Wheeles; or, Oddes betwixt Carts and Coaches* (London, 1623), sig. B3v.
3. Henry Peacham, *Coach and Sedan Pleasantly Disputing for Place and Precedence* (London, 1636), sigs. C1r–v. For a more detailed discussion of Peacham's possible debt to Caroline drama and literature in the fashioning of his playlet pamphlet, see my introduction to Richard Brome's *The Sparagus Garden* in The Complete Works of Richard Brome Online (forthcoming 2010).
4. Andrew Gurr, 'Who Is Lovewit? What Is He?', in Richard Cave, Elizabeth Schafer and Brian Woolland (eds.), *Ben Jonson and Theatre* (London: Routledge, 1999), p. 7.
5. Joan Thirsk, *Horses in Early Modern England: For Service, for Pleasure, for Power* (Reading: University of Reading, 1978), p. 5.
6. Thirsk, *Horses in Early Modern England*, p. 7.
7. Thirsk notes that in 1574 Sir Henry Sidney spent 1s 5d for stabling in Reading for one night and 2s 7d for another night in Warwick (*Horses in Early Modern England*, p. 7).
8. Peacham, *Coach and Sedan*, sig. F3r.
9. Michelle O'Callaghan, *The English Wits: Wit and Sociability in Early Modern England* (Cambridge: Cambridge University Press, 2007), p. 28. See also Karen Newman, 'Walking Capitals: Donne's First Satyre', in *The Culture of Capital: Properties, Cities, Knowledge in Early Modern England* (London: Routledge, 2002), pp. 203–21.

10. Anne Wallace, *Walking, Literature and English Culture* (Oxford: Clarendon Press, 1993), p. 54.
11. King James himself referred to the journey as 'salmon-lyke' in a letter from Newmarket, 15 December 1616 to the Privy Council of Scotland. Quoted in John Nichols, *The Progresses of King James the First*, 4 vols. (London, 1828), vol. III, p. 309. On the detailed preparations for the journey, see William A. McNeill and Peter G. B. McNeill, 'The Scottish Progress of James VI, 1617', *The Scottish Historical Review*, 75 (1996): 38–51.
12. John Taylor, *The Carriers Cosmographie* (London, 1637), sig. A4v.
13. John Aubrey, *Brief Lives,* edited by J Buchanan Brown (London: Penguin, 2000), pp. 171–2; cited in Aileen Ribiero, *Fashion and Fiction: Dress in Art and Literature in Stuart England* (New Haven, Conn.: Yale University Press, 2005), p. 40.

CHAPTER 31

Money and consumerism

Christopher Burlinson

A proper understanding of money in the economic and cultural history of late sixteenth- and early seventeenth-century England, of its different forms and transactions as well as its denominations, allows us better to grasp the financial references and playfulness within Ben Jonson's works, the chequins and angels and crowns that change hands in so very many of his plays,[1] and also to understand their philosophical and ethical force: Jonson's defining interest in trust and exchange, honesty and deceit, credit and coining.

But it is curious that one should speak of reassessing Jonson's financial preoccupations, for at least two very good reasons. The first is very clear to any spectator or reader of his plays: namely, that almost all of them are so explicitly about money. Volpone's pile of gold, the swindles of *The Alchemist*, Merecraft's projects in *The Devil is an Ass* and his dreams of the millions that he will make from them, the transactions and purchases of *Bartholomew Fair*, of *Eastward Ho!*, of *Every Man In His Humour*, and so on; how could anyone miss this? Furthermore, Jonson's own financial biography, his renowned commercial control over his published texts,[2] the archival information that we possess about the expenditure that was lavished on the masques and entertainments on which he worked, his apparently autobiographical remarks in *Discoveries* about the mockery that his own poverty had occasioned from certain accusers and enemies ('I confess [poverty] is my domestic' [970]) – all make it difficult for us to fail to be alert to the financial contexts and concerns of his writings.

The second reason why it is difficult for any of Jonson's spectators or readers to remain oblivious to commercial matters has to do with the history of Jonsonian criticism itself, in which the importance of the world of finance – commerce and the market, consumerism and confidence tricks – has been well attested and studied since at least the early twentieth century. L. C. Knights, in his *Drama and Society in the Age of Jonson*, a precursor of the more recent historical turn in Renaissance studies, provided critics with a definitive assertion of the importance of the economic history of the English Renaissance to its literature. Knights argued that Jonson's writings provided not just a reflection of their times but a critical, nay condemnatory, commentary upon them. Quoting T. S. Eliot's remark that the logic of Jonson's imaginary worlds 'illuminates the actual world, because it gives us a new point of view from which to inspect it',[3] Knights replied that 'The connexion between Jonson's plays and "the actual world" is much closer than that sentence allows it.'[4]

What Knights believed Jonson was writing about, and moreover criticizing, was what he described as the 'acquisitive' society of his time: an emergent capitalism, marked by a growing 'money market', increased overseas trade and the rise of 'new men', and the social disruptions that accompanied these changes. The late sixteenth century was, as Joan Thirsk has argued more recently with a breadth of detail and analysis that extends and corroborates Knights's point, a commonwealth whose economy was increasingly based on *projects,* schemes for the manufacture of goods, household or otherwise, for the domestic and export markets. In the contemporary treatises that defended such projects, for instance Sir Thomas Smith's *Discourse of the Common Weal* (1549), it was argued that they mixed public and private interest, since they would not only stimulate the domestic economy at the same time as they satisfied the population's increasing desire for consumer goods but would also provide 'a tailor-made solution to the problem of finding work for the poor'.[5] Whereas Knights sees writers in the age of Jonson viewing these projects with a critical eye, then, and taking them to task as examples of an increasingly acquisitive world, Thirsk shows that for many politicians and thinkers, not merely the investors themselves, they seemed to be a worthwhile and beneficial economic development. Investment in ironworks in the Sussex Weald in the 1540s, in the growing of woad on Nottinghamshire estates in the 1580s, in the spinning of woollen cloth, and in the hundreds of other projects that Thirsk describes ('everyone with a scheme... had a project'[6]) not only filled the pockets of the successful adventurers but also reinvigorated the local and national economies of the sixteenth century.

What Thirsk's analysis brings to that of Knights, then, and what it allows us to see all the more clearly, is the contact between three economic terms that have informed a great deal of work on Jonson and on early modern English drama in general – projection, consumption and money. 'In short', Thirsk writes, 'The majority of the population in many local communities did not begin to accumulate much cash in hand until they began to produce commodities other than the staple necessities of life.'[7]

That extra income did not simply come from satisfying a public demand for goods: it also permitted a nascent consumer culture that was based upon the purchase of such goods. So, in *The Devil is an Ass,* for instance, Merecraft's projects deal not just with the ambitious reclaiming of fenland but with the manufacture of luxury and household goods: dog skins for gloves, wine from blackberries and so on. And at the same time as Merecraft imagines taking advantage of all ranks of society, in a swelling bubble of investment and credit – 'we'll take in citizens, commoners, and aldermen / To bear the charge' (2.1.42–3) – his production of goods also supposes a commonwealth of purchasers, of consumers, ready to buy them. And while Jonson's shops, markets and tradespeople are not always the purveyors of fashion that one sees, for instance, in Middleton and Dekker's *The Roaring Girl,* the abundance of goods makes consumerism an obvious subject of interest.

The origin of the consumer society has preoccupied cultural historians for the past twenty or thirty years: located variously in the sixteenth century (as by Joan Thirsk), in the eighteenth century,[8] in modern urban culture,[9] or at other historical moments. As Paul Glennie suggests in an article that surveys these varying accounts, what seems to be at stake in them is the establishment of a historiographical framework that can posit the period in question as one of unique change and transition.[10] What was it that changed in the culture and economy of the early seventeenth century? What did Jonson, or the people who came to see his plays, stand to gain from these changes? Accounts of consumer culture tend, as Glennie goes on, to stress the growing consumption of commodities and consumer acquisitiveness, often tied to fashion or advertising, and the development of mass culture, or 'systematic manipulation by capital of consumer knowledges through mass media and advertising images'.[11] They also frequently, as in the case of Jean Baudrillard, ask us to reconsider the relationship between needs and appetites, as both arise from a proliferation of consumer goods: 'when communication becomes total, "needs" grow exponentially – not from the growth of *appetite* but from *competition.*'[12]

Knights's analysis, too, seems to confirm the importance of a consumer culture – not just an acquisitive one – to Jonson's drama, even though such a historiographical term was clearly not available to either Knights or Jonson. Knights argues that Jonson's criticism of the acquisitive society of Elizabethan and early Stuart England finds its consummate expression in the extraordinary hyperbolic rhetoric of Sir Epicure Mammon, a rhetoric that 'generate[s] an intensely critical activity in the reader, make[s] him aware that he is called on to judge a mode of experience as well as to enjoy the representation'.[13] But Mammon's language also suggests a society in which the proliferation of domestic goods generates a desire for them: 'all my beds blown up, not stuffed', 'mine oval room / Filled with such pictures as Tiberius took / From Elephantis, and dull Aretine / But coldly imitated', 'my glasses / Cut in more subtle angles, to disperse / And multiply the figures as I walk / Naked between my *succubae*' (*The Alchemist*, 2.2.41–8). This is indeed, as Knights's argument suggests, absurdly inflated rhetoric, a satire upon greed and acquisitiveness, but what Mammon imagines is no mere accumulation of pelf, as Volpone's hoard of treasure is; rather, it is a hyperbolic version of consumer spending power.

A consideration of consumerism, then, and the possible beginnings of a consumer society in the early seventeenth century, might allow us to articulate a first criticism of Knights's work in *Drama and Society*, a first way of reassessing Jonson's concern with money; namely, that what Knights identifies in Jonson is not so much an accurate account of the early modern English economy, or of early modern economic analysis, but rather a particularly striking version of a conventional critique of *wealth*, and of a certain attitude to it. Knights is undoubtedly correct to point out Jonson's criticism of acquisitiveness; it has numerous medieval and classical precedents (Knights notes Lucian, Petronius, and others), but Jonson often expresses it explicitly, as in *Discoveries*:

Money never made any man rich, but his mind. He that can order himself to the law of nature is not only without the sense but the fear of poverty. Oh, but to strike blind the people with our wealth and pomp is the thing! What a wretchedness is this, to thrust all our riches outward, and be beggars within; to contemplate nothing but the little, vile, and sordid things of the world, not the great, noble, and precious! We serve our avarice, and, not content with the good of the earth that is offered us, we search and dig for the evil that is hidden. God offered us those things and placed them at hand and near us, that He knew were profitable for us; but the hurtful He laid deep and hid. Yet do we seek only the things whereby we may perish, and bring them forth, when God and nature hath buried them. We covet superfluous things, when it were more honour for us if we would contemn necessary. What need hath nature of silver dishes, multitudes of waiters, delicate pages, perfumed napkins? (*Discoveries*, ll. 980–92)

But this is a passage in which the point of criticism changes from 'money' to wealth and riches (something that might be coveted, hoarded, displayed); it alerts us to the relation, and the differences, between *wealth* and *money*, both in Jonson's writings and in the world from which he emerged.

Recent studies of the early modern economy, for instance Craig Muldrew's *The Economy of Obligation* (1998), have shown that it was increasingly dependent upon credit, and that notions of credit were beginning at that time to acquire a particularly significant cultural resonance.[14] But Muldrew also shows that in the early seventeenth century there was a strong conceptual and literal separation between credit and *money*, a word which at the time was used to refer only to hard cash and not to more abstract concepts of wealth or purchasing power (a use of the word which, the *OED* suggests, came into being only at the end of the seventeenth century). A dearth of cash, in particular of coins, had precipitated one of the economic crises of the early modern period. The growth in population during the sixteenth century, as well as a rapid inflation in food prices (approximately 300 per cent between 1540 and 1600), meant that the early modern economy had grown faster than the amount of money in circulation and that the demand for coins was at an extraordinary height by the end of Elizabeth's reign.[15] But another peculiarity of the status of money, in particular coins, at that time was the way in which their value was conceived. The value of money, seventeenth-century economists stressed, could consist in two different things: coins could have value as tokens of exchange (that is, they could stand in for the value of two different things or sums that were exchanged) or they could have value in themselves: in other words, the precious metal of which coins were made meant that their value could be strictly what they, as objects, were worth. Laws against minting and clipping of coins, and the widespread refusal among tradespeople to accept clipped currency (as well as the custom of paying poor employees in clipped currency) originated from the anxiety that damaged or diminished coins were no longer actually worth what they purported to be worth.

In other words, the proliferation of references to money in Jonson's plays, and the consequent presence of coins as props on the Jonsonian stage, should alert us to two things. First, they register the unprecedented importance that coins had in the lives of the people who would have attended Jonson's plays. If it was true that the conspicuous consumption of gold was an uncommon luxury in a world in which gold supplies were limited, it was also the case that money was in extremely short supply during the period, and especially during times (e.g. 1594–7) when economic crisis led to the calling in of debts that needed to be paid in cash. And second, such references remind us that transactions in money might actually have been seen as moments at which trust was required or called into question – not only because such transactions made demands upon the trustworthiness of the partners that engaged in them, and symbolically required that trust, but also because money itself bespoke a true correspondence between an object and its value. The satirical point of Jonson's account of dishonest financial exchanges might lie partly in the truthfulness of exchange that money ideally promised. In the exchange that takes place between Brainworm and the foolish Stephen in *Every Man In His Humour* (Folio), for instance, in which Brainworm attempts to sell a sword for an inflated sum, the conversation begins by emphasizing the exchange of coins for goods that is to take place: 'Gentlemen, please you change a few crowns for a very excellent good blade here?' (2.4.43–4). It continues with numerous references to coins – crowns, angels, shillings – and concludes with Stephen swearing upon the very money that he is handing over that what he is buying is not worth it:

KNOWELL: You shall not buy it, I say.
STEPHEN: By this money, but I will, though I give more than 'tis worth.
(2.4.79–80)

In another contemporary text, *Coryats Crudities* (1611), for instance, for which Jonson wrote a dedicatory poem, English travellers to Venice are warned about a breakdown in this system of coins and exchange. 'Now whereas the Venetian duckat is much spoken of, you must consider that this word duckat doth not signifie any one certaine coyne. But many seuerall pieces doe concurre to make one duckat .... So that a duckat is sometimes more, sometimes lesse.'[16] The untrustworthiness of the Venetian mercantile system comes from the uncertainty of ascertaining what any such coin 'signifies'. And the practices of currency exchange in Venice also mean that exchange will no longer be an act of trust but one of loss and exploitation:

I would Counsell thee whatsoeuer thou art that intendest to trauell into Italy, and to returne thy money in England by bill of exchange that thou maiest receiue it againe in Venice; I would counsell thee (I say) so to compound with thy merchant, that thou maiest be paide all thy money in the exchange coyne, which is this brasse piece called the Liuer. For otherwise thou wilt incurre an inconuenience by receiuing it in peeces of gold of sundry coines, according to the pleasure of the Merchant that payeth thee in Venice.[17]

An awareness of the cultural and economic importance of money in early modern England should not take the edge off Jonson's satire of greed and individualism. Indeed, it contributes to that satire by reminding us that money could carry with it the implication of trustworthiness. The coins that appear at dramatic and comedic moments of exchange as well as acquisition remind us that trust and honesty were bound up in Jonson's understanding of money. And this reassessment of money also modifies our understanding of a final economic term that has proliferated in criticism of Jonsonian and early modern drama – the *market*. Recent critics of Jonson, and of Knights's analysis of him, have argued that Jonson's personal financial involvement in his masques and authorship rendered his satire of greed and acquisitiveness uncertain, even paradoxical. As Don Wayne has argued, for instance, his works after *Volpone*:

> show signs of a disturbed awareness that his own identity as poet and playwright … depended on the same emerging structure of social relationships that he satirized in his plays. … There is an interesting tension in Jonson's work between, on the one hand, the designation of rampant individualism as the origin of social disorder in Jacobean England, and, on the other, the poet's constant assertion of his own individuality and independence.[18]

And such ambivalence, according to Wayne, influences the comic conclusions of Jonson's plays, for example that of *The Alchemist*, 'not a judgement and an action founded on an ethical absolute, but one founded on the exigencies of power, self-interest, and reciprocal exchange'.[19]

But considering Jonson as a man of the market, as well as a critic of the market, has also forced a succession of critics to think about the manifestation of the market in various physical and metaphorical places: the 'ritually defined threshold[s]' and liminal spaces of Jean-Christophe Agnew,[20] the new financial institutions and buildings of sixteenth- and seventeenth-century London, such as Thomas Gresham's Royal Exchange, which forms a prominent part of the geography of *Every Man In His Humour*,[21] the negotiations between the producers and buyers of books. What a renewed concentration on money allows us to see is that a particular kind of commerce, and of ethical observations and failings, takes place at moments of monetary exchange, that Jonson's critique of money, or at least of certain uses of it, had as much to do with exchange and transactional ethics as with acquisitiveness and the hoarding of wealth.

NOTES

1. For a glossary of these terms, see Sandra K. Fischer, *Econolingua: A Glossary of Coins and Economic Language in Renaissance Drama* (Newark, Del. and London: University of Delaware Press and Associated University Presses, 1985); see also D. F. Allen and W. R. Dunstan, 'Crosses and Crowns: A Study of Coinage in the Elizabethan Dramatists', *British Numismatic Journal*, 23 (1938–41): 287–99, David C. Baker, 'The "Angel" of English Renaissance Literature', *Studies in the Renaissance*, 6 (1959): 85–93.
2. See, for example, Joseph Loewenstein, 'The Script in the Marketplace', *Representations*, 12 (Fall) (1985): 101–14.

3. T. S. Eliot, *Elizabethan Essays* (London: Faber, 1934), p. 79.
4. L. C. Knights, *Drama and Society in the Age of Jonson* (London: Chatto & Windus, 1937), p. 206.
5. Joan Thirsk, *Economic Policy and Projects: The Development of a Consumer Society in Early Modern England* (Oxford: Clarendon Press, 1978), p. 18.
6. Thirsk, *Economic Policy and Projects*, p. 1.
7. Thirsk, *Economic Policy and Projects*, p. 7.
8. See, for instance, Neil McKendrick, John Brewer and J. H. Plumb, *The Birth of a Consumer Society: The Commercialization of Eighteenth-Century England* (London: Hutchinson, 1982).
9. See, for instance, Jean Baudrillard, *The Consumer Society: Myths and Structures* (originally published 1970; London: Sage, 1998).
10. Paul Glennie, 'Consumption within Historical Studies', in Daniel Miller (ed.), *Acknowledging Consumption: A Review of New Studies* (London: Routledge, 1995), pp. 164–203. For another survey, see Sara Pennell, 'Consumption and Consumerism in Early Modern England', *Historical Journal*, 42 (1999): 549–64.
11. Glennie, 'Consumption within Historical Studies', p. 165.
12. Baudrillard, *The Consumer Society*, p. 65.
13. Knights, *Drama and Society in the Age of Jonson*, p. 208.
14. Craig Muldrew, *The Economy of Obligation: The Culture of Credit and Social Relations in Early Modern England* (Basingstoke: Macmillan, 1998).
15. See Craig Muldrew, '"Hard Food for Midas": Cash and its Social Value in Early Modern England', *Past and Present*, 170 (2001): 78–120.
16. Thomas Coryate, *Coryats Crudities* (1611), p. 286.
17. Coryate, *Coryats Crudities*, p. 286.
18. Don E. Wayne, 'Drama and Society in the Age of Jonson: An Alternative View', *Renaissance Drama*, 13 (n.s.) (1982): 103–29; pp. 107–8.
19. Wayne, 'Drama and Society', p. 112.
20. Jean-Christophe Agnew, *Worlds Apart: The Market and the Theater in Anglo-American Thought, 1550–1700* (Cambridge: Cambridge University Press, 1986), p. 32.
21. See Janette Dillon, *Theatre, Court and City, 1595–1610: Drama and Social Space in London* (Cambridge: Cambridge University Press, 2000).

CHAPTER 32

Land

Garrett A. Sullivan, Jr

Land lies at the heart of Ben Jonson's ethical ideal. Jonson represents land both as the locus of a moral economy and, satirically, as readily exchangeable. His work is marked by resistance to land's commodification even as it imaginatively explores how different understandings of land, including a commodified one, lend themselves to the formation of distinct models of society and self.

Jonson's ideal is explicitly championed in 'To Penshurst'. Strictly speaking, Jonson does not write of a superseded past in his tribute to Robert Sidney and his estate. However, the many virtues of house, land and landlord emerge out of the contrast between this 'ancient pile' (l. 5) and those manors, tacitly of newer vintage, that are 'built to envious show' (l. 1). The organizing distinction, which the poem clearly articulates in its final line, is between *building* and *dwelling* (l. 102) – between building a 'prodigy house' that functions as the expression of the landlord's social position, and *dwelling* on an estate that sustains a community extending outward from family to tenants to visiting poet and even to King James and Prince Henry when they came 'hunting late, this way' (l. 76).[1] It is Sidney's hospitality to both his inferiors and superiors that marks him as one who dwells.

'To Penshurst' offers an influential vision of the estate-centered moral economy at its most salubrious. While the poem begins and ends with the 'ancient pile', it encompasses the entire physical and social world of the estate through the depiction of a reciprocal relationship among landlord, tenantry and natural resources. The Sidney family's hospitality is mirrored by self-offerings made by all the estate's inhabitants: the partridge 'willing to be killed' (l. 30), the carp that 'run into thy net' (l. 33), the fruit that 'Hang[s] on thy walls, [so] that every child may reach' (l. 44) and even the 'ripe daughters' whose 'baskets bear / An emblem of themselves, in plum, or pear' (ll. 54–6). This emphasis on fecundity – of land, of 'ripe daughters', and, towards the end, of Lady Sidney herself (ll. 90–2) – binds together the estate's topography with the reproductive abilities of its human inhabitants. The land is tacitly gendered female, and Jonson's vision of a potent, licit fertility – he emphasizes the certainty of Sidney's paternity (ll. 91–2) – encompasses all elements of manorial life, with the Sidneys as the source of this generative capacity. The behaviour of the Sidneys is reflected even in the estate's superior microclimate: it has 'better marks, of soil, of air, / Of wood, of water' (ll. 7–8).

Jonson's conception of Penshurst as simultaneously exemplary and redolent of an all-but-vanished social order is informed by changes in land use and management that were routinely understood as erosive of the kind of moral economy Jonson champions. The practice of enclosure (the fencing in of land, often to graze sheep, previously leased to tenants or held in common) remained controversial and was understood by many as doing great harm to the tenantry. Moreover, the broader rationalization of land use, especially as represented by estate surveying, was perceived to damage customary relations between landlord and tenant. A character in John Norden's *The Surveyor's Dialogue* says that it is through the surveyor's activities that 'customes are altered, broken, and sometimes peruerted or taken away … [The surveyor] looke[s] into the values of mens Lands, whereby the Lords of Mannors doe racke their Tenants to a higher rent and rate than euer before'.[2] For many, the most important broken custom was the one still performed by Jonson's Sidney, that of extending hospitality to one's superiors and, especially, inferiors. According to Felicity Heal, it is during Jonson's lifetime that 'housekeeping' or hospitality ceases to serve as a primary aristocratic practice and value, not to mention as a source of poor relief.[3] Emblematic of hospitality's decline was the relocation of the landlord from country to city or court. This practice was deemed so erosive of social relations that James VI and I, like Elizabeth I before him, issued a proclamation exhorting landlords to return to their estates, with the necessity of housekeeping being a primary reason.[4] Taken together with a land market that had long flourished, these phenomena all troubled the vision of a self-sufficient moral economy expressed in 'To Penshurst'; they also underscore the fabular elements of the poem, in which the willing partridge and the carp eager to be netted manifest the merits of 'dwelling'. Such fabular elements intimate the extent to which Penshurst is more ideal than reality, and indeed, as critics have suggested, the poem is shadowed by significant occlusions and negations.[5] For example, the often harsh reality of agrarian labour is nowhere to be found in the poem. (Jonson even insists that Penshurst's walls were 'reared with … no man's groan' [l. 46)]. Similarly, Sidney's estate was anything but a self-sustaining rural community sealed off from a comparatively debased urban world: 'The country elite used their country estates as a power base for political office in London, and their political office in London in turn enhanced their standing in the country, in their county ... [T]he country house was a place from which one acted with a view to the court.'[6]

'To Penshurst', along with 'To Sir Robert Wroth', exemplifies the country-house poem, a subgenre, extended by the likes of Lanyer, Herrick and Marvell, which focuses upon and trumpets the virtues of the well-run estate. Land also figures prominently in other poems and plays of Jonson's, often in the service of satirizing fallings off from the ideal. One sees this in a trope dear to Jonson's heart, that of land's transformation into expensive clothing or fashionable objects. A typical example is found in *Epicene* (1609), when Truewit underscores to Morose the potentially deleterious effects of marriage:

[Your would-be wife] must have that rich gown for such a great day, a new one for the next, a richer for the third; be served in silver, have the chamber filled with a succession of grooms, footmen, ushers, and other messengers, besides embroiderers, jewellers, tirewomen, sempsters, feathermen, perfumers; while she feels not how the land drops away, nor the acres melt, nor foresees the change when the mercer has your woods for her velvets. (2.2.77–83)

The hierarchical and reciprocal social order instantiated in 'To Penshurst' contrasts intriguingly with the bevy of attendants and tradespeople serving the vanity of Morose's imagined wife. Most important, though, is the transmutation of acres into velvets and other dear commodities. In Jonson's 'Epistle. To Katherine, Lady Aubigny', the titular heroine is praised for not 'follow[ing] fashions and attires', unlike those women who 'for foreign wires, / Melt down their husbands' land, to pour away / On the close groom and page on new year's day' (*The Forest*, 13, ll. 71–4). And in *Every Man Out of His Humour* (1599), Carlo Buffone provides Sogliardo with instructions necessary to his achieving his dearest wish:

First, to be an accomplished gentleman, that is, a gentleman of the time, you must give o'er housekeeping in the country and live altogether in the city amongst gallants, where, at your first appearance, 'twere good you turned four or five hundred acres of your best land into two or three trunks of apparel – you may do it without going to a conjurer. (1.2.33–7)

Buffone explicitly juxtaposes the moral economy ('housekeeping in the country') with elegant city life, which requires the landed gentleman's abnegation of his responsibilities to his tenants. In his aspirations, Sogliardo appears as Robert Sidney's opposite.[7]

These satirical examples are marked by some striking commonalities. The commodification of land is figured in terms of the frictionless transformation of one form of property into another: woods turn to velvets, acres become trunks of apparel or New Year's gifts. Buffone says Sogliardo may effect this transformation 'without going to a conjurer', but Jonson's metaphors all evoke a magical, even alchemical transmutation of substance. Changes occur not only at the level of matter, however; the objects into which land is alchemized usher us into a fashionable milieu. That is, whereas 'To Penshurst' represents a social world built upon 'housekeeping in the country', these works present us with one predicated upon vanity and the desire for social advancement. If maintaining one's land – and the social relations built upon it – is the basis for the Jonsonian moral economy, selling land enables social relations that are fundamentally immoral.

The trope of land turned into apparel (or 'foreign wires') builds upon several significant assumptions: first, a putative opposition between the country and the city or court (explicitly developed in 'To Sir Robert Wroth'); second, a distinction between two models of gentlemanly behaviour, one predicated upon hospitality and the latter upon fashionable display in the service of social advancement; and finally, the treatment of land not as a renewable resource but as an object of exchange for which economic benefits are to be gleaned only at the moment of 'melting'. All of these assumptions are developed fully in *Every Man Out of His Humour*, a work centrally concerned with turning land into clothing.

Clothing's desirability lies in the way it enables the performance of what we might call Buffonian masculinity. After Macilente, the envious scourge, is decked out in elaborate garb, he opines:

> Be a man ne'er so vile
> In wit, in judgement, manners, or what else,
> If he can purchase but a silken cover,
> He shall not only pass, but pass regarded.
>
> (3.3.9–12)

Whereas in a land-based moral economy hospitality is constitutive of gentlemanliness, in the court it is the 'silken cover', afforded the Sogliardos of the world by the translation of acres into apparel, that makes the man.

While Sogliardo is advised to sell his lands in order to become a gentleman, his brother, Sordido, holds on to his but offers no hospitality. Instead, he hoards his crops so that, in an anticipated dearth, their value will go up. As for the social implications of this, Sordido says, 'Oh, but (say some) the poor are like to starve. / Why, let 'em starve; what's that to me?' (1.3.94–5). Sordido's son Fungoso seeks his father's money to buy clothes; he obsessively emulates the foppish Fastidious Brisk, who opines that 'your good face is the witch and your apparel the spells that bring all the pleasures of the world into their circle' (2.3.242–3). Fastidious soon makes clear the connection between real estate and clothing, with money introduced as an agent in the alchemical process: 'I am come to have you play the alchemist with me, and change the species of my land into that metal you talk of' (2.2.279–81). Given Fastidious's overriding association with sartorial excess, we know that land's conversion into 'metal' (that is, cash) is only a step in its translation into clothing. In short, the logic articulated in Buffone's lines about 'trunks of apparel' governs the actions and aspirations of numerous characters in the play. Additionally, the figure who does not sell his land is the one who cries 'let 'em starve'. For Sordido, land provides not the basis for a timeless ideal but the means by which he hopes to make a timely and time-sensitive intervention into the commodities market.

By the play's end, each of these characters has been driven out of his humour. Sordido, for example, reforms his relations to the poor after he is saved from suicide by a group of 'rustics'; his 'barns and garners shall stand open still / To all the poor that come' (3.2.89–90). Such changes occur at the level of character, in accordance with Jonson's theatrical modification of the Galenic humoural scheme.[8] However, the social world of *Every Man Out of His Humour* turns upon the (ab)use or sale of land; the play offers a reverse image of the world of 'To Penshurst'. *Every Man Out of His Humour*'s characters might change, but the cultural logic that animated their actions remains intact. This logic is marked by rampant commodification, for which land is the perfect emblem.

But how can land be both central to a static moral economy and the emblem of a fluid and alchemical one? We can understand this by reading *Every Man Out of His Humour* next to 'To Penshurst'. In the latter, land is inextricable from the web of estate-based social relations: the salubrious nature of the Sidney's hospitality is mirrored in the 'better marks, of soil, of air'; the estate's fecundity is expressed in that of 'noble, fruitful, chaste' Lady Lisle (l. 90). Land is one interconnected element among many that together comprise the social organism of the Sidney estate. At the same time, the estate is an expression of Sidney's authority and identity. If, as Thomas Greene has influentially argued, Jonson's ethical ideal is that of 'centred selfhood', the proper management of one's estate is integral to the achievement of that ideal.[9] Centred selfhood depends upon and is expressed through interconnectedness; the centred self (usually masculine in Jonson) lies at the centre of a social world. The well-managed estate indexes the well-regulated self and, in turn, is a key element for the health of the commonwealth as a whole.[10] From this point of view, land represents that which is or should be uncommodifiable.

This brings us back to Jonson's satiric inversion of his land-based social ideal. As *Every Man Out of His Humour*, *Epicene* and other plays show, Jonson also places land at the core of a set of social relations comprised not of 'centred selves' but of con artists, fops and rural folk aspiring to become urban(e) gentlemen. Jonson figures land's commodification in terms of its 'melting' into apparel, but the real alchemical process involves not acres but people. As in 'To Penshurst', land is inextricable from social relations; its transformation figures the transformation of its seller, who 'to be an accomplished gentleman' turns his 'best land' into 'two or three trunks of apparel'. The alchemy of property is an alchemy of personhood; it enables the production of a self not centred but protean, a 'gentleman of the time' whose frequent changes of clothing (as in the cases of Fastidious Brisk and the hapless Fungoso) bespeak an absence of fixity and an essential fluidity of self.[11]

Jonson's poetry and plays have often been read through the lens of the significant historical developments that they so eagerly engage, especially in the case of the emergence of entrepreneurial capitalism. It should be stressed, though, that Jonson's works are less a transparent register of historical change than figurations of such change in relation to Jonson's literary and ethical aims. This chapter has focused on two powerful Jonsonian fantasies of the land and of the social worlds in which land is imbricated. The centred and protean selves are the purest expressions of these fantasies; they register and imaginatively develop Jonson's recognition of profound changes being wrought in land's relation to both society and self.

NOTES

1. On the architecture of Penshurst, see Don Wayne, *Penshurst: The Semiotics of Place and the Poetics of History* (Madison, Wisc.: University of Wisconsin Press, 1984).
2. John Norden, *The Surveyors Dialogue* (London,1610), sig. B2r.
3. Felicity Heal, *Hospitality in Early Modern England* (Oxford: Clarendon Press, 1990).
4. James I, 'A Proclamation Enjoyning All Lieutenants, and Justices of the Peace, to Repair into Their Countreys, and All Idle Persons to Depart the Court', 29 July 1603, in James F. Larkin and Paul L. Hughes (eds.), *Stuart Royal Proclamations*, 2 vols. (Oxford: Clarendon Press, 1973), vol. I, p. 44.
5. See especially Raymond Williams, *The Country and the City* (Oxford: Oxford University Press, 1975); Wayne, *Penshurst*.

6. Martin Elsky, 'The Mixed Genre of Ben Jonson's "To Penshurst," and the Perilous Springs of Netherlandish Landscape', *Ben Jonson Journal*, 9 (2002): 1–36; especially p. 23. Not discussed in this essay is Jonson's satire of land reclamation projects in *The Devil is an Ass*; see Leah Marcus, *The Politics of Mirth* (Chicago, Ill.: University of Chicago Press, 1986), pp. 64–105; Robert C. Evans, *Ben Jonson and the Contexts of His Time* (Lewisburg, Pa.: Bucknell University Press, 1994), pp. 62–94; Julie Sanders, *Ben Jonson's Theatrical Republics* (Basingstoke: Macmillan, 1998), pp. 107–22.
7. For more on this trope, see Garrett A. Sullivan, Jr., *The Drama of Landscape: Land, Property, and Social Relations on the Early Modern Stage* (Stanford, Calif.: Stanford University Press, 1998); Julie Sanders, '"Wardrobe Stuffe": Clothes, Costume and the Politics of Dress in Ben Jonson's *The New Inn*', *Renaissance Forum*, 6 (1) (2002): 1–27. Available online at www.hull.ac.uk/renforum/v6no1/sanders.htm.
8. On the Galenic humours and the metaphoric use to which they are put, see the play's Induction, ll. 86–120.
9. Thomas M. Greene, 'Ben Jonson and the Centered Self', *Studies in English Literature, 1500–1900*, 10 (1970): 325–48. See also Lawrence Danson, 'Jonsonian Comedy and the Discovery of the Social Self', *PMLA*, 99 (1984): 179–93; Ann C. Christensen, 'Reconsidering Ben Jonson and the "Centered Self"', *South Central Review*, 13 (1996): 1–16.
10. 'Knowing one's place, in the double sense of recognition and disposition in a hierarchical order, marks both the human and the "natural"': in the poem (Nancy S. Leonard, 'Knowing One's Place: The "Natural" Landscape of Jonson's "To Penshurst,"', in Jürgen Kleist and Bruce A. Butterfield (eds.), *Re-Naming the Landscape* [New York: Peter Lang, 1994], p. 111). See also Kari Boyd McBride, *Country House Discourse in Early Modern England* (Aldershot: Ashgate, 2001).
11. The most developed examples of the protean self are Jeremy/Face in *The Alchemist* and Mosca in *Volpone*.

CHAPTER 33

Patronage

Helen Ostovich

Patronage networks were still a vital part of the socio-literary and political arenas in the early modern period, when writers were beginning to claim a new status as independent professionals. Deborah C. Payne lays out the obligations of the patron in relation to the artist as 'direct financial support; exchange of gifts . . .; appointment to a post . . .; or recommendation to someone who can secure such an exchange for social and political allegiance';[1] to this list, I would add that Jonson's patrons also required diplomatic and political skills to get their poet out of trouble, or out of jail. Many of his lifelong friendships originated at the Inns of Court: John Hoskyns, Sir Francis Beaumont, John Donne, Sir Walter Ralegh, John Marston and others. Richard Martin, the Christmas prince of the 1597/8 Middle Temple revels, extricated Jonson from threats of prosecution over the 'Apologetical Dialogue' appended to *Poetaster* in 1601; Jonson dedicated the play to him in the 1616 folio, and dedicated the folio *Every Man Out of His Humour* to the Inns of Court at large. David Riggs emphasizes how much Jonson benefited from patronage even in his very early life, when an unknown gentleman paid for his education at Westminster School, thus introducing him to another patron and later friend, his schoolmaster William Camden.[2] Through Camden, to whom he dedicated the revision of *Every Man In His Humour*, Jonson met Sir Robert Cotton, and through him other members of the upper class who became invaluable in helping to shape Jonson's career – although Jonson, as he might insist and as seems to be true, also assisted the political careers of those patrons, especially those who pleased the King by introducing Jonson's plays to the court and by commissioning and dancing in Jonson's masques. For Jonson, at least, patronage seems to have developed into a mutually beneficial exchange in which the patron's power and influence nurture the poet's talent, based on an ideology of service and interdependency sustained by their mutual agreement; that is, it is a system that potentially gives dignity to both sides of the equation. Jonson implies this balance when he points out in his various dedicatory epistles or prefaces that patron and poet work on a basis that is completely unlike the marketplace, since quality of mind, not just quantity of cash, creates the relationship between the two. The patron's gift is the investment in the poet – whether artistic, intellectual, social, political or domestic, this last exemplified in Lord Aubigny's permitting Jonson to live in his house for some years – but the poet's return gift may confer grace and immortality through his art. According to Arthur Marotti, 'The intellectual and cultural authority he desired for authorship' allowed Jonson to address his patrons 'from a position of strength, often offering moral and intellectual instruction as well as the requisite expressions of humble gratitude and devotion'.[3]

The list of Jonson's friends and patrons is impressive, and we should not forget that, aside from his intellectual and artistic powers, Jonson was a man of immense personal charm. David Kay suggests that Jonson's habit of creating poetry of praise and dedicating his work to courtiers who were either current patrons or potential patrons was unusual for the period, propelling him into royal favour.[4] His career moved forward with the performance of his *Every Man* plays at court, where, over the Jacobean and Caroline years, he gained the patronage of such men as Esmé Stuart, Lord Aubigny, the King's cousin and one of the Gentlemen of the Bedchamber, and Robert Cecil, Earl of Salisbury, Secretary of State and subsequently Lord Treasurer, for whom Jonson wrote four entertainments and three poems of praise in gratitude for Salisbury's rescue of himself and Chapman from the *Eastward Ho!* incarceration in 1605. Other patrons were members of Sir Philip Sidney's family circle: his brother, Sir Robert Sidney, Lord Lisle, was the Queen's Lord Chamberlain, and uncle of William Herbert, Earl of Pembroke (he gave Jonson £20 a year for books) and his brother Philip Herbert, Earl of Montgomery. Both brothers also pushed for the playwrights' release from prison in 1605, and by 1615, along with George Villiers, Duke of Buckingham, became Gentlemen of the Bedchamber. By 1616, King James gave Jonson a pension of 100 marks for life as quasi-poet laureate. After the phenomenal success of *The Gypsies Metamorphosed*, written at Buckingham's request, Jonson received the reversion to the post of Master of the Revels. He had also acquired another influential patron, William Cavendish, Earl of Newcastle. He may have met Cavendish earlier, since Cavendish was a companion of Prince Henry's, and both William and Charles Cavendish toured Europe with Sir Henry Wotton, another friend of Jonson's, while Jonson himself was chaperoning Walter Ralegh's son in 1613 through France and the Netherlands. Although it seemed that Jonson's financial future was secure by the early 1620s, King Charles was less generous, and, despite a poetic supplication in 1628/9 that prompted him to raise Jonson's pension to £100, he seems to have forgotten to pay it most of the time. Luckily, Jonson had also won City of London approval and had been awarded the post of City Chronologer at £33 a year. That income was supplemented by William Cavendish's interest in Jonson, who wrote the memorial for his father Sir Charles Cavendish's monument in 1617; in 1619 or 1620, he also created *The Cavendish Christening Entertainment* either for William's son or for his cousin the Duke of Devonshire's son born the same year. Later, Jonson wrote the royal entertainments for Charles at Welbeck and Bolsover, as well as epigrams on William's talents as horseman and architect.

Some of Jonson's significant early patrons were female. Most of his poetry about women praises intelligence and strength. Of Margaret Ratcliffe, he wrote, 'Rare as wonder was her wit, / And like Nectar ever flowing' (*Epigrams* 40, ll. 9–10), and Lucy Countess of Bedford, he admired for having 'a learnèd and a manly soul' (*Epigrams* 76, l. 13). His admiration for the women of the Sidney circle is clear not only in poetry written for them but also in the personal friendship they extended, in part related to their own writing. Lady Mary Wroth's sonnet sequence, *Pamphilia to Amphilanthus,* written and revised between 1612 and 1621, owes a debt to Jonson's reading and praise of her work, especially in *The Underwood* 28, in which he claims – in sonnet form, a form he otherwise never used – that her work made him 'A better lover, and much better poet' (l. 4). He regarded Wroth as beyond praise, 'Nature's index' (*Epigrams* 105, l. 19), proficient in the arts and sciences, and thus capable of fully appreciating the intellectual satire of *The Alchemist,* dedicated to her in the year following his dedication of *Catiline* to her cousin William Herbert. Elizabeth Countess of Rutland, 'nothing inferior to her father, Sir P. Sidney, in poesy' (*Informations* 12, ll. 159–60), he considered a superior female tribute to a poet whom no mere man could succeed. Admittedly, his verses to patronesses had to express admiration, but his praises might have stopped at physical beauty, wifely chastity or charity, as they did when he wrote epitaphs for women he did not know. The women of the Sidney circle, however, he did know and admire, just as later in his career he came to know and admire women in the Cavendish circle. It is a moot point whether Wroth or the Countess of Rutland was the Charis of Jonson's *A Celebration of Charis in Ten Lyric Pieces,* but, as I have argued elsewhere, one lyric in that poetic sequence appears also as a song in *The Devil is an Ass,* a play in which the predicament of the wife Frances Fitzdottrel suggests that Mary Wroth was a key shadowy original of that character.[5]

Jonson's presentation copy of *Cynthia's Revels* to Lucy Countess of Bedford, the Queen's closest lady-in-waiting, may have paved the way for his masque-writing career. Jonson was not reluctant to take a stand with daring female wit, perhaps most clearly declared in the 1608 publication of *The Queenes Masques,* or *Two Royall Masques. The One of Blacknesse, the Other of Beautie. Personated by the Most Magnificent of Queenes, ANNE Queene of Great Britaine, & C., with Her Honorable Ladyes, 1605 and 1608 at Whitehalll.* Jonson states in his preface that he wants to give full credit to the Queen for having the concepts and the 'will' to perform them and also to demonstrate both his 'duty ... to that majesty who gave them their authority, and grace ... [and] to redeem them as well from ignorance as envy, two common evils, the one of censure, the other of oblivion' (*The Masque of Blackness,* ll. 8–12).[6] In other words, Jonson wanted to respond publicly to those critics at court who disapproved of the masques as indecorous or grotesque and wanted the embarrassment of at least the first masque forgotten. The Queen's object in presenting herself and her ladies in blackface as African princesses, Jonson declares, was 'her Highness' pleasure ... to glorify the court' by celebrating the kingdom's power to absorb the mysterious, foreign, and feminine other into a loyal and well-integrated national self. Both masques may be understood as Queen Anna's statement about her own power as a foreign-born authority whose court had significant artistic and political influence conjoining James's. Similarly, with *The Masque of Queens,* performed in 1609 by Anna and her ladies, showing her elegant court as virtuous queens of history subduing and controlling vice, represented as witches: Jonson inscribed the presentation copy 'To her sacred Majesty', in whose name he created 'this invention' and 'hath since been careful to give it life, and authority'; he credited her with the idea of the anti-masque as a 'foil' to the masque proper.[7] The published text he dedicated to Prince Henry, who requested the annotations in order to appreciate fully the masque's intention of honouring his mother and the royal court with its 'beauties, and strengths'.[8] So Jonson seizes the moment to represent himself as an advocate for, or interpreter of, assertive, active and powerful women.

By 1618, Lady Mary Wroth was out of favour at court, although the Herberts continued in successful careers, and Jonson's Cavendish patrons were also on the rise. Anne Barton and, later, David Riggs agree that Lovel in *The New Inn* is based on William Cavendish, made Earl of Newcastle in 1628 after his successful term as Lord Lieutenant of Nottinghamshire;[9] the Act 4 oration on valour in fencing seems to refer to Cavendish's expertise as a swordsman, but the same talent was even more famously true of

Cavendish's father. William's mother, Lady Katherine Ogle Cavendish, had designed her husband's burial monument, with the 'Sad and Weeping Remembrance of his Sorrowful Lady Katherine', at Bolsover with her sons in 1617, and continued to be a strong influence on Cavendish family interests, including patronage, although she moved from Welbeck up to her Bothal estate in Northumbria. In 1625, Jonson wrote an epitaph for her sister, Jane Ogle Talbot, Countess of Shrewsbury, and in 1629 wrote one for Katherine Ogle herself, describing her as a 'magnetic' force – the first figurative use of that word – who reinvigorated the family's fortunes by acquiring, in her own right, the title of Baroness Ogle, a barony left in abeyance since her father's death in 1597 for lack of a male heir ('Epitaph, l. 19). When she died, William became Baron of Ogle, a title he transmitted to his own son. The acquisition of this title is significant in that the Ogle barony, unlike some Tudor and Stuart titles, was ancient, a true confirmation of 'blue blood' and gentlemanly status. It is Katherine, Lady Ogle who provides the character of the magnetic Lady Loadstone in Jonson's *The Magnetic Lady*, and her sons whose accomplishments reflect Cavendish family skills in the characters of Compass and Ironside. Compass, the 'scholar mathematic' from Oxford, combines the diplomatic, philosophical and scientific skills of the Cavendish brothers, William and Charles, whose circle of friends and correspondents included Oughtred, Hobbes, Descartes and Fermat.

The poetic exchanges with the Cavendishes did not end with *The Magnetic Lady;* William Cavendish admired the play so much that he wrote an imitation of it in his own play, *The Variety*, drawing on support from other Jonson plays to fill out his own script: the jeerers in *The Staple of News*, and the Manly/Wittipol ideal of a good man from *The Devil is an Ass*, as Anne Barton has already suggested. William's other works – *The Humourous Lovers* and *The Triumphant Widow; or, The Medley of Humours* – suggest his adherence to Jonsonian humours comedy. Jonson's *A Tale of a Tub*, a rural comedy, and *The Sad Shepherd*, set in Sherwood Forest near Welbeck, compliment the Cavendish family interest in country life. William's daughters, Lady Jane Cavendish and Lady Elizabeth Cavendish Brackley, also wrote in the pastoral mode in their plays, *A Pastorall* and *The Concealed Fancies*, as well as in verse.[10] Their style, unlike their father's, was not so much an imitation of Jonson as it was a compliment influenced by the respect given to the poet patronized by their father; in the Cavendish family, cultural and intellectual pursuits, self-expression through poetry and drama, witty considerations of performance as well as scripting, all had favour within the family milieu. And they experienced Jonson's theatrical spectacles at first hand in their own homes with the masques for Charles during two of his royal progresses: *The King's Entertainment at Welbeck* in 1633, and *Love's Welcome at Bolsover* in 1634. The income for Jonson was vital, since his masque-making had been out of favour at court since 1631, and he had also lost his post as City Chronologer through ill-health, in addition to having difficulty collecting his royal pension from Charles. From a patronage point of view, William Cavendish outdid himself in hiring Jonson to write these pieces which did indeed please the King, and spending for both masques combined the huge sum of £15,000.[11]

Unfortunately, the exchange of mutuality between Jonson and Cavendish, his last and perhaps best patron, did not echo the same exchange value between Cavendish and Charles, who did not give Cavendish the political job he was angling for, despite the large outlay of cash to promote Cavendish interests and to demonstrate his loyalty to the Stuart monarchy. But the ideal relation between the patron and the patronized, as Jonson implicitly argued throughout his career, cannot flourish in a money market that in itself pledges no allegiance to reciprocal service bound by intellectual or artistic ties. *Every Man Out of His Humour*'s Grex made just such a point in 1599, as did the later *Bartholomew Fair*'s attempt to draw up a contract between the audience and the playwright. Poor reception of gifts, like the Intermean ladies' behaviour in *The Staple of News,* and Damplay's rejection of twists of plot in *The Magnetic Lady,* are simply a by-product of the patronage system gone awry, a system in which honour, obligation and reward no longer figure in the larger and crasser scheme of things.

NOTES

1. Deborah C. Payne, 'Patronage and the Dramatic Marketplace under Charles I and II', *The Yearbook of English Studies,* 21: *Politics, Patronage and Literature in England, 1558–1658,* special volume (1991): 137–52. Several chapters in this volume pertain to Jonson's career.
2. David Riggs, *Ben Jonson: A Life* (Cambridge, Mass.: Harvard University Press, 1989), p. 11.
3. Arthur F. Marotti, 'Patronage, Poetry, and Print', *The Yearbook of English Studies,* 21, *Politics, Patronage and Literature in England, 1558–1658,* special volume, edited by Andrew Gurr and Phillipa Hardman (1991): 1–26. See also Kathleen E. McLuskie, 'The Poets' Royal Exchange: Patronage and Commerce in Early Modern Drama', *The Yearbook of English Studies,* 21, *Politics, Patronage and Literature in England, 1558–1658,* special volume (1991): 53–62; Martin

Butler, '"We Are One Mans All": Jonson's *The Gipsies Metamorphosed*', *The Yearbook of English Studies*, 21, *Politics, Patronage and Literature in England, 1558–1658*, special volume (1991): 253–73; and M. D. Jardine, 'New Historicism for Old: New Conservatism for Old? The Politics of Patronage in the Renaissance', *The Yearbook of English Studies*, 21, *Politics, Patronage and Literature in England, 1558–1658*, special volume (1991): 286–304.

4. W. David Kay, *Ben Jonson: A Literary Life* (Basingstoke: Macmillan, 1995), p. 114. Chapter 8 is a very useful discussion of 'The Poet and His Patrons' (pp. 114–35).

5. For the full argument, see Helen Ostovich, 'Hell for Lovers: Shades of Adultery in *The Devil is an Ass*', in Julie Sanders with Kate Chedgzoy and Susan Wiseman (eds.), *Refashioning Ben Jonson: Gender, Politics, and the Jonsonian Canon* (New York: St Martin's Press, 1998), pp. 155–82.

6. The edition of *The Masque of Blackness* cited is from Ben Jonson, *The Complete Masques*, edited by Stephen Orgel (New Haven, Conn.: Yale University Press, 1969).

7. The edition of *The Masque of Queens* cited is from Ben Jonson, *The Complete Masques*, edited by Stephen Orgel (New Haven, Conn.: Yale University Press, 1969), p. 12. The spellings in the dedication of the presentation copy have been modernized.

8. The dedication is reprinted in the notes to Orgel's edition; see Jonson, *The Complete Masques*, p. 478.

9. Anne Barton, 'Harking Back to Elizabeth: Ben Jonson and Caroline Nostalgia', *English Literary History*, 48 (1981): 706; pp. 707–9 discusses other Cavendish influences; see also Riggs, *Ben Jonson*, pp. 302 ff.

10. Alexandra G. Bennett, '"Now Let My Language Speake": The Authorship, Rewriting, and Audience(s) of Jane Cavendish and Elizabeth Brackley', *Early Modern Literary Studies*, 11 (2) (2005): 3.1–13, available online at http://purl.oclc.org/emls/11–2/benncav2.htm.

11. Julie Sanders, 'Jonson's Caroline Coteries', in Takashi Kozuka and J. R. Mulryne (eds.), *Shakespeare, Marlowe, Jonson: New Directions in Biography* (Aldershot: Ashgate, 2006), pp. 279–94; p. 285.

Figure 33.1 *Lucy (Percy) Hay, Countess of Carlisle,* by Pierre Lombart, after Sir Anthony Van Dyck. One of the circle of Henrietta Maria in the Caroline period.

CHAPTER 34

Architecture

Mimi Yiu

Despite a famously acrimonious break with Inigo Jones, the pre-eminent architect and scenographer credited with introducing neo-classical style to England, Ben Jonson maintained a constructive dialogue with architecture throughout his career.[1] Forced by financial straits in youth to take up his stepfather's trade as bricklayer, Jonson eventually forged a successful literary career that brought if not wealth at least royal patronage and admiring followers. Such a wilful rise from manual labour to intellectual and social prestige reflects the trajectory of early modern architecture, which sought to surpass physical construction and achieve recognition as a liberal art. To justify its place in humanist philosophy, architecture turned to writing; reviving and refining the claims of Vitruvius's *De architectura,* the only surviving text from antiquity detailing the philosophy and practice of building, early modern Europe nurtured a learned architectural discourse that explored principles of proportion, harmony, decorum and ornamentation. Before the Grand Tour became popular post-Restoration, these treatises offered armchair travellers in England the opportunity to explore Roman ruins while engaging with an emergent discourse of design.

As an indicator of Jonson's interest in this field, his library assembles an unusual number of architecturally significant texts, including John Dee's introduction to Euclid and two personally annotated editions of Vitruvius in Latin.[2] Not surprisingly, then, Jonson spoke the language of architecture, perhaps more fluently than any of his literary contemporaries. In his notebooks, published posthumously as *Discoveries* (1641), Jonson muses on parallels between constructing architecture and plotting poetry, contending that 'what is place in the one, is action in the other'; indeed, Jonson explains that epics are to other poems as palaces are to private residences, since 'The difference is in space' (ll. 1911–12). Elsewhere in *Discoveries,* Jonson breaks down this literary architectonics to the even more foundational level of grammar, crafting a metaphor that seemingly draws on his early experiences with masonry:

The congruent and harmonious fitting of parts in a sentence hath almost the fastening and force of knitting and connection; as in stones well squared, which will rise strong a great way without mortar. (ll. 1400–2)

At every level, then, from syntactical articulation to emplotment to generic considerations of scale, Jonson envisions the process of writing as intimately linked to the process of building, yoking the author's mind to the architect's. Unlike the classical art of memory, which uses imagined palaces as a mnemonic device for oratory, Jonson's architectural tropes look outward to his physical environment, to the changing landscape of early modern England.

Indeed, beyond conceptualizing language as a kind of built space, Jonson speaks directly to architecture. 'Thou art not, Penshurst, built to envious show' (l. 1): so begins his seminal country-house poem, 'To Penshurst'. Like the emergence of landscape paintings as a distinct genre in this period, the rise of country-house poetry foregrounds space itself as a worthy aesthetic subject, bringing into focus not Romantic scenes of pastoral beauty but the choreography of 'humanized nature'.[3] Although 'To Penshurst' immediately scorns any 'envious show', Jonson's eye seeks out the elemental 'better marks, of soil, of air / Of wood, of water' (ll. 7–8) that act as building blocks to another kind of spectacle, a theatrical display in which natural abundance offers itself to a surveyor's gaze. What ought to induce envy, in the ideology of this poetic encomium, is the idyll of a harmonious, labour-free world where 'fat, agèd carps ... run into thy net' (l. 33) and walls are 'reared with no man's ruin, no man's groan' (l. 44). Disdaining the distant pleasures of an elevated, enclosed lantern 'whereof tales are told' (l. 4), the rhapsodic poet wanders through orchards and fields to recount the earthy delights of a 'blushing apricot, and woolly peach' (l. 43), a seasonal cornucopia that feasts his eyes before overflowing indoors onto the table of his hosts, the Robert Sidney family. In promoting a reciprocal gift economy that binds nature and nurturer, tenant and landlord, patron and poet, 'To Penshurst' tries to dissolve domestic boundaries to form a common hall of hospitality, downplaying architectural artifice to promote an ageless ecological system.

Indeed, at both the beginning and end of his poem, Jonson negates Penshurst's architecture by emphasizing what it is not: 'a row / Of polished pillars, or a roof of gold', surfaces 'Of touch or marble' (ll. 2–3). Thus effacing Penshurst's architecture at the poem's threshold of visibility, Jonson forces us to penetrate a figurative façade to access the estate's organic concordance, to discover a circulatory system of natural and social plenitude anchored by a lord who truly 'dwells' (l. 102). Despite reducing superficially grand houses to a mere envelope in the poetic structure,

Jonson nevertheless draws attention to an important development in early modern architecture: the adoption of a highly fenestrated, outward-looking façade. In contrast to the fortified walls of a more insecure medieval era, the Renaissance façade presents an aestheticized mask designed to please the eye, establishing a public identity while fostering an increasing sense of privacy. In a post-Reformation building boom where wealthy courtiers and merchants competed for status, the English countryside witnessed a rise of 'prodigy houses' that strove to outdo one another in their extravagant exteriors; often, these palatial houses were intended not as primary residences but as staging grounds to entertain Queen Elizabeth and her retinue during their regular progresses through the countryside. Pitting these novelties of conspicuous and politicized consumption against the humility of Penshurst's 'ancient pile' (l. 5), Jonson's poem laments how such architectural prodigies transform dwellings into monstrous spectacles, defying nature to become men's ruin and groan.

As these cosmetically enhanced buildings assume gendered overtones, 'To Penshurst' emerges as a kind of perversely non-Petrarchan love poem, an ode to masculine utility rather than feminine beauty. In comparison, we might examine the opening of Sonnet IX from Philip Sidney's *Astrophil and Stella,* a sonnet sequence penned by the brother of Penshurst's owner:

> Queen Virtue's court, which some call Stella's face,
> Prepar'd by Nature's choicest furniture,
> Hath his front built of alabaster pure;
> Gold is the covering of that stately place.[4]

Constructing an architectural conceit that extends throughout the poem, Sidney praises his beloved in terms that evoke grandiose prodigy houses, outfitting Stella's face with cheeks like marble porches and eyes like prospect windows that not only look 'o'er the world', but are made of touch 'that without touch doth touch'.[5] By superimposing an architectural onto a facial 'front', Sidney clads a queen's masculine court ('his') with feminine ornament, this 'stately place' troubling gender boundaries in a manner reminiscent of Elizabeth's physical and political bodies.[6] In contrast, a native masculinity often permeates Jonson's sensibility, as epitomised by Epigram 78's portrait of Sir Kenelm Digby:

> In him all virtue is beheld in state,
> And he is built like some imperial room
> For that to dwell in, and be still at home,
> His breast is a brave palace, a broad street,
> Where all heroic ample thoughts do meet.
>
> (*The Underwood* 78, ll. 6–10)

The virtue 'beheld' in Digby's heroic front, unlike Stella's, manifests itself in amplitude and public orientation rather than a fine aesthetics, a 'brave Palace' whose magnificence lies in its stately *gravitas* rather than garish bravery. Such a masculine philosophy of architecture echoes that of Inigo Jones, who opined in his notebooks that 'every wyse man carrieth a graviti in Publicke Places... so in architecture, ye outward ornaments oft [ought] to be sollid, proporsionable according to the rulles, masculine and unaffected'.[7]

Although 'Penshurst' decries self-important houses 'whereof tales are told', Jonson intimately intertwines theatre and architecture in his numerous masque collaborations with Jones. Heeding Vitruvius's decree that *scaenographia* belongs in an architect's repertoire, Jones designed stage locales as varied as the House of Fame (*Masque of Queens*, 1609), Oberon's palace (*Oberon the Fairy Prince*, 1611), a Roman atrium (*Albion's Triumph*, 1632), even his own banqueting hall (*Time Vindicated*, 1623). Spectacles first and foremost, these masques featured elaborate sets where boards painted in single-point perspective create a sense of three-dimensional space. Framed by a proscenium arch, a façade for façades that Jones introduced from Continental sources, these masque sets crucially develop a consciousness of architecture as theatrical tableaux. Since masques typically offer idealized representations of their courtly viewers, Jones's scenography advertises to potential patrons in the audience that he can house their fantasy selves on the English landscape, that he can build a scaffold for their social and architectural aspirations.

Jonson seems amenable to promoting this architectural ideology that takes Jones's Palladian style as its apotheosis. In *Prince Henry's Barriers* (1610), Jonson eulogizes the fallen House of Chivalry, which represents Britain's Arthurian past, by rendering its architecture the emblem of truth and knowledge:

> More truth of architecture there was blazed,
> Than lived in all the ignorant Goths have razed.
>
> (ll. 54–5)

Just as Prince Henry, the masque's hero, will soon essay forth to win honour and glory in jousting ('barriers'), the flowering of a golden Stuart age hinges on restoring a lost 'truth' realized only through Jones's architecture on stage and off. To fulfil this dream of blazing truth in architecture, of inscribing harmonious social spaces upon the nation, Jones was appointed Surveyor to Prince Henry later that same year. Had the noble-minded heir to the throne not suffered an untimely death in 1612, Henry's patronage might have allowed an erstwhile scenographer to transcend the 'barriers' of theatre by attempting to fashion a New Troy in Albion.

Jones overcame this temporary setback to become Surveyor to both James I and Charles I, his purview at the King's Works embracing the construction of spectacular architecture for both the masque stage and the national stage. Likewise reaching beyond the proscenium arch, Jonson created several site-specific, occasional entertainments that exploited the possibilities of three-dimensional architecture as a platform for theatre. Having contributed text to James's triumphal entry into London in 1604, a magnificent procession through seven custom-built arches with allegorical tableaux enacted en route, Jonson accepted a commission from Robert Cecil, Lord Salisbury, to collaborate with Jones on an entertainment inaugurating the New Exchange, a grand shopping complex being hurried to completion in 1609. Located within the royal precinct of Westminster, the New Exchange marked out 'another kingdom' ruled not by the divine figure of a sovereign but by the impersonal principles of a market economy.[8] In stark contrast to Penshurst's home-grown, pastoral pleasures, the New Exchange dedicated itself to the pursuit of luxury consumerism in an age of global trade; not only did merchants hawk an array of exotic, fetishized wares in rows of shops but the building also provided a gallery where Londoners could parade in all their purchased finery.

Several years earlier, Jones had produced a dramatic but rejected design for the New Exchange, proposing an Italianate façade with elaborate scrolls and towers that, according to the architectural historian John Summerson, 'might do well enough in a scene for a masque but are unrealizable in building terms'.[9] Jones's return to the site as scenographer thus underscores how architecture repeats itself with a difference: the first time as visionary, the second time as theatre. Indeed, Jonson's *Entertainment* exploits the New Exchange's spatial dynamics by structuring its narrative upon a tour led by the Key Keeper, who guides James's party through the building to a specially mocked-up shop where a banner proclaims: 'All other places give for money, here all is given for love.'[10] Despite this facetious gesture towards an economy of love, Cecil's project cannily deploys an architectural semiotics for mercenary motives, pasting a classically inspired façade with niches and statues onto a jumbled half-timbered backside more familiar to a Tudor sensibility. This veneer of stylistic sophistication evidently generated much public bewilderment during its construction, since the Key Keeper's speech pointedly decries rumours that the building exists merely to furnish 'a fair front, built only to grace the street and for no use'.[11] By defining the New Exchange's use value through a physical and rhetorical exploration of its spaces, Jonson's *Entertainment* not only allows a foreign-

Figure 34.1 View out from the Little Castle, Bolsover, Derbyshire.

based economics and architecture to signify locally but also mobilizes a performative act of inscription whereby James's every footstep demarcates and legitimizes an alternative kingdom of capitalism.

Such an embodied, unifying experience of architecture takes another turn in *Love's Welcome at Bolsover* (1634), an entertainment for William Cavendish, Earl of Newcastle, on the occasion of Charles I's visit to Bolsover Castle. If the New Exchange tries to turn a financial venture into a stage for loving, paternalistic exchange, then Bolsover Castle turns an aristocratic country home into a theatre for escapist pleasure, promoting a love that Jonson calls 'a lifting of the sense' (l. 1).[12] As a mock-medieval castle in miniature, Bolsover strongly resembles a masque set with its crenellated parapets and towers, and its allegorically painted walls throughout the interior (see Figures 34.1 and 34.2). Indeed, since the devising of *Love's Welcome* overlaps with the period of Bolsover's construction, Timothy Raylor speculates that 'Jonson's masque may have influenced the scheme of the castle': tellingly, we cannot determine whether architecture imitates theatre, or vice versa.[13] *Love's Welcome* certainly makes full use of its setting as guests enjoy a series of banquets, songs and dances while progressing through house and grounds. Jonson carefully matches each segment

Figure 34.2 Painted panels in the Little Castle, Bolsover, Derbyshire.

Figure 34.3 Panel in the Pillar Chamber in the Little Castle, Bolsover, Derbyshire.

to the allegorical theme of each site; for example, the opening banquet of the senses likely took place in the Pillar Chamber, where lunettes depicted each of the five senses (see Figure 34.3).[14] Within this consonance of performance and space, however, a jarring note sounds when Jonson introduces the overweening 'Coronel Vitruvius', an obvious Jones caricature who herds his hapless workmen into dance formations, exhorting them to 'work upon that ground' as time is beaten on an anvil (l. 48). Tellingly exiled to the garden, 'Iniquo Vitruvius' and his 'mathematical boys' (l. 57) execute a travesty of architectural design in this anti-masque-like dance of the mechanicals;[15] yet by translating spatial harmony into music and spatial figures into movement, Jonson unwittingly underscores the essentially performative nature of architecture.

Evidently, Jonson and Jones had fallen out by the time of *Love's Welcome*, having dissolved their partnership some time in the early 1630s. Although their final masque collaboration, *Chloridia* (1631), ranked Architecture alongside Poesy as fame-worthy endeavours, Jonson soon churned out scathing poems denouncing Jones's ambitions. 'An Expostulation with Inigo Jones' mocks 'an asinigo' (l. 20) who not only 'mistook names out of Vitruvius' (l. 8) but also prized 'spectacles of state' (l. 42) over textual sense.[16] In the poem's castigation of a simple-minded artificer, 'smiling at his feat / Of lantern-lerry' (ll. 71–2), we might hear Jonson attacking both the ingenious lighting effects that Jones devised for masques as well as the architectural lanterns and glassy lantern-houses once contrasted with Penshurst.[17] These twinned theatrical and architectural critiques culminate in Jonson's last play, *A Tale of a Tub*, as the joiner In-and-In Medlay transforms an old tub into both a parodic edifice and a lantern projecting a shadow play ('motion'). A self-designated *'Architectonicus professor'* and masque-maker (4 Scene Interloping, 10) Medlay apparently replaces a character named Vitruvius Hoop that the Revels Office censored for offending Jones;[18] as these hybrid names suggest, Jonson takes umbrage at how Jones adulterates a Vitruvian aesthetic with his mechanical and materialistic 'shop-philosophy' ('An Expostulation with Inigo Jones', l. 74). That is, in projecting these negative shadow puppets of Jones, Jonson always measures his foe against an ideal architect who builds palaces, forums, or 'some Colossus to bestride the seas' ('To Iniquo Marquis Would-Be', ll. 9–13), a pure Vitruvian who exists only in the mind's eye, or on paper. While Jonson may indeed believe that 'architecture is safer inside poetry than outside it', as Gail Kern Paster argues, his corpus perpetually lives on the edge between textual and spatial construction, insistently dwelling *on* and *in* architecture.[19]

NOTES

1. The classic account of this quarrel is D. J. Gordon's 'Poet and Architect: The Intellectual Setting of the Quarrel between Ben Jonson and Inigo Jones', *Journal of the Warburg and Courtauld Institutes*, 12 (1949): 152–78.
2. A. W. Johnson, *Ben Jonson: Poetry and Architecture* (Oxford: Clarendon, 1994), pp. 9–10.
3. G. R. Hibbard, 'The Country House Poem of the Seventeenth Century', *Journal of the Warburg and Courtauld Institutes*, 19 (1956): 159–74; p. 165. Don Wayne provides a superb analysis of how the poem deconstructs the boundary between cultured Nature and natural Culture; see Chapter 3 of *Penshurst: The Semiotics of Place and the Poetics of History* (Madison, Wisc.: University of Wisconsin Press, 1984), pp. 45–80. Simon Schama discusses the etymology and rise of landscapes in *Landscape and Memory* (New York: Knopf, 1995), p. 10 and *passim*.
4. Sir Philip Sidney, *The Major Works* (Oxford: Oxford University Press, 2002), no. 156, ll. 1–4.
5. Sidney, no. 156, ll. 10 and 12.
6. Although 'his' could be construed as a neutral pronoun in earlier usage, Sidney's diction in this context seems to be deliberately gendered.
7. Inigo Jones, 'Roman Sketchbook', Chatsworth House Collection, entry dated 20 January 1614. Author's own transcription, but see also John Peacock, *The Stage Designs of Inigo Jones: The European Context* (Cambridge: Cambridge University Press, 1995), p. 232. A full transcription and fascimile of Jones's notebook has recently been published by Edward Chaney in *Inigo Jones's 'Roman Sketchbook'*, 2 vols. (London: Roxburghe Club, 2006).
8. James Knowles, 'Jonson's *Entertainment at Britain's Burse*', in Martin Butler (ed.), *Re-Presenting Ben Jonson: Text, History, Performance* (New York: St Martin's Press, 1999), p. 132. Knowles discovered an incomplete copy of this hitherto-lost entertainment (also known as *The Key Keeper*) in 1997; all citations come from his annotated edition of this text (spellings modernized).
9. John Summerson, *Inigo Jones* (Harmondsworth: Penguin, 1966), pp. 26–7.
10. According to a Venetian ambassador's report of the event; see the Calendar of State Papers, Venetian, vol. XI, No. 497.
11. Knowles, 'Jonson's Entertainment', p. 133 (spellings modernized).
12. The edition of *Love's Welcome at Bolsover* cited throughout is that which appears in David Lindley (ed.), *Court Masques* (Oxford: Oxford University Press, 1995).
13. Timothy Raylor, '"Pleasure Reconciled to Virtue": William Cavendish, Ben Jonson, and the Decorative Scheme of Bolsover Castle', *Renaissance Quarterly*, 52 (1999): 402–39; p. 415.
14. Raylor, 'Pleasure Reconciled to Virtue', p. 416. For a counter-argument, see Cedric Brown, 'Courtesies of Place and Arts of Diplomacy in Ben Jonson's Last Two Entertainments for Royalty', *The Seventeenth Century*, 9 (1994): 159–60.

15. Only the manuscript version of *Love's Welcome* specifies that the King and Queen 'retir'd into a Garden' (Harley MS 4955); see C. H. Herford and Percy and Evelyn Simpson (eds.), *Ben Jonson,* 11 vols. (Oxford: Oxford University Press, 1925–52), vol. x, p. 806.
16. In 'An Expostulation with Inigo Jones', Jonson seems to indicate some malfunction when this part was performed (ll. 35–9).
17. We might also recall Lantern Leatherhead from *Bartholomew Fair,* who runs a puppet-show. John Selden calls Leatherhead 'Inigo Lanthorne'; see *Table-talk* (London: E. Smith, 1689), p. 52.
18. Since no version of Vitruvius Hoop remains in print, we cannot determine the exact relation of Hoop to Medlay.
19. Gail Kern Paster, 'Ben Jonson and the Uses of Architecture', *Renaissance Quarterly,* 27 (1974): 306–20; p. 320.

CHAPTER 35

Food

Robert Appelbaum

Ben Jonson was a big man in an age when obesity was a rare accomplishment. Access to food and drink was limited, and the day-to-day demands of living – moving about and keeping warm – burned off a good many calories. Moreover, all the guidebooks to good health and civilized behaviour, going back to Hippocrates and the famous Graeco-Roman physician Galen, emphasized moderation. One of Jonson's most illustrious acquaintances, Sir Francis Bacon, came up with a new-fangled biological theory that made strict moderation in the diet necessary for keeping the 'vital spirits' of a person's intelligence aflame.[1] Another illustrious contemporary, the poet George Herbert, prepared the first English translation of Luigi Cornaro's *A Treatise of Temperance and Sobriety*, which recommended a regime of radically reduced food consumption as a key to a long and happy life.[2] There were variations, but there was no dissent from the basic principle, promoted equally by doctors and philosophers, by ministers and mothers: to live well one should eat and drink with moderation. So Ben Jonson's obesity required a good deal of stubborn effort. Even after a long and arduous walk from London to Scotland in 1618–19, Jonson managed to retain his enormous bulk, apparently; Jonson himself referring at the time to his 'mountain belly', which got in the way of his wooing of women ('My Picture Left in Scotland', *The Underwood* 9, l. 17).

About Jonson's actual tastes in food and drink, however, we have little information. We only know that, in his prime, he ate and drank a lot of it. If he dined in those years like most of his prosperous contemporaries – the food of the poor offered a very different set of options – his diet involved a lot of white or almost white bread and a lot of meat, washed down with ale or wine. Fruits and vegetables were becoming more prominent in the English diet in Jonson's lifetime, especially items such as artichokes and leaf vegetables (served raw or cooked in salads with oil and vinegar), but meat and bread took pride of place at any prosperous individual's table, the meat served in whole joints, or baked in pie crusts or seethed in stews with various seasonings and garnishes, and served alongside a variety of spicy and aromatic sauces and condiments such as mustard. Sometimes fricassees or other 'made dishes' were prepared in a skillet. The meat itself was most commonly mutton or beef but could also be pork or veal or (more rarely) venison, or it could be taken from any of a number of game birds, domestic fowl, especially chicken, or (again more rarely) rabbit. Eggs too played a large part in the diet, as did butter and cheese and pulses and nuts and a variety of sweets made from sugar or honey and fruit (plums, apricots, apples), themselves often washed down with strong sweetened wine. Many of the staples of the modern European diet were missing – tea, coffee, chocolate, tomatoes, common beans and, for the most part, potatoes. And the kind of ready availability of a variety of foodstuffs that modern Europe takes for granted was missing. Seasonal variation was the rule of thumb – preserved pork and root vegetables in the winter, fresh beef and strawberries in the summer – and so were daily and yearly fluctuations in the weather and the market. Jonson lived through years of dearth in the 1590s and years of plenty in most of the early 1600s. And one thing more: in this pre-modern world two to three days of the week, as well as the six weeks of Lent, the English were required by law to abstain from meat and to eat fish instead: fresh fish for the rich, in great variety from carp and trout to sturgeon and lamprey, and mainly salt-fish (usually herring or cod) for everyone else.

So we know what Jonson's choices in food probably were, and we know that his diet was rhythmically organized. We also know that he was an avid eater and drinker, even in defiance of the science of the day. He may have been aware of the fact that a good deal of expansion in the variety of foods available was underway and almost certainly he was aware of new trends in cookery. Gardeners were cultivating more and more varieties of edible plants. Foreign dishes were becoming more sought after. Especially popular was the *olla podrida,* a stew from Spain, made in England from as many as a half dozen different meats. And more and more people were concerned to eat *à la mode,* in imitation of the French. French-trained cooks had been sought after for decades, and at least one food writer of the time boasted that his *New Booke of Cookerie* would 'set forth the newest and most commendable fashion for dressing or sousing either flesh, fish, or fowl', along with 'all sorts of jellies and other made dishes, some recipes following the principles of the most exquisite London cookery', and all of it 'set forth according to the now new English and French fashion'.[3] It is likely that Jonson was familiar with the latest trends for he had travelled himself to France; he was well known as a frequenter of taverns in fashionable London (which served food as well as drink); he was an enthusiastic attender of social dinners among players and poets; and he frequently dined as a guest of the rich and powerful.

Jonson was aware, too, of the ambitions (or pretensions) of prominent cooks. Cooks had their own guild in London. They could hire out their services for specially catered events, or work in cook shops and taverns or bourgeois households. Best of all would be the position of 'master cook' of an aristocratic family, a position of power and prestige since it meant overseeing an operation responsible for the daily feeding and entertaining of hundreds. The head chef played an important role in the family's presentation of itself to the world. Entertainments great and small were about distributing bounty and healthfulness, but they were also about culture and hegemony and deference and the illusions of power. And so we have in Jonson not only the most famous poem of the Renaissance about household feasting, 'To Penshurst', but the Master-Cook of the masque *Neptune's Triumph* (1624) who reappears as a fleshed-out character, Lick-finger, speaking some of the same lines, in *The Staple of News* (1626).

The Cook in *Neptune's Triumph* lets us know what he thinks of himself and his labours:

> A master-cook! why he is the man of men
> For a professor! He designs, he draws,
> He paints, he carves, he builds, he fortifies,
> Makes citadels of curious fowl and fish;
> Some he dry-ditches, some moats round with broths,
> Mounts marrowbones, cuts fifty-angled custards,
> Rears bulwark pies, and for his outer works,
> He raises ramparts of immortal crust,
> He teacheth all the tactics at one dinner,
> What ranks, what files to put his dishes in:
> The whole art of military! Then he knows
> The influence of the stars upon his meats,
> And all their seasons, tempers, qualities,
> And so, to fit his relishes and sauces!
> He'as nature in a pot!
>
> (ll. 61–75)[4]

The cook compares himself to other professionals such as artists, architects, military engineers and physicians, not to mention poets, like the one to whom he is speaking. The point is that he knows not only how to make food taste good but also how to make of it an impressive social experience, and that he does so not only out of experience but also out of art and science. The master-cook knows how to orchestrate a feast, and he can do so because he knows both how to do it and why, even to the point of using astrology, agronomy and chemistry to understand the 'seasons, tempers, qualities, and so' of his ingredients.

Behind what the cook is saying there lies the actual practices of culinary festivity in Jonson's lifetime. What he names in his account – fowl and fish, some roasted ('dry-ditched'), some seethed and served with their broth, along with marrowbones and custards and pies – were part of the usual Jacobean feast. What he does with the things he names – serves them in a certain order, presents them in decorative displays, arranges the whole of a table in complex array, and garnishes everything with appropriate relishes and sauces – were part of the feast as well. And so we can see that when Jonson writes about food and food practices, he does so in the context of a specific framework of culinary experience. Jonson was enthusiastic about food; he was knowledgeable about food; and he was a keen observer of the food manners and matters of his time, all the way to appreciating the relationship between food and power.

But still, we don't know much directly about Jonson's personal tastes and habits. And when we look at what Jonson wrote about food, we find that Jonson was mainly interested in food as a *literary* subject. That meant that he was mainly interested, too, in the *social meanings* of food. Being the kind of artist he was, Jonson was interested in playing with literariness and asserting scholarly authority while scrutinizing and critiquing the social life of his contemporaries – not only having fun with things such as food and food practices but also putting them into a literary, moral, political and scientific perspective.

Take the case of one his comic catalogues of foodstuffs, in the speech by Sir Epicure Mammon in *The Alchemist*. This is what Mammon says, as he anticipates the wealth he is going to amass in his partnership with Face and Subtle:

> My meat shall all come in in Indian shells,
> Dishes of agate, set in gold, and studded
> With emeralds, sapphires, hyacinths, and rubies.
> The tongues of carps, dormice, and camels' heels,
> Boiled i'The spirit of Sol [gold] and dissolved pearl
> (Apicius's diet 'gainst the epilepsy),
> And I will eat these broths with spoons of amber,
> Headed with diamond and carbuncle.
> My foot-boy shall eat pheasants, calvered [sliced] salmons,
> Knots [a game bird], godwits [another game bird], lampreys.
> I myself will have
> The beards of barbels served instead of salads,
> Oiled mushrooms, and the swelling unctuous paps

> Of a fat pregnant sow, newly cut off,
> Dressed with an exquisite and poignant sauce[.]
>
> (2.2.72–85)

Obviously, Mammon's desire has much less to do with the taste and enjoyment of food than with price and rarity and conspicuous consumption. Some of the items – pheasants, salmon, 'poignant sauce' – were a regular part of the English diet of the seventeenth century, at least among the wealthy, but most were not, and would have sounded strangely taboo: dormice, camels heels, sow's paps. What Jonson has managed to produce here is a funny, enticing and disturbing juxtaposition. Mammon is a caricature of the greedy, materialistic English gentleman, pretending to be forward-looking. What Mammon desires, however, is transgressive and impossible, in food as in everything else. Mammon openly refers to Apicius, a legendary Roman gourmet whose name was attached to the only surviving cookbook of antiquity, the fourth-century *De re coquinaria*, where items such as dormice are delicacies. Most of the details, however, are adopted from *The Life of Heliogabalus*, by Lampridius, the Emperor Heliogabalus being very much a man who liked to feast on delicacies like fish tongues and make a show of his wealth and power with elaborate feasts. But Heliogabalus, for Lampridius, is the model of the Roman tyrant. Lampridius accuses him of just about every crime one could accuse a tyrant of, from sexual perversity, incest and murder to theft, graft and sacrilege. Lampridius itemizes the Emperor's sumptuary habits as a testament to his degeneracy. So where does that leave Sir Epicure Mammon?

An apparently more down-to-earth example comes in Jonson's Epigram 101, 'Inviting a Friend to Supper'. 'To rectify your palate', Jonson says to his invitee, you shall have:

> An olive, capers, or some better salad
> Ush'ring the mutton; with a short-legged hen,
> If we can get her, full of eggs, and then
> Lemons and wine for sauce: to these a cony
> Is not to be despaired of, for our money;
> And, though fowl now be scarce, yet there are clerks,
> The sky not falling, think we may have larks.
>
> (ll. 9–16)

This food is not unlike what a middling sort of host, like Ben Jonson at home or at one of his taverns, would order for dinner. And it betrays some of the characteristics of food before the modern era mentioned above. The host is uncertain what exactly he will be able to acquire: fowls are 'scarce', a short-legged hen may or may not be available. (The 'short-legged hen' refers to a breed of chicken whose better specimens would have lots of leg meat; the eggs would be hard-boiled and stuffed inside the bird's cavity.) Again, this is a meat-centred diet, where vegetables are 'ushers' and fruits (the lemon) are a garnish. We have a dinner that is unlavish and uncertain, but one that is nevertheless substantial, varied, aesthetically balanced (with palates properly 'rectified') and not unpricey. Cheese and more fruit, the poem continues, will follow, along with a lot more wine – the prestigious drink of the day.

But the whole of the poem is paraphrased from the epigrams of one of Jonson's favourite Latin poets, Martial. Jonson has anglicized the dinner. The rarities he jokes about, wishing he could offer them – partridge, pheasant, woodcock, godwit, knat or 'knot', rail and ruff – are English game birds; and there is nothing else in the menu that would not be associated with the English table. But the spirit of the dinner is Roman, and the spirit of the invitation is Roman too. As Robert Cummings has put it, 'The food, however Englished it may be, is rendered as something to be remembered from other poems, not something to be eaten.'[5] As for the social relations that the poem prescribes, where a poorer man invites a richer man to dinner, where a spirit of austerity is seamlessly blended into a spirit of extravagance, and where a kind of equality is established among unequals through hospitality and festivity, even as their inequality is also emphasized – those too are to be remembered from other poems rather than to be practised. Even if what Jonson is inviting his friend to is an occasion for indulgent conviviality, readers are assured that a kind of moral order with a classical pedigree will reign, a politically moral order, as well as an aesthetic order ranging from the presentation of the dishes to the entertainment provided. That the invitation is an elegant poem only further frames the dinner morally, politically and aesthetically.

'To Penshurst' also plays this kind of game. The food in 'To Penshurst' is all English and local, and the dining custom of the great house that the poem describes was an old English institution. The picture presented of Jonson himself dining at a good spot in the room, not too far from the hosts and their most honoured guests, and eating as much as he likes, without a household butler trying to spoil his pleasure lest Jonson eat everything up, may speak very much to what it was like to dine as a subordinate on an occasion such as this. But the vision is the poet's projection onto the scene; much of the language even here is adopted from classical sources. The occasion has hence been elevated to something new by reference to something old, and the poet does not want us to forget any of this. Austerity and extravagance, equality and inequality, generosity and hegemony, sensual indulgence and literary delight all come together in an account not so much of what Jonson was actually doing at the great hall of Penshurst as of the ideal of hospitality and social order which he wishes to construct.

The one major work where Jonson seems to give free reign to his own predilection for over-indulgence and the joys that go along with it would appear to be the comedy *Bartholomew Fair*. There the whole action seems to turn on the desire of the main characters to eat their fill of roast pork. But it is obvious that in this case too Jonson is pushing the desire to eat to some sort of moral conclusion. Pork itself is milked, as it were, for as many ethical and behavioural associations as possible, ranging from the Jewish prohibition of pork to the secret cravings of pregnant women and Puritan ministers. Very much a staple of the English diet (though never so plentiful as beef and mutton), and a well-known speciality of Smithfield, where the Fair was held, pork in this play is nevertheless made into a sign of transgressive excess. The pursuit of pork even takes the upstanding young petty bourgeois of the play into the midst of a whorehouse, as the young bride Win goes in search of a place where she can politely urinate.

But not only excess is signalled by this; poetic and scientific control is signalled by it too. Of course, it is not a common thing for a player to try to urinate on stage; doing so is and was quite outrageous. And one critic has pointed out the excessive sexism inherent in the representation, since it makes the woman on stage into a 'leaky vessel'.[6] True it is that a simple meditation on food at a fair causes Jonson to think about the insides and outsides of bodies, and the comical, grotesque nature of people's relation to them; and these things are inevitably gendered and therefore, from our own perspective, biased. But Jonson also knew what physicians since the time of the classical author Galen had been saying. 'Of all foods', Galen wrote, 'pork is the most nutritious.' Among its other favourable qualities was the fact that pork had the life-enhancing ability to 'provoke urine'.[7]

So Jonson was a big man with big appetites who loaded his work with images of food and consumption and excess. And he knew what he was talking about. But a lot of what he was talking about offered something in addition to the plain facts of foodstuffs and their preparation. He was talking about the outrageousness of wisdom.

NOTES

1. Francis Bacon, *History Naturall and Experimentall, of Life and Death; or, Of the Prolongation of Life* (London, 1638).

2. Luigi Cornaro, *A Treatise of Temperance and Sobrietie,* trans. George Herbert, in *Leonardus Lessius, Hygiasticon; or, The Right Course of Preserving Life and Health unto Extream Old Age* (London, 1636).
3. John Murrell, *A New Booke of Cookerie* (London, 1615), title page.
4. The edition of *Neptune's Triumph* cited is from Ben Jonson, *The Complete Masques*, edited by Stephen Orgel (New Haven, Conn.: Yale University Press, 1969).
5. Robert Cummings, 'Liberty and History in Jonson's "Invitation to Supper"', *Studies in English Literature, 1500–1900*, 40 (1) (2000): 103–22; p. 105.
6. Gail Kern Paster, *The Body Embarrassed: Drama and the Disciplines of Shame in Early Modern England* (Ithaca, NY: Cornell University Press, 1993).
7. Galen, *On the Powers of Food*, in Mark Grant (trans.), *Galen on Food and Diet* (London: Routledge, 2000), p. 154.

CHAPTER 36

Alchemy, magic and the sciences

Margaret Healy

> FITZDOTTEREL: Ay, they do now name Bretnor, as before
> They talked of Gresham, and of Doctor Foreman,
> Franklin, and Fiske, and Savory – he was in too –
> But there's not one of these that ever could
> Yet show a man the devil in true sort.
> They have their crystals, I do know, and rings,
> And virgin parchment, and their dead men's skulls,
> Their ravens' wings, their lights, and pentacles,
> With characters; I ha'seen all these. But –
> Would I might see the Devil.
>
> *(The Devil is an Ass,* 1.2.1–10)

In *The Devil is an Ass,* Fitzdotterel's mere 'longing' to see a devil proves more productive than the combined efforts of England's best 'artists' including this interesting roll-call of London's alleged real 'conjurers'. Arriving without cloven feet and occupying the body of a common 'cut-purse' recently hanged, Pug – a lesser devil from Derbyshire – is a disappointment: he fails to live up to Fitzdotterel's fantasies about Beelzebub and his mates, not least because London's vices, even in Satan's estimation, are a fair match for Hell. Time and again, Jonson's city comedies present demonic magic and its close associates alchemy and astrology in this manner as the product of delusions entertained only by madmen and fools motivated by greed, lust and thirst for power. At the mercy of his burlesquing pen, such activities seem impossible to take seriously, and it is easy for modern audiences to assume that Jonson was in the vanguard of a changing culture, increasingly sceptical of 'mumbo-jumbo' superstition while embracing an emerging, objective scientific mentality that would culminate in the 'Enlightenment'. Such an interpretation would, however, be erroneous: there was no simple correlation between a rise of something resembling modern science and the decline of magic in early modern England. On the contrary, it can even be argued that alchemy nurtured the mentality that gave birth to that venerable establishment, the Royal Society for the promotion of science.[1]

Certainly, c. 1600, there was no clear intellectual boundary separating alchemy and magic from 'the sciences'; all were incorporated under the umbrella of natural philosophy, and 'science' was very vaguely defined. John Securis's medical treatise declares, for example, 'science is a habit ... [a] ready, prompt and bent disposition to do any thing confirmed and had by long study, exercise, and use.'[2] It was a mental outlook, to do with knowledge acquisition associated with proof and application, and it was not owned by any specific philosophy of the body or the universe. With the aid of a modern lens it is possible to identify three competing but overlapping cosmologies rubbing shoulders, not without friction, in early modern Europe, and all had ancient origins; these are now associated with distinctive scientific traditions.

The dominant model for understanding the universe at the outset of the Renaissance is frequently termed the 'organic' tradition. It rested upon a triple base of ancient Greek biology, Roman medicine and Roman astronomy. By roughly 1500 the philosophies of Aristotle, Galen and Ptolemy, respectively, had largely been enmeshed with those of Christian doctrine to produce a comforting world picture in which God, man, angels, animals, planets and elements all had their divinely allotted place (known as 'The great chain of being'), with man at the centre of the universe. Of course much literature from the period engages, often playfully, with this poetically rich and evocative earth-centred worldview: John Donne's *The Sun Rising* is a prime example of this. In Aristotelian natural philosophy and Galenic medicine, the world of matter was composed of four elements (earth, air, fire and water) and the human body was imagined as composed of fluid substances called humours (yellow bile, black bile, phlegm and blood), which corresponded to them. Depending on which humour dominated the body, a person might be choleric, melancholic, phlegmatic or sanguine in 'complexion'. The God of this tradition was a providential deity whose designs were revealed in the ordered workings of the universe; this was religious orthodoxy, and its knowledge base was identified with Aristotle and scholasticism. It was taught in all Catholic and most Protestant universities, supported by the power and resources of church and state.[3]

However, in the same period, this model of the universe faced its most serious challenges since classical times; Donne gave moving poetic expression to this in his poem *The First Anniversary,* declaring 'And new Philosophy calls all in doubt'.[4] The 'new Philosophy' was drawn from two rival traditions that operated at the margins, under pressure and sometimes persecution. One alternative cosmology was that of the atomists or mechanists who shared the belief of the ancient Greek philosopher, Democritus, that the universe was composed of tiny particles called atoms and that man was little more than a sophisticated machine (Leonardo de Vinci was in this tradition, also Galileo, Descartes and Hobbes). The other rival tradition, which gained enormous ground in the fifteenth, sixteenth and seventeenth centuries was, by contrast, highly mystical and had its roots deep in the interwoven philosophies of Platonism, Pythagoreanism, Hermeticism and alchemy. Somewhat surprisingly, it was this cosmology that nurtured mathematics and the discoveries of Copernicus, Boyle, Kepler and Newton. Maynard Keynes famously called Newton the last of the magicians – the notebooks of this brilliant mathematician reveal that he was obsessed with alchemy.[5] However, this rising, mystical cosmology simultaneously encouraged ideas compatible with thinking demons, and witchcraft persecutions reached their height in England in the late sixteenth century.[6]

In fact, witches and magicians were a very substantial feature of Ben Jonson's London but all self-respecting conjurors, like the celebrated magus John Dee, were much more intent on summoning angels than devils. In many ways Dee (1527–1608) embodied the eclectic mystical-scientific mentality of the emerging intellectual climate of his age. He was one of the most remarkable polymaths associated with the Elizabethan court: from the 1560s he was England's leading mathematician and experimental scientist and a noted theologian and geographer; but he was also a magician in Shakespeare's Prospero's mould immersed in the most extreme forms of occultism. He had been imprisoned under Mary I for his conjuring activities – she obviously thought him more of a Faustus type – but under Elizabeth I he became court astrologer. In this role, he was asked to select the most propitious day for Elizabeth's coronation, and, when an image of the Queen with a pin stuck in its heart was found in Lincoln's Inn Fields, an anxious Privy Council asked Dee to counteract any harm against her. But the court employed more than his magic: Dee was frequently consulted before voyages of exploration, about affairs of state and on scientific matters. The Queen admired him greatly, and some of the finest intellects in England visited his home in Mortlake, which functioned as an intellectual centre dedicated to mathematical and experimental pursuits, especially alchemy and natural magic. Dee's London circle seems to have included important literary figures including Sidney, Marlowe, Raleigh and Donne.[7]

In fact, in spite of Jonson's apparent thorough-going scepticism, it is not inconceivable that he showed his face at Mortlake on occasion too. He certainly knew a great deal about the mystical knowledge system pursued there – particularly about Hermetic Neoplatonism and its science of alchemy – and to deride and mock alchemy as practised by covetous and foolish types (called Geber's 'cooks' after a famous alchemist) was not necessarily to register disbelief in the 'science'; on the contrary, adepts did it all the time in their treatises in order to distinguish their own higher pursuits from those of greedy men seeking to transmute gold from base metal. But if 'true' alchemists were not pursuing material riches, what were they up to?

Two fifteenth-century works, *The Compound of Alchymie* by George Ripley,[8] Canon of an Augustinian Priory in Yorkshire, and *The Ordinall of Alchemy* by Thomas Norton,[9] businessman and Privy Councillor, were regarded as key alchemical treatises throughout the early modern period, and this quest for understanding should begin here. Ripley was the most famous of the medieval alchemists; his treatise went into print in 1591 and was one of a clutch of alchemical treatises published that decade to meet a new thirst for alchemical knowledge (the famous *Mirror of Alchemy* appeared in 1597); as Deborah E. Harkness's *The Jewel House* describes, late Elizabethan London was bristling with budding students of nature including fledgling chemists labouring over smoky backstreet furnaces.[10] Written in deliberately obtuse doggerel verse, Ripley's *The Compound of Alchymie* nevertheless works hard to convey the seriousness of its quest and its religious orthodoxy: it concludes, for example, 'kepe thy Secretts in store unto thy selve; / And the comaundements of God looke thou fulfill'.[11] I say quest, because it describes the alchemical work as a journey – a foray into a philosophical castle of secret wisdom. The adept has to pursue his work through twelve 'gates' or stages. These 'gates' are described in turn as 'calcination' (the reduction of matter to powder), 'solution' (the solid is rendered liquid and returned to the first matter of creation), 'separation' (the breaking apart of the four elements), 'conjunction' (the joining together of opposite properties in a 'chemical wedding'), 'putrefaction' (the nadir of the journey entailing purgatorial suffering and the matter turning black), 'congelation' (the stone is now congealed and white), 'cibation' (a process of fortification) and, finally, 'sublimation', 'fermentation', 'exaltation', 'multiplication' and 'projection'. The last five mysterious processes serve to deliver from the castle stronghold 'The Red Man and his White Wife' – the perfect Philosopher's Stone.[12]

Cutting through Ripley's indigestible terminology – so brilliantly parodied to serve the ends of comedy in Jonson's *The Alchemist* and in the masque, *Mercury Vindicated from the Alchemists at Court* – it would seem that through applying heat by means of a furnace, the alchemist repeatedly dissolves and destroys the substance in his flask and then resurrects and unites it again in altered, purified form (parallels were made with Christ's crucifixion and resurrection). However, in spite of Ripley's liberal deployment of terms that sound to the modern ear as though they should be associated with practical chemistry, *The Compound of Alchymie* reads much more like a philosophical tract with pronounced spiritual implications than a chemical recipe book. If anything, Norton's treatise, *The Ordinall of Alchemy*, which ostentatiously declares itself 'A Booke of secrets given by God; / To men Elect'[13] – those who love justice with 'spotles-Minde' – serves to deepen this sense of a frustratingly vague divine 'Art'.[14] Norton revels in his numerous paradoxes and obscurities – a feature, as he suggests, of most alchemical works. To write clearly would be to reveal the secrets of the holy 'science' to unworthy, covetous fools – 'Gebars Cookes' seeking only to make silver and gold from lead 'for Mony, Cupp or Ring'.[15] This is not, he repeatedly insists, the goal of 'holy Alkimy' which 'treateth of a precious Medicine', a red 'elixir' that is achieved, at great cost, by a painful, dangerous 'Pilgrimage'-like journey.[16]

In fact, as the historian of chemistry John Read points out, the ancient art of alchemy was a double quest involving both 'outer' and 'inner' work. Exoteric alchemy evolved from ancient metallurgy, glass-working and dyeing practices and involved purification processes through fire, smelting and distillation, while esoteric alchemy used the same vocabulary to describe a journey of spiritual purification through memory work and contemplation in the furnaces of the head and heart – it was philosophical soul work. It might thus be construed as pre-psychology as well as pre-chemistry.[17] 'Alchemy' derives from the ancient name for Egypt meaning dark soil ('Khem'), and if Egypt gave alchemy its name, it was also associated with its legendary founding father, the thrice great, Hermes Trismegistus, 'identified with Thoth, the Egyptian god of revelation and wisdom'.[18] Thought to have been active around the time of Moses, he was a priest-philosopher-king closely connected with the dissemination of Egyptian religion (inscribed in hieroglyphs) but also with natural philosophy, law and the arts; the latter made Hermes a good candidate for his Renaissance cloning with the Roman god, Mercury.

The 'sons of Hermes', alchemical adepts, based their art on thirteen precepts that were said to have been inscribed in Phoenician characters on the 'Emerald Tablet' taken from the tomb of Hermes by none other than Alexander the Great.[19] As might be anticipated, the 'Emerald Tablet' has a pronounced mystical aura: the first precept states, 'That which is above is like to that which is below, and that which is below is like to that which is above, to accomplish the miracles of one thing', the second talks of 'The contemplation of one', and another promises, 'Thus thou wilt possess the glory of the brightness of the whole world, and all obscurity will fly far from thee.'[20] It will be clear by now that the crazed and overblown dreams of Jonson's would-be possessors of the Philosopher's Stone resonate with such Hermetic aphorisms.

Jonson's burlesques aside, for many early modern intellectuals, Hermeticism's stress on one religion and inner spirituality provided a peaceful-seeming contrast to the strife and factionalism they were witnessing around them.[21] Marsilio Ficino, the fifteenth-century translator of the Greek *Hermetic Corpus* into Latin, had speculated that Hermes had been born a little after Moses and that his esoteric knowledge had been passed to Orpheus and then on to Pythagoras and Plato. Egyptian hieroglyphs, Greek myths and Platonic dialogues might therefore encode pristine religious wisdom. Ficino was unaware that the pronounced Platonic influences he found in the Hermetic writings derived from their having actually been penned by Christian Neoplatonists in approximately the third century AD rather than in ancient times. We can now begin to see why in *The Advancement of Learning* Francis Bacon saw fit to commend James I as 'invested of that triplicity which in great veneration was ascribed to the ancient Hermes; the power and fortune of a King, the knowledge and illumination of a Priest, and the learning and universality of a Philosopher', and proceeded to list alchemy, along with astrology and natural magic, as sciences with 'noble' ends. He singled alchemy out as having 'brought to light a great number of good and fruitful inventions and experiments, as well for the disclosing of nature as for the use of man's life'.[22]

According to the Hermetic text, *Asclepius,* the book of Nature was, in effect, a second work of divine revelation (after Holy Scripture), and the devout philosopher was thus duty bound to study Nature's works and to seek out the treasures which became hidden after man's expulsion from Eden. In Hermeticism, the celestial bodies are a link between God and mankind: they transmit divine efficacy to earthly matter which the skilled scientist can access. Bacon described natural magic in the following terms: 'I ... understand it as the science which applies the knowledge of hidden forms to the production of wonderful operations; and by uniting (as they say) actives with passives displays the wonderful works of nature'.[23] In this scheme of things, the scientist assisted the work of nature encouraging it to yield its secrets, which gave him enhanced 'powers' that could be deployed, in Bacon's words, to 'The effecting of all things possible'.[24] This vision included England's regeneration into the golden world of New Jerusalem. As Lauren Kassell's *Medicine and Magic in Elizabethan London* stresses, natural magic was not considered 'a perversion of religion' but rather 'a perfection of it'.[25]

Like Jonson, Bacon abhorred extremism and delusions of any kind, and his writings frequently shape him as a sceptic and rationalist, yet the vision of his *New Atlantis* – the blueprint for the Royal Society – is deeply Hermetic. Against this complex backdrop it would be unwise to speculate too far about Jonson's own beliefs. His writings reveal that he had an extensive knowledge of Hermetic philosophy and its partner alchemy and that he was a master of exploiting the comic potential of their bizarre lexicon and more fantastical claims. He sniffed out the sectarian 'enthusiasm' that beliefs in inner purification and enlightenment could and did breed, yet at the same time as he poured scorn on these for public consumption, he crafted court masques celebrating golden worlds restored by the Hermetic powers of his royal masters. His approach was certainly protean.

NOTES

1. Paolo Rossi, *Francis Bacon: From Magic to Science*, trans. Sacha Rabinovitch (originally published in 1957; London: Routledge, 1968).
2. John Securis, *Detection and Querimonie of the Daily Enormities and Abuses Committed in Physick* (London, 1566), sig. B4v.
3. See Margaret Healy, *Fictions of Disease in Early Modern England: Bodies, Plagues and Politics* (Basingstoke: Palgrave, 2001).
4. John Donne, 'An Anatomy of the World: The First Anniversary', in *The Poems of John Donne*, edited by Herbert Grierson (Oxford: Oxford University Press, 1912), pp. 229–45.
5. Charles Webster, *From Paracelsus to Newton: Magic and the Making of Modern Science* (Cambridge: Cambridge University Press, 1982), p. 9.
6. See Stuart Clark, *Thinking with Demons: The Idea of Witchcraft in Early Modern Europe* (Oxford: Clarendon Press, 1997).
7. Peter J. French, *John Dee: The World of an Elizabethan Magus* (originally published in 1972; London: Routledge & Kegan Paul, 1984).
8. George Ripley, *The Compound of Alchymie* in Elias Ashmole (ed.), *Theatrum Chemicum Britannicum* (London, 1651); all citations are to this edition.
9. Thomas Norton, *The Ordinall of Alchimy*, in Elias Ashmole (ed.), *Theatrum Chemicum Britannicum* (London, 1651); all citations are to this edition.
10. Deborah Harkness, *The Jewel House: Elizabethan London and the Scientific Revolution* (New Haven, Conn.: Yale University Press, 2007).
11. Ripley, *The Compound of Alchymie*, p. 186.
12. Ripley, *The Compound of Alchymie*, p. 185.

13. Norton, *The Ordinall of Alchimy,* Preface, sig. C2r.
14. Norton, *The Ordinall of Alchimy,* sig. C2r.
15. Norton, *The Ordinall of Alchimy,* ll. 15, 103, 13.
16. Norton, *The Ordinall of Alchimy,* ll. 20, 105.
17. John Read, *Through Alchemy to Chemistry* (London: G. Bell & Sons Ltd., 1961), pp. 12–40.
18. Lyndy Abraham, *A Dictionary of Alchemical Imagery* (Cambridge: Cambridge University Press, 1998), p. 100.
19. Read, *Through Alchemy to Chemistry,* pp. 22–3.
20. Cited in Stanton Linden (ed.), *The Alchemy Reader* (Cambridge: Cambridge University Press, 2003), p. 28.
21. Frances Yates, *Giordano Bruno and the Hermetic Tradition* (Chicago, Ill.: Chicago University Press, 1964).
22. Francis Bacon, *The Advancement of Learning,* Book I, in *Collected Works of Francis Bacon,* edited by James Spedding, Robert Ellis and Douglas Heath (originally published in 1876; London: Routledge, 1996), Vol. III, Part 1, pp. 263, 289.
23. Francis Bacon, *De dignitate et augmentis scientarum,* Sp. I, 573, quoted in Paolo Rossi, *Francis Bacon: From Magic to Science,* trans. Sacha Rabinovitch (London: Routledge & Kegan Paul, 1968), p. 21.
24. Cited in Rossi, *Francis Bacon,* p. 21.
25. Lauren Kassell, *Medicine and Magic in Elizabethan London: Simon Forman – Astrologer, Alchemist, and Physician* (Oxford: Clarendon Press, 2005), p. 9.

CHAPTER 37

Clothing and fashion

Eleanor Lowe

When *The New Inn* was performed in 1629 to an unreceptive audience, Jonson's blame for the play's failure in the printed quarto is partially directed at the stage-sitters: '"What did they come for, then?" thou wilt ask me. I will as punctually answer: "To see and to be seen. To make a general muster of themselves in their clothes of credit, and possess the stage against the play"' (*The New Inn* (printed 1631), 'Dedication to the Reader', ll. 5–7). Jonson's scorn compares these audience members (dressed in clothes yet to be paid for) with the tapestries hung behind them, faces fixed and unmoved, positioning themselves as the prime focus of attention to the detriment of the play's action in what is described as an aggressive military manoeuvre. Jonson's account sees clothing – and its superficial mannequins – turn the stage into a catwalk, privileging the visual over the aural, appearance over substance. His satiric portrait of sartorially fixated London is vividly drawn in the plays: this chapter will discuss in particular *Epicene* and *The New Inn*, where clothing and identity, class and taste, are an integral part of social commentary.

Jonson's audience had benefited from an increased commercialization and commoditization of clothing in the sixteenth and early seventeenth centuries. In tandem with newly accessible cloths, accessories and fashions, concern rose that the carefully structured, pyramidal ordering of society (with God at the top, filtering power through the monarch to the people below) might be disrupted. This prompted various attempts to legislate what differing ranks of people could and couldn't wear in the sumptuary laws of Elizabeth's reign. In *Epicene,* Daw's 'box of instruments' are a necessity 'to draw maps of every place and person where he comes' (5.1.14, 17–18). Julie Sanders has clearly outlined the important significations of clothing as part of a sign system, leading to identification 'of profession, rank, gender, age and even nationality'.[1] In Jonson's plays this can be observed clearly on multiple occasions, but most pertinently in 5.2 of *Every Man In*

His Humour (Quarto), where Musco disguises himself as a varlet. Bobadilla and Matheo recognize the 'varlet' by his clothing, but not Musco. A similar incident occurs when Stephano, wearing Giuliano's fallen cloak, is arrested as Giuliano. These examples illustrate how clothing and costume might be linked with generic persons and specific individuals. Daw's cartographically taxonomic practice in *Epicene* is essential in an increasingly commercialized city society where each item of clothing carries its own semiotic message and shopping becomes a pastime in its own right.[2]

The semiotics of clothing both on and off stage in early modern England have been well documented. Alan C. Dessen identifies the metonymic use of clothing as theatrical shorthand in place of elaborate exposition, so that, for example, the Host from an ordinary or tavern can be represented by placing a napkin upon his shoulder.[3] Jonson's *Epicene* contains a similar circumstance: in 3.3, Dauphine instructs La Foole to dress like a sewer, who supervises the serving of a meal: 'clap me a clean towel about you, like a sewer, and bare-headed, march afore it with a good confidence' (3.3.50–1).

Peter Stallybrass has identified early modern England as a cloth and livery society, both of which involve encoded networks of social obligations.[4] Earlier in *Epicene,* La Foole boasts of another kind of cloth label: his coat of arms, a rather garish-sounding affair of yellow, red and blue, 'and some three or four colours more' (1.4.32–3) which does nothing to escape the thinly veiled meaning of his family name. In a cloth society, one piece can easily overlay another, an idiotic knight such as La Foole displaying his *true* 'colours' with the simple addition of a serving towel. His cousin is married to Captain Otter: *'animal amphibium'* (1.4.20); as Dauphine observes, the name is a hotch-potch, neither one thing nor the other, a fitting representative symbol of Jacobean London society. A similar description befits La Foole's description of his coat of arms: an amalgamation which disassociates itself from true nobility and taste, the equivalent, in Gordon Campbell's opinion, of a fool's motley coat.[5] For a real sewer, the addition of livery badge and serving towel to his clothing would function as a mark of honour, a symbol of ownership by, and responsibility to, his master. For a knight, it ridicules him, downgrading his status by displaying a sign of subservience to another when he should be in command of servants wearing his own livery.

The multi-layered semiotics of clothing and fashion are reflective of their practical construction from layers of lining, interlining, outer material, stiffening (buckram, reeds or whalebone), made in panels and sewn together to form fashionable shapes. Silhouettes were in transition through the three reigns of Jonson's life, from the angular outlines of Elizabethan dress, through elaborate, structured Jacobean ensembles, to the softer lines of Charles's reign. Items of clothing, themselves individually constructed from pieces, were layered onto the blank canvas of the body, linen lying next to the skin (to absorb its natural odours and dirt, and easily cleaned by washing) over which were placed various items: pairs of bodies (corsets), partlets, farthingales, petticoats, skirts, bodices or gowns for women, doublet and hose of some kind for men. Sleeves could be attached with laces or pins, as could women's foreparts (a highly decorated panel visible in the gap between the openings of the overskirt), and points (laces with metal tips called aglets) attached doublet to hose and bodies to underskirts.

The effect of piecing and layering enabled the greatest effect to be gained from purchasing a small piece of expensive cloth: the point of the forepart was to suggest a highly decorated (and thus extortionately expensive) whole underskirt, when a much smaller piece of cloth could intimate this extravagance without the outlay. Each piece of layered clothing therefore had its own significance, contributing to the overall effect of the outfit and communicating essential information to the viewer regarding gender, status, profession and age. The richer the wearer, the more likely that even undergarments would be constructed of high-quality materials with additional ornamentation, such as embroidery, which went unseen in public but were appropriate nevertheless to the wearer's status. In this context, the desire of Pinnacia Stuff the tailor's wife in *The New Inn* to show off her clothing (borrowed from one of her husband's clients, Lady Frampul) by stopping for him to tie a shoe is inappropriate vulgar behaviour, the equivalent of a gaudy coat of arms.

The sinister side to an obsession with transient objects is revealed by Clerimont's Boy in *Epicene,* who complains how the gentlewomen wish to make him their plaything:

The gentlewomen play with me and throw me o' the bed, and carry me in to my lady, and she kisses me with her oiled face and puts a peruke o' my head and asks me an I will wear her gown, and I say 'No'. And then she hits me a blow o' the ear and calls me innocent, and lets me go. (1.1.10–14)

The women want to dress the Boy, in a manner akin to girls playing with dolls, and when he refuses to play her game, Lady Haughty sulks. There is something inherently repulsive in this description: the desire of the women to accessorize their plaything, the demand for compliance, bordering on the abuse of gender, status and age. The key element is the gentlewoman's desire for the Boy to wear her gown, urging him to change his shape (quite literally, for the construction of the gown would give him a woman's silhouette) and his sex and to assume a higher status translated by the materials of which the gown is made.

Moreover, the cloth would be impregnated with the smell of another human being, normal odour and sweat combined in close proximity to his body in an intimacy usually experienced in sexual relations. When the Boy declines, Lady Haughty's response is to hit him, symptomatic not only of sexual rejection but perhaps also jealousy, since it is revealed that the Boy is Clerimont's 'ingle' (1.1.19), happier to function as his master's favourite. The Boy's speech also serves the self-reflexive function of reminding the audience of the players' status as their, quite literal, 'play' thing, the flexible boundaries crossed by actors playing female roles and the title, *Epicene*, pointing to indeterminacy of gender.

Similar tension is found in *The New Inn*, where Prudence's beautiful new clothes have been defiled by the tailor's wife, Pinnacia, who is stripped of the now 'polluted robes' (4.3.92) and their status. Lady Frampul is clear on the direct correlation between expensive clothing and appropriate status:

> Rich garments only fit
> The parties they are made for; they shame others.
> (5.2.3–4)

Prudence describes the smell of the tailor's wife lingering on the clothes: the taint is 'of his wife's haunches, / Thus thick of fat; I smell 'em, o' the 'say' (5.2.13–14).[6] The reference neatly combines a description of Pinnacia as large and greasy, with haunches like an animal, base and vulgar in contrast with the costly fabrics, whilst also acknowledging the difficulty of washing them. While linen was cleaned by being beaten with battledores in the laundering process, silk or wool would need more careful treatment. Prudence's exorcism of Pinnacia's scent from her garments is likely to require more time and care than Lady Frampul optimistically suggests.

Jonson's plays often articulate a contrast between the performance of clothed beauty in public, and its application, or the 'manner' of the artifice which 'must be private' (*Epicene*, 1.1.90), a ceremony to which only the chosen are invited to attend. Captain Otter, himself privy to his wife's nightly ritual, describes her artificial features and their origins thus: 'All her teeth were made i' the Blackfriars, both her eyebrows i' the Strand, and her hair in Silver Street. Every part o' the town owns a piece of her … She takes herself asunder still, when she goes to bed, into some twenty boxes' (4.2.75–80).[7] The description is an act of exposure, a revelation of truths and the naked honest body beneath the artifice. It also has much in common with a depiction of anatomization, the dissection of character upon which Jonson was intent, or, worse, akin to the punishment of quartering the body and positioning it as a warning in different parts of the city. Here, instead of body parts sent forth, adornments for the imperfections of the body are collected from various city artificers. Mistress Otter is 'made' by London: her china-shop provides income which is spent on acquiring London's fashions.

In contrast with the consumerism of the living, the play is set against the contemporary backdrop of mortality in 1609: Clerimont points to 'The perpetuity of ringing' of bells in plague time as Morose's tipping point (1.1.146). In this context, the reference to 'some twenty boxes' (4.2.80) brings to mind several coffins and a reminder of what will remain once bodily flesh decays. This point is most pertinent 400 years later, since the preserved contents of upper-class burials in particular have informed the study of clothing. Johannes Pietsch's recent article in *Costume* contains photographs of the surviving clothing from the burial of Margaretha Franziska de Lobkowicz, her skull still crowned with hair.[8] When Mistress Otter dies, her artificial accessories of beauty will remain within boxes, either their own containers or the box within which she will be buried, unless they are divided and dispersed as were Queen Elizabeth's wardrobe belongings.[9]

Jonson's characters often express themselves in composite lists. In *Epicene* these describe inventories of clothing, beautification procedures and accessories, mimicking the effect of layering present in the construction of both individual articles of clothing and their placement on the body. Morose's list carefully dictates the pattern of dressing undergone by a woman standing in her undergarments of smock, corset and stockings: 'that bodice, these sleeves, those skirts, this cut, that stitch, this embroidery, that lace, this wire, those knots, that ruff, those roses, this girdle, that fan, the tother scarf, these gloves' (2.5.59–61). In other circumstances, Morose's list might constitute the imaginings of a newly married man who has enjoyed his first night with his wife and the morning after her ceremonial undressing. However, in consideration of Morose's oppositional nature to noise, life and companionship, it seems that he is more keen to cover her up, imagining the expense of this shopping list into the bargain.

Early modern plays were *heard* as well as *seen,* two essentials of theatre being sound and visuals. Jonson comments on plays that 'Their fate is only in their hearers' ears' (*The New Inn,* Epilogue, l. 2). The importance of sound as well as sight is foregrounded by Morose's affliction in *Epicene*. Inventories of clothing, dress-related artisans and processes of beautification are coupled with composite lists of sounds: Truewit's catalogue of domestic noises (for example, spitting, coughing, laughter, farting and music, 4.1.5–7) sits beside Morose's account of the agonizing noise at court when he goes to seek a lawyer. His description is of a layered aural impression of speech and sound, 'such speaking and counter-speaking' (4.7.12–15). Sound dresses space, clothes it, furnishes it, just as clothed bodies furnish space, not only domestic and public spaces of the city but also the naked stage of the theatre. Morose's silence is also penetrated by the sound of clothing: 'He turned away a man last week for having a pair of new shoes that creaked. And this fellow waits on him now in tennis-court socks, or slippers soled with wool' (1.1.148–50). The account points to an additional element of the soundscape of both Jonson's London and therefore the stage: the sound made by items of clothing.

Bruce R. Smith describes how spoken sound is encoded in early modern England by 'speech communities' which are distinguished by social station, dialect, variety or register, by code, or a combination of these.[10] Clothing similarly serves as an identity marker, functioning as an overlooked participant in the Renaissance soundscape. Perhaps this is one reason why Morose notices and objects to the sound of squeaking shoes. Smith uses this information as inspiration to read early modern maps of London and Kenilworth as aural guides to early modern soundscapes. He imagines the early morning sounds of waking up in the country and the business of the city streets. One aspect Smith does not appear to consider but which is signalled by the sensitive Morose, is the sound of clothing. The everyday sounds of waking would begin with dressing: struggling into a bodice, lacing, pushing of woollen hose into leather shoes on a rush-matted floor, leather shoelaces being tied, layering of skirts in linen and wool, more lacing, pinning of cloth and the sound of footsteps walking away to begin the day. These sounds are called to mind when Lady Frampul is dressing Prudence: the whipping sound of a lace through eyelets and the human response to being squeezed into clothes too tight (*The New Inn*, 2.1).[11] The communal aspect of dressing heightens the probability that these sounds were extremely familiar: the lower classes shared sleeping spaces and might help each other dress; the wealthy employed formal assistance with dressing. It was a shared ritual of morning and evening, a soundscape of layering and unlayering.

In the same way as clothing visually serves as a status marker, it might also aurally convey status: the sound of hobnail boots is quite different to new (squeaky) shoes or even heeled shoes (accompanied by attendants). Individuals could be identified through voice or specific footfall, just as Smith suggests that people would be able to *read* the sounds of whistle, voices and dogs in a small community where sounds lack anonymity and have both audibility and legibility.[12] In addition, the sounds of cloth could be differentiated: silk's quiet rustling luxuriantly different to wool or linen. Like Morose, Thorello wonders why he ever married: 'I that before was ranked in such content, / My mind attired in smooth, silken peace' (*Every Man In His Humour,* Quarto, 3.3.15–16), an enjoyable luxury.

Jonson's writing invites his plays to be heard and seen. They enfold anxiety about presenting 'untruth' by dressing above rank, such as Prudence in *The New Inn:*

> Or judge of me,
> To be translated thus, 'bove all the bound
> Of fitness or decorum?
>
> (2.1.53–5)

In the same play, sturdy, reliable characters display their 'truth' on the body: the Nurse wears an old-fashioned French hood (2.2.42), the Host, a long sword (2.5.74). For the revelation of true identity, a simple theatrical transformation suffices: the removal of Laetitia's headdress and the Host's cap and beard unmasks 'Frank' and Lord Frampul. Robbed of the opportunity to gain a fair 'reading' in the theatre by idiotic gallants, the final words of Jonson's 'Dedication' of *The New Inn* express his second chance (through print) clearly: 'Fare thee well, and fall to. Read' (l. 14). Ironically, though, to read the text is to experience the play without the multi-layered distractions made much of in its content, theatrical essentials of visuals and sound. Instead, Jonson implores his readers to embark on a semiotic 'reading' of his text, of aural and visual signs in sound and clothing, supplementing the stage action with multiple interpretational and experiential layers.

NOTES

1. Julie Sanders, '"Wardrobe Stuffe": Clothes, Costume and the Politics of Dress in Ben Jonson's *The New Inn*', *Renaissance Forum,* 6 (1) (2002): paragraph 13. Available online at www.hull.ac.uk/renforum/v6no1/sanders.htm.
2. For an account of references to shops and female shopkeepers on the stage, see Leslie Thomson, '"As Proper a Woman as Any in Cheap": Women in Shops on the Early Modern Stage', *Medieval and Renaissance Drama in England,* 16 (2003): 145–61.

3. Alan C. Dessen, *Elizabethan Drama and the Viewer's Eye* (Chapel Hill, NC: University of North Carolina Press, 1977), pp. 72–3.
4. Peter Stallybrass, 'Worn Worlds: Clothes and Identity on the Renaissance Stage', in Margreta de Grazia, Maureen Quilligan and Peter Stallybrass (eds.), *Subject and Object in Renaissance Culture* (Cambridge: Cambridge University Press, 1996), pp. 289–320; p. 289.
5. *Epicene,* in *Ben Jonson: The Alchemist and Other Plays,* edited by Gordon Campbell (Oxford: Oxford University Press, 1995); 1.4.38n.
6. 'Say' can be silk or wool cloth.
7. Charles Nicholl suggests that Jonson might be referring specifically to Christopher Mountjoy's tyre-making business on Silver Street, in whose house Shakespeare lodged for a time; see *The Lodger: Shakespeare on Silver Street* (London: Penguin, 2008), p. 141.
8. See Johannes Pietsch, 'The Burial Clothes of Margaretha Franziska de Lobkowitz, 1617', *Costume,* 42 (2008): 30–49. Janet Arnold's work produced patterns from grave clothes for her Patterns of Fashion series.
9. See Janet Arnold, *Queen Elizabeth's Wardrobe Unlock'd* (Leeds: Maney, 1988), pp. 174–5 for discussion of this issue.
10. Bruce R. Smith, *The Acoustic World of Early Modern England: Attending to the O-Factor* (Chicago, Ill.: University of Chicago Press, 1999), p. 42.
11. See also Julie Sanders's analysis of this scene as social inversion of a dressing ritual ('Wardrobe Stuffe').
12. Smith, *The Acoustic World of Early Modern England,* p. 76.

Figure 38.1 Old man with a long coat and a large hat by Rembrandt Harmenszoon van Rijn.

CHAPTER 38

Gender and sexuality

Mario DiGangi

In the first scene of Jonson's *Volpone,* there is a puzzling moment in which Volpone boasts of receiving visits from '[w]omen and men, of every sex and age' who hope to be made his heirs (1.1.77). Volpone here seems to hint at the existence of a plurality of 'sexes' ranged within the bland taxonomy of 'women' and 'men'. But to what does 'every sex' refer? Does it denote the kind of anatomical peculiarities that distinguish Volpone's servants Castrone (a eunuch) and Androgyno (a hermaphrodite)? Does it refer to the permutations of gender traits that run the spectrum from (feminine) 'women' to (masculine) 'men'? Perhaps 'every sex' glances at the multiple ways of enjoying the sex organs, including those non-reproductive sexual practices that leave Volpone childless. The 1983 Revels edition of *Volpone,* which, like most criticism of its time, does not consider issues of sexuality, simply ignores this line.[1] Instead, we might see in the strange formulation of 'women and men of every sex' an emblem of the plurality of gender and sexuality in Jonson that is the subject of this chapter.

One critical context for understanding the cultural parameters within which gender plurality emerges is provided by Judith Butler's definition of 'gender' as 'The apparatus by which the production and normalization of masculine and feminine take place along with the interstitial forms of hormonal, chromosomal, psychic, and performative that gender assumes.'[2] Jonson's contemporaries lacked the knowledge of hormones and chromosomes, but Butler's account of biological sex as an *effect* of gender also holds true for the Renaissance, in that male and female bodies were differentiated in terms of the gendered concepts of genital morphology, humoural disposition and internal heat. Butler also theorizes gender as the social enactment through which idealized norms of masculinity and femininity get reproduced – sometimes in deviant, displaced or approximate forms. Hence, 'those permutations of gender' that fall outside the masculine/feminine binary are 'as much a part of gender as its most normative instance'.[3] Jonson's plays are rich with the 'daily social rituals of bodily life' that can serve to 'reidealize' gender norms as well as to express the gender permutations that fuel the transgressive energies of some of Jonson's most memorable characters.[4]

Jonson's texts do frequently assert an idealized patriarchal understanding of gender that defines the 'manly' in terms of truth, orderliness, independence and reason, as opposed to the qualities of artificiality, excess, dependence and passion derided as 'womanish' or 'effeminate'.[5] A prescriptive ideal of femininity for women in the period centred on the modest virtues of chastity, silence and obedience, codes that guide the conduct of Jonson's more conventional female characters, such as Celia in *Volpone*. Daw's song in *Epicene* articulates the orthodox view:

> Silence in women is like speech in man,
> Deny't who can ...
>   Nor is't a tale
> That female vice should be a virtue male,
> Or masculine vice, a female virtue be.
>
>   (2.3.102–7)

Maintaining sharp distinctions between male and female gender norms is more difficult than such crude schemes imply, however, since for women to achieve 'manliness' in the sense of discipline and moral virtue (but not aggression or licence) is commendable: Jonson praises the Countess of Bedford for possessing a 'learnèd and a manly soul', as well as a woman's 'softer bosom' (*Epigrams* 76, ll. 12–13). Conversely, moralists and theologians admonished men as well as women to be chaste and to speak modestly and behave submissively towards social superiors. Pushing against this orthodox ideal of patient conformity to hierarchical norms, manliness in Jonson's plays tends to accrue from intellectual competitiveness, conversational mastery and strident display of social entitlement.[6] Manly in *The Devil is an Ass* indignantly rejects the company of frivolous women and impudently challenges the compromised authority of Justice Eitherside. Through his virtuous outrage, Manly earns the right to voice the rather timid concluding moral that it 'is not manly to take joy or pride / In human errors', but to live 'a true life' (5.8.169–74).

Ironically, however, in the exuberance with which his characters pursue 'humours' and vices, and in the sharpness with which they are punished, Jonson often appears to 'take joy' in exposing 'human errors'. The easiest satiric targets are domineering women who usurp male authority and frivolous men who cede their male authority. In *Epicene,* Truewit ridicules the Collegiates for judging fashions and poets 'with most masculine, or rather hermaphroditical authority' – 'hermaphroditical' paradoxically suggesting that the Collegiates are at once typical (feminine) and unnatural (masculine) women (1.1.62–3). As his name suggests, the 'perfumed courtier' Amorphus in *Cynthia's Revels* conforms to the effeminate type whom Jonson derides for being 'always kempt and perfumed and every day smell[ing] of the tailor ... too much pickedness is not manly' (*Discoveries*, ll. 1009–14).

Despite Jonson's efforts to define and apply particular standards of gendered comportment, his dramatic characters enact gender in ways that are not always legible simply in terms of affirmation or censure. For instance, *The New Inn* features Frank, a boy who disguises himself as a girl and marries a young lord but who is finally revealed actually to be a girl. In *The Alchemist*, we hear of the 'boy of six year old, with the great thing', a freak-show attraction whose hyper-masculine attributes might earn grudging respect (5.1.24). Conversely, when Face shaves off his 'Captain's beard' to turn himself back into 'smooth Jeremy' the butler, he survives adversity through an act of symbolic self-emasculation (4.7.130–1). In *Bartholomew Fair*, the puppets, who are 'neither male nor female' in terms of anatomical sex, reinforce normative gender roles during a burlesque performance of Marlowe's *Hero and Leander* by shaming each other as 'whore-master' and 'whore' (5.5.83; 5.4.288, 262). It is difficult to say if such a scenario is subversive or just silly.

In the masques Jonson wrote for Queen Anna, gender norms are reproduced through the mobilization of both popular and elite cultural archetypes and through the gendered distinction between silence and speech. *The Masque of Queens,* for instance, opens with an anti-masque of witches: types of malignant, unruly and sexually deviant femininity. Led by a 'Dame' in the classical guise of Ate (goddess of strife in *The Iliad*), the homely witches perform an act of perverse maternity, chanting grotesque charms in a failed attempt to generate a creature fashioned from bones, body parts and herbs and nourished with 'milk and blood' (l. 236).[7] Performed by the professional actors of the King's Men, the witches are spectacularly verbal, though ineffective. Performed by Queen Anna and her ladies, the Amazon queens who enter on a pyramidal throne, scattering the witches, are visually glorious, but speechless. Perseus, 'expressing heroic and masculine virtue', blazons the Amazons' accomplishments (l. 342). Although the noblewomen thus embody a feminine ideal of silence, their impersonation of warlike Amazons risks being read as a provocative appropriation of 'masculine' might and sovereignty.

In *Volpone*, the protagonist's agency in choosing silence or speech as strategies of manipulation complicates the issue of his gender identity.

Problematically, recent critics have attached both masculine and feminine gender traits to Volpone's theatrical behaviours while downplaying the social and material basis of his male privilege. For instance, Mary Beth Rose describes as 'phallic heroism' Volpone's 'energetic wit' and 'absurdly brave assumption of control', yet observes that his fake illness places him in a 'female' role, 'passive, immobilized, silenced'.[8] Peter Parolin concurs that 'through his theatricality, he comes to occupy a culturally feminized position', and Richmond Barbour finds Volpone both 'phallic and effeminate' in his elaborate wooing of Celia.[9] Although Volpone might play or occupy the culturally normative feminine position of silence and objectification, however, the power and pleasure he derives from that performance are functions of his social, economic and gender privileges as a Venetian gentleman. While Volpone is not the sober patriarch of early modern didactic literature, he embodies patriarchal masculine gender norms in his management of household, servants and goods.[10] The choice to play a 'feminine' theatrical role is itself a function of masculine privilege, a point underscored by Celia's inability to escape her position of wifely dependence. When courting Celia, Volpone sings, 'Why should we defer our joys? / Fame and rumour are but toys. / Cannot we delude the eyes / Of a few poor household spies?' (3.7.173–6). That a wife could transgress with such impunity is the fantasy of a 'voluptuary' (4.6.25); the complementary fantasy is the husband's certainty that his wife will be seduced by the voluptuary's fantasy. Both fantasies are predicated on the wife's silence about her own desires.

Volpone is typical of Jonsonian characters who experience eroticism as a species of voracious appetite. In Jonson's plays, erotic passions enact the impulse to possess, control and consume another person; they do not emanate, as the modern concept of sexual orientation would have it, from a core 'sexuality' directed towards persons of a particular gender. Instead of identifying themselves with a particular modality of sexual desire understood as the expression of an essential self, Jonson's characters express desire in highly theatrical scenarios of sexual seduction, bargaining or cajoling. Jonson's texts thus corroborate the historicist argument that in the early modern period, one's erotic dispositions and practices were not organized through a 'homosexual' or 'heterosexual' identity. Moreover, in Jonson's demystifying treatment of sexual relations between men and women, there is 'no endorsement of heterosexual love, no celebration of heterosexual romance' as there is in Shakespeare.[11] Given its relentlessly social and material quality, Jonsonian eroticism is aptly described by Judith Butler's definition of sexuality as neither 'fully captured by any regulation' nor 'by nature, free and wild', but as 'an improvisational possibility within a field of constraints'.[12]

In Jonson's plays, the constraints upon sexuality often take the form not of opposition to mutual romantic desire as found in Shakespeare (for example, in *A Midsummer Night's Dream* or *Othello*) but of contests of will among those who are differently positioned in terms of sexual agency and socio-economic opportunity. Grace Wellborn in *Bartholomew Fair* demonstrates some of the improvisational possibilities that emerge from within the socio-economic constraints on female sexuality in early modern England. As Justice Overdo's ward, Grace is betrothed to the idiotic Bartholomew Cokes, but the unruly atmosphere of the fair provides her the opportunity to choose as her husband one of two gentlemen she has just met. Yet choice is precisely what Grace sacrifices to the gendered dictates of 'modesty' and 'wit', for not knowing either man, she is 'indifferently affected' towards them both (4.3.24, 27–8). Leaving her choice of husband to fate or arbitrary chance, she has each of her suitors write down a name; she will ask the first passer-by to pick a name, and on the victor she promises to 'fix [her] resolution, and affection, without change' (ll. 43–4). In the event, a madman picks the name chosen by Winwife, whose own surname foretells his success. Although this scenario appears to demand an ironic reading, particularly in terms of the comic plot's apparent hijacking of female sexual agency, Jonson draws on the conventions of romantic comedy to suggest that the marriage might, in fact, be happy.

If *Bartholomew Fair* thus appears to reward a modest female initiative in choosing a marriage partner,[13] *The Devil is an Ass* explores the much more difficult circumstance of an unhappily married woman – not an uncommon premise in Jonson's comedies – drawn into an intimate relationship with another man. Courted by Wittipol in the presence of her husband, Frances Fitzdottrel says nothing. But like Volpone, who thinks that to forgo rape is to admit to being 'cold, / Frozen, and impotent' (3.7.259–60), Frances worries about being perceived as without desire:

> I would have not him think he met a statue
> Or spoke to one not there, though I were silent.
> (2.2.69–70)

Here Frances subversively translates the norm of female chastity, silence and obedience into an imposition of inhuman rigidity. Having slyly arranged to meet Wittipol, she allows him to court her while he *plays with her paps* and *kisseth her hands,* but she hints at some further circumstance regarding her 'fortune' that prompts her to seek his company (2.6.70 s.d., 54). It is only later that she reveals her need for Wittipol's friendly counsel to save her from financial ruin. By remaining faithful to her doltish husband, Frances escapes the fate of Fallace, the unhappy wife in *Every Man Out of His Humour,* who is humiliated as a 'lascivious strumpet' for having pursued her palpably sexual attraction to the courtier Fastidious Brisk (5.6.47). Through Wittipol's help, moreover, Frances secures possession of her husband's estate. But the price she pays for her conformity to the constraints of female virtue is disappearance from the play. It is as if, once outside the boundaries of the adultery plot, Frances becomes incapable of possessing a viable dramatic subjectivity.

In Jonson's plays, extravagant expressions of erotic desire are usually the preserve of elite men. These men experience identity itself as a sexual constraint, perhaps, paradoxically enough, because the gender and status privileges attendant on their elite identities offer relative freedom from more material forms of sexual constraint. In *The Alchemist,* Sir Epicure Mammon, tempted by the possibility of a sexual encounter with a noblewoman (actually Doll Common), imaginatively transforms himself into the gold that will lure her into sin:

> She shall feel gold, taste gold, hear gold, sleep gold,
> Nay, we will *concumbere* [generate] gold.
> (4.1.29–30)

Mammon's fantasy of epicurean banqueting melds into the fantasy of a perpetual cycle of erotic stimulation and satisfaction:

> [we will] set ourselves high for pleasure,
> And take us down again, and then renew
> Our youth, and strength, with drinking the elixir,
> And so enjoy a perpetuity
> Of life, and lust.
> (4.1.162–6)

Similarly, when Volpone woos Celia, his fantasies aim at self-transformation, the prodigious consumption of all imaginable roles:

> we, in changèd shapes, [will] act Ovid's tales,
> Thou like Europa now and I like Jove,
> Then I like Mars and thou like Erycine;
> So of the rest, till we have quite run through
> And wearied all the fables of the gods.
> (3.7.220–4)

Gender and sexuality

Dispersing identity into a dynamic field of erotic pleasures and positions, such expressions of desire have the sheen of liberation. And yet, as Jonson writes in *Discoveries,* such fantasies might also be seen as a form of bondage, for 'we make ourselves slaves to our pleasures' (l. 1000).

Jonson's epigrams on Sir Voluptuous Beast succinctly represent such capacious anti-identitarian sexual pleasures as a form of self-enslavement. In 'On Sir Voluptuous Beast', Beast instructs his wife how to re-enact his past sexual experiences with a prostitute, boy and goat. Although Beast's fantasies require the refraction of his wife's identity – in acting out the 'varied shapes' of her husband's former lovers, she commits adultery on herself – his sexual aims are at once narcissistic and self-shattering: 'What doth he else but say "Leave to be chaste, / Just wife, and, to change me, make woman's haste"' (*Epigrams* 25, ll. 7–8). The two-line answer poem 'On the Same Beast' unfolds the consequences of that desire for change: 'Than his chaste wife, though Beast now know no more, / He adulters still: his thoughts lie with a whore' (*Epigrams* 26, ll. 1–2). Through the pun on 'adulters still' as 'adulters unmoving' (i.e. while lying only with his wife) and 'adulters ceaselessly', the epigram aptly illustrates how for Jonson the vicious are 'singularly mobile'.[14] The satiric bite of 'He adulters still' – in the sense of 'to corrupt; debase'[15] – comes from the implication that the voluptuary's restless craving for self-transformation moves only in one direction: downward.

The punitive account of sexuality in the 'Beast' poems is largely a function of genre. Whereas satiric epigrams foreground the constraints crashing in on sexual pleasures, theatrical texts accommodate multiple voices and allow a fuller airing of gender and sexual improvisations of all kinds. The collaborative nature of theatre, moreover, decentres and demystifies authorial control (as Jonson frequently complained), potentially exposing the *process* by which normative gender and sexual meanings are reproduced. Thus it is in Jonson's plays and masques that feminist critics have recently posited more room for the assertion of female agency than earlier accounts of Jonson's misogyny had allowed. Sophie Tomlinson finds that *The Masque of Queens* acknowledges the 'female masquer's capacity for self-transformation'; hence 'The theatrical spectacle *is* one of female empowerment', though such empowerment also threatens 'patriarchal government'.[16] Likewise, Alison Findlay concludes that even though *Epicene* 'confines female spectators as silent women', its exposure of 'The unnaturalness of such a situation' demystifies patriarchal ideology.[17] And in an analysis of women's sexual and economic agency in *The Devil is an Ass,* Helen Ostovich argues that Jonson's sympathetic treatment of Frances

Fitzdottrel's dilemma indicates his awareness of 'complex models of female behaviour' in contemporary London.[18] This is not, then, a Jonson who wantonly celebrates the violation of gender norms and sexual constraints, but whose participation in dynamic urban and courtly cultures necessarily impresses on his work the insistent desires of 'every sex and age'.

NOTES

1. Ben Jonson, *Volpone*, edited by R. B. Parker (Manchester: Manchester University Press, 1983), p. 101.
2. Judith Butler, *Undoing Gender* (New York: Routledge, 2004), p. 42.
3. Butler, *Undoing Gender,* p. 42.
4. Butler, *Undoing Gender,* p. 48.
5. As Alexandra Shepard argues, however, there were 'competing forms of manhood' in early modern England, and they 'could and did undermine patriarchal ideals' of manhood defined in terms of 'discretion, reason, moderation, self-sufficiency', and so on; see *Meanings of Manhood in Early Modern England* (Oxford: Oxford University Press, 2003), p. 2.
6. Regarding conversational mastery, Lorna Hutson argues that Jonson's ideal 'manly speaker' is an 'anticipator and master of inference and rumor' ('Civility and Virility in Ben Jonson', *Representations,* 78 (Spring) (2002): 1–27; p. 16).
7. The edition of *The Masque of Queens* cited is that from Ben Jonson, *The Complete Masques,* edited by Stephen Orgel (New Haven, Conn.: Yale University Press, 1969).
8. Mary Beth Rose, *Gender and Heroism in Early Modern English Literature* (Chicago, Ill.: University of Chicago Press, 2002), pp. 16–17.
9. Peter Parolin, '"A Strange Fury Entered My House": Italian Actresses and Female Performance in Volpone', *Renaissance Drama,* 29 (1998): 107–35, p. 126; Richmond Barbour, '"When I Acted Young Antinous": Boy Actors and the Erotics of Jonsonian Theater', *PMLA,* 110 (October) (1995): 1006–22; p. 1009.
10. Shepard, *Meanings of Manhood in Early Modern England,* p. 74.
11. Kate Chedgzoy, Julie Sanders and Susan Wiseman, 'Introduction: Refashioning Ben Jonson', in Julie Sanders, with Kate Chedgzoy and Susan Wiseman (eds.), *Refashioning Ben Jonson: Gender, Politics and the Jonsonian Canon* (Basingstoke: Macmillan, 1998), pp. 1–27; p. 19.
12. Butler, *Undoing Gender,* p. 15.
13. Historian Amy Erickson observes that young women who lived apart from their parents were more likely to conduct their own marriage arrangements and to marry men closer to their own age; see *Women and Property in Early Modern England* (London: Routledge, 1993), p. 94.
14. Victoria Silver, 'Totem and Taboo in the Tribe of Ben: The Duplicity of Gender and Jonson's Satires', *English Literary History,* 62 (Winter) (1994): 729–57; p. 735.

15. *Oxford English Dictionary,* adulter v. 2.
16. Sophie Tomlinson, *Women on Stage in Stuart Drama* (Cambridge: Cambridge University Press, 2005), pp. 33, 35.
17. Alison Findlay, *A Feminist Perspective on Renaissance Drama* (Oxford: Blackwell, 1999), pp. 115–16.
18. Helen Ostovich, 'Hell for Lovers: Shades of Adultery in *The Devil is an Ass*', in Julie Sanders, with Kate Chedgzoy and Susan Wiseman (eds.), *Refashioning Ben Jonson: Gender, Politics and the Jonsonian Canon* (Basingstoke: Macmillan, 1998), pp. 155–82; p. 155.

Further reading

LIFE AND BIOGRAPHY

Davis, Lloyd, 'The Love Life of Ben Jonson', in Takashi Kozuka and J. R. Mulryne (eds.), *Shakespeare, Marlowe, Jonson: New Directions in Biography* (Aldershot: Ashgate, 2006), pp. 227–40.

Hirschfeld, Heather, *Joint Enterprises: Collaborative Drama and the Institutionalization of the English Renaissance Theater* (Amherst, Mass.: University of Massachusetts Press, 2004).

Hutson, Lorna, 'Civility and Virility in Ben Jonson', *Representations*, 78 (2002): 1–27.

'Liking Men: Ben Jonson's Closet Opened', *English Literary History*, 71 (2004): 1065–96.

Riggs, David, *Ben Jonson: A Life* (Cambridge, Mass.: Harvard University Press, 1989).

THE ELIZABETHAN PERIOD

Bednarz, James P., *Shakespeare and the Poets' War* (New York: Columbia University Press, 2001).

Evans, Robert C., *Ben Jonson and the Poetics of Patronage* (Lewisburg, Pa.: Bucknell University Press, 1989).

Haynes, Jonathan, *The Social Relations of Jonson's Theater* (Cambridge: Cambridge University Press, 1992).

Martin, Randall, 'Stepping into Risky Business: Jonson's Canine Ventures in *Every Man Out of His Humor*', *The Ben Jonson Journal*, 12 (2005): 1–21.

Scolnicov, Hanna, *Experiments in Stage Satire: An Analysis of Ben Jonson's 'Every Man Out of His Humour', 'Cynthia's Revels' and 'Poetaster'* (Frankfurt: Peter Lang, 1987).

THE JACOBEAN PERIOD

Butler, Martin, '"Servant, but Not Slave": Ben Jonson at the Jacobean Court', *Proceedings of the British Academy*, 90 (1996): 65–93.

Helgerson, Richard, *Self-Crowned Laureates: Spenser, Jonson, Milton and the Literary System* (Berkeley, Calif.: University of California Press, 1983).

Norbrook, David, *Poetry and Politics in the English Renaissance*, 2nd edn (Oxford: Oxford University Press, 2002).
Perry, Curtis, *The Making of Jacobean Culture: James I and the Renegotiation of Elizabethan Literary Practice* (Cambridge: Cambridge University Press, 2006).

THE CAROLINE PERIOD

Butler, Martin, 'Late Jonson', in Gordon McMullan and Jonathan Hope (eds.), *The Politics of Tragicomedy: Shakespeare and After* (London: Routledge, 1992).
Maxwell, Julie, 'Ben Jonson among the Vicars: Cliché, Ecclesiastical Politics, and the Invention of "Parish Comedy"', *The Ben Jonson Journal*, 9 (2002): 37–68.
McRae, Andrew, 'The Poetics of Sycophancy: Ben Jonson and the Caroline Court', in David Brooks and Brian Kiernan (eds.), *Running Wild: Essays, Fictions and Memoirs Presented to Michael Wilding* (Delhi: Manohar Press, 2004), pp. 29–42.
Sanders, Julie, 'Jonson, *The Sad Shepherd*, and the North Midlands', *The Ben Jonson Journal*, 6 (1999): 49–68.
Veevers, Erica, *Images of Love and Religion: Queen Henrietta Maria and Court Entertainments* (Cambridge: Cambridge University Press, 1989).

GENRE

Cousins, A. D. and Scott, Alison V. (eds.), *Ben Jonson and the Politics of Genre* (Cambridge: Cambridge University Press, 2009).
Harp, Richard and Stewart, Stanley (eds.), *The Cambridge Companion to Ben Jonson* (Cambridge: Cambridge University Press, 2000).

FRIENDS, COLLABORATORS AND RIVALS

Evans, Robert C., *Ben Jonson and the Poetics of Patronage* (London and Toronto: Associated University Presses, 1989).
O'Callaghan, Michelle, *The English Wits: Literature and Sociability in Early Modern England* (Cambridge: Cambridge University Press, 2007).
Raylor, Timothy, *Cavaliers, Clubs, and Literary Culture: Sir John Mennes, James Smith, and the Order of the Fancy* (London and Toronto: Associated University Presses, 1994).
Riggs, David, *Ben Jonson: A Life* (Cambridge, Mass.: Harvard University Press, 1989).
Steggle, Matthew, *Wars of the Theatres: The Poetics of Personation in the Age of Jonson*, ELS Monograph Series, No. 75 (Victoria: University of Victoria Press, 1998).

JONSON AND SHAKESPEARE

Barton, Ann, *Ben Jonson, Dramatist* (Cambridge: Cambridge University Press, 1984).

Donaldson, Ian (ed.), *Jonson and Shakespeare* (Atlantic Highlands, NJ: Humanities Press, 1983).
  'Jonson and the Tother Youth', in *Jonson's Magic Houses: Essays in Interpretation* (Oxford: Oxford University Press, 1997), pp. 6–25.
  '"Not of an Age": Jonson, Shakespeare, and the Verdicts of Posterity', in James Hirsh (ed.), *New Perspectives on Ben Jonson* (London: Associated University Presses, 1997), pp. 197–214.
McDonald, Russ, 'Jonson and Shakespeare and the Rhythm of Verse', in Richard Harp and Stanley Stewart (eds.), *The Cambridge Companion to Ben Jonson* (Cambridge: Cambridge University Press, 2000), pp. 103–18.
  Shakespeare and Jonson/Jonson and Shakespeare (Lincoln, Nebr.: University of Nebraska Press, 1988).

EDITIONS

Herford, C. H., and Percy and Evelyn M. Simpson (eds.), *Ben Jonson*, 11 vols. (Oxford University Press, 1925–52).
Bevington, David, Martin Butler and Ian Donaldson (eds.) *The Cambridge Edition of the Works of Ben Jonson* (Cambridge University Press, in press).

Brady, Jennifer and W. H. Herendeen (eds.), *Ben Jonson's 1616 Folio* (Newark, Del.: University of Delaware Press, 1991).
Butler, Martin (ed.), *Re-Presenting Ben Jonson: Text, History, Performance* (Basingstoke: Macmillan, 1999).
Jowett, John, 'Jonson's Authorization of Type in *Sejanus* and Other Early Quartos', *Studies in Bibliography*, 44 (1991): 254–65.

JONSON AND CRITICISM

Barish, Jonas (ed.), *Ben Jonson: A Collection of Critical Essays* (Englewood Cliffs, NJ: Prentice Hall, 1963).
Craig, D. H. (ed.) *Ben Jonson: The Critical Heritage, 1597–1798* (London: Routledge, 1990).
Evans, Robert C. 'Jonson's Critical Heritage', in Richard Harp and Stanley Stewart (eds.) *The Cambridge Companion to Ben Jonson* (Cambridge: Cambridge University Press, 2000), pp. 188–201.
Lockwood, Tom, *Ben Jonson in the Romantic Age* (Oxford: Oxford University Press, 2005).
Loxley, James, *Complete Critical Guide to Ben Jonson* (London: Routledge, 2002).

JONSON AND PERFORMANCE

Cave, Richard, Elizabeth Schafer and Brian Woolland (eds.), *Ben Jonson and Theatre: Performance, Practice and Theory* (London: Routledge, 1999).
Potter, Lois, 'The Swan Song of the Stage Historian', in Martin Butler (ed.), *Re-Presenting Ben Jonson: Text, History, Performance* (Basingstoke: Macmillan, 1999).

Woolland, Brian (ed.), *Jonsonians: Living Traditions* (Aldershot: Ashgate, 2003).

LONDON AND URBAN SPACE

Ayers, P. K., '"Dreams of the City": The Urban and the Urbane in Jonson's *Epicoene*', *Philological Quarterly*, 66 (1987): 73–86.
Howard, Jean, *Theater of a City: The Places of London Comedy, 1598–1642* (Philadelphia, Pa.: University of Pennsylvania Press, 2006).
Inwand, Theodore, *The City Staged: Jacobean City Comedy from 1603–1613* (Madison, Wisc.: University of Wisconsin Press, 1986).
Manley, Lawrence, *Literature and Culture in Early Modern London* (Cambridge: Cambridge University Press, 1995).
Orlin, Lena Cowen (ed.), *Material London, ca. 1600* (Philadelphia, Pa.: University of Pennsylvania Press, 2001).
Turner, Henry, *The English Renaissance Stage: Geometry, Poetics, and the Practical Spatial Arts, 1580–1630* (Oxford: Oxford University Press, 2006).

THE GLOBE THEATRE AND OPEN-AIR THEATRES

Barish, Jonas A., 'Jonson and the Loathed Stage', in W. Blisset, Julian Patrick and R. W. Van Fossen (eds.), *A Celebration of Ben Jonson* (Toronto: University of Toronto Press, 1972), pp. 27–53.
Barnes, Peter, 'Staging Jonson', in Ian Donaldson (ed.), *Jonson and Shakespeare* (London: Macmillan in association with Humanities Research Centre, Australian National University, 1983), pp. 156–62.
Cave, Richard, Elizabeth Schafer and Brian Woolland (eds.) *Ben Jonson and Theatre: Performance, Practice and Theory* (London: Routledge, 1999).
Kirsch, Arthur C., *Jacobean Dramatic Perspectives* (Charlottesville, Va.: University Press of Virginia, 1972).
Ostovich, Helen, '"To Behold the Scene Full": Seeing and Judging in *Every Man Out of His Humour*', in Martin Butler (ed.), *Re-Presenting Ben Jonson: Text, History Performance* (Basingstoke: Macmillan, 1999), pp. 76–92.

THE WHITEFRIARS THEATRE AND THE CHILDREN'S COMPANIES

Ayers, P. K., 'Dreams of the City: The Urban and the Urbane in Jonson's *Epicoene*', *Philological Quarterly*, 66 (1) (1987): 73–86.
Munro, Lucy, *Children of the Queen's Revels: A Jacobean Theatre Repertory* (Cambridge: Cambridge University Press, 2005).
Shapiro, Michael, 'Audience vs. Dramatist in Jonson's *Epicoene* and Other Plays of the Children's Troupes', *English Literary Renaissance*, 3 (1973): 400–17.
Yui, Mimi, 'Sounding the Space between Men: Choric and Choral Cities in Ben Jonson's *Epicoene; or the Silent Woman*', *Publications of the Modern Language Association of America*, 122 (1) (2007): 72–88.
Zucker, Adam, 'The Social Logic of Ben Jonson's *Epicoene*', *Renaissance Drama*, 33 (n.s.) (2004): 37–62.

THE BLACKFRIARS THEATRE AND INDOOR THEATRES

Armstrong, William A., 'The Audience of the Elizabethan Private Theatres', *Review of English Studies*, 10 (n.s.) (1959): 234–49.
Donaldson, Ian, *Jonson's Magic Houses: Essays in Interpretation* (Oxford: Clarendon Press, 1997).
Gurr, Andrew, 'London's Blackfriars Playhouse and the Chamberlain's Men', in Paul Menzer (ed.), *Inside Shakespeare: Essays on the Blackfriars Stage* (Selinsgrove, Pa.: Susquehanna University Press, 2006), pp. 17–30.
Smallwood, R. L., '"Here, in the Friars": Immediacy and Theatricality in *The Alchemist*', *Review of English Studies*, 32 (n.s.) (1981): 142–60.

PROVINCES, PARISHES AND NEIGHBOURHOODS

Fletcher, Anthony, *Reform in the Provinces: The Government of Stuart England* (New Haven, Conn.: Yale University Press 1986).
Hindle, Steve, *The State and Social Change in Early Modern England, c. 1550–1640* (Basingstoke: Palgrave Macmillan, 2000).
Wrightson, Keith, 'Mutualities and Obligations: Changing Social Relationships in Early Modern England', *Proceedings of the British Academy*, 139 (2006): 157–94.
  'The "Decline of Neighbourliness" Revisited', in N. L. Jones and D. Woolf (eds.), *Local Identities in Late Medieval and Early Modern England* (Basingstoke: Palgrave Macmillan 2007), pp. 19–49.

THE COURT

Bevington, David and Peter Holbrook (eds.), *The Politics of the Stuart Court Masque* (Cambridge: Cambridge University Press, 1998).
Marcus, Leah, 'Jonson and the Court', in Richard Harp and Stanley Stewart (eds.), *The Cambridge Companion to Ben Jonson* (Cambridge: Cambridge University Press, 2000), pp. 30–42.
Riggs, David, *Ben Jonson: A Life* (Cambridge, Mass.: Harvard University Press, 1989).
Sanders, Julie, 'Jonson, King and Court', in Patrick Cheney, Andrew Hadfield and Garrett A. Sullivan Jr. (eds.), *Early Modern English Poetry: A Critical Companion* (Oxford: Oxford University Press, 2007), pp. 253–63.
Smuts, R. Malcolm Smuts, 'Progresses and Court Entertainments', in Arthur Kinney (ed.), *A Companion to Renaissance Drama* (Oxford: Oxford University Press, 2002), pp. 266–80.

MASQUES, COURTLY AND PROVINCIAL

Butler, Martin, *The Stuart Court Masque and Political Culture* (Cambridge: Cambridge University Press, 2009).

McManus, Clare, *Women and the Renaissance Stage: Anna of Denmark and Female Masquing in the Stuart Court (1590–1619)*, (Manchester University Press, 2002).
Orgel, Stephen, and Roy Strong, *Inigo Jones: The Theater of the Stuart Court*, 2 vols. (Berkeley, Calif.: University of California Press, 1973).
Parry, Graham, *The Golden Age Restor'd* (Manchester: Manchester University Press, 1981).
Sharpe, Kevin, *Criticism and Compliment* (Cambridge: Cambridge University Press, 1987).
Shohet, Lauren, *Reading Masques: The English Masque and Public Culture in the Seventeenth Century* (Oxford: Oxford University Press, 2010).

MUSIC

Butler, Martin, *The Stuart Court Masque and Political Culture* (Cambridge: Cambridge University Press, 2009).
Chan, Mary, *Music in the Theatre of Ben Jonson* (Oxford: Clarendon Press, 1980).
Duffy, John, *The Songs and Motets of Alfonso Ferrabosco, the Younger (1575–1628)* (Ann Arbor, Mich.: UMI Research Press, 1980).
Lindley, David, 'The Politics of Music in the Masque', in David Bevington and Peter Holbrook (eds.), *The Politics of the Stuart Court Masque* (Cambridge: Cambridge University Press, 1996), pp. 273–95.
Ravelhofer, Barbara, *The Early Stuart Masque: Dance, Costume, and Music* (Oxford: Oxford University Press, 2006).
Walls, Peter, *Music in the English Courtly Masque, 1604–40* (Oxford: Oxford University Press, 1996).

DANCE

Brissenden, Alan, *Shakespeare and the Dance* (London: Macmillan, 1981).
Daye, Anne, 'Torchbearers in the English Masque', *Early Music*, 26 (2) (1998): 246–62.
Payne, Ian, *The Almain in Britain, c. 1549–c. 1675: A Dance Manual from Manuscript Sources* (Aldershot: Ashgate, 2003).
Ravelhofer, Barbara, *The Early Stuart Masque: Dance, Costume, and Music* (Oxford: Oxford University Press, 2006).
Ward, John, 'Newly Devis'd Measures for Jacobean Masques', *Acta Musicologica*, 60 (2) (1988): 111–42.

MANUSCRIPT CULTURE AND READING PRACTICES

Johns, Adrian, *The Nature of the Book: Print and Knowledge in the Making* (Chicago, Ill.: University of Chicago Press, 1998).
Knowles, James, '"Songs of Baser Alloy": Jonson's *Gypsies Metamorphosed* and the Circulation of Manuscript Libels', *Huntington Library Quarterly*, 69 (2006): 153–76.

Loewenstein, Joseph, 'The Script in the Marketplace', *Representations*, 12 (1985): 101–14.
Love, Harold, *The Culture and Commerce of Texts: Scribal Publication in Seventeenth-Century England* (Amherst, Mass.: University of Massachusetts Press, 1998).

PRINT CULTURE AND READING PRACTICES

Brady, Jennifer and Herendeen, W. H. (eds.), *Ben Jonson's 1616 Folio* (London and Toronto: Associated University Presses; Newark, Del: University of Delaware Press, 1991).
Brooks, Douglas, *From Playhouse to Printing House: Drama and Authorship in Early Modern England* (Cambridge: Cambridge University Press, 1998).
Donovan, Kevin, 'Forms of Authority in the Early Texts of *Every Man Out of His Humour*', in Martin Butler (ed.), *Re-Presenting Ben Jonson: Text, History, Performance* (Basingstoke: Macmillan, 1999), pp. 59–75.
Evans, Robert C., *Habits of Mind: Evidence and Effects of Ben Jonson's Reading* (Lewisburg, Pa.: Bucknell University Press, 1995).
Loewenstein, Joseph, *Ben Jonson and Possessive Authorship* (Cambridge: Cambridge University Press, 2002).

VISUAL CULTURE

Gordon, D. J., 'Poet and Architect: The Intellectual Setting of the Quarrel between Ben Jonson and Inigo Jones', in Stephen Orgel (ed.), *The Renaissance Imagination* (Berkeley, Calif.: University of California Press, 1975), pp. 77–101.
Johnson, Anthony. W., *Ben Jonson: Poetry and Architecture* (Oxford: Clarendon Press, 1994).
Peacock, John, *The Stage Designs of Inigo Jones* (Cambridge: Cambridge University Press, 2006).
Peterson, Richard S., *Imitation and Praise in the Poems of Ben Jonson* (New Haven, Conn.: Yale University Press, 1981).

THE BODY

Cave, Richard, '*Poetaster:* Jonson and His Audience', in B. Woolland (ed.), *Jonsonians: Living Traditions* (Aldershot: Ashgate, 2003), pp. 13–26.
 'Ben Jonson and the Theatre', in Richard Cave, Elizabeth Schafer and Brian Woolland (eds.), *Ben Jonson and Theatre: Performance, Practice and Theory* (London: Routledge, 1999), pp. 21–78.
Mardock, James D., *Our Scene Is London: Ben Jonson's City and the Space of the Author* (New York: Routledge, 2008).
Steggle, Matthew, *Laughing and Weeping in Early Modern Theatres* (Aldershot: Ashgate, 2007).

LAW, CRIME AND PUNISHMENT

Cockburn, J. S. and Green, Thomas A. (eds.), *Twelve Good Men and True: The Criminal Jury in England, 1200–1800* (Princeton, NJ: Princeton University Press, 1988).

Cromartie, Alan, 'The Constitutionalist Revolution: The Transformation of Political Culture in Early Stuart England', *Past and Present*, 163 (1999): 76–120.

Hindle, Steve, *The State and Social Change in Early Modern England, c. 1550–1640* (Basingstoke: Palgrave Macmillan, 2000).

Langbein, John, *Prosecuting Crime in the Renaissance* (Cambridge, Mass.: Harvard University Press, 1974).

Shapiro, Barbara J., *A Culture of Fact: England, 1550–1720* (Ithaca, NY: Cornell University Press, 2003).

RELIGION

Donaldson, Ian, *Jonson's Magic Houses: Essays in Interpretation* (Oxford: Clarendon Press, 1997), pp. 47–65.

Dutton, Richard, 'Introduction', in Richard Dutton (ed.), *Ben Jonson's 'Epicene'* (Manchester: Manchester University Press, 2003), pp. 26–42.

Maxwell, Julie, 'Ben Jonson among the Vicars: Cliché, Ecclesiastical Politics, and the Invention of "Parish Comedy"', *The Ben Jonson Journal*, 9 (2003): 37–68.

Walsham, Alexandra, *Church Papists: Catholicism, Conformity and Confessional Polemic in Early Modern England* (Woodbridge: Boydell Press, 1999).

POLITICS

Cain, Tom, 'Jonson's Humanist Tragedies', in A. D. Cousins and Alison V. Scott (eds.), *Ben Jonson and the Politics of Genre* (Cambridge: Cambridge University Press, 2009), pp. 162–89.

Riggs, David, *Ben Jonson: A Life* (Cambridge, Mass.: Harvard University Press, 1989), pp. 184–6.

Sanders, Julie, *Ben Jonson's Theatrical Republics* (Basingstoke: Macmillan, 1998).

Wayne, Don E., *Penshurst: The Semiotics of Place and the Poetics of History* (Madison, Wisc.: University of Wisconsin Press, 1984).

Worden, Blair, 'Ben Jonson among the Historians', in Kevin Sharpe and Peter Lake (eds.), *Culture and Politics in Early Stuart England* (Basingstoke: Macmillan, 1994), pp. 67–89.

RANK

Kastan, David Scott, 'Is There a Class in This (Shakespearean) Text?', *Renaissance Drama*, 25 (1993): 101–21.

Parolin, Peter, '"A Strange Fury Entered My House": Italian Actresses and Female Performance in *Volpone*', *Renaissance Drama*, 29 (1998): 107–35.

Ravelhofer, Barbara, *The Early Stuart Masque: Dance, Costume, and Music* (Oxford: Oxford University Press, 2006).

Tylus, Jane, 'Women at the Windows: Commedia Dell'arte and Theatrical Practice in Early Modern Italy', *Theatre Journal*, 49 (3) (1997): 323–42.

HOUSEHOLDS

DiGangi, Mario, *The Homoerotics of Early Modern Drama* (Cambridge: Cambridge University Press, 1997).

Donaldson, Ian, *Jonson's Magic Houses: Essays in Interpretation* (Oxford: Oxford University Press, 1997).

Richardson, Catherine, *Domestic Life and Domestic Tragedy in Early Modern England: The Material Life of the Household* (Manchester: Manchester University Press, 2006).

Wall, Wendy, *Staging Domesticity: Household Work and English Identity in Early Modern Drama* (Cambridge: Cambridge University Press, 2002).

FOREIGN TRAVEL AND EXPLORATION

Bach, Rebecca Ann, *Colonial Transformations: The Cultural Production of the New Atlantic World, 1580–1640* (New York: Palgrave, 2000).

Fuchs, Barbara, 'Jonson's Commendatory Poetry and the Translation of Empire', *Modern Philology*, 99 (2002): 341–56.

Harris, Jonathan Gil, '"I Am Sailing to My Port, Uh! Uh! Uh! Uh!": The Pathologies of Transmigration in *Volpone*', *Literature and Medicine*, 20 (2001): 109–32.

Murphy, Andrew, *But the Irish Sea Betwixt Us: Ireland, Colonialism, and Renaissance Literature* (Louisville, Ky.: University of Kentucky Press, 1999).

DOMESTIC TRAVEL AND SOCIAL MOBILITY

Capp, Bernard, *The World of John Taylor, the Water-Poet, 1578–53* (Oxford: Clarendon Press, 1994).

Donaldson, Ian, *Jonson's Walk to Scotland* (Edinburgh: Quadriga Press, 1992).

Knowles, James, 'Jonson in Scotland: Jonson's Mid-Jacobean Crisis', in Takashi Kozuka and J. R. Mulryne (eds.), *Shakespeare, Marlowe, Jonson: New Directions in Biography* (Aldershot: Ashgate, 2006), pp. 259–77.

Mcrae, Andrew, *Literature and Domestic Travel in Early Modern England* (Cambridge: Cambridge University Press, 2009).

Newman, Karen, 'Walking Capitals: Donne's *First Satyre*', in *The Culture of Capital: Properties, Cities, Knowledge in Early Modern England* (London: Routledge, 2002), pp. 203–21.

Sullivan Jr., Garrett A., *The Drama of Landscape: Land, Property and Social Relations on the Early Modern Stage* (Stanford, Calif.: Stanford University Press, 1999).

MONEY AND CONSUMERISM

Dillon, Janette, *Theatre, Court and City, 1595–1610: Drama and Social Space in London* (Cambridge: Cambridge University Press, 2000).
Fischer, Sandra K., *Econolingua: A Glossary of Coins and Economic Language in Renaissance Drama* (Newark, Del.: University of Delaware Press, 1985).
Knights, L. C. *Drama and Society in the Age of Jonson* (London: Chatto & Windus, 1937).
Muldrew, Craig, *The Economy of Obligation: The Culture of Credit and Social Relations in Early Modern England* (Basingstoke: Macmillan, 1998).
  '"Hard Food for Midas": Cash and Its Social Value in Early Modern England', *Past and Present*, 170 (2001): 78–120.
Thirsk, Joan, *Economic Policy and Projects: The Development of a Consumer Society in Early Modern England* (Oxford: Clarendon Press, 1978).

LAND

Elsky, Martin, 'The Mixed Genre of Ben Jonson's "To Penshurst," and the Perilous Springs of Netherlandish Landscape', *The Ben Jonson Journal*, 9 (2002): 1–36.
McRae, Andrew, *God Speed the Plough: The Representation of Agrarian England, 1500–1660* (Cambridge: Cambridge University Press, 1996).
Olwig, Kenneth Robert, *Landscape, Nature, and the Body Politic: From Britain's Renaissance to America's New World* (Madison, Wisc.: University of Wisconsin Press, 2002).
Sullivan Jr., Garrett A., *The Drama of Landscape: Land, Property, and Social Relations on the Early Modern Stage* (Stanford, Calif.: Stanford University Press, 1998).
Wayne, Don, *Penshurst: The Semiotics of Place and the Poetics of History* (Madison, Wisc.: University of Wisconsin Press, 1984).

PATRONAGE

Evans, Robert C., *Ben Jonson and the Poetics of Patronage* (Lewisburg, Pa.: Bucknell University Press, 1989).
Gurr, Andrew and Hardman, Phillipa (eds.), *The Yearbook of English Studies, 21, Politics, Patronage and Literature in England 1558–1658*, special volume (1991): 137–52.
Kay, W. David Kay, 'The Poet and His Patrons', in *Ben Jonson: A Literary Life* (Basingstoke: Macmillan, 1995), pp. 114–35.
Riggs, David, *Ben Jonson: A Life* (Cambridge, Mass.: Harvard University Press, 1998).
Rowe, Nick, '"My Best Patron": William Cavendish and Jonson's Caroline Drama', *The Seventeenth Century*, 9 (2) (1994): 197–212.
Sanders, Julie, 'Jonson's Caroline Coteries', in Takashi Kozuka and J. R. Mulryne (eds.), *Shakespeare, Marlowe, Jonson: New Directions in Biography* (Aldershot: Ashgate, 2006), pp. 279–94.

ARCHITECTURE

Anderson, Christy, *Inigo Jones and the Classical Tradition* (Cambridge: Cambridge University Press, 2007).

Dubrow, Heather, 'Guess Who's Coming to Dinner? Reinterpreting Formalism and the Country House Poem', *Modern Language Quarterly*, 61 (2000): 59–77.

Girouard, Mark, *Robert Smythson and the Elizabethan Country House* (New Haven, Conn.: Yale University Press, 1983).

Mardock, James, *Our Scene Is London: Ben Jonson's City and the Space of the Author* (New York: Routledge, 2008).

Peacock, John, *The Stage Designs of Inigo Jones: The European Context* (Cambridge: Cambridge University Press, 1995).

Summerson, John, *Architecture in Britain, 1530–1830*, 9th edn (New Haven, Conn.: Yale University Press, 1993).

Turner, Henry, *The English Renaissance Stage: Geometry, Poetics, and the Practical Spatial Arts, 1580–1630* (Oxford: Oxford University Press, 2006).

FOOD

Appelbaum, Robert, *Aguecheek's Beef, Belch's Hiccup, and Other Gastronomic Interjections: Literature, Culture, and Food among the Early Moderns* (Chicago, Ill.: University of Chicago Press, 2006).

Boehrer, Bruce Thomas, *The Fury in Men's Gullets: Ben Jonson and the Digestive Canal* (Philadelphia, Pa.: University of Pennsylvania Press, 1997).

Heal, Felicity, *Hospitality in Early Modern England* (Oxford: Oxford University Press, 1990).

Loewenstein, Joseph, 'The Jonsonian Corpulence; or, The Poet as Mouthpiece', *English Literary History*, 53 (1986): 491–518.

Mennell, Stephen, *All Manners of Food: Eating and Taste in England and France from the Middle Ages to the Present*, 2nd edn (Urbana, Ill.: University of Illinois Press, 2000).

Thirsk, Joan, *Food in Early Modern England: Phases, Fads, Fashions, 1500–1760* (London: Hambledon Continuum, 2007).

ALCHEMY, MAGIC AND THE SCIENCES

Kassell, Lauren, *Medicine and Magic in Elizabethan London. Simon Forman: Astrologer, Alchemist, and Physician* (Oxford: Clarendon Press, 2005).

Mebane, John S., *Renaissance Magic and the Return of the Golden Age* (Lincoln, Nebr.: University of Nebraska Press, 1989).

Nicholl, Charles, *The Chemical Theatre* (London: Routledge & Kegan Paul, 1980).

Sherman, William, *John Dee: The Politics of Reading and Writing in the English Renaissance* (Amherst, Mass.: University of Massachusetts Press, 1995).

CLOTHING AND FASHION

Arnold, Janet, *Queen Elizabeth's Wardrobe Unlock'd* (Leeds: Maney, 1988).
Patterns of Fashion 4: The Cut and Construction of Linen Shirts, Smocks, Neckwear, Headwear and Accessories for Men and Women, c. 1540–1660 (London: Macmillan, 2008).
Jones, Ann Rosalind and Stallybrass, Peter, *Renaissance Clothing and the Materials of Memory* (Cambridge: Cambridge University Press, 2000).
Richardson, Catherine, *Clothing Culture, 1350–1650* (Aldershot: Ashgate, 2004).
Sanders, Julie, '"Wardrobe Stuffe": Clothes, Costume and the Politics of Dress in Ben Jonson's *The New Inn*', *Renaissance Forum*, 6 : 1 (2002). Available online at www.hull.ac.uk/renforum/v6no1/sanders.htm.
Stallybrass, Peter, 'Worn Worlds: Clothes and Identity on the Renaissance Stage', in Margreta De Grazia, Maureen Quilligan and Peter Stallybrass (eds.), *Subject and Object in Renaissance Culture* (Cambridge: Cambridge University Press, 1996), pp. 289–320.

GENDER AND SEXUALITY

Digangi, Mario, *The Homoerotics of Early Modern Drama* (Cambridge: Cambridge University Press, 1997).
Dutton, Richard, 'Introduction', in Ben Jonson, *Epicene; or, The Silent Woman*, edited by Richard Dutton (Manchester: Manchester University Press, 2003).
Mitchell, Marea, 'Jonson's Politics of Gender and Genre: Mary Wroth and "Charis"', in A. D. Cousins and Alison V. Scott (eds.), *Ben Jonson and the Politics of Genre* (Cambridge: Cambridge University Press, 2009), pp. 115–33.
Orgel, Stephen, *Impersonations: The Performance of Gender in Shakespeare's England* (Cambridge: Cambridge University Press, 1996).
Sanders, Julie, with Kate Chedgzoy and Susan Wiseman (eds.), *Refashioning Ben Jonson: Gender, Politics and the Jonsonian Canon* (Basingstoke: Macmillan, 1998).
Tomlinson, Sophie, *Women on Stage in Stuart Drama* (Cambridge: Cambridge University Press, 2005).

Index

N.B. All Ben Jonson plays, masques and poems are indexed by title.

A Celebration of Charis in Ten Lyric Pieces, 298
A Tale of a Tub, xxiv, 34, 36, 37, 56, 100, 128, 137, 221, 222, 223, 226, 235, 300, 311
Act of Uniformity, 230
Admirals Men, 52, 107
Alchemist, The, x, 15, 19, 21, 44, 45, 66, 67, 84, 86, 87, 88, 90, 91, 100, 102, 103, 107, 111, 112, 113, 114, 117, 120, 127, 128, 132, 139, 196, 197, 213, 222, 225, 234, 245, 247, 250, 254, 255, 256, 258, 267, 269, 272, 275, 281, 284, 287, 298, 317, 325, 341, 344
alchemy, 294, 322–8
'An Epistle to Master John Selden', 49
'An Execration Upon Vulcan', 189, 277
Anna of Denmark, Queen Consort, xxi, 25, 44, 144, 154, 155, 158, 176, 186, 187, 207, 232, 246, 247, 300, 341
Apollo Room, 48, 53, 54, 55
Aristotle, 41, 172, 323
Aubrey, John, 279

Bacon, Sir Francis, 314, 327, 328
　New Atlantis, 328
Bakhtin, Mikhail, 78
ballet de cour, 34, 147, 172, 175
Banqueting Hall, 154, 307
Barksted, William, 118, 119, 121
Barnes, Peter, 80, 81, 90, 91
Barry, Lording, 117
　Ram Alley, 117
Bartholomew Fair, xxii, 15, 19, 26, 31, 44, 45, 46, 53, 86, 90, 100, 102, 103, 107, 109, 111, 113, 136, 168–9, 204–5, 212, 221, 226, 234, 254, 275, 281, 301, 320, 341, 343
Beaujoyeulx, Balthasar de, 171
Beaumont, Francis, 6, 51, 120, 121, 192, 194, 296
Beaumont, Francis and John Fletcher,
　Coxcomb, The, 121
　Cupid's Revenge, 121
Bell, Thomas, 232

benefit of clergy, 225, 230
Benson, Frank, 88
Blackfriars Theatre, xxi, 32, 58, 88, 107, 116, 120, 125–4, 126, 127, 198, 250, 272
Blaney, John, 119
Bogdanov, Michael, 90
Bolsover, 300
Bolsover Castle, 159, 309
Bond, Edward, 1
book culture, 184
'Book of Sports', 1632, 38
Brackley, Lady Elizabeth Cavendish, 301
Brett, Robert, 7
Brome, Richard, 54, 55, 120, 276
　City Wit, The, 120
Burbage, James, 125, 126
Burbage, Richard, 119

Caird, John, 92
Cambridge Ben Jonson, 71–2
Camden, William, 7, 11, 12, 50, 146, 147, 169, 278, 296
　Britannia, 278
Campion, Thomas, 162
　Lord Hay's Masque, 162
Carleton, Sir Dudley, 158, 246, 250
Caroso, Fabritio, 179
Carroll, Pat, 90
Cartwright, William, 54, 75
Cary, Giles, 119, 120
Cary, Lucius, Viscount Falkland, 33, 42, 54, 56, 74, 176, 177
Cary-Morison Ode, 176, 181
Case is Altered, The, xxi, 18, 19, 66, 221, 258
Castiglione, Baldassare, 201
　Courtier, The, 201
Catiline, xxii, 45, 47, 85, 93, 171, 193, 196, 197, 205, 206, 222, 298
Cavendish Christening Entertainment, The, xxiii, 128, 298
Cavendish family, 299–301

360

Index

Cavendish, Lady Jane, 300
Cavendish, Sir Charles, 297
Cavendish, William, Earl of Newcastle, 33, 85, 154, 159, 188, 277, 297, 298, 299, 300, 302, 309
   Humourous Lovers, The, 300
   Triumphant Widow, The, 300
   Variety, The, 300
Cecil, Sir Robert, Earl of Salisbury, 27, 119, 186, 297, 308
Chapman, George, 6, 10, 11, 12, 51, 52, 66, 117, 120, 121, 126, 192, 224, 275, 297
   Bussy D'Ambois, 121
   May Day, 121
   Revenge of Bussy D'Ambois, The, 121
   Widow's Tears, The, 121
Charles I, King, xxiii, 2, 28, 31, 33, 35–6, 99, 135, 144, 154, 159, 172, 226, 227, 234, 298, 308, 309
Charles II, King, 84, 85
Chettle, Henry, 52, 107
Children of the King's Revels, 116, 128
Children of the Queen's Revels, 116, 118, 194
Chloridia, xxiii, 34, 311
Cicero, 49, 193, 205, 206, 238
City Chronologer, role of, 31, 298, 301
classicism, 1, 46, 74, 146, 148, 149, 197, 218, 219, 239
coach travel, 271–4
Cock Lorel ballad, 186, 188
Cockain, Aston, 107
Cockpit Theatre, Drury Lane, 84, 128
coins, 284–5
Coke, Edward, Lord Chief Justice, 226
collaborative writing practices, 48, 52
community, ideas of, 134–5, 256
Condell, Henry, 119
Contarini, Gaspare, 225
Conway, Sir Edward, 187
Cooke, George Frederick, 88
cooks, 316
Cornaro, Luigi, 314
Coryate, Thomas, 52, 249
   Coryats Crudities, 52, 286
Cotton, Sir Robert, 50, 52, 146, 296
   library, 50
country house poetry, 26, 42, 257, 291
Crane, Ralph, 188
Cranmer, Thomas, 229
criminal-justice system, 221–7
Cromwell, Thomas, 134
Curtain Theatre, 107, 225
Cynthia's Revels, xxi, 16, 17, 18, 19, 21, 66, 68, 126, 165, 166, 167, 172, 173, 174, 176, 184, 196, 198, 202, 207, 233, 299, 341

Daborne, Robert, 121
   A Christian Turned Turk, 121
dance, 147, 148, 154, 156, 158, 159, 162, 163, 164, 165, 171, 209, 245, 246, 267, 309
Daniel, Samuel, 145, 155, 194
   Philotas, 194
   Vision of the Twelve Goddesses, 155
   Works, The, 194
Davenant, William, 34
   Britannia Triumphans, 202
Dee, John, 304, 324
Dekker, Thomas, 16, 17, 22, 48, 52, 53, 107, 116, 126, 145, 192, 216, 231, 245, 283
   Bellman of London, The, 116
   Satiromastix, 53, 126
Denham, Sir John, 84
Derrida, Jacques, 57, 60
Descartes, René, 300, 324
Devereux, Robert, Earl of Essex, 21, 148
Devil is an Ass, The, 42, 45, 89, 92, 100, 128, 129, 130, 167, 171, 212, 221, 226, 245, 247, 250–1, 256, 269, 281, 283, 298, 300, 322, 340, 343, 345
Dickens, Charles, 8, 88, 235, 236
Digby, Sir Kenelm, 33, 189, 306, 307
Discoveries, 27, 45, 59, 172, 201, 202, 207, 281, 284, 304, 341, 345
Dolce, Lodovico, 208
Donne, John, 51, 52, 189, 206, 276, 296, 323, 324
Doran, Gregory, 93
Drayton, Michael, 6, 191, 277
Drummond, William, of Hawthornden, 1, 5, 6, 7, 8, 9, 10, 11, 12, 13, 14, 21, 42, 48, 56, 169, 185, 206, 225, 277
Dryden, John, 75, 76
d'Urfé, Honore
   L'Astrée, 34
Dyce, Alexander, 69

Eastward Ho!, xxii, 8, 10, 11, 12, 14, 52, 87, 100, 117, 126, 127, 148, 192, 247, 251, 275, 278, 281, 297
education, 1, 7, 50, 146, 278, 296
Egerton, Alice, Dowager Countess of Derby, 155
Elgar, Sir Edward
   The Spanish Lady, 89
Eliot, T. S., 61, 62, 76, 77, 79, 80, 282
Elizabeth I, Queen, xxii, 2, 15, 19, 20, 43, 45, 99, 141, 145, 154, 160, 186, 229, 290, 324, 330, 334
Elyot, Sir Thomas, 202
Entertainment at Althorp, 155, 158, 159
Entertainment at Britain's Burse, 119, 308
Entertainment at Theobalds, 182, 186–8

Epicene, xxii, 15, 19, 43, 45, 46, 51, 57, 59, 60, 79, 84, 85, 86, 87, 88, 90, 91, 100, 101, 116, 117, 118, 119, 120, 121, 128, 149, 167, 174, 222, 245, 247, 251, 254, 255, 259, 261, 263, 264, 266, 276, 291, 294, 320, 330, 331, 332, 333, 334, 335, 340, 345
Epigrams, xxiii, 23, 24, 25, 27, 50, 51, 53, 117, 203, 214, 215, 232, 237, 239, 264, 269, 298, 318, 340, 345
'Epistle. To Katherine, Lady Aubigny', 291
Every Man In His Humour, xxi, 7, 16, 17, 18, 19, 65, 66, 68, 87, 88, 92, 100, 107, 109, 110, 221, 222, 224, 225, 226, 254, 256, 258, 268, 281, 286, 287, 296, 297, 331
Every Man Out of His Humour, xxi, 16, 17, 18, 19, 22, 42, 43, 51, 53, 65, 68, 72, 107, 109, 110, 111, 113, 192, 194, 195, 196, 197, 206, 230, 231, 265, 266, 291–4, 296, 297, 301, 344
'Expostulation with Inigo Jones, An' 35, 163, 174, 210, 311

Fanthorpe, U. A., 1
Farrant, Richard, 125
fashion, 49, 79, 126, 127, 130, 155, 166, 172, 251, 260, 263, 265, 266, 267, 278, 283, 291, 292, 330–6
feminist criticism, 78
Fermat, Pierre de, 300
Ferrabosco, Alphonso, 162, 163, 164, 165, 167, 168
Field, Nathan, 118, 119, 120, 121, 128
  A Woman is a Weathercock, 120, 121
  Amends for Ladies, 121
film versions, 89, 90
Fish, Stanley, 77, 78
fisher play, 277
Fletcher, John, 6, 7, 12, 58, 120, 121, 192, 194, 197
  Faithful Shepherdess, The, 197
  Scornful Lady, The, 120, 121
folio, 1616 *Works*, xxii, 5, 7, 13, 14, 16, 17, 22, 26, 31, 39, 44, 46, 52, 56, 65, 67, 68, 69, 70, 71, 116, 181, 185, 192–4, 197, 199, 239, 296
food, 171, 237, 285, 314–20
foreign trade, 263, 264, 268
Forest, xxiii, 26, 44, 239, 291
Foucault, Michel, 78
four humours, theory of, 323
Freeman, Thomas, 99
friendships, 48–56, 184, 185, 237, 238–9, 242, 298
Fuller, Thomas, 7

Galen, 314, 320, 323
Galileo Galilei, 324
Garrick, David, 86, 87, 88, 91

Gascoigne, George, 194
Gelbart, Larry
  Sly Fox, 90
genre, 1, 16, 17, 39–46, 48, 145, 146, 147, 154, 162, 165, 168, 199, 213, 218, 219, 220, 246, 247, 254, 260, 291, 305, 345
Gentleman, Francis
  Tobacconist, The, 87
Gifford, William, 69, 70, 71, 76
Globe Theatre, xxi, 107–15, 198
Godolphin, Francis, 88
Godolphin, Sidney, 73
Goodyere, Sir Henry, 52, 187
Gosson, Stephen, 245
Greenblatt, Stephen, 62
Gresham, Sir Thomas, 287, 322
Guiness, Alec, 87
Gunpowder Plot, xxii, 10, 13, 45, 232
Guthrie, Tyrone, 91
Gwyn, Nell, 85
Gypsies Metamorphosed, The, xxiii, 28, 32, 171, 188, 297

Haddington Masque, xxii, 163
Hampton Court, 246
Harington, Lucy, Countess of Bedford, 51, 146, 151, 158, 184, 298, 299, 340
Harington, Sir John, 247
Hawkins, Sir Thomas, 33
Heath, Sir Robert, 159
Henrietta Maria, Queen Consort, 33, 34, 172
Henry VIII, King, 91, 134, 147, 149, 229
Henry, Prince of Wales, xxii, 150, 155, 157, 176, 187, 289, 297, 300, 307
Henslowe, Philip, 6, 7, 8, 13, 52
Herbert, George, 314
Herbert, Philip, Earl of Montgomery, 297
Herbert, Susan de Vere, Countess of Montgomery, 45
Herbert, William, Earl of Pembroke, 45, 297, 298
Herford, C. H., 5, 6, 13, 14, 70, 71, 72, 89
Herrick, Robert, 54, 107, 110, 291
Heywood, Jasper, 196
Heywood, Thomas, 192
Hill, Geoffrey, 271
Hilliard, Nicholas, 204
Hobbes, Thomas, 300, 324
Holland, Hugh, 50, 51, 52, 66, 269
Holme, William, 65
Hope Theatre, 103, 107
Horace, 1, 16, 192, 196, 216, 219
Hoskyns, John, 50, 51, 52, 296
Hot Anger Soon Cold, 107
households, 137–8, 254–61

Howard, Henry, 1st Earl of Northampton, 9, 10
Howard, Thomas, 1st Earl of Suffolk, 246
Howell, James, 54
Howes, Edmund, 99
Hymenaei, xxii, 45, 163, 164, 174, 182, 198, 209
Hytner, Nicholas, 91

Informations, xxiii, 6, 7, 8, 9, 10, 11, 12, 13, 14, 21, 42, 48, 53, 169, 206, 243, 277, 298
Inns of Court, 51, 126, 154, 276, 296
'Inviting a Friend to Supper', 44, 237, 239, 318
Irish Masque The, 164, 263
Isle of Dogs, The, xxi, 52, 107, 238, 279

James VI and I, King, xxii, 1, 2, 10, 15, 19, 23, 24, 26, 28, 31, 45, 52, 53, 78, 98, 99, 104, 128, 135, 144, 145, 150, 154, 158, 186, 193, 226, 231, 232, 234, 242, 244, 245, 277, 289, 290, 308, 327
  Basilikon Doron, 150
Johnson, Robert, 167
Jones, Inigo, xi, 14, 31, 32, 34, 48, 52, 53, 55, 56, 99, 140, 142, 146, 147, 148, 158, 159, 163, 164, 175, 176, 201, 202, 208, 209, 210, 246, 271, 304, 307, 308, 311
Jonsonus Virbius, 56, 73, 75
juries, 223, 225
Justices of the Peace, 136, 221–2, 223, 227
Juvenal, 1, 46, 149, 205

Kean, Edmund, 88
Keysar, Robert, 119, 128
King's Men, 102, 107, 119, 126, 127, 128, 129, 168, 188, 251, 341
King's Entertainment at Welbeck, xxiv, 33, 159, 298, 301
Knights, L. C., 78, 281, 282, 283, 284, 287

Lady Elizabeth's Men, 119
Lady Elizabeth's Servants, 107
Lampridius, 318
language, 50, 201, 217, 220, 266, 267, 268, 269, 284, 292
Lanier, Nicholas, 165
Lanyer, Aemilia, 291
Laud, William, Archbishop of Canterbury, 12, 33, 235
law, i, 35, 53, 98, 101, 102, 137, 139, 140, 149, 221–7, 234, 267, 284, 315, 326
Lawes, William, 162
Lewkenor, Lewis, 225
Libanius, 46
libels, 27
Livy, 237, 238
  History of Rome, 238

local officials, 135, 136, 221–2, 226
London as setting, 18, 26, 43, 45, 46, 68, 97–105, 127, 251, 322
Lord Chamberlain's Men, 125
Love Freed from Ignorance and Folly, xxii
Love's Triumph through Callipolis, xxiii, 34, 55, 210
Lovelace, Richard, 54
Lovers Made Men, xxiii, 165
Love's Welcome at Bolsover, xxiv, 33, 154, 159, 175, 298, 301, 309
Lucan, 73
  Pharsalia, 73
Lucian, 46, 284
Lyly, John, 18

Machin, Lewis, 121
Macready, William, 88
Magnetic Lady, The, xvii, 32, 36–7, 42, 45, 56, 92, 127, 128, 129, 130, 131, 133, 235, 236, 300
Malone, Edward, 69
Manners, Elizabeth Charlton, Countess of Rutland, 298
manslaughter charge, 225, 230, 231
manuscript transmission, 183, 189
Marlowe, Christopher, 58, 238, 239, 324, 341
Marston, John, 9, 10, 11, 12, 14, 48, 51, 52, 53, 66, 117, 121, 126, 153, 155, 159, 166, 167, 192, 216, 231, 275, 296
  Entertainment at Ashby, 155
  Fawn, The, 11
  Histriomastix, 53
  Insatiate Countess, The, 153, 159, 160
  What You Will, 53
Martial, 1, 237, 319
Martin, Richard, 52, 296
Mary I, Queen, 229, 324
masculinity, 292
masculinity, idea of, 13, 256, 306, 339
Masque of Beauty, The, xxii, 158, 207, 208, 299
Masque of Blackness, The, xxii, 146, 147, 158, 182, 207, 208, 209, 250, 299, 300
Masque of Queens, The, xxii, 47, 158, 163, 182, 183, 246, 300, 307, 341, 345
masques, 1, 6, 15, 23, 25, 28, 32, 34, 44, 45, 52, 68, 70, 72, 76, 78, 79, 98, 128, 144, 145, 147, 148, 153–60, 162, 163, 164, 165, 169, 171, 172, 174, 175, 181, 182, 185, 189, 192, 198, 201, 207, 208, 209, 210, 235, 245, 246, 247, 259, 269, 277, 279, 281, 287, 296, 300, 301, 307, 311, 328, 341, 345
Master of the Revels, 144, 297
May, Thomas, 73
Mayne, Jasper, 74, 113

Mendes, Sam, 91
Mercer, Johnny
   Foxy, 90
Mercury Vindicated from the Alchemists at Court, xxii, 326
Meres, Francis, 17
Mermaid tavern, 48, 51
Merry Devil of Edmonton, The, 129
Middleton, Thomas, 116, 121, 188, 192, 245, 283
   A Trick to Catch the Old One, 121
   Black Book, The, 116
Middleton, Thomas and Thomas Dekker
   Roaring Girl, The, 245
military service in the Netherlands, 269
Milton, John, 154
   Masque at Ludlow, A, 154
mobility, 251, 271–5
Montagu, Sir Edward, 156
Morison, Henry, 42, 176
Morley, Thomas, 166
Mortimer His Fall, 42, 69, 221
mountebanks, 267
musical versions, 89–90
'My Picture Left in Scotland', 186, 314

Nashe, Thomas, 52, 107, 238
neoplatonism, 33, 34, 324, 325
Neptune's Triumph, xxiii, 189, 316
New Exchange, 98, 308, 309
New Inn, The, i, 31, 32, 33–4, 36, 42, 58, 63, 92, 127, 128, 131, , 202, 205, 212, 254, 259, 260, 263, 272, 273, 274, 275, 278, 299, 330, 332, 333, 334, 335, 336, 341
News from the New World Discovered in the Moon, xxiii, 184, 185
Nobody and Somebody, 157
Norden, John, 290
   Surveyor's Dialogue, The, 290
Norton, Thomas, 325

Oberon, the Fairy Prince, xxii, 176, 307
'Ode to Himself', 31, 32, 58, 131
'Of Life, and Death', 232
Ogle, Lady Katherine, 300
Old Bailey, 225
'On English Monsieur', 263
'On Poet-Ape', 215, 216
'On Sir Voluptuous Beast', 345
'On the Famous Voyage', 43, 51, 104
operatic versions, 91
Ostler, William, 119
Oughtred, William, 300
Oxford Ben Jonson, 70–1, 89

Page of Plymouth, 107
pageant books, 146

Panegyre, 21, 149, 182
parish politics, 136–7, 278
Parrot, William, 115, 237, 238
patronage, 13, 24–5, 27, 42, 48, 50, 51, 67, 79, 135, 136, 144, 145, 146, 149, 155, 158, 181, 184, 185, 226, 239, 246, 277, 296–301, 304, 307
Peacham, Henry, xi, 202, 272, 275
   Coach and Sedan, 272
   Compleat Gentleman, The, 202
Pembroke's Men, 107
Penn, William, 119
Penshurst estate, 239–42, 257, 289, 290, 308
Perkins, William, 255, 260
Petronius, 46, 284
plague, 12, 15, 102, 121, 126, 272, 334
Plautus, 46
Pleasure Reconciled to Virtue, xxiii, 165, 171, 209
Pliny, 207
Plutarch, 50, 201
Pocahontas, 263
Poel, William, 88
poet laureateship, 1, 24
Poetaster, xxi, 16, 17, 18, 21, 43, 53, 66, 88, 126, 149, 165, 167, 177, 196, 198, 212, 213, 216, 217, 296
Poley, Robert, 238, 239
Porter, Henry, 107
postal networks, 278
Prince Charles's Men, 119
Prince Henry's Barriers, 307
Privy Council, 9, 10, 29, 126, 324
prodigy houses, 289
projectors, 226
projects, 282
Prynne, William, 12, 171
Ptolemy, 323
punctuation, 67, 68, 69, 70, 71
Purchas, Samuel, 269
Puttenham, George, 39
   The Arte of English Poesie, 39

Queen Anna's Men, 119
Queen Henrietta Maria's Men, 119, 128
Quintilian, 56, 207, 224

Ralegh, Sir Walter, 296, 324
Ralegh, Wat, 269, 297
Randolph, Thomas, 54
Ratcliffe, Margaret, 298
Reade, Emmanuel, 118
religion, 6, 9, 10, 229, 230, 326, 327, 328
   Catholicism, 6, 33, 149, 189, 229, 231, 232
   Protestantism, 189, 229
   Puritanism, 33, 136
republican values, 150, 239, 242
Restoration performances, 84–6

Revels editions, 71
Richard Crookback, 17, 107
Ripley, George, 325
rivalries, 48–56, 202, 304
Robert II, 17, 107
Robinson, Richard (Dick), 129, 251
Roe, Sir John, 12, 246
Rose Theatre, xxi, 52, 107
Rowley, William, 119
Royal Entertainment (1604), 181, 308
Royal Exchange, 287
Royal Society, 323, 328

Sad Shepherd, The, xxiv, 34, 37–8, 42, 69, 71, 88, 277, 300
Scaliger, Julius Caesar, 39
Securis, John, 323
Sejanus, xxii, 8, 9, 10, 11, 13, 14, 28, 29, 45, 52, 66, 68, 88, 93, 104, 107, 111, 112, 114, 148, 149, 150, 196, 197, 212, 222, 224
Selden, John, 11, 12, 49, 50, 51, 269
Seneca, 196
Shaa, Robert, 52
Shakespeare, William, xxii, 1, 5, 13, 14, 18, 44, 57–63, 65, 67, 68, 69, 70, 71, 74, 75, 76, 80, 86, 87, 88, 90, 107, 125, 168, 169, 177, 192, 194, 199, 258, 324, 342, 343
 A Midsummer Night's Dream, 343
 Antony and Cleopatra, 59
 Comedy of Errors, The, 59, 68
 Cymbeline, 167
 Hamlet, 224
 Othello, 87, 343
 Pericles, 59
 Romeo and Juliet, 59, 177
 Troilus and Cressida, 59
 Two Gentleman of Verona, The, 59, 167
 Venus and Adonis, 59
 Winter's Tale, The, 168
Shirley, James, 192, 276
Sibbald, Sir Robert, 5, 6
Siddons, Sarah, 87
Sidney family, 239, 240, 242, 289, 298, 305
Sidney, Sir Philip, 10, 39, 41, 240, 297, 324
 Astrophil and Stella, 240, 306
 The Defence of Poetry, 39
Sidney, Sir Robert, Lord Lisle, 45, 240, 242, 257, 289, 297, 305
Simon, Barney
 Phiri, 89
Simpson, Evelyn, 70
Simpson, Percy, 5, 6, 7, 70
Smith, Sir Thomas, 223
 De republica anglorum, 223
 Discourse of the Common Weal, 282
sonnets, 42, 298

Sons of Ben, 53, 54, 107, 239
Spencer, Gabriel, xxi, 6, 7, 9, 52, 53, 225
Spencer, Sir Robert, 155, 156, 160
Spenser, Edmund, xiii, 29, 154, 189
Stainer, C. L., 5, 6, 7, 11
Staple of News, The, xxiii, 42, 45, 92, 100, 104, 127, 128, 129, 130, 173, 205, 300, 301, 316
Star Chamber, 136
Stephens, John, 193
 Cynthia's Revenge; or Menander's Ecstasy, 193
Stow, John, 99
 A Survey of London, 99
Strachey, William, 52
Stuart, Esmé, Lord D'Aubigny, 125, 127, 145, 297
Stuart, James, Duke of Lennox, 146
Stuart, Lady Arbella, 128
Swan Theatre, xxi, 93, 107
Swinburne, Algernon, 76

Tacitus, 1, 28, 149, 237, 238
Talbot, Jane Ogle, Countess of Shrewsbury, 300
Taylor, John, 10, 14, 122, 123, 152, 271, 272, 273, 276, 278
 Carriers Cosmographie, The, 278
 Pennyles Pilgrimage, The, 278
 World Runnes on Wheeles, The, 271, 276
Theatre, the, xxi, 107
Tieck, Ludwig, 89
Time Vindicated, xxiii, 307
title pages, 39, 46, 197–8
'To Captain Hungry', 269
'To Heaven', 233
'To My Book', 23, 214
'To My Bookseller', 23, 215, 216
'To Penshurst', xxii, 26, 42, 44, 136, 156, 239–43, 254, 257–8, 259, 289–91, 292, 293, 294, 305–6, 316, 319–20
'To Sir Robert Wroth', 26, 239, 242, 291, 292
tobacco, 102, 264, 265, 268
Tourneur, Maurice, 89
Townshend, Aurelian, 34
 Albion's Triumph, 307
Tresham, Sir Thomas, 156
Tylers and Bricklayers company, 7, 8

Underwood, 32, 33, 35, 41, 44, 49, 50, 53, 177, 178, 277, 298, 306, 314
union of England and Scotland, 25

Villiers, George, Duke of Buckingham, 28, 32, 159, 171, 297
Virgil, 88, 149, 193, 219, 237, 238
Virginia colony, 263, 270, 279
Vision of Delight, xxiii, 165

Vitruvius, 34, 175, 304, 307, 311
Volpone, xxii, 13, 15, 26, 42, 46, 59, 60, 61, 62, 66, 77, 86, 88, 89, 90, 91, 104, 107, 109, 112, 114, 117, 120, 125, 149, 167, 168, 193, 196, 197, 201, 213, 222, 225, 247, 248–9, 250, 254, 256, 258, 259, 263, 264, 265, 267, 268, 281, 284, 287, 339, 340, 341, 342, 343, 344

walk to Scotland, 1618, 1, 5, 21, 277, 314
War of the Theatres, 45, 53, 55, 126
Welbeck Abbey, 159, 300
Westminster School, 50, 278, 296

Weston, Richard, Earl of Portland, 32, 33, 189
Whalley, Peter, 69
Wheatley, William, 235
Whitefriars Theatre, xxii, 116–22
Wilson, Robert, 194
   Three Ladies of London, The, 194
Wotton, Sir Henry, 151, 297
Wright, Thomas, 232
Wroth, Lady Mary, 45, 67, 242, 298, 299

Zoffany, Johann, 91
Zweig, Stefan, 89, 90, 91